Government and Politics in South Asia

SECOND EDITION

Government and Politics in South Asia

Craig Baxter,
Yogendra K. Malik,
Charles H. Kennedy, and
Robert C. Oberst

Westview Press

BOULDER • SAN FRANCISCO • OXFORD

Copyright © 1987, 1991 by Westview Press, Inc.

Published in 1991 in the United States of America by Westview Press, Inc., 5500 Central Avenue, Boulder, Colorado 80301, and in the United Kingdom by Westview Press, 36 Lonsdale Road, Summertown, Oxford OX2 7EW

Library of Congress Cataloging-in-Publication data
Government and politics in South Asia/Craig Baxter . . . [et al.].—
  2nd ed.
    p. cm.
  Includes bibliographical references and index.
  ISBN 0-8133-7905-9.   ISBN 0-8133-7906-7 (pbk.)
    1. South Asia—Politics and government.   I. Baxter, Craig.
JQ98.A2G68   1991
320.3′0954—dc20

90-43083
CIP

Printed and bound in the United States of America

∞ The paper used in this publication meets the requirements
of the American National Standard for Permanence of Paper
for Printed Library Materials Z39.48-1984.

10   9   8   7   6   5   4   3   2   1

This book is dedicated to our wives

Barbara Baxter
Usha Malik
Patricia A. Poe (Kennedy)
Kathy Shellogg (Oberst)

in thanks for their patience, help, and encouragement

CONTENTS

List of Tables   ix
List of Illustrations   xi
Preface to the Second Edition   xiii
Preface to the First Edition   xv

INTRODUCTION   1

1   THE GOVERNANCE OF SOUTH ASIA UNDER THE BRITISH   5

PART 1
INDIA

2   SOCIETY'S HERITAGE AND ITS MEANING FOR THE PRESENT   21

3   SOCIAL STRUCTURE AND POLITICAL CULTURE   41

4   LEADERS AND SUCCESSIONS   58

5   POLITICAL INSTITUTIONS AND GOVERNMENTAL PROCESSES   78

6   POLITICAL PARTIES   102

7   GROUPS AND INTEREST ARTICULATION   120

8   THE EXECUTIVE AND THE BUREAUCRACY: POLICY
     FORMULATION AND IMPLEMENTATION   135

9   MODERNIZATION AND DEVELOPMENT: PROSPECTS AND PROBLEMS   146

PART 2
PAKISTAN

10   SOCIETY'S HERITAGE AND ITS MEANING FOR THE PRESENT   161

11   ISLAM AND THE POLITICAL CULTURE OF PAKISTAN   172

12   REGIONALISM   181

13   PARTIES AND LEADERS   190

14   CONSTITUTIONAL STRUCTURES AND POLICY IMPLEMENTATION   204

15   THE FUTURE OF PAKISTAN   220

PART 3
BANGLADESH

16   SOCIETY'S HERITAGE AND ITS MEANING FOR THE PRESENT   229

17   SOCIALIZATION AND POLITICAL CULTURE   236

18   LEADERS AND FOLLOWERS   246

19   INSTITUTIONS AND GOVERNMENTAL PROCESSES   257

20   PARTIES AND GROUPS   267

21   THE MILITARY   279

22   MODERNIZATION AND DEVELOPMENT: PROSPECTS AND PROBLEMS   286

PART 4
SRI LANKA

23   SOCIETY'S HERITAGE AND ITS MEANING FOR THE PRESENT   297

24   THE SOCIAL AND ECONOMIC FABRIC OF THE SOCIETY   303

25   LEADERSHIP AND FAMILY   310

26   THE POLITICAL PROCESS AND GOVERNMENT INSTITUTIONS   317

27   THE POLITICAL PARTY SYSTEM   329

28   GROUPS AND INTEREST ARTICULATION   339

29   MODERNIZATION AND DEVELOPMENT: PROSPECTS AND PROBLEMS   345

PART 5
SOUTH ASIA

30   NEPAL, BHUTAN, AND THE MALDIVES   357

31   SOUTH ASIA AS A REGION AND IN THE WORLD SYSTEM   372

CONCLUSION: DEMOCRACY AND AUTHORITARIANISM IN SOUTH ASIA   393

Statistical Appendix   401
About the Book and Authors   403
Index   404

TABLES

3.1 Religious distribution of the population (India)   45

3.2 Languages specified in the constitution of India and their speakers   48

4.1 Prime ministers of India: 1947–1990   72

5.1 Presidents of India   83

5.2 Voter participation in Indian parliamentary elections, 1952–1984   88

5.3 Poll expenditure for the Lok Sabha elections   89

6.1 1989 Lok Sabha election by state and union territory   105

10.1 Pakistan: Population by province, 1981   163

10.2 Pakistan: Language usually spoken in the household, 1981   165

10.3 Pakistan: Religion by province, 1982   166

13.1 Pakistan National Assembly elections, 1970–1971   191

13.2 National Assembly results, 1977   192

13.3 National Assembly results, 1988   193

13.4 Heads of state and of government   197

19.1 Bangladesh local government   265

20.1 Elections in eastern Bengal, East Bengal, East Pakistan, and Bangladesh   268

24.1 Voter turnout rates in national elections   304

24.2 Ethnic population of Sri Lanka 305

24.3 Religious composition of the Sri Lankan
population 306

25.1 Heads of government of Sri Lanka 313

26.1 1988 presidential election results 323

27.1 Results of Sri Lanka parliamentary elections 330

ILLUSTRATIONS

Maps

South Asia   xvi

India   20

3.1   Official and other important languages (India)   49

Pakistan   160

Bangladesh   228

Sri Lanka   296

30.1   Nepal   358

30.2   Bhutan   366

Figures

5.1   Organization of the central government (India)   81

5.2   Organization of the state government (India)   95

14.1   Structure of Pakistan's government   210

19.1   Bangladesh central government   263

26.1   Structure of the Sri Lankan government   320

PREFACE TO
THE SECOND EDITION

In the four years since the first edition of this book was published, there have been a number of major changes in South Asia. These have included the defeat of the Rajiv Gandhi government in India, the death of Zia-ul-Haq and the coming to power and subsequent dismissal of Benazir Bhutto in Pakistan, the changing of the guard in Sri Lanka, and the withdrawal of Soviet troops from Afghanistan as well as the many events that are important even if less likely to draw worldwide headlines.

We have, therefore, felt that a second edition of the work is necessary. In preparing this edition we have followed the pattern described in the preface to the first edition in that the book is a collective effort although each author had specific responsibilities.

We wish to add our thanks to Susan McEachern of Westview Press with whom we have worked cordially and successfully in bringing out this new edition.

Craig Baxter
Yogendra K. Malik
Charles H. Kennedy
Robert C. Oberst

PREFACE TO
THE FIRST EDITION

The authors of this book, who all teach courses in the politics of South Asia and in political development in the Third World, have been concerned that there is no text book that contains information on the major countries of South Asia. Such a book, we believe, would be valuable for use both in courses specifically about the region and those broader in scope. To fill this gap, we have combined to write a book that should be useful to our students and to students of others in the field of political development.

The book is a combined effort. In the initial draft, however, the sections were assigned to individual writers. Malik was responsible for India and the three smaller countries, Kennedy for Pakistan, and Oberst for Sri Lanka. Baxter was responsible for Bangladesh, the historical introduction, the international and regional relations chapter, and the introduction and conclusion and also served as coordinator. The chapters were circulated among all the other writers, each of whom made contributions to each section. The result is, therefore, the combined work of all four of us.

The authors wish to thank especially those at Westview Press who worked with us patiently and carefully. Holly Arrow was a particularly close associate and saw the book through the final stages of the ultimate draft. Senior editor Libby Barstow and copy editor Christine Arden also aided us greatly in the preparation of the text for typesetting.

Professor Malik wishes to express his thanks to Bonnie Ralston of the University of Akron for her assistance in preparing his section of the manuscript; Professor Kennedy similarly extends his appreciation to Elide Vargas of Wake Forest University. Our thanks and appreciation for the patience of our wives is shown in the dedication of this work to them.

C.B.
Y.K.M.
C.H.K.
R.C.O.

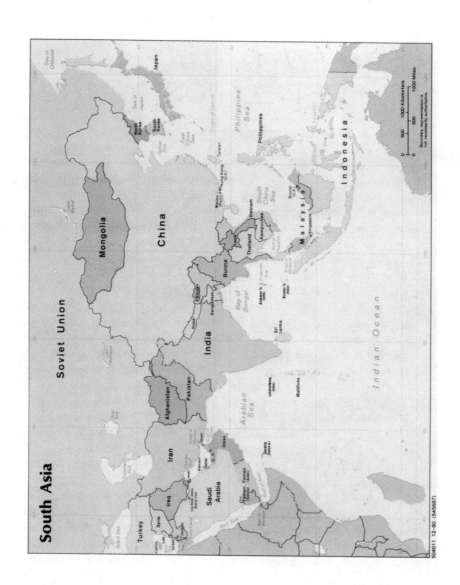

South Asia

INTRODUCTION

Should South Asia be a subject for study? Can we effectively survey an area remote from our Western experiences, one with a new vocabulary of politics and society coupled with unfamiliar names (many of them seemingly unpronounceable)? Is it appropriate for those of us from such prosperous nations as the United States and Canada, which are at the center of world affairs, to study nations that are poverty stricken and, it often appears, far from the mainstream of international activity?

Each of these questions must be answered in the affirmative, for several reasons. The size of the region's population is perhaps the most important consideration. A second consideration is the rising importance of the region's contribution to the productive capacity of the world. South Asia's location alone makes it strategically important. Further, the region provides examples of different forms of political development ranging from the open and democratic—but not entirely perfect—systems of India and Sri Lanka to the frequently authoritarian governments of Pakistan and Bangladesh and to the changing traditional polities of Nepal, Bhutan, and the Maldives. In addition, the wide range of political development examples in a compact area permits comparison among the seven countries and between South Asia and other developing nations.

With respect to population size, the region contained over 1 billion people in mid-1987.[1] According to estimates published by the World Bank, this number will increase to almost 2 billion by the year 2025, meaning that more than one-fifth of the world's people will live in South Asia. On this basis alone the region cannot be disregarded; indeed, it must be looked upon as one of the key areas of the world.

In 1987, India ranked twelfth in terms of annual gross national product (GNP). When the relatively much smaller economies of the other six countries were taken into account as well, the collective GNP of South Asia was more than one-quarter trillion dollars. Excluding the communist nations, for which comparable data is not available in World Bank reporting, India ranked third—behind China and the United States—in value added in agriculture. Further, the growth in the GNPs of Pakistan, Bangladesh, and Sri Lanka

1

exceeded the average growth of all low-income economies during the period 1973–1983, although, admittedly, this growth occurred in each case from a much smaller base than that of India. Nonetheless, in constant dollars the collective GNP of the seven nations will exceed a half-trillion dollars by 2000 if past rates of growth are approximated in the next ten years.

In the chapters that follow, these data will be amplified to show where growth has taken place and is expected to take place in the future as the South Asian nations work toward greater economic development and the provision of a better standard of living for their people.

When the nations of the Third World (the developing nations) are considered, it is clear that the attention of the West is riveted on the Middle East and perhaps on Latin America and East Asia. Nonetheless, the location of South Asia is important to the West and to Japan. The air and sea routes that connect Europe and the Middle East with the Far East and Australasia pass through or near the subcontinent that we call South Asia. India borders China along the Himalayas. Pakistan plays host to more than 3 million Afghan refugees as the civil war in neighboring Afghanistan continues despite the Soviet withdrawal of its troops. Pakistan also forms the eastern flank of the vital Middle East with its oil riches, and several countries of South Asia supply significant (though now decreasing) numbers of workers to the labor-poor Middle East. Bangladesh and Sri Lanka look both to South Asia and to Southeast Asia for trade and cultural ties. It was not without reason that Pakistan, which then included Bangladesh, was the link member of the Central Treaty Organization and the Southeast Asia Treaty Organization, nor is it insignificant that both the United States and the Soviet Union have greatly increased naval presence in the Indian Ocean in the past two decades.

For almost two centuries South Asia was under the domination of Great Britain, as the Indian Empire, the Crown Colony of Ceylon (now Sri Lanka), and the protectorates over Nepal, Bhutan, and the Maldives. The defense of South Asia and the mediation of disputes among various parts of the region were the concerns of Whitehall and of Calcutta and New Delhi. The withdrawal of British power in 1947 and 1948 left the region without an umpire, so to speak—not that an umpire would have been welcome, although such a figure could have settled or at least postponed some disputes. Nevertheless, each of the four major states has kept in place many of the institutional structures inherited from the British—structures that have contributed significantly to stability and continuity, especially in the administrative system. Parliamentary institutions have not fared as well in Pakistan and Bangladesh as in India and Sri Lanka.

South Asia has been slow to set up regional institutions and has only recently done so on a limited basis, such that political and bilateral issues have been excluded from the purview of the South Asian Association for

Regional Cooperation (SAARC). The issue of regional cooperation will be explored in Chapter 31; then, in the conclusion, some of the reasons for the failure of the continuance of the British heritage in domestic politics will be considered.

The routes taken toward political, social, and economic development by the nations of South Asia have diverged widely. Three major religious systems—Hinduism, Buddhism, and Islam—each one dominant in one or more of the nations, account for part, often a major part, of the political culture of the nation concerned. Two of these systems, Hinduism and Buddhism, are indigenous to the region, while the third, Islam, has had a major impact for almost a millenium. These religious systems, along with other important aspects of the social systems—for example, the caste system, which is inherent in Hinduism—provide a traditional basis for the political system that is only partly offset by the later accretions from the British period. The study of the mix of traditional and modern is one of the most important aspects of the study of politics and society in these seven nations.

Of special interest in this study are the variations in political development as measured by structural differentiation and cultural secularization in each political system. These two keys to modernization are thus investigated in relation to each of the countries of South Asia. A society that makes many and varied demands on its political system requires also that the system contain sufficiently specialized (or differentiated) structures, both governmental and nongovernmental, to provide the means to place and aggregate those demands as well as to respond to them with authoritative decisions. In addition, a modern society requires that the demands be answered by decisions that are made on a rational or secular basis using data that are as objective as possible. In our discussion of the South Asian nations, secularism is taken to mean rationalism—that is, the knowledge that people, through their own initiative, are able to modify the environment in which they live. Secularism does *not* mean the absence of religion (or of ideology, for that matter), for religion is a key ingredient of the political cultures in which the political systems must operate. Moreover, the political cultures themselves are neither stagnant nor static, for they tend to change along with the societies of which they are a part.[2]

Both the culture and the political system have much to do with the degree of the autonomy experienced by the nongovernmental structures in the system. For instance, India and Sri Lanka, though generally open polities (e.g., the press in both countries has usually, but not always, been free), have undergone periods of limitation of autonomy.

Each of the states of South Asia faces five critical areas of political development: nation building, state building, participation, economy building, and distribution. (1) Although India, Pakistan, and Sri Lanka inherited fairly effective state apparatuses, they are facing difficult challenges in the process of building unified nations. These challenges include the problems pertaining to the Sikhs and Kashmiris in India, the Sindhis in Pakistan, and the Tamils in Sri Lanka. (2) Economy building is, of course, another difficult challenge for the Third World nations, and those of South Asia are no exception. (3) Periodic and free elections, an important form of participation in India and Sri Lanka, are not regularly available to the people of the other states. Finally, (4) the distribution of resources in each of the nations is badly skewed; moreover, steps being taken to remedy this problem lack uniformity among the seven countries.

In the chapters that follow, we shall look first at the political heritage of the British past (Chapter 1) and then at each of the countries. The four largest countries are dealt with in Parts 1 through 4: Part 1, India; Part 2, Pakistan; Part 3, Bangladesh; and Part 4, Sri Lanka. The three smallest countries—Nepal, Bhutan and the Maldives—are considered together in Chapter 30. Chapter 31 reveals the interrelationships among the seven states in the region and the roles they play in the international system. Finally, the conclusion ties the threads together in a discussion of the political development of the region as a whole.

Notes

1. Data in this introduction are taken from the annex to World Bank, *World Development Report, 1989* (New York: Oxford University Press, 1989).

2. The concepts used in this paragraph and the following one are developed from Gabriel A. Almond and G. Bingham Powell, Jr., *Comparative Politics: System, Process and Policy,* 2d ed. (Boston: Little, Brown, 1978).

1
THE GOVERNANCE
OF SOUTH ASIA
UNDER THE BRITISH

Newly independent nations do not spring into the world as did Athena from the head of Zeus. Instead they bring to their new status a baggage of traditional and changing societal patterns, an economic infrastructure that often may be classed as "less developed," and a political system that is usually at least partially modeled on that of the colonial power from which independence has been won. In the chapters that follow, the political and social systems for each of the South Asian nations will be discussed separately. In this introductory chapter, to set the background for political change, we will briefly sketch the system of British colonial rule before 1947 in India and before 1948 in Sri Lanka (then called Ceylon). The British Indian Empire embraced the area that is now the independent republics of India, Pakistan, and Bangladesh, the territory that is now the independent nation of Sri Lanka was governed as a "crown colony," and the relationship between Great Britain and the smaller nations of Nepal, Bhutan, and the Maldives was something approaching a "protectorate." Although each pattern must be looked at separately, the bulk of this chapter pertains to the British Indian Empire. Shorter descriptions of the Crown Colony of Ceylon and the three smaller countries follow.

British Expansion: The Dual System of "States" and "British India"

The British were not the first Europeans to arrive in India and to begin to set up trading stations (called "factories"—places where "factoring," a rather antiquated term for trading, took place). Beginning with the circumnavigation of Africa by the Portuguese Vasco da Gama in 1498 and the establishment of the first Portuguese station at Cochin on the southwestern coast of India in 1506, other Europeans, particularly the French, Dutch, and British, began to follow the Portuguese example and establish stations along the Indian coast.

In 1600, the British East India Company was chartered in London to carry out British trade with India and the East. The Company was given a monopoly over trade between India and British territory—as will be recalled from descriptions of the Boston Tea Party of 1773. The right of the Company to govern came almost by accident. As the British began to establish their factories (the first at Surat, north of Bombay, in 1612), some form of administration and protection became necessary; these matters came to be the responsibility of the Company. The Indian territories directly controlled by Britain as well as the princely states subordinate to the British eventually came under the authority of the Company. Its Indian headquarters were located in Calcutta until 1858, when the Company was dissolved and its powers were transferred to the Crown (a legalism referring to the British government).

When the British and the other Europeans arrived in India, the major local power was the Mughal empire. This empire did not control all of the subcontinent; several independent Hindu kingdoms remained in the southern part. But the bulk of northern India from Afghanistan to Bengal and as far south as the Deccan plateau was under Mughal rule. The Mughals were the latest in a series of Muslim dynasties to rule northern India beginning in the eleventh century.

Mughal rule began when Babur, the first of the dynasty, defeated a declining Delhi sultanate in 1526 at Panipat. Babur and his five successors have been described as the "Great Mughals" because they expanded and retained power in the areas mentioned above. The greatest of these was Akbar (who reigned from 1556 to 1605), but the empire began to decline after the death of the sixth emperor, Aurangzeb, in 1707. The empire technically continued to exist until 1858, although it was under British domination for most of its last century and a half. It was the Mughals who set up a major aspect of the administrative system that the British would follow later: the division of the territory into provinces (*subas*) and districts (*zillas*). The Mughals also provided a framework for British rule in Bengal inasmuch as the British rulers initially operated, at least *de jure*, under the aegis of a grant of power from the emperor.

British expansion occurred not steadily but in spurts, by a process that has been described as gaining an empire in a fit of absent-mindedness. Madras became the principal seat of British presence in 1639; Bombay was acquired in 1661 as part of the dowry brought by the Portuguese wife of Charles II; and Calcutta became a station in 1690. It was from these three major sites that British expansion would take place. The power of Portugal declined during the seventeenth century until that nation was left with three small enclaves along the western coast (Goa, Daman, and Diu), which were annexed by India after a brief conflict in 1961. The French continued to be a major rival of the British, and the wars between the two powers that occurred in Europe and North America also had their Indian counterparts. French power in India, however, was diminished by the end of the Napoleonic period, although France retained a number of small enclaves, the most important of which was Pondicherry, located south of Madras. These enclaves were transferred by the French to India during the decade following Indian independence. With the exception of the French and Portuguese dots on the map, all of the territory now in India, Pakistan, and Bangladesh was under British control in 1947 and subject to a transfer of power by the British.

British expansion took two routes, however, thereby confusing the development of more representative institutions in India prior to independence and complicating the integration of India especially and Pakistan to a limited degree after independence. Some of the territory acquired by the Company (and the Crown after 1858) was annexed by the British, ruled directly through the governor general and his subordinates and described as "British India." It constituted about 60% of the territory of India and about two-thirds of the population. This territory can properly be termed a British colony (even though it was officially described as the British Indian Empire), and the reforms discussed later in this chapter applied only to this directly ruled area.

Other territories were acquired through agreements with local Indian rulers (usually termed "maharaja" if Hindu or Sikh and "nawab" if Muslim, although other titles were occasionally used). These areas were known variously as "princely India," "the princely states," and "the native states." At the time of Indian independence in 1947, there were more than 500 of these states, ranging in size from Jammu and Kashmir and in population from Hyderabad to tiny tracts in the Saurashtra region of Gujarat.[1] The agreements between the British and the princes were not uniform, but all provided that the British would have control of foreign affairs, defense, and communications. In return, the princes would have internal autonomy, subject to reasonable behavior by the rulers. The British did intervene in numerous cases when the princes exceeded the bounds of decency as defined by the Victorian and Edwardian British. British "residents," officials of the British Indian government, were located in the major states, whereas the smaller states were grouped together geographically with residents assigned to them collectively.

The Mutiny and the Transfer
of Power to the Crown

The Crown did not abolish the Company and assume full control of Indian affairs until 1858, but beginning in the latter part of the eighteenth century, a series of "regulating acts" passed by the British parliament curtailed the powers of the Company, placed it under closer parliamentary supervision, and cut into and finally abolished the trade monopoly held by the Company. A key step along this path was the act passed in 1784 during the prime ministership of William Pitt. It set up what has been called a "double government" system in which the directors of the Company were severely limited in their actions by a Board of Control under parliament. An earlier act, in 1774, had established the primacy of the governor of Bengal in Calcutta over the governors in Madras and Bombay and created the title of governor general, first held by Warren Hastings (1774–1785). The first governor generalship of Lord Cornwallis (1786–1793) brought the beginnings of what was to become the "steel frame" of British rule, the Indian Civil Service (ICS), the predecessor of the Indian Administrative Service (IAS), and the civil services of Pakistan and Bangladesh. In 1793, Cornwallis also decreed the "permanent settlement" system of land revenue rooted in the *zamindar* (landlord) arrangement for the areas under Bengal control, which then extended well up the Ganges river as far as Benares (present-day Varanasi). In effect, the permanent settlement made landowners out of persons who had been tax collectors. The Madras land tenure system, however, was based on direct payment of land revenue by the *ryots* (peasants), and the long-standing problem of landlordism was avoided there.

The Indian Mutiny (called by many Indian nationalists the First War of Independence) of 1857–1858 was the result of a number of long-term and proximate causes, one of which related to British expansionism. This was the doctrine of "lapse," which, as decreed by the governor general, Lord Dalhousie (1848–1856), declared that the states of rulers who died without natural heirs would be annexed directly to the British territories. During Dalhousie's term in office seven states, including sizable Nagpur and Oudh, were annexed through the doctrine, and lower Burma was added through war. The ultimate British victory over the mutineers resulted in the termination of the remnant of the Mughal Empire in 1858. It also led to the British theory that some Indian groups belonged to the "martial races" and others to the "nonmartial races," a theory that would have long-lasting consequences in independent India and Pakistan. Because the Punjabis, both Muslims and Sikhs, came to the assistance of the British in the mutiny, they were considered the principal group among the "martial races" and remained so as long as the British ruled; the Bengalis and other north Indians who had rebelled were henceforth known as "nonmartial."

On September 1, 1858, the British East India Company was terminated and all of its remaining powers were transferred to the British crown. The governor general added the title of viceroy, clearly indicating that he was the representative of the British monarch. He also remained governor general with respect to British India and became "crown representative" with respect to the princely states; the latter title was seldom used, however—partly because it was, in effect, a translation of viceroy. In her statement on the Crown's assumption of power, Queen Victoria declared that there would be no discrimination before the law with regard to her subjects in India. On January 1, 1877, the queen was proclaimed empress of India.

Under the India Councils Act of 1861, the British parliament made possible a very limited Indian participation in the governance of India. The act added a legislative council to the executive council (in effect, a cabinet) of the viceroy and to each of the heads of the provinces (these heads were designated at this time as governors in Bombay and Madras, and as lieutenant governors in other provinces). At each level, the members of the executive council would continue to be entirely British; they would also be members of the legislative council. But the other members of the legislative council included "nonofficials"—that is, persons not in the employ of the British *raj* (government)—and some of those appointed were Indians. This development was not a great advance, but it did permit the voices of very carefully selected Indians to be heard at the central and provincial levels. The founding of the Indian National Congress in 1885 (the Muslim League was founded in 1906) led to increasing and insistent demands by Indians for greater and elective representation and for an Indian share in the highest level of administration, the Indian Civil Service.

During the viceroyalty of Lord Ripon (1880–1884) laws were passed permitting the election, by a severely limited franchise, of local councils at the district level. But this scheme was not immediately introduced throughout British India; indeed, it was well into the twentieth century before local government had spread across all British territory. Nonetheless, the participation of Indians in local affairs was admitted, first in Bengal. During the same period, especially following the Aitchison Report of 1887, steps were taken to increase Indian membership of the central and provincial services.

A new councils act in 1892 expanded Indian representation at the central and provincial levels but fell short of allowing elections through which members could be chosen. Instead, certain recognized groups were permitted to make nominations to the viceroy and the provincial heads of government— nominations that may or may not have been accepted. The movement toward possible election, however, concerned Muslims who saw clearly that they would be a permanent minority at the center and in most provinces if the principle of direct election were applied. The Muslims, who made up slightly more than one-quarter of the population, were concentrated in the northwest and the east (where they formed a majority); hence the term "Muslim-majority provinces" applied, in 1947, to the Punjab, the North-West Frontier Province, Sind, Baluchistan, and Bengal. The other provinces were "Muslim-minority provinces" (or, if one prefers, "Hindu-majority provinces").

In 1906, a delegation of Muslims called on the viceroy, Lord Minto, at Simla and demanded that the next parliamentary act include a system of separate representation for Muslims. This demand was endorsed by Minto and was incorporated in the Government of India Act of 1909, often called the Morley-Minto Act as Viscount Morley was the secretary of state for India in London at the time.

The Morley-Minto Reforms: Separate Electorates

The new act greatly expanded Indian participation in the governance of India at the central and provincial levels, although it fell far short of Indian demands and left control firmly in the hands of the British rulers. An Indian was added to the executive council of the viceroy and the legislative council included twenty-seven elected Indian members and five appointed nonofficial Indian members in addition to thirty-six appointed officials, mainly British. Election at the central and provincial levels was by a severely restricted electorate who qualified for the privilege principally through taxpaying or educational attainment. At the provincial level also Indians were added to the executive councils, and in the legislative councils the elected Indian members and the appointed Indian nonofficials together slightly outnumbered the official (i.e., government) members, who were mostly British, in each council. In addition, two (later three, after 1919) Indians were appointed to the council of the secretary of state for India (a member of the British cabinet) in London.

In electoral systems in the West (e.g., the United States and Canada) elections are held without reference to the religious affiliation either of the voters or of the candidates. In India the system was different in that each seat in the legislature was assigned to a specific religious community and only those voters who belonged to that community were eligible to contest as candidates or to vote for candidates for that seat. Thus Muslims voted for and were represented by Muslims and Sikhs for and by Sikhs. The remainder of the population was lumped together as "general" and included the majority Hindu population. In later acts other religious minorities were also given separate representation so that the "general" remainder came closer to meaning only Hindus. The central and provincial seats were assigned roughly in accordance with the ratio of each community in the population, although smaller minorities were given some "weightage" (i.e., the percentage of seats was somewhat higher than that community's share of the total population).

This system of separate electorates recognized the Muslims' demand of 1906 that they be given adequate representation in legislative bodies. It was initially opposed by the Congress, but when the Muslim League and the Congress met in their annual sessions at the same time and in the same place, Lucknow, in 1916, an agreement was signed between the two parties. Under this agreement, the Congress accepted the demand of the Muslims and agreed to proportions of Muslim (and Sikh) seats in each province in anticipation of further reforms following World War I. The Lucknow Pact was negotiated largely on the Muslim League side by Muhammad Ali Jinnah (1876–1948) and for the Congress by Motilal Nehru (1861–1931), whose son (Jawaharlal Nehru, 1889–1964), granddaughter (Indira Gandhi, 1917–1984), and great-grandson (Rajiv Gandhi, b. 1944) would all serve as prime ministers of independent India.

Although the Liberal Morley had stated that Great Britain had no intention at the time of taking steps to grant India self-government (or "dominion status," as it was termed in the cases of Canada, Australia, New Zealand, and South Africa), the 1909 act was seen by many in both India and Great Britain as a step along that path. During World War I, on August 20, 1917, the then secretary of state for India, Edwin Montagu, declared in the British parliament that the policy of the British government with regard to India was the gradual development of self-governing institutions leading to the introduction of self-government. This decision confirmed to the Indians that the postwar period would see a new reform act. Montagu visited India in 1918 and joined with the viceroy, Lord Chelmsford (1916–1921), in a report that would form the basis of a new act.

During the war the British rulers had imposed a number of severe restrictions on Indian political activity and on the Indian press. These were largely understood by the moderates in the Indian national movement as being required during an emergency period. The death of several moderate leaders and the return from South Africa of Mohandas K. Gandhi (1869–1948) were factors involved in the change of the Indian movement from one characterized by elitism, constitutionalism, and gradualism to one based on mass participation. The British unwittingly aided this shift by reinstating wartime restrictions through a pair of anti-sedition acts (the Rowlatt acts) in March 1919. Gandhi proclaimed a movement of nonviolent passive resistance, noncooperation, and civil disobedience (*satyagraha*) to protest the new acts. The movement was centered in the Punjab and culminated in the Jallianwala Bagh massacre of April 13, 1919, in Amritsar, and in the imposition of martial law in the province of the Punjab. The Gandhi-led movement coincided with Congress support for the Muslim demand that the victorious allies retain the Islamic caliphate in Constantinople (Istanbul). Gandhi called off the movement in February 1922, when Indians assaulted and killed Indian policemen in a small town in the United Provinces and violated the principle of nonviolent noncooperation. The demand for the maintenance of the caliphate ended for all practical purposes when the new Turkish government abolished the office in 1924.

During this period of turmoil, the new Government of India Act, 1919 (often referred to as the Montagu-Chelmsford reforms) was passed by the British parliament and became effective on December 23, 1919. Indian representation was increased at both the central and provincial levels. At the center, the viceroy would be assisted in his executive council by four British and three Indian members. The legislature was made a bicameral one consisting of an "upper" Council of State and a "lower" Central Legislative Assembly, with the property qualifications made significantly higher for the electorate and membership of the Council of State. That body had 60 members, of whom 32 were elected Indians and 2 elected Britons. Also present were 20 government officials (some of whom could be Indians) and 6 nominated nonofficials (5 of them Indians), who represented various sectors of society (e.g., retired servicemen). The body thus had a majority of elected Indians. The same was true of the Central Legislative Assembly. The 145-member assembly had 105 elected members of whom 97 were Indian and 8 British. Of the 26 official members, as many as 10 could be Indian and as few as 16 British. There were also 14 nominated Indian nonofficials. The powers of the legislature were extended, but ultimate legislative power remained in the hands of the viceroy, who could decree ordinances when he declared the subject to be of utmost importance. At the center in India, there was no provision for responsible government, as existed in the parliamentary ("Westminster") system of Great Britain.

At the provincial level, however, there did exist an element of responsible government. The governor remained at the apex of power, but his executive council was divided into two parts under the system of *dyarchy* (dual rule) introduced by the act. The "nation-building departments," including agriculture, education, health, and public works, were placed in charge of ministers who were chosen by the governor from among the members of the legislative council. Although these ministers were not legally responsible to the council, it was incumbent on the governor to choose ministers who enjoyed the confidence of the council, with consideration given to the communal makeup of his ministerial group. The finance, revenue, and home departments, which remained directly under the governor, were headed by executive councilors responsible to the governor. The British were not yet prepared to surrender control of the key departments, although in fact some executive councilors were Indian political figures. The legislative councils included approximately 70% Indian elected members, the exact number of whom varied from province to province.

The Government of India Act, 1919, called for a review of its effectiveness by 1929, with the clear implication that further steps would be taken to carry out the Montagu declaration that self-government was the goal of British rule. Although the act could have been seen as a step along the road toward full Indian responsibility, it was rejected by the Congress, the formal leadership of which, including Gandhi, was determined not to cooperate with the reforms. The result was a split within the Congress and the creation of the Swaraj ("self-rule") party, of which Motilal Nehru was a leader. The Swarajists, who contested the second and succeeding elections under the act, comprised the largest bloc in the Central Legislative Assembly and in some provincial legislative councils.

During the same period (the 1910s and 1920s), the recruitment patterns of both the civil and the military services were changed. The fact that Indian Civil Service examinations were held in both India and London made it less difficult for Indians to enter the highest administrative system. The officer ranks of the military were also opened to Indians; during the 1920s the first Indian cadets were graduated from Sandhurst, the British military academy, as well as from an academy in India at Dehra Dun. The first part of the twentieth century also saw a significant increase in industrial, commercial, and financial activity by Indians, including the opening of the first steel mill at Jamshedpur, Bihar, in 1907. Although the period can be seen as a time of advance for Indians in many fields, that advance, not surprisingly, was less rapid than many Indians desired.

The commission promised under the Montagu-Chelmsford act was appointed in 1927 under the leadership of Sir John Simon. The omission of Indian members was a tactical error that led to its boycott by the Congress, the Muslim League, and many other parties. In 1928, the Congress, under the chairmanship of Motilal Nehru, prepared a report containing a proposed constitution for India as a dominion. Its rejection by the British led the Congress to demand complete independence at its annual meeting in 1929. The report was also rejected by the Muslim League, headed by Jinnah, as it proposed the ending of separate electorates without, in Jinnah's view, providing adequate substitute safeguards for the Muslims. Civil disobedience began anew in 1930, but the British government announced at the same time that a round-table conference would be held in London with British and Indian delegates to frame a new constitution for India. Gandhi boycotted the first meeting in 1930 but compromised with the British and attended the second in 1931. The communal question between Hindus and Muslims proved to be a major stumbling point, and, even with a third conference in 1932, no agreed plan could be reached. A "communal award" made by British Prime Minister Ramsey MacDonald in 1932 continued the system of separate electorates and set the ratios of seats for each community at the center and in each province.

The 1935 Reforms: Provincial Autonomy and Federalism

The British parliament passed the Government of India Act of 1935 on August 2 of that year; it became fully effective at the provincial level and partially effective at the central level on April 1, 1937. The federal provisions, with a few exceptions, were not made effective, and the system of the 1919 act continued at the center until independence. The federal concept, which, in effect, would have introduced dyarchy at the center, was intended to embrace British India and the princely states. The princes were unwilling to accede even in the limited matters of defense, foreign affairs, and currency, the responsibility for which would have been transferred under the act from the viceroy (as Crown representative) to the central authority for federal India. A federal unified judiciary was established. Burma was separated from India and made a crown colony. Sindh was taken from Bombay and made a separate province, one of a total of eleven in British India.

The principal changes came at the provincial level, where cabinet governments with ministers responsible to the legislative assembly[2] were formed. Emergency powers were reserved for the governors who, in answer to a complaint by the Congress, agreed to use them sparingly. Elections, according to the system of separate electorates, were held during the winter of 1936–1937. The Congress won clear majorities in six Hindu-majority provinces (Bihar, United Provinces, Central Provinces, Bombay, Madras, Orissa) and was able for a time to form a ministry in a seventh (Assam). It also formed a ministry in the Muslim-majority North-West Frontier Province. The Muslim League fared poorly in the elections in the Muslim-majority provinces although it was able to join a coalition in Bengal and to form a ministry in Sindh. The Punjab was ruled until 1947 by the multicommunal Unionist party. (The Muslim League's movement toward a separate Muslim state [Pakistan] will be described in Chapter 10.)

World War II brought several constitutional issues to the fore. In September 1939, the viceroy, exercising his legal powers if not the best judgment, declared India at war without consulting the provincial premiers. The Congress, showing its capability for poor judgment as well, then resigned from the ministries in the provinces it ruled and lost the opportunity for continuing experience and the chance to participate in the war effort. The ministries were restored as the war ended. At the urging of the United States, the British sent Sir Stafford Cripps to India in 1942, with an offer of independence when the war was won by the allies. The offer contained the seed of Pakistan as it provided the provinces an opportunity to withdraw from the federation and to gain independence either separately or in groups. The Congress rejected the plan, renewed demonstrations (in the "Quit India" movement), and found most of its leaders in jail for the duration.

Independence and Partition

The end of the war brought a change in British policy: Great Britain now wished to withdraw from India. The discussions thereafter centered on the means by which this withdrawal could be accomplished. The British preferred to transfer power to a united India, one in which the princes would also play a part. A mission of the British cabinet visited India in 1946 and proposed a three-tier system for an Indian federation. The greatest share of power would be vested in the provinces, and the center would be limited to foreign affairs, defense, communications, currency, and taxation to the extent necessary to carry out these functions. The provinces would be permitted to form groups or zones and to delegate upward such powers as the associating provinces thought desirable. For example, the group including the Indus river basin might delegate irrigation and hydroelectric matters to the group administration. Three groups were contemplated: one would comprise the Punjab, Sindh, the North-West Frontier Province, and Balochistan and would clearly be a Muslim-majority area; a second would consist of Bengal and Assam and would also be Muslim-majority; the third would encompass the remainder of India and would be Hindu-majority. Reluctantly accepted by the Muslim League but rejected by the Congress, the plan ultimately failed.

Viceroy Lord Wavell (1943–1947), through difficult negotiations, had transformed the executive council into a de facto cabinet in 1946 with Jawaharlal Nehru as leader. But it became evident that the partition of India was the only acceptable solution—a solution accepted by the Muslim League despite its failure to gain all the territory it wanted (Bengal and the Punjab were partitioned as provinces), opposed but finally accepted by the Congress, and implemented with great speed by the new viceroy, Lord Mountbatten (also governor general of India, 1947–1948).

India and Pakistan thus entered their independence with the heritage of the governmental systems of the British period, modified to transfer all power to the newly elected constituent assemblies of each dominion under the India Independence Act of 1947. The partially effective democratic background as well as the viceregal system and "steel-frame" method of administration would affect the governance of each new nation. The Government of India Act of 1935, as modified, would serve as the constitutional document for each dominion until it passed its own constitution.

Ceylon as a Crown Colony

Although the framework for Ceylon was parallel to that of India in certain respects, the island was governed by the British as a separate entity. The Portuguese in 1505 were the first Europeans to arrive, but they gave way to the Dutch East India Company by the mid-seventeenth century. During the Napoleonic wars, during which time the Dutch were allied with the French, the British arrived and with some difficulty eventually established the coastal areas as a crown colony in 1802. This development was confirmed by the settlements at Vienna in 1815. The local Ceylonese kingdom of Kandy continued to exist until it was defeated by the British in 1818. From then until independence in 1948, all of Ceylon was a British crown colony.

Ceylon progressed more rapidly than India in education and its administration and law-making sectors were at least as advanced as those in the larger British area. In the latter part of the nineteenth century and the early part of the twentieth, increasing numbers of Ceylonese were admitted to the civil services. In 1833, as a result of the Colebrooke Commission, governmental reforms were made through the establishment of an executive council and a legislative council, the latter including some Ceylonese nonofficial nominated members. Little reform was seen thereafter until 1912 when elections were used for the selection of Ceylonese members. Political changes in 1920 and 1924, which occurred partly in response to demands by the Ceylon National Congress, led to a nonofficial majority in the legislative council and to a measure of financial control that greatly exceeded the degree of such control in India under the 1919 act.

A royal commission in 1928 recommended extensive changes, which were implemented in 1931. A state council elected by universal suffrage served as the instrument of self-government, and a body similar to a council of ministers was formed. Although final control remained in the hands of the governor, Ceylon had become a self-governing colony.

World War II delayed further constitutional advance, but another royal commission was sent to Ceylon in 1945 to discuss the demands of the now ruling United National party. A new constitution, modeled on Westminster, came into effect in October 1947. Four months later on February 4, 1948, Ceylon became independent as a dominion in the British commonwealth.

Nepal, Bhutan, and the Maldives

Nepal, Bhutan, and the Maldives were not British colonies as such, but they were protected by the British in the sense that their foreign relations were under British control.

Present-day Nepal dates from the expansion of the territory of the king of Gorkha, which culminated in the capture of the Kathmandu Valley by Prithvi Narayan Shah in 1768. The ambitions of the Nepalese kings and the British East India Company conflicted, and the two entities were at war from 1814 to 1816. The result of this war was the designation of a boundary between Nepali and Company territories and the acceptance by Nepal of a British resident in Kathmandu. From 1846 until 1951, the kings of Nepal were overshadowed by the power of the hereditary prime ministers in the Rana family. The Ranas were ousted in 1951 by King Tribhuvan, and Nepal moved into what can be called the modern period of its administration. Great Britain recognized the complete independence of Nepal by the Treaty of 1923. Although a degree of tutelage by Britain continued until 1947, Nepal was free to act in its own interests, and the treaty permitted it to escape the integration of the princely states that ended the rule of the maharajas and nawabs elsewhere in the subcontinent.

Bhutan escaped the same fate although its status as a protectorate was continued by India after 1947. Bhutan's military contacts with the Company predated those of Nepal, as the two were at war in 1772. A treaty in 1774 recognized that Tibet claimed Bhutan as a dependency. Difficulties between the Company and Bhutan continued, but a treaty in 1865 finally settled the border and provided a Company subsidy to Bhutan. British influence increased at the expense of China and Tibet, and in 1910, despite Chinese protests, a new treaty was signed under which Bhutan agreed to be "guided" by Britain in foreign relations and Bhutan was paid a subsidy. This arrangement with India was continued through another treaty in 1949. Neither Great Britain nor India interfered in the traditional Bhutanese government. Indian control of foreign affairs gradually decreased, and Bhutan was admitted to the United Nations in 1971.

The Maldive Islands had both Portuguese and Dutch intervention before the British extended a protectorate over the sultanate. With Ceylonese independence came the agreement that the British would continue to conduct the foreign affairs of the islands and be responsible for their defense but would not interfere with internal administration. In July 1965, Britain and the Maldives agreed that the islands were completely sovereign. The Maldives were admitted to the United Nations the same year.

Notes

1. The term *states* is used here to mean the princely states; territorial divisions of British India were termed *provinces*—the term is still used in Pakistan and was used in India until the 1950 constitution was enacted. Since then, in India the major divisions are termed *states*.

2. The provincial legislative council was renamed the legislative assembly, but a few provinces had bicameral legislatures in which the upper house retained the name of legislative council.

Suggested Readings

A recently published and useful overview of Indian history is Stanley Wolpert, *A New History of India*, 2nd ed. (New York: Oxford University Press, 1982). For almost encyclopedic coverage the venerable *Oxford History of India*, 3rd ed. (New York: Oxford University Press, 1958) is valuable; this is an update of the original work by Vincent A. Smith. Still a standard work is Arthur Berriedale Keith, *A Constitutional History of India* (Allahabad: Central Book Depot, 1961).

For information regarding Ceylon (Sri Lanka) see W. Howard Wriggins, *Ceylon: Dilemmas of a New Nation* (Princeton, N.J.: Princeton University Press, 1960). For Nepal, see Leo E. Rose and John T. Scholz, *Nepal, Profile of a Himalayan Kingdom* (Boulder, Colo.: Westview Press, 1980).

For further discussion of specific topics in this chapter and generally throughout the book see Maureen L. P. Patterson, *South Asian Civilizations: a Bibliographic Synthesis* (Chicago: University of Chicago Press, 1981), which can be supplemented by the annual *Bibliography of Asian Studies*, published by the Association for Asian Studies.

PART 1

INDIA

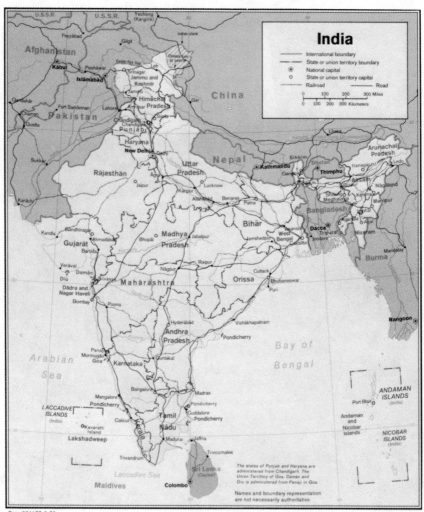

2
SOCIETY'S HERITAGE
AND ITS MEANING
FOR THE PRESENT

India's difficulties in nation building, economic development, and political stability have been strongly influenced by a host of complex factors. Of these the most prominent are its geographic setting and its sociocultural history. India is the largest state on the South Asian subcontinent. One-third the size of the United States—about 1,127,000 square miles—it is a country of great distances: From the Himalayan mountains in the north to the Indian Ocean in the south is 2,000 miles and some 1,700 miles from the western border with Pakistan to the eastern border with Burma. These distances and elevational changes mean that India has a wide variety of climates and landscapes, from snow-covered mountains and lush green forests to dry brown plains and sandy deserts.

Geographically, India is divided into three main regions, each having its own culture, traditions, and history. The various subregions add to the country's variety of life-styles and traditions. The first region consists of the vast plains of north India, irrigated by the Ganges and its tributaries. Originating in the Himalayas, the sacred Ganges River runs more than 1,500 miles through several states of India until it reaches the Bay of Bengal. The silt deposited by this river enriches the soil of the vast northern plains, where agriculture is the main livelihood of the people. It was in the Ganges Valley in ancient times that the Hindu civilization flourished.

The second region, the Deccan plateau, is separated from the north by the Vindhya hills and from the coastal areas by the Eastern and Western Ghats, which form a kind of mountain wall. Although rich in mineral resources, the plateau is short in rainfall; hence it is not heavily populated, in contrast to the other regions of India. In this region the people and the cultures of north and south intermingle.

The third region, farther south near the port city of Madras, is the ancient land of the Tamils and the heartland of the Dravidian people. This southern peninsula has been free from any extended domination of invaders and has preserved the ancient traditions of Hinduism.

India's society is basically agrarian. Despite rapid strides in industrialization since 1947, when India became independent, 80% of its population still relies upon agriculture for a living. The fortunes of Indian farmers, who live in thousands of tiny villages, are dependent on the erratic monsoon, which can cause disastrous floods or droughts. Although with recent improvements in irrigation, varieties of seeds, and petroleum-based fertilizer the government has succeeded in increasing the country's agricultural output, the majority of Indian farmers are still untouched by these developments. Efforts by India's political elites to raise the standard of living of the country's more than 800 million people and to bring them into the modern age are complicated by ancient traditions and culture.

Sociocultural Plurality: Historical Roots

Historians often divide Indian history into three distinct periods: Hindu, Muslim, and British. Each of these periods has left its impact on the cultural and sociopolitical structure of the country, leading to a composite culture enriched by these diverse sources.

Ancient Hindu Heritage

The origins of Hindu India trace back to the Aryans, who migrated to India from central Asia around 1500 B.C., entering India through Afghanistan and the Hindu Kush mountains. The Aryans, who have been described as sharp featured, handsome, tall, and fair skinned, were nomadic. Their early settlements were located in northwest India, particularly in the Punjab, the land of five rivers. They developed a language known as Sanskrit, which philologists subsequently discovered was Indo-European, or similar to the languages spoken by the people settled in Iran and various parts of Europe. The languages spoken in present-day north India and in the western states of Maharashtra and Gujarat belong to this Indo-European family of languages; the Aryans of India belong to the same racial and ethnic group that settled in Iran and parts of Europe.

As colonists in northwest India, the Aryans clashed with the Dravidians, who lived in India before the Aryan invasion. The Dravidians had founded a sophisticated culture called the Indus Valley civilization of Harappa and Mohenjodaro, two towns located respectively in the present-day Punjab and Sind provinces of Pakistan. The Aryans pushed the Dravidians into the south, where Dravidian languages still flourish. Over several centuries the Aryans were able to conquer most of India, which was populated by the non-Aryans and indigenous tribes. Fair-skinned Aryans intermarried with

Dravidians, who were short, broad nosed, and dark, and one can still discern the predominant Dravidian features among the south Indians.

The Aryans were the first Hindus in India. The development of Hinduism took centuries; the religion is evolutionary in nature and reflects a great deal of local and regional variation. Around 1200 B.C. the Aryans started composing hymns that were collected into the *Vedas*, the early Hindu scripture. The *Vedas* are the "oldest known literature in any Indo-European language."¹ Later, in the post-Vedic period, the Aryans began discussing fundamental philosophical questions and speculating about the nature of the universe and the meaning of human life. These discussions have been summed up in the *Darshanas*, the literature that provides the intellectual heritage of Hindus.

Although there is no one source of Hindu religious thought, the two great epics composed in Sanskrit, the *Ramayana* and the *Mahabharata*, have profoundly influenced the religious, cultural, and literary worlds of the Hindus. These two epics describe the period between 1000 and 700 B.C., and their heroes and heroines have been the subjects of writings in all Indian languages, including the languages of south India. Even today the stories in these two epics are told to children in Hindu families. The *Bhagavadgita* (Song of God), which is a part of the *Mahabharata*, is the most frequently cited sacred work of the Hindus.

It was in the Vedic period that the Aryans developed a complex social structure based on the caste system, wherein the priests (Brahmins) and the warriors (Kshatriyas) occupied the highest positions, the traders (Vaishyas) the middle, and the menials (Sudras) the lowest. Despite repeated attacks on the caste system by subsequent reform-oriented social and religious movements, it still exists in India and has a strong impact on the sociopolitical behavior of Hindus. (This aspect of Hindu society is discussed in detail in the following chapter.)

Although ancient Hinduism was not equalitarian—it asserted that different classes were needed to perform different social functions—it nevertheless placed considerable emphasis on kindliness and tolerance of other human beings. The ethics of Hinduism required ritualistic sacrifices but also emphasized such personal virtues as honesty, hospitality, and "piety, in the sense of such religious acts as worship, pilgrimage, and the feeding of cows and brahmans."²

The most important challenge to the teachings of Hinduism and its hierarchical social order in ancient India came from Buddhism and Jainism, which were founded almost at the same time by two princes born into Kshatriya families. In the late sixth and early fifth centuries B.C., Gautama Buddha (563–483 B.C.) turned ascetic, propounded his teachings, and established a new order of followers. These followers placed emphasis on truthfulness, nonviolence, eschewing of hatred, purity of heart, and love for fellow human beings irrespective of caste or class considerations. Vardhaman Mahavir (599–527 B.C.), the founder of Jainism, was equally emphatic on personal virtues as opposed to the ritualistic sacrifices practiced by Hindu Brahmins, but Mahavir placed far greater emphasis on self-discipline and nonviolence than the Buddha had done. Most of the religious writings of Buddhism and Jainism were in vernaculars rather than in Sanskrit. Even though royal patronage was extended to Buddhism, Hinduism was able to reassert itself and become the predominant religion of the subcontinent. Buddhists and Jains survive today as small religious minorities.

The cultural heritage of Hindus was also influenced by pre-Islamic Persia and especially by ancient Greece. Even before the invasion of India by Alexander the Great in 326 B.C., India was in touch with Greece through Persia. Many scholars find close parallels between early Greek and Indian schools of philosophy. After the Greek invasion several Greek imperial outposts were set up in India; many were eventually absorbed into the cultural groups of north India.

Although various Hindu kingdoms were founded from time to time in both the north and the south, they were never able to establish their control over the entire subcontinent of India. Most of these kingdoms were regional in nature, and the founders were unable to build a type of government that could survive the demise of the ruling dynasty.

There was little discussion of the theoretical basis of politics and political institutions in Hindu India. Unlike the ancient Greeks, the ancient Hindus did not develop a formal political philosophy. The authors who wrote on state and government actually expounded the elements of statecraft rather than the theoretical issues of politics.

Evidence suggests the existence of both monarchical and republican forms of government. In some cases monarchs were advised by a council of ministers; in others they were absolute rulers. In essence the Hindu system was authoritarian and feudalistic in structure. Even in republics the power belonged to the elders of the tribes or to the leaders of the guilds and community groups rather than to the ordinary citizens.[3] In any case, the Hindus, who had made rich contributions to the development of civilization in India, largely failed to display a constructive ability to build stable political institutions.[4]

By the end of the tenth century A.D., Hindu civilization had lost its dynamism and creativity. Hindu society had become stagnant and rigid. The rulers of the various Hindu kingdoms displayed no sense of nationalism or patriotism and were unable to withstand the onslaught of hardy Muslim invaders from the northwest.

The Muslim Heritage

The advent of Islam in India proved to be a different story. Broadly speaking, the interaction between Islam and Hindus in India followed three patterns. The first was one of terrorism: Muslim invaders came to plunder and to slaughter the native population, leaving in their wake a trail of death and destruction. Mahmud of Ghazni, a Turk by descent, typifies this early aspect of India's contact with Islam. In A.D. 1000, he repeatedly invaded India in order to plunder its wealthy towns and cities and particularly the fabulous offerings of gold and cash stored in Hindu temples. A devoted Muslim, Mahmud concentrated his destructive tactics on nonbelievers. His example was later followed by Tamerlane, by Nadir Shah of Persia, and by Ahmad Shah Abdali of Afghanistan, although they were less religiously motivated than Mahmud and discriminated little between Muslim and Hindu gentry while looting. Most of these invaders went back to their native lands and did not settle in India.

The second pattern of Muslim invasion was characterized by the Muslim conquest, settlement, and founding of kingdoms in parts of western and northern India. This pattern is evident, for example, in the Arab conquest of Sind in 712 by Mohammad bin Qasim, who founded an Arab kingdom and forced the Hindus to convert to Islam. This pattern of conquest was followed from the twelfth to the sixteenth centuries until the establishment of the Mughal empire. During this period, divided Hindu kingdoms fell, one after the other, to the Muslim invaders of Turkish, Persian, and Afghan origin. Although the Muslims left a majority of the resident Hindu population alone, there were instances in which Hindus were subjected to humiliation, discrimination, and occasional torture and forcible conversion to Islam. Many of these Muslim kingdoms were short lived and ruled by transient dynasties, and most of them were unstable. The early Muslim rulers failed to build an efficient system of administration, and the organizational abilities they displayed were no better than those of their Hindu predecessors.

The founding of the Mughal empire in the sixteenth century represented the third pattern of interactions. Not only did the Mughal rulers conquer most of India, but they established a stable and centralized administration directed from Lahore, Agra, and Delhi. The founder of the Mughal empire was Babur, who conquered Delhi in 1525–1526. But it was Babur's grandson, Akbar, who during his long rule (1556–1605) laid the foundation of the Mughal empire in north India. During his reign and those of his three successors, India achieved political stability unmatched in the history of Muslim India.

The Mughals were not only the new rulers; they were also the newest settlers in India. In the process they actively integrated the Hindus into both the civil and military administrations. In addition, they tried to reach across the religious divide to create a more coherent society by making matrimonial alliances with the Hindu princely houses of Rajasthan. Many of the Mughals, especially Akbar (who was highly rationalist in his orientation), were opposed to the orthodox and dogmatic Islamic traditions. They tried to create a composite Indian culture incorporating both Hindu and Muslim values. But

Islam, unlike many other religious movements of the past, was a young, vibrant, and aggressive religious force that could not be absorbed by Hinduism.

Some progress was made during this period in uniting Hindus and Muslims in a composite culture. A powerful part of the Bhakti (devotional) movement criticized the orthodoxies of both Hindu Brahmins and Muslim Ulema (religious scholars). Nanak, Kabir, and many other saint poets emphasized a devotee's personal relationship with his god and tried to synthesize the teachings of Islam and Hinduism. Among the Muslims, similar efforts were made by the Sufis, who were influenced by Hindu mysticism.[5] As a result, many places of worship were established that were frequented by both Muslims and Hindus. Yet, despite these efforts, the fundamental division and a sense of latent hostility continued among the Hindus and Muslims throughout India. No religious or social movement was able to bridge the deep gulf between the two religious communities.

The Mughal empire brought progress in other areas, however. In addition to building forts and beautiful palaces and mausoleums, the Persian-speaking Mughal rulers patronized Urdu, which is written in Persian script. As a language it is rich in literary traditions, and it was spoken by cultivated people in and around Delhi, the principal seat of the Mughal empire. But even though both Hindus and Muslims contributed to the development of Urdu literature, a majority of Hindus considered Urdu and its literature to be symbols of Muslim culture.

In contemporary India the Hindu nationalists regard the Muslim period of Indian history as a period of alien rule and subjugation. For them the desecration of Hindu temples and the slaughter of innocent followers of Hinduism are too painful to be forgotten and the defeats of Hindu kings at the hands of Muslim invaders are shameful episodes of Indian history. The religious tolerance of Akbar, they assert, was only an exception, for his successors gave up this policy. Instead, following Islamic orthodoxy, they prohibited interreligious marriages, pulled down Hindu temples, and even imposed *Jizya* (poll tax) on Hindus. Hindu nationalists today have disowned Urdu language and literature and instead consider Hindi to be the language of north India.

In contrast, secularist Hindus and nationalist Indian Muslims emphasize the positive side of the Muslim rule in India. They look upon the Mughal empire, its architectural achievements, and Urdu literary traditions as an important part of the cultural heritage of India. For example, Jawaharlal Nehru, a leader of the freedom movement and the first prime minister of India, displayed a high regard for the Muslim contributions to Indian civilization. Nevertheless, the two contradictory attitudes toward the Muslim period persist in the contemporary politics of India.

British Rule and the Contact with the West

In the third period of Indian history, British supremacy was firmly established in 1858, when the queen-in-council took over the direct administration of India, replacing the East India Company (see Chapter 1). British rule brought India face to face with a much more dynamic, creative, and vibrant culture. The British displayed far better administrative and organizational skills than did any of the earlier ruling classes of India. Not only did they establish control over India and achieve territorial integration, they also founded a centralized administration that could not be challenged easily.

The territorial integration of the country was strengthened by the building of an extensive network of highways, railroads, and post and telegraph systems. Such a system not only enabled the British to exploit India as a vast market for the sale of its manufactured goods, but it also gave the Indians a mobility within their own country that they had never before experienced. Trade between different parts of India expanded rapidly, and by the time the British left, India had developed a national economy that strengthened the unity among different regions of the country.

The efficient administrative machinery built by the British and the merit-based system of recruitment to bureaucracy they introduced are two of the important traditions inherited by the Indians from this period. The foundation of this system of administration at the district level had been laid earlier by the Mughals, wherein the local and the provincial administrators would act as the agents of the central government. But the British introduced a high degree of uniformity, in both the civil and the judicial administration; in addition, the administrative system possessed objectivity and impersonality, qualities not found in the previous system of administration. Such a system established rule of law, respect for personal liberty, and equality of all persons of Indian origin, regardless of religion. Administratively, India became one— an achievement unparalleled in the political history of India.

The Western system of education brought a slow though radical transformation of the value structure and behavior patterns of Indian intellectuals. The new system of civil and judicial administration made the English language and education a very valuable avenue for achieving political influence, economic power, and social mobility. Thus it came as no surprise when thousands of Indians started flocking to the newly established institutions of higher learning that provided instruction in English. This system of education produced a new class of professionals and enlarged the size of the urban middle class; it also exposed Indian elites to the constitutional liberalism and democratic socialism propounded by English utilitarians and Fabian socialists. The democratic ideals of liberty, equality, and social justice gradually took root among the members of the intellectual establishment of the country. In short, the knowledge of English brought the upper classes of India in contact with the West, thus injecting a new dynamism into an ancient civilization.

The British impact, however, was not uniform throughout India. Princely India, with a few notable exceptions, remained feudal and isolated, and many regions of the country were slow to respond to the new ideas and values. In some parts of the subcontinent the feudal order was dismantled, although in other areas it survived.

In the nation-building and modernization process, the unevenness of the British impact created problems for the elites in the post-independence period. The pace of modernization and development of a national identity has been faster in those communities that experienced a higher exposure to the Western impact.

Quest for National Identity: The Cultural Revival and the Nationalist Movement

One of the most remarkable developments of the British period of Indian history was the development of a national sense of unity among the elites from urban areas who practiced law or medicine or other professional occupations. These professionals received their training in English, but, although they were as qualified as their English counterparts, they were never considered their equals. The average British ruler in India looked down upon the native culture and its practitioners. The resultant sense of humiliation and status deprivation brought these Indian people together and forced them, despite their diverse ethnic and religious origins, to think about the political issues in all-India terms.

The English system of education and contact with the West brought the Indian elites in touch with nationalism as an ideological force at a time when it was at its zenith in Europe. Moreover, the English language provided communication links among the urban elites, who originated from different provinces and therefore spoke different native languages. It was the members of this elite class who rose above the ascriptive and primordial ties characteristic of traditional India and propagated a national vision of India.

Nationalism as a movement was preceded by cultural revivalism and a social reform movement. Contact with the West through the British forced Indians, especially Hindus, to examine critically the structure of Hindu society. Through this process of self-examination, Hindu elites became painfully aware of the deficiencies of Hindu society, which was permeated with social customs that could not be justified on rational or even religious grounds.

The elites saw Hindu society as dominated by superstitions, idolatry, magical myths, and many reprehensible social customs. If Hinduism was to save itself from the onslaught of Western culture and proselytic Christian missions supported by the British empire, its critical need was not only to get rid of social evils but also to reorganize its structure on a more rational basis. Consequently, an upsurge of social reform movements occurred in different parts of the country. Some reformers sought a synthesis of Hinduism, Western liberalism, and selective principles of Christianity while others emphasized the glories of Hindu India and hoped to restore to it the essential Vedic values they felt had been lost in the course of subjugation of Hindus during the Muslim rule.

Raja Ram Mohan Roy (1774–1833), a Bengali thinker and reformer, exemplified the first group of reformers. A learned person who had studied the scriptures of Christianity, Islam, and Hinduism and who knew many languages including Sanskrit, Arabic, English, Hebrew, and Persian, he was deeply influenced by the rationalist philosophies of the West. He strongly disapproved of idol worship, the caste system, the inferior status of women, untouchability, and other social evils of Hinduism. In order to propagate his reformist views he founded the Brahmo Samaj, an organization that contributed a great deal to social reform and to the stimulation of cultural and intellectual activities in Bengal and in several other parts of India.

The second type of social reform movement, seeking social reforms coupled with Hindu revivalism, was reflected in the writings and activities of Swami Dayanand (1824–1883), a Gujarati Brahmin who sought to legitimize the reform of Hindu society on the basis of a reinterpretation of the *Vedas*. These ancient Hindu scriptures, Dayanand felt, not only contained sacred knowledge but were the source of all philosophical and scientific thought as well. He glorified the Hindu past and sought to purify contemporary Hinduism by getting rid of the caste system, untouchability, idol worship, and other superstitions. Such evil social practices, he stressed, were introduced into Hinduism by selfish Brahmins, who used them to perpetuate their dominance on Hindu society. In his quest to create a sense of pride among Hindus, he virulently attacked both Islam and Christianity. Dayanand was a staunch nationalist who thought social reform should precede *Swarajya* (self-rule).

The Arya Samaj, a social reform movement founded by Dayanand in 1875, became closely associated with educational activities, especially with the spread of English education through the Dayanand Anglo-Vedic (DAV) college movement in northwest India. In subsequent years many leaders of the Arya Samaj movement joined hands with the protagonists of Hindu nationalism.

In south India, the Theosophical Society became instrumental in both cultural revival and social reform among Hindus. The Society worked to establish the superiority of Hindu philosophy over Western. Annie Besant (1847–1933), an Englishwoman who was deeply influenced by Hindu philosophy, became a major spokesperson for the society; she helped popularize its teachings and thereby created a great degree of cultural pride among middle-class Hindus of south India.

But there was another group of reformers, consisting of intellectuals and professionals, who were deeply influenced by the rationalist thinking of the West. Although they were committed to the preservation of the basic institutions of Hindu society and its value system, they believed that it needed reform and reorganization in order to face the challenge of modern times. They held that patience, endurance, and understanding were needed to accomplish such changes, not a frontal assault on the traditional Hindu leadership. They sought these gradual changes by founding educational institutions, cultural organizations, research foundations, science and religious study groups, reading rooms, libraries, and so on. Justice M. G. Ranade (1842–1901) and R. C. Bhandarkar in Maharashtra and Debendranath Tagore (1817–1905) in Bengal represented this more secular route toward social reform among Hindus.

Originally, contact with the West had created a sense of cultural inferiority among the English-educated Hindus. Swami Vivekanand (1863–1902) and his associates sought to counter this image by comparing Hinduism and Western culture. A powerful speaker and a charismatic personality, Vivekanand called upon Hindus to take pride in their spiritual heritage and attacked Western culture as inferior. For him, "the backbone, the foundation and the bedrock of India's national life was India's spiritual genius,"[6] which the West did not possess.

The overall consequence was an unprecedented cultural revival among Hindus. Interest in classical Sanskrit writings and in Hindu art and philosophy was stimulated by an outpouring of European scholarship in praise of India's cultural heritage. It was not surprising, therefore, that the glorification of Indian history became a staple of writings in various regional languages of India. In addition, literary elites and political leaders used Hindu religious symbols to arouse patriotism. They identified Indian nationalism with Hinduism and deified the motherland. Recollection of the glories of the past was essential to the creation of a sense of national respect and a new national identity.

But in this process of cultural revival and resurgence of Hindu nationalism, Muslims were left out. Initially, the Indian Muslims' reaction to British rule was to withdraw within the shell of their own community and their self-imposed isolation from the new ideas that British rule had generated within Indian society. Sir Syed Ahmad Khan (1817–1898) brought the Muslims into the modern world by establishing in 1875 the Mohammadan Anglo-Oriental College at Aligarh (now known as Aligarh Muslim University). Syed Ahmad

Khan placed strong emphasis on the revival of the Muslims' pride in their heritage, on preservation of the Muslim subnational identity, and on the reconciliation of the Muslims' interests with British rule in India. Aligarh produced the main elements of Western-educated Muslim intelligentsia, who became the vanguard of Muslim separatism in Indian politics.

In a politically and administratively united India, the cultural revitalization movement, as in other parts of South Asia, especially in Sri Lanka, led to the rise of a well-organized nationalist movement. The impetus for the organization of a national association that would speak on behalf of all Indians was provided, ironically, by the racially motivated policies of the British government, which discriminated against Indians in their land. Even though, for instance, recruitment of Indians into the Indian Civil Services (ICS), the most prestigious bureaucratic organization in British India, was promised as early as 1858, all efforts were made to block the Indians' entry into such services. When an Indian such as Surendranath Banerjea (1848–1926) was successful in entering the ICS, he was dismissed on flimsy grounds. Indians faced further humiliation when Englishmen living in India were successful in withdrawing the Ilbert Bill of 1883, which had permitted the trial of a European in a court presided over by an Indian judge. Events such as this forced Indians to seek a national forum not only to articulate their demands and to protest this discrimination but also to consolidate their ranks to force the attention of the British government in India to their needs. The result was the establishment of the Indian National Congress in 1885.

From its very inception, the Indian National Congress became intertwined with the nationalist movement in the country. This movement, however, underwent several phases and revealed considerable tension among its various leaders and factions with respect to both the ultimate goals of the movement and the methods to achieve these goals. Fortunately for India, its struggle for freedom was spread over a long period of time; the leaders of the movement were thus permitted the opportunity to debate openly the kind of society and polity to be built once India achieved independence. By contrast, the Pakistan movement was not only single-issue-oriented, it was also dominated by one powerful leader, Mohammad Ali Jinnah, who displayed little tolerance for dissent within his ranks. Not surprisingly, then, the Indian political elites at the time of India's independence were much better prepared to tackle the issues of institution building and economic development than were the leaders of Pakistan.

The first phase of the nationalist movement was dominated by the well-to-do segment of Indian society. The leaders representing this segment were steeped in British traditions and education and depended upon the British sense of justice; they sought to ameliorate the conditions of Indians through an appeal to the British sense of fairness. Their main objective was to seek greater representation of educated Indians in the civil services and to introduce representative institutions at the provincial and local levels. They did not entertain the hope of complete independence from British rule; rather, they believed that continued association with the British empire was in the interests of Indians. Surendranath Banerjea, who was twice elected president of the Indian National Congress, asserted that English civilization was the "noblest the world has ever seen . . . a civilization fraught with unspeakable blessings to the people of India."[7] These nationalists took pride in their citizenship in the British empire and sought to propagate values of British liberalism throughout the country. During this period such men as Dadabhai Nauroji (1825–1917), Justice M. G. Ranade (1842–1901), and Pherozshah Mehta (1845–1915), all products of the British system of education, led the Indian National Congress and pressured the British government to address the problems. The British tried to diffuse this pressure by passing the Government of India Act of 1909 (see Chapter 1), which expanded political participation and electoral representation at both the provincial and central government levels. The representatives to the legislative councils were to be elected by voters holding property or having high educational qualifications. This measure also introduced separate representation for the Muslims, who were to elect their representatives from their own community.

In the second nationalist phase, starting in 1905, the struggle for the control of the Indian National Congress was divided between the "moderates" led by Gopal Krishana Gokhale (1866–1915) and the "extremists" led by Bal Gangadhar Tilak (1856–1920). These two leaders, both Maharashtrian Brahmins, differed not only in their personalities and ideological orientations but also in their approaches to achieving self-rule for the country. Gokhale was a disciple of Ranade, a moderate, and even though he was much more vocal in his criticism of British government than Ranade, he believed in constitutional methods. He did not hesitate to work with British rulers and tried to represent Indians in the Imperial Legislative Council, where he was a member.

Bal Gangadhar Tilak and his extremist associates, on the other hand, did not trust the British government. Tilak was a Hindu nationalist and an ardent believer in the superiority of Hindu culture over Western. In his opposition to the moderates, Tilak was supported by Lala Lajpat Rai of the Punjab and Bipan Chandra Pal and Aurobindo Ghose of Bengal. These extremists were militant and provided philosophical justification for the use of violence against the alien rulers of India. Unlike the moderates, the extremists asserted that political freedom could be won only by waging a war against the enemy. Whereas the moderates believed that they would be able to achieve self-government with the blessings of British rulers, the extremist Tilak declared that "Swaraj [self-rule] is my birthright and I will have it." Also unlike Gokhale and his associates, the extremists openly used Hindu religious symbols and traditions to stimulate nationalist sentiments among the masses. They never stopped attacking the moderates for their subservience to the Western culture.

In 1907 the extremists lost out to Gokhale and his moderate associates in their struggle to control the Congress organization. But British suppression, Tilak's confinement in Mandalay, the arrest of B. C. Pal and Aurobindo Ghose, and the political exile of Lala Lajpat Rai turned the extremists into popular heroes. By 1915 a reconciliation between the two factions had occurred, and Tilak and his associates once again became active within the Congress party. The united nationalist leadership of the Indian National Congress demanded and was promised by the British a large measure of self-government at the end of World War I.

This second nationalist phase also witnessed the rise of self-assertiveness among the minorities. The emergence of the Hindu-dominated Indian National Congress at the center stage of Indian politics and the fear that Hindus would become the rulers of the country owing to their overwhelming majority in the population spurred the Muslims into political activity, resulting in the organization of the All-India Muslim League in 1906. The Muslims demanded separate representation and allied themselves with the British, seeking their favor and protection against what the Muslims perceived as the aggressiveness of the Hindu-dominated Indian National Congress. Given the pluralistic structure of Indian society, the rise of such particularistic movements was not surprising. The leaders of the nationalist movement, however, under-estimated the strength of these subcultural and regional movements in perceiving the problem of national integration to be primarily a political one.

The end of World War I brought about a radical transformation in the political expectations and aspirations of Indians. The British government responded by enacting the Government of India Act of 1919 (known as the Montague-Chelmsford Reforms). As previously noted, this act introduced partial responsible government in the provinces; increased the number of elected representatives in the central legislative assembly; gave separate representation to the Sikhs, the Europeans settled in India, and the Anglo-Indians (Eurasians); and extended voting rights to almost 10% of the adult population of the country. Even though these steps provided opportunities for Indians to learn about parliamentary government, to organize voters for electoral purposes, and to gain experience in self-government, they did not satisfy the political aspirations of the nationalist leaders. Their alienation from the British rulers in India was increased by the continuation of the repressive policies that the government had adopted during the war. The British government still possessed enormous powers to restrict civil liberties, to imprison politically active Indians, and to declare martial law. Increased protests against such repressive measures after World War I resulted in the declaration of martial law and in the Amritsar tragedy (April 13, 1919), in which more than three hundred Indians were killed and more than a thousand wounded when General Dyer ordered troops to fire on peaceful and unarmed protestors. This brutal action shocked the Indian nationalists, but the House of Lords, ignoring Indian sentiments, passed a resolution in 1920 in appreciation of General Dyer's services to the empire.

The conflict between the Indian extremists and the British left the moderates outside the mainstream of the nationalist movement. As the extremist faction led by Tilak took over the Congress organization in 1917, the moderates withdrew from the party and founded their own organization, the Indian Liberal Federation. Tilak then became the undisputed leader of the nationalists. After Tilak's death in 1920, the leadership passed into the hands of Mohandas Karamchand Gandhi (1869–1948). Gandhi rejected the moderates' gradualist approach to political reforms, but he also rejected the extremists' philosophical justification of violence. His nonviolent approach, using mass mobilization and peaceful defiance of British authority, radicalized Indian politics far beyond the expectations of Tilak's followers.

During the twenty years he lived in South Africa practicing law among the Indian settlers, Gandhi developed his concept of *satyagraha* (loosely translated as "soul force") and the technique of civil disobedience. On his return to India, before he plunged into Indian politics, Gandhi traveled widely throughout the country, observing the culture, traditions, and living conditions of the people. He felt that the leaders of the nationalist movement were out of touch with the people who lived in India's many villages. He realized that in order to win freedom from Britain, the nationalist movement required a mass base; it needed to involve the people living in the countryside. Accordingly, Gandhi not only established his headquarters in rural India but also sent the nationalist leaders and party workers to live in the villages, to undertake social service, and to lead simple and austere lives. He enforced strict discipline, emphasized nonviolence, and demanded sacrifices from his followers. This pacifist approach, austere and rigorous life, and complete identification with the common man earned Gandhi the saintly title of the *Mahatma* (the great soul).

Thus it was only after prolonged observation that Gandhi applied his concept of *satyagraha* and the technique of civil disobedience to the Indian situation. He called for peaceful breaching of unjust laws; protesting through strikes, fasting, and noncooperation with the authority; and boycotting not only of imported goods but also of British educational institutions. But he insisted on peaceful defiance of authority, seeking arrest by breaking laws. Soon, thanks to his charismatic personality and simple and saintly life-style, Gandhi was able to build a formidable nationwide following for himself as well as for the Indian National Congress. Under his leadership the elitist nationalist movement became a mass movement. Although the top leaders of the Congress organization were still English-educated and upper-class Indians, they were nevertheless able to identify with the cause of the common man. In addition, the second tier of leadership at the provincial and local levels was more attuned to the sensitivities of the masses than any other group in the country. A well-organized vernacular press and an articulate vernacular-speaking intelligentsia established strong links between these national leaders in the center of Indian politics and the mass of Indians living on the periphery.

Thus began the third phase of the nationalist movement in which the nationalist leadership, with an expanded mass base, started to press for complete independence. During its Lahore session in 1929, the Indian National Congress, no longer willing to accept dominion status and membership in the British Commonwealth of Nations, adopted a resolution demanding complete independence for India. During this phase of the nationalistic movement, Gandhi launched several mass drives: the noncooperation movement of 1921, the breaking of salt laws (the salt march) in 1930, and the civil disobedience of 1933. Although the sudden suspension of these movements was criticized by many young and leftist leaders, each of them succeeded in enhancing mass political consciousness and demonstrated Gandhi's ability to mobilize the country. The British government responded by passing the Government of India Act of 1935, which established complete provincial autonomy and proposed partial responsible government at the center. These concessions were no doubt a substantial improvement on the institutional setup created by the Government of India Act of 1919, but they were too little and too late. The nationalist movement had taken deep roots in Indian soil, and Gandhi's Indian National Congress had caught the imagination of the masses. The popularity of the Congress became evident when in the elections of 1937 it won the majority of legislative seats in six provinces; it had become the single largest party and formed the government in eight out of eleven provinces in British rule. For the next twenty-eight months (1937–1939), during which time the party's leadership ran the provincial governments, it not only gained administrative experience but also made substantial progress in social and economic programs for the masses.

It should be noted, however, that while the Indian National Congress represented the nationalist aspirations of a majority of Indians, there were several smaller movements representing the aspirations of religious and regional minorities that could not be absorbed by the nationalist group led by Mahatma Gandhi. The Muslim League, for example, under the able leadership of Mohammad Ali Jinnah, became a powerful rival of the Indian National Congress, claiming to be the sole representative of the Indian Muslims. Similarly, in Kashmir, the National Conference under the dynamic leadership of Sheikh Mohammad Abdullah and, in the Punjab, the Akali Dal led by Master Tara Singh represented the Kashmiri Muslims and Punjabi Sikhs, respectively. During the 1940s the subnational movements gained momentum and became a major challenge to the nationalist goals of the leaders of the Indian National Congress.

The final phase of the nationalist movement (1940–1947) was dominated by the Congress leaders' two concerns: complete independence from British rule and preservation of the territorial unity of India through accommodation of the aspirations of these subnationalist movements, especially the leaders of the Muslim League.

By 1942 it had become evident to the leaders of the Indian National Congress that the British government was in no mood to meet its demands for independence despite the Congress's offer to support the British war efforts against Japan and Germany. In August 1942, therefore, Mahatma Gandhi planned to launch a massive Quit India movement. But before the leaders could organize this movement, the British government arrested many of the leaders of the Indian National Congress, including Gandhi. The British were always baffled by the success of Gandhi's methods of nonviolence and uncertain as to how to deal with them. However, a preemptive strike by the government in August 1942 saved it from the unpleasant task of brutalizing Gandhi's nonviolent soldiers. Despite some disruption of the administration, order was restored in a short time.

While the Congress leaders were in jail, the leaders of such subnationalist parties as the Muslim League and the Akali party of the Sikhs were able to consolidate their positions within their respective communities. Toward the end of World War II it became evident to the British government that it would not be able to keep India under control and that it would have to reach an agreement with the nationalist leaders. In 1944, therefore, first Gandhi and later many of his associates were released.

Once out of jail, the nationalist leaders were confronted with the prospect of independence but also with the possibility that the country might become divided on a religious basis. In 1940 the Muslim League had demanded the creation of a Muslim-majority state out of British India consisting of those provinces in which the Muslims formed a majority. The Sikhs, on the other hand, sought the creation of a Sikh homeland in Punjab, where the Sikh religion had originated. The leaders of the Indian National Congress were ill prepared to face the challenges of rival nationalist groups based upon religion; their nationalist ideology, in fact, sought to downgrade the importance of religious divisions in the Indian population.

During the 1945–1946 elections the Muslim League emerged as the representative body of the Muslims of India, capturing 446 out of 496 provincial seats in the Muslim majority provinces of the country. In addition, the Muslim League launched a massive campaign to press its demand for the division of the country. This action resulted in widespread Hindu-Muslim rioting; indeed, there emerged a real threat of civil war in India. Ultimately, therefore, the Congress leaders agreed in 1947 to a division of the country on the basis of religion: The demand for Pakistan was conceded, Punjab and Bengal were divided, Muslim-majority areas went to Pakistan, and the rest became parts of India. Such religious and ethnic minorities as the Sikhs were not able at the time to manage sovereign states for themselves, but the desire for separate states persists to this day, especially among a section of the Sikh community. On August 15, 1947, India became independent from Britain; the aspirations of the nationalist leaders were realized. Despite this triumph, however, the religious division of the country proved to be a major setback for their ideology of nationalism. Independence and partition were accompanied by massive Hindu-Muslim rioting and migration in which an estimated half-million Hindus, Muslims, and Sikhs perished.

The Indian people still have bitter memories of the partition of the subcontinent and the consequent exchange of population between West Pakistan and the East Punjab State of India. Indeed, the independence movement left a smoldering hostility between the Hindus and the Muslims. The Indian leaders' adherence to the preservation of a multicultural and multireligious society in India has caused them to become wary of politicians and parties that make religious demands or seek to alter state boundaries along religious lines. The disintegration of the nationalist movement following independence and the experience of the division of the country have made Indian leaders highly sensitive about the territorial integrity and unity of the country.

Quest for Institution Building and Modernization: The Development of New Goals

Even before independence, questions regarding the future setup of an independent India were frequently discussed among the Indian elites. The dominant sector of the Indian National Congress, the modernists, agreed on the form of government they wanted: Their experience with representative government during the British rule and their observation of the parliamentary system in the United Kingdom fixed their choice on the Westminster model of government.

The elites were convinced that if people could participate in the political process, national unity would be consolidated and the national identity that had been nourished by the cultural revival and the nationalist movement would be strengthened. The establishment of a liberal democracy in India thus became the modernists' new goal, reflecting the Indian leaders' desire for citizen participation in the political process. Freedom of speech and expression were also to become essential attributes of the new system. Conscious of the social and economic disparities in Indian society, the leaders believed that the ideals of democratic socialism would help achieve some degree of social and economic equality within the society, with the state actively helping the poor, the backward, and the helpless. The ideology of socialism, they believed, would also strengthen the principles of secular nationalism that they had so ardently championed. In subsequent chapters we will see how successful the contemporary political elites have been in adhering to these ideals.

With independence, India needed modernization and economic development. The nationalist leaders inherited from the British rulers a primarily agricultural economy; an overwhelming majority (80%) of the population depended on the land to earn their living. Furthermore, Indian agriculture was one of the most inefficient and backward systems in the world. Indians were hardly able to feed themselves. The land was tormented by frequent droughts, famines, floods, and pestilence. Most of the industries the British had set up were established merely to meet consumers' needs for cotton textiles, sugar, and jute. Despite India's possession of certain strategic raw materials, such as iron ore, coal, mica, bauxite, magnesite, chromite, titanium, and refractory materials, the country lacked a significant capital goods industry. It was heavily dependent on Great Britain and other industrialized countries of the West for its machinery and engineering goods.

The elites agreed on the need to end poverty and raise the standard of living of the people. However, they differed as to the approach which they should undertake to achieve these goals. There were two main viewpoints— one advocated by Gandhi and his followers, the other by a more modernist and secular-minded group. Gandhi's approach was the product of his moral and religious orientations. He strongly disapproved of the profit motive, favored strict limits on private property, and opposed the tyranny of machines and the ruthless competition of a market economy. He also favored the development of agricultural and consumers' cooperatives. According to Gandhi, India needed to maintain its agricultural, rural-based economy while redeveloping and expanding its traditional cottage and small-scale industries, which would once again make the village society self-sufficient. His vision of India also recognized the need for low consumption of resources and the development of indigenous technologies suitable for its environment and culture. As the society of India was primarily agricultural and rural, Gandhi's strategy of economic development would have resulted in a higher investment of resources in rural India, where 80% of its population lives. Although a labor-intensive development process might not have made India an industrial giant, the belief was that such an effort would have generated more job opportunities for the poorer segment of Indian society. Such a vision of

India, however, was incompatible with the model of a modern industrial state.

Jawaharlal Nehru and his modernist and secularist associates, influenced by Marxist and socialist thought, disagreed with the Gandhian approach to the economic development of India. Nehru looked upon science and technology as the key elements in the transformation of the character of Indian society. Technology was perceived as the handmaiden of science; when effectively linked together, the two could remove poverty from India and radically change its face. These modernists attributed underdevelopment of societies such as that of India to the insufficiency of technological development. They sought to modernize India through the application of science and technology and through heavy investment in capital goods industries. They believed in centralized planning, increased output of technically skilled manpower and importing of technical know-how to make India ultimately a technologically self-sufficient country. In such a system the state would play a key role; it would set the development priorities. Although no wholesale takeover of industries and businesses would occur, and while private initiative and investment would be allowed, the private sector of the economy was to be subservient to the public needs, which the government alone was capable of defining.

Of these two ideological approaches to India's economic and industrial development, it was Nehru's approach rather than Gandhi's that the political elites preferred. As a result, in industrial and economic development the new goal became the development of an extensive scientific and technological infrastructure based on the model of advanced industrialized societies.

*   *   *

In sum, India's sociocultural background, its history, its geographic diversities, and its nationalist movement have rendered the task of nation building and modernization extremely difficult for its leaders. Unlike the political leaders of Pakistan, India's leaders were very clear about the direction in which they wanted their newly independent country to move. Reflecting the religious division of the country, India's political leaders—in contrast to those of Pakistan—refused to adopt the religion of the majority as the state religion. Instead they opted to build a modern nation-state upon the twin principles of democracy and socialism.

Notes

1. Percival Griffiths, *The British Impact on India* (London: Archon Books, 1953), p. 22.

2. A. L. Basham, *The Wonder that Was India* (New York: Grove Press, 1954), p. 341.

3. Ibid., pp. 80–137.

4. Griffiths, *The British Impact*, p. 26.

5. H. G. Rawlinson, *India: A Short Cultural History* (New York: Praeger Publishers, 1968), p. 245.

6. Dennis Dalton, "The Concept of Politics and Power in India: Ideological Traditions," in J. R. Wilson and Dennis Dalton (eds.), *The States of South Asia: The Problem of National Integration* (London: C. Hunt & Co., 1982), p. 177.

7. D. Mackenzie Brown, *The Nationalist Movement: Indian Political Thought from Ranade to Bhave* (Berkeley: University of California Press, 1965), p. 15.

Suggested Readings

Brown, Judith M. *Modern India: The Origins of an Asian Democracy* (New York: Oxford University Press, 1980).

Chand, Tara. *History of the Freedom Movement in India* (Delhi: Publication Division, Ministry of Information and Broadcasting, 1972).

Gallagher, John, Gordon Johnson, and Anil Seal. *Locality, Province and Nation: Essays on Indian Politics 1870–1940* (Cambridge: Cambridge University Press, 1973).

Gupta, A. K. *Myth and Reality: The Struggle for Freedom in India 1945–47* (New Delhi: Manohar Publications, 1987).

Hardy, P. *The Muslims of British India* (Cambridge: Cambridge University Press, 1972).

Kumar, R. *Essays on Gandhian Politics* (Oxford: Oxford University Press, 1971).

McLane, John R. *Indian Nationalism and the Early Congress* (Princeton: Princeton University Press, 1977).

Mehrotra, S. R. *The Emergence of Indian National Congress* (New Delhi: Vikas, 1971).

Menon, V. P. *The Transfer of Power in India* (Princeton: Princeton University Press, 1957).

Moore, R. J. *Escape from Empire: The Attlee Government and the Indian Problem* (Oxford: Clarendon Press, 1980).

Mujeeb, M. *The Indian Muslims* (Montreal: McGill University Press, 1967).

Nanda, B. R. (ed.). *Essays in Modern Indian History* (Delhi: Oxford University Press, 1980).

Rawlinson, H. G. *India: A Short Cultural History* (New York: Frederick A. Praeger, 1968).

Schwartzberg, Joseph E. *A Historical Atlas of South Asia* (Chicago: University of Chicago Press, 1978).

Spear, Percival (ed.). *The Oxford History of India,* third edition (London: Oxford University Press, 1967).

Wolpert, Stanley. *A New History of India* (New York: Oxford University Press, 1982).

3
SOCIAL STRUCTURE
AND POLITICAL CULTURE

The stability of a political system is dependent upon the support that it enjoys from its citizens. In return, social institutions transmit sociopolitical values and norms of political behavior. They become instrumental in creating support for the system and enhancing its legitimacy. A description of India's social structure and the nature of its political culture can help us understand the conditions under which the system operates.

India is an ancient civilization but a new nation; therefore, the values and attitudes of its citizens, the nature of its political culture, and its political processes are influenced by both its traditional past and its contemporary experience. Indians are proud of the operation of their contemporary democratic institutions and of the uniqueness of their culture, which gives its people a distinct identity.

Through a complex network of primary and secondary structures, the people of India have successfully transmitted several key elements of their cultural and political structure from generation to generation. It is through this process of socialization that India has developed its distinct political culture.

The Dominant Cultural Pattern:
The Hindu Worldview

Despite the confluence of the various cultures that have affected the Indian people, the Hindu worldview constitutes the most dominant cultural force in the society. The religious teachings of Hinduism and its belief system deeply influence the social behavior and political attitudes of its followers.

Hindus have often been described as other-worldly and fatalistic because Hinduism teaches that an individual is bound in the cycle of birth and death. It is the *karma* (the actions in one's life) that determines the nature of one's following life. In order to end the earthly cycles of birth and death, an individual needs salvation through an ultimate union of his soul (*atman*) with the Supreme Reality (*parmatman*).

Even though acquisition of material wealth and a desire for enjoyment and reproduction are important for the survival of this world, spiritual salvation through this union of the soul with the Supreme Reality is superior to all other life goals. Therefore, to Hindus the quest for political power and secular activities ought to be secondary to spiritual affairs. In actual life, however, there is a considerable gap between religious prescriptions and an individual's behavior. Thus, despite their emphasis on spiritual values, Hindus continue to pursue vigorously material goals in their lives.

Hinduism, however, is known for its flexibility, sectarian organizations, and religious tolerance. Because there is no organized church or clerical authority among the Hindus as there is among the Christians, there is no uniform enforcement of the rules among Hindus. God may be perceived and worshipped in many ways. Not only may individuals choose different paths to reach the Supreme Reality, but they are also free to worship deities of their own choice. Hindus are therefore divided into numerous sects, each having its own deity, temples, and rituals. This kind of flexibility is nowhere more evident than in the villages of India, where the majority of Indians live. Their belief system enables Hindus to live side by side with the followers of such other religions as Buddhism, Jainism, and Christianity without friction. Peaceful coexistence between Hinduism and Islam, however, has been difficult to achieve.

Although Hindus are flexible in their religious practices, they do tend to separate politics from religion. These characteristics of Hinduism have enabled the predominantly Hindu political elites of India to build the political institution of the new republic on secular principles.

The Caste System

Despite its flexibility in other areas, Hinduism retains one of the world's most highly structured and stratified social orders, the caste system. This traditional social order divides Hindus into a hierarchical structure consisting of four castes: the Brahmins (priests and custodians of sacred knowledge), Kshatriyas (warriors and rulers), Vaishyas (traders), and Sudras (persons performing manual labor and menial jobs). In this hierarchical social order the Brahmins occupy the top position and the Sudras the lowest. Today the caste system has become ascriptive in its nature; high caste origin and high social status usually go together. Thus a person born into a particular caste rarely has an opportunity to change status within the society, regardless of his or her talent and achievements. In rural India the system has also created a highly segregated residential pattern in which the Sudras live on the outskirts of the villages or towns, away from the high-caste neighborhood.

Some sections of Sudras have been treated as "untouchable" by the members of the upper castes because their hereditary occupations (such as scavenging and leather working) have been considered unclean. Even after the legal abolition of untouchability in post-independence India, the practice is still prevalent in many sections of Hindu society, especially in rural India. In addition, many native tribes who earlier did not believe in Hinduism have now adopted many of its practices and traditions but are not yet considered part of mainstream Hindu society.[1] Thus, although in theory Hinduism may be one of the most tolerant and flexible religions in the world, in its social order it displays a high degree of rigidity.

The Hindu caste system in reality, however, does not exist in these simple fourfold divisions. The four main castes are actually formal names for the organizational structure consisting of 3,000 subcastes into which the present Hindu society is divided. In rural India, where the caste system is most pervasive, a close interrelationship exists among social status, economic power, and occupational divisions. In the thousands of villages the landowners traditionally make up the upper castes—the Kshatriyas and the Brahmins. In south India the situation is different in that non-Brahmins constitute the landowning castes. Money lending, banking, and trading are done mostly by the Banias, a term used almost interchangeably with Vaishyas. Landholding and well-to-do castes are traditionally expected to look after the well-being of the members of lower castes, who in turn perform services for the upper castes. In this kind of *jajmani* (superordinate-subordinate) relationship, both the upper and lower castes have rights and obligations toward each other. Both the caste obligations and the occupational differentiations have religious sanctions. In this way each caste group is obligated to fulfill its role within the society, whatever its status and the nature of the work it is obliged to perform.

The status, functions, and organizations of the subcastes (*jatis*), vary considerably from one region of the country to another. Many of the subcastes are confined only to a subregion of the country and others only to a locality or village. Yet despite these variations, the caste system is deeply imbedded in the subconscious of the individual Hindu. Indeed, caste affiliations influence and often determine the social and political behavior of all citizens.

The organization of the members of one caste to protect and promote their common sociopolitical interests has been a frequent phenomenon. Caste group activity has long been in evidence, even before the introduction of representative institutions in India. Since independence in 1947 some castes have become highly politicized. Whether the castes infiltrate the parties or the parties use the existing caste associations to mobilize the voters is a debatable question, but there is little doubt that candidates for public office, regardless of their ideological orientations and party affiliations, are attuned to the sensitivities of caste groups. According to A. H. Somjee, "the fact that a caste is horizontally integrated and continues to hold itself together for the pursuit of its primary social concerns, despite rapid change in all other aspects of Indian life since independence, indicates an effective network of communication integrating its members towards common social goals."[2] It is not surprising, therefore, that in the selection of candidates for political offices the parties are deeply influenced by the caste composition of the population of an electoral district.

Castes and subcastes are very important instruments of political socialization. In the formation of the political attitudes of young adults and children, the caste affiliation plays an important role. Empirical evidence suggests that persons originating from the upper castes (i.e., from the Brahmins and Kshatriyas) show a higher level of personal efficacy and interpersonal trust; they also seem to have a stronger commitment to the operation of democracy than do the members of the Jats (an agriculturist subcaste) and the low castes.[3] There is a clear tendency on the part of children and young adults to identify themselves with the national political leaders originating from their own caste rather than with those from other castes. Mahatma Gandhi, for instance, is a political hero more favored by the members of his own caste, the Vaishya, than, say, by the Jats.[4]

Family and Kinship

Along with his or her caste, a factor likely to influence an Indian's sociopolitical behavior is family and kinship group. The basic unit of Hindu society in particular and of religious communities of India in general is not the individual but the extended or joint family, which consists of three generations living under the same roof.[5]

Kinship is one of the most important organizational structures within the Indian religious groups—a structure that includes numerous real or supposed uncles, aunts, brothers, sisters, and cousins, as well as grandparents from both maternal and paternal sides. Each person is accorded a status in the kinship hierarchy and receives due respect. Indian children brought up under this complex structure of kinship relations learn about politics from their families, which are characterized by frequent exchanges of political views and a high degree of trust between parents and children. Various surveys of Indian children indicate that the process of political socialization in India does indeed reflect familial transmission of party identification and political orientations to the children. An overwhelming majority of the young respondents in one recent study not only were aware of the party affiliations of their parents but also identified with the parties that their parents preferred.[6]

TABLE 3.1   Religious Distribution of the Population (India) (in percentages)

Hindus	82.64
Muslims	11.32
Christians	2.43
Sikhs	1.96
Buddhists	.71
Jains	.48
Others	.43

Figures do not total 100 percent due to rounding.

Source: Census of India data in Francis Robinson, ed., The Cambridge Encyclopedia of India, Pakistan, Bangladesh and Sri Lanka (Cambridge: Cambridge University Press, 1989).

Minority Religions and Subgroup Identities

Although Hinduism is the religion of the majority of Indians (see Table 3.1), there are important religious minorities such as Muslims and Sikhs who have been able to preserve their group identities. In societies such as that of India, minority religions provide "each group with a focal point of identity and social solidarity, and large areas of its culture are associated with its religion."[7] By the same token, religion and aspects of cultural life such as language, art, literature, and social institutions become intertwined and lead to the development of powerful group identities that often inhibit the development of a cohesive political community.

Unlike the Muslims and Sikhs, other religious minorities such as the Jains, Buddhists, and Christians have shown little or no religious fundamentalism and have stayed in the mainstream of Indian politics.

Muslims. Muslim religious doctrine is based upon the belief that the Quran contains the ultimate truth and the revelation of the Divine Will. Muslims believe in the ultimate establishment of a divinely ordained social order. In institutional structures and value systems, Hinduism and Islam seem incompatible. Many Muslims sought the creation of Pakistan as a Muslim nation so as to escape from the tyranny of the Hindu majority. Even after the partition of British India on a religious basis, the Muslim population of India constitutes the single most important minority of the country. Political elites in power in India after independence sought to lessen the anxiety of the Muslim minority by creating a secular state. The separation between religion and state was expected to reduce Hindu-Muslim antagonism and lead to the development of greater political integration.

In post-independence India, Muslims have freely participated in the political process of the country. They have used their votes as leverage for political bargaining, seeking accommodation from the majority community. Sectarian hostility between Hindus and Muslims persists, however; the electoral and institutional mechanisms created to reduce group conflict have had only limited success. There is an overwhelming domination of the political institutions by the majority community. Despite the fact that the Muslims constitute the largest minority of the country, they form one of the depressed segments of Indian society. Nevertheless, they have displayed greater assertiveness as well as group awareness in recent years. The orthodox and traditional Muslim leaders have been joined by the more educated and younger members in seeking to mobilize the community in order both to preserve its identity and to acquire a greater share of the society's goods and services.

Sikhs. Another example of the assertion of religious identity concerns the rise of Sikh fundamentalism. Sikhism, which was born out of a fusion of Hinduism and Islam, is a young and vibrant religion. Guru Nanak Dev (1469–1539), who founded Sikhism, advocated monotheism and opposed the idolatry and caste system practiced by Hindus. He was followed by nine *gurus* (teachers). It was Guru Gobind Singh (1666–1708), the tenth *guru*, who gave the Sikhs a distinct organization and turned them into militant fighters against the Muslim rulers. The Sikhs believe in one sacred book, the *Adi Granth*, a collection of hymns written mainly by Nanak, Kabir, and Hindu saints. The practice of the caste system is still prevalent among them despite its denunciation by the Sikh *gurus*. An overwhelming majority of the followers of Sikhism came from the fold of Hinduism. Sikhs and Hindus intermarried and celebrated each others' religious festivals. But the early part of the twentieth century witnessed the rise of numerous Sikh sectarian organizations that emphasized the distinct Sikh identity. Claiming Punjabi as their religious language and looking upon the Punjab, a northwestern state in India, as their homeland, the Sikhs have developed a very strong subnational identity.

In 1982, the members of the Akali Dal, a moderate Sikh political party, launched a peaceful agitation in which they demanded certain religious concessions. They also wanted greater political autonomy for the Sikh majority state of Punjab than had been granted by the constitution of India. Soon, however, the militant Sikhs, led by a fundamentalist preacher, Sant Jarnail Singh Bhindranwale (1947–1984), resorted to terrorism. They converted the Golden Temple, the holiest shrine of the Sikhs, into an armed fortress. In June 1984, Prime Minister Indira Gandhi sent the army to flush out the terrorists from the temple. The result was considerable loss of life: In addition to the large number of terrorists killed were many innocent pilgrims fatally entrapped in the temple. The Sikhs as a community felt humiliated and angered. They became alienated from the national government, and some even sought the establishment of an independent and sovereign Sikh state called Khalistan. The subsequent assassination of Indira Gandhi by two Sikh bodyguards, on October 31, 1984, resulted in widespread Hindu retaliation against the Sikhs.

In July 1985, however, an agreement was signed between Sant Harcharan Singh Longowal, the president of the Sikh moderate Akali Dal, and the prime minister, Rajiv Gandhi. Most of the demands of the Sikhs were conceded.

In September 1985, elections were held in Punjab. The Akali Dal won a massive majority, and a government headed by moderate Sikhs has since been installed in the state. In 1987, the central government not only failed to implement the terms of the agreement reached between the moderate Sikh leadership and the Rajiv government, but it also dismissed the Punjab ministry led by Surjit Singh Barnala, the moderate Sikh leader, imposing central rule on the state. The repressive measures adopted by the central government further alienated the Sikh population of the state and intensified political violence leading to thousands of casualties. The 1989 elections for the national parliament resulted in impressive victories for militant Sikh leaders, resulting in the ouster of many moderates. The events of the last several years have created an unprecedented gulf between the Hindus and the Sikhs, despite the close and cordial relations they had maintained in the past. The future place of the Sikhs in Indian politics remains uncertain.

Subnational Solidarities: Linguistic and Cultural Divisions

India's problems in attaining national integration and political cohesion have been further complicated by the existence of strong subnational identities based along linguistic-cultural lines. The constitution of India recognizes fourteen major languages spoken by a large majority of the people (see Table 3.2), and hundreds of other languages and dialects are spoken by the people in rural areas (see Map 3.1). Many people, however, can speak more than two or three languages, and in urban areas bilingualism is common.

Linguistic and cultural identities are very strong among the regions that are far removed from the Hindi heartland of north India. Even though they are listed separately in the constitution, the Hindi, Urdu, and Punjabi languages are closely related. People are often able to shift speaking from one language to another without much difficulty. Hindi, the plurality language, was chosen in 1950 by the body that framed the constitution of free India as the official language of the country; then, in 1965, after the constitution had been in force for fifteen years, Hindi was to become the sole official language of the country. But there was strong cultural and practical opposition to Hindi in the south, because Hindi is a north Indian language and a language of Indo-European origin. To south Indians, the adoption of Hindi symbolized

TABLE 3.2   Languages Specified in the Constitution of India and Their Speakers

Languages	Number of Persons (in millions)	Percentage of Total
Hindi[a]	162.6	29.7
Telegu	44.8	8.1
Bengali	44.8	8.1
Marathi	42.3	7.7
Tamil	37.7	6.9
Urdu	28.6	5.2
Gujarati	25.9	4.7
Malayalam	21.9	4.0
Kannada	21.7	4.0
Oriya	19.9	3.6
Punjabi	16.5	3.0
Assamese	8.9	1.6
Kashmiri	2.4	.4
Sanskrit	.002	—

[a]Hindi, Urdu, and Punjabi, as spoken languages, are very closely related.

Source: Pocket Book, Population Statistics (based on the Census of India, 1971) (New Delhi: Office of the Census Commissioner, 1977).

the domination of the Dravidian south by the Aryan north. Hindi is as foreign to the people in south India as English is. Hindi remains only a regional language, however; it is not yet well enough developed to take the place of English as the interregional and commercial language of India. As English is a global language, knowledge of English enhances job opportunities for educated persons in India as well as in other parts of the world. Preferring English, the south Indians therefore resented the forced imposition of Hindi. As a result of violent opposition to Hindi in the south, the government of India agreed in 1965 to an indefinite continuation of English as the second official language of the country.

Regional divisions solidified by common language, literary traditions and culture have deep historical roots in India. Even though various vernacular literary traditions took shape in the thirteenth and fourteenth centuries, such regional identities were politically diffused and unorganized until recent times. It was only during the British period that vernacular literary traditions matured; the literary elites chose native symbols and myths and glorified the history, the land, and the people who spoke their own languages. In this way they became instrumental in developing subnational identities. Many of the literary elites became torn between pan-Indian nationalism and regional loyalties based upon cultural-linguistic identities. But when India became independent, the regional elites became the strongest protagonists of the subnational movements, immediately putting strong pressure on the national

Map 3.1

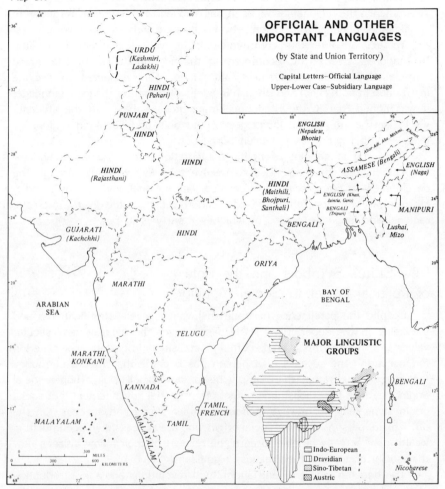

Source: Ashok K. Dutt and M. Margaret Geib, *Atlas of South Asia* (Boulder, Colo.: Westview Press, 1987). Reprinted by permission.

government to reorganize the states on a linguistic basis. They sought equal treatment and status for all regional languages. The national political elites initially resisted these demands, fearing the balkanization of the country. However, Indian political elites showed political flexibility by meeting the aspirations of the leaders of linguistic groups. In 1956, the government of India agreed to their demands and carried out a vast reorganization of the state boundaries on a linguistic basis. In each of the unilingual states of India today, the regional language is used both for administrative and educational purposes. The creation of unilingual states, however, has further strengthened the regional identities; it has also led to an increase in interstate conflict and enhanced the tension between the state and national governments.

To facilitate interstate communication as well as population mobility, the national government recommended the adoption of a three-language formula. Under this arrangement, the states were expected to provide instruction in both Hindi and English in addition to that for the local language. It was hoped that in the Hindi-speaking states of the north the students would learn some of the languages of the non-Hindi-speaking regions of India. But this hope has not been borne out.

From the standpoint of political integration, this situation may look bleak. India has, however, tried to resolve this divisive issue through the development of complex political devices. The national government in India, for example, consists of broad-based coalitions reflecting the diverse interests, regions, and language groups of whichever party is in power.

New Status Symbols and the Role of Political Power in Social Mobility

Despite the persistence of traditional values, caste stratifications, and the belief in the superiority of the sacred over the secular, new secular values and status symbols are becoming increasingly important. The criterion for measuring the success of a person has become the amount of money that person has, rather than simply his or her social origin. Higher social origin may help in establishing contacts for material advancement, but social origin alone may not always guarantee higher status and success. On the other hand, persons of lower social origin who are successful in accumulating wealth may actually be able to earn the respect of their fellow citizens now that social origin is somewhat less significant.

The ongoing industrial and agricultural revolutions and the introduction of the electoral process based upon universal suffrage have increased the opportunities for social mobility. Education, knowledge of the English language, political power, material wealth, and higher social status have become interdependent. Higher education, as in other modern societies, is considered one of the primary means of achieving upward social mobility. In India an understanding of English and proficiency in writing and speaking English give a person a head start over others. Although many people might criticize a westernized Indian, in urban areas they can hardly disguise their eagerness to accept him as their role model. If they cannot adopt his values and lifestyle in their own lives, they would like their children to emulate him. Moreover, the image of such an Indian as an ideal to emulate has been reinforced by television, movies, magazines, and newspapers. Both the politically influential people and the members of the "nouveau riche" classes send their children to the exclusive private schools that provide education in English.

With the diversification of political activity in several areas of national life, the competition for elective positions has increased immensely. Naturally this process has enhanced the demand for and the status of people who are politically ambitious and who possess organizational abilities. As the older generation of leaders who commanded authority because of their age and contributions to the independence movement has almost disappeared of late, reliance on the new type of political leaders who are willing to use all means to acquire power has increased. In India, most politicians are not trusted by the people: They have a cynical attitude toward politicians, even though their services are constantly in demand.

At present, social stratification and class divisions in India are based upon a mixture of ascription and personal ability. The upper class in India is small and consists of members of the landed aristocracy, former rulers of princely states, industrial proprietors, businesspeople, and English-educated westernized groups holding top positions in the administration as well as in the business and intellectual establishment of the country.

The post-independence period has also witnessed the emergence of a middle class. Aside from the lower echelon of the bureaucracy, the middle class includes the members of the business community, the managerial-political elites, and the powerful, wealthy, and influential farmers of the countryside. According to one estimate, this class constitutes about 20% of the population of the country. It is also estimated that the members of this class are gradually "adopting similar life-styles and values [and] are being steadily woven together by a web of communication, trade and commercial economic development."[8] This growing middle class provides strategic political support for the ruling elites by accepting the legitimacy of the system. The rest of the population constitutes the lower classes, of which approximately 44% live below the poverty line.[9]

A Mixed Political Culture

Given the enormous complexity of the Indian sociocultural structure, it is not surprising that Indian political values and norms of behavior often give contradictory signals. There is a considerable intermixing of modern and traditional values. For example, one may find hero worship verging on idolatry along with an expression of strong democratic impulses; supersensitive nationalism along with strong parochialism; egalitarianism along with the existence of a hierarchical social order; a high degree of tolerance and passivity along with occasional outbursts of violence; and so on. These contradictory tendencies may be attributed to the vast size of the country and to its diversities, as well as to the uneven levels of exposure to modern values in the different segments of the population.

The introduction of democratic institutions in India, as is well known, was not the result of an internal groundswell. The ordinary person in India has little awareness of the advantages of a democracy. It was the Western-educated and Anglicized elites who made the deliberate choice for democracy over other forms of government. John Osgood Field put it well: "Indians struggled against Englishmen for the right to run a British system in India."[10] The political elites believed that through the introduction of universal suffrage and consequent mass political participation, a traditional society based upon an ascriptive oligarchic structure would transform itself into an egalitarian and open society. In addition, the spread of mass media and industrialization would help internalize democratic values and lead to the development of an egalitarian political culture. Various surveys suggest that these values are in fact becoming increasingly integrated into the personality structure of the newer generation of the population.[11]

The frequent elections held at the state and national levels on the basis of adult franchise have broken the traditional isolation in which most of the villagers of India had lived. Many of the groups on the periphery of the village society have developed political awareness and are learning to use their political power, and the members of the backward castes are becoming increasingly restive and challenging the domination of the land-owning upper castes. Consequently, electoral participation and voter turnout are quite impressive. Whereas in the first national election of 1951–1952 the voter turnout was around 45%, since then it has consistently risen. In the last three national elections, about 61% of the voters turned out to cast their ballots.

Even though the degree of politicization is higher in urban than in rural areas, issue awareness among the rural poor is increasing. Average citizens, while often illiterate and relatively ill-informed, are not ignorant. In fact, they tend to display sound common sense in politics. They have also been highly politicized. They may or may not always be aware of the national issues involved in the elections, but pocketbook issues have a strong impact on their voting behavior.[12] Moreover, they are capable of penalizing politicians and the parties for their highhandedness and insensitivity toward them. In a village society the elected representative is an easily accessible spokesperson for the citizens, serving as an important link between the citizens and the complex world of administration. By contrast, administrators are often English educated and come from urban areas; hence illiterate villagers do not have easy access to them.

Egalitarian values emphasized by the elites have found expression both in the constitution and in the laws of the country. Strong efforts have been made to provide not only equal voting rights granted to all citizens regardless of sex and social origin but also greater educational and job opportunities for India's millions of untouchables, the people Mahatma Gandhi called *Harijans* (the children of God), and the members of the backward castes. But despite these efforts, the equality of "citizenship in the economic field whereby . . . irrespective of his place in the social hierarchy an individual would be able to claim the right to economic advancement and distributive justice has yet to take place."[13]

The resilience of the Indian system and its capacity to face internal and external challenges seem to be rooted in the strong sense of nationalism that pervades it. This nationalism, rooted in turn in the cultural revival movement of the nineteenth century and nurtured and promoted by the political stalwarts who led the independence movement, has been further consolidated and strengthened by the policies adopted by the elites in the post-independence period. Despite the divisions within Indian society, Indians on the whole display a very positive attitude toward the system as well as its accomplishments. They express pride in the creation and operation of its democratic political institutions; indeed,"India's achievements in the area of foreign policy and the emphasis on non-alignment have become symbols of political pride. . . . Nehru's period of neutralist policy and his defiance of John Foster Dulles [President Dwight Eisenhower's Secretary of State] and, by extension, American power, are described . . . as the days of national glory and pride."[14] The system also seems to have "shown a remarkable capability to create several technological, scientific and industrial symbols which evoke a great degree of emotional response"[15] among the elite and nonelite segments of the population. In a 1974 survey in which young students were asked to list the achievements of the system about which they felt a sense of pride, 96% were able to indicate one or more achievements they thought were worthy of their pride. The most frequently mentioned achievements included the peaceful nuclear explosion, victories in the wars with Pakistan, the Green Revolution, industrial developments, and the successful working of democracy.[16] Such pride in the achievements of the system and emotional attachment to its leaders, charismatic or otherwise, are expressions not only of strong nationalism but also of the high degree of system support that exists among the citizens.

An emphasis on consensus, conciliation, compromise, and accommodation is a tradition that Indians have inherited from their past. In particular, conflict management through consensus or arbitration has been widely used by the community and caste leaders. Gandhi employed this method to resolve intraparty disputes as well as a variety of conflicts arising in national politics. In fact, the Gandhian approach to politics based upon nonviolence, or *ahimsa,* was "not only a technique of protest, defiance, and change, but also the major support for consensual decision-making and conflict resolution in intergroup and interpersonal context."[17] This unique Indian tradition of conflict management continued to operate even in the post-independence democratic process. Most of the successful Indian leaders have been conciliators and consensus builders who were able to balance conflicting political interests based upon religious, linguistic, and cultural diversities. It is widely believed that the unity and integrity of India have been preserved primarily through the practice of the politics of consensus and conciliation as opposed to the politics of confrontation and partisan divisions.

Another dominant trait of Indian political culture, shaped by its religious traditions and literature as well as by the behavior of such political leaders as Mahatma Gandhi and his followers, is a negative attitude toward the acquisition of political power. Indian ethics places emphasis on self-negation— that is, on the renunciation of desire for power, money, and status. In general, both repression of desires and cleanliness of mind have been traditionally emphasized in India.[18] According to the ancient Hindu ordering of personal virtues, *satogun* (purity of heart and absence of desire for power and wealth) ranks higher than *rajogun* (the desire to acquire power or wealth); a *sanyasi* (a person who has renounced such desires and devotes himself entirely to social service) is superior to a king. Indians therefore tend to revere those persons who seek to influence politics and public policy without seeking political power. Hence India has witnessed the introduction of what W. H. Morris-Jones has called the "language of saintly politics," a kind of politics that "is important as a language of comment rather than of description of practical behavior."[19] It sets up very high standards of public behavior, with the Mahatma as the role model.

The recent professionalization of politics, however, has reduced Mahatma Gandhi's moralistic approach to public affairs to a mere marginal importance in the Indian political process. As politics has become an important avenue of social mobility and political ambition is playing an increasingly important role in the acquisition of political power, Indian politics has become what could be termed "amoral politics." This brand of politics is characterized by a decline of the political values associated with democratic institutions and political leaders during the early stages of independent India. For example, both the elected officials and the people know that the high-sounding moral phrases of politics serve rhetorical purposes only; they are not likely to be put into practice. In addition, the giving and accepting of bribes are normal ways of political life; elected officials frequently seek and receive monetary rewards for the services they render, and persons hoping to acquire elective positions frequently purchase votes and distribute liquor to uneducated voters on or before polling days. Indeed, there is the widespread belief in India that with money and political influence, rules can be bent and laws can be broken. Many politicians and their children are in league with black marketeers or other criminal elements and yet are rarely penalized for their transgressions. Such politicians are considered to be "free looters" interested only in "plunder and power";[20] they have also been called "half-educated, money-making simpletons."[21] The intellectuals of India look upon the power-hungry professional politicians as a new breed of pundits, priests, and practitioners of witchcraft, out to perpetrate deception and fraud on common people. Moreover, the so-called black money (undeclared income) flows freely in the party coffers and in the state legislative assemblies. In this respect the politicians and political representatives in India are not much different from those characteristic of the early stages of political development in many Western societies: Indeed, the societies based upon representation rather than coercion tend in general to develop patron-client relationships rooted in amoral politics. As James Scott has noted, "self-interest thus provides the necessary political cement when neither a traditional governing elite nor a ruling group based upon ideological or class interest is available."[22]

In addition to its use of constitutional means to influence the political process, the pre-independence tradition of Gandhian politics provided the moral basis underlying the agitational approach. Disregarding the institutional procedure set up for the resolution of conflict, political and community leaders to this day frequently resort to the use of such nonviolent methods of protest as civil disobedience, satyagraha, strikes, walkouts, gherao (blockades), and sometimes even fasts until death. These methods usually disrupt normal administration and occasionally paralyze the government in a state or a region, frequently producing results where other methods have failed.

*   *   *

In sum, the Indian elites' efforts toward nation building and the establishment of a stable political system have faced frequent challenges from the divisive forces existing within the political culture; loyalties based upon subgroup identity are pervasive. But these elites have shown considerable flexibility in dealing with the demands of diverse groups. Their strategy of conciliation and accommodation has enabled the system to meet several internal challenges successfully. New national symbols in conjunction with the pride expressed over the achievements of the system have provided the Indian system far greater legitimacy than is enjoyed by any other system in South Asia.

As subnational loyalties have historic origin, they are likely to persist; hence complete secularization of the political culture is unlikely. Occasionally, therefore, the demands of these subnational groups cause tension within the system. Such tension may be further aggravated by the continuation of the tradition of agitational politics. So far, however, the system has demonstrated its ability to withstand these pressures, although not without paying a price.

Notes

1. With respect to representation in legislative bodies, the legal term for "untouchables" is "Scheduled Castes"; the unassimilated tribals are called "Scheduled Tribes."

2. A. H. Somjee, "Caste and the Decline of Political Homogeneity," *American Political Science Review,* vol. 67, no. 3 (September 1973), p. 816.

3. Yogendra K. Malik, "Efficacy, Values, and Socialization: A Case Study of North Indian Youth," *Political Science Review,* vol. 19, no. 1 (January–March 1980), p. 84; and "Trust, Efficacy and Attitude Toward Democracy: A Case Study from India," *Comparative Education Review,* vol. 23, no. 3 (October 1979), pp. 433–442.

4. Yogendra K. Malik, "Sub-Cultural Variations and Political Socialization: The Case of North Indian Youth," *Journal of Asian and African Studies,* vol. 16, no. 1-2 (1981), p. 230.

5. T. N. Madan, "The Joint Family: A Terminological Clarification," *International Journal of Comparative Sociology,* vol. 3, no. 1 (September 1962), pp. 10–11.

6. Yogendra K. Malik, "Party Identifications and Political Attitudes Among the Secondary School Children of North India," *Asia Quarterly,* vol. 4 (1979), p. 265.

7. Donald E. Smith (ed.), *Politics and Religion in South Asia* (Princeton, N.J.: Princeton University Press, 1966), p. 22.

8. Bhabani Sen Gupta, "Indian Society: An Unromantic Journey," *India Today,* January 15, 1983, p. 50.

9. *Economic and Political Weekly,* August 1979, p. 1220.

10. John Osgood Field, *Consolidating Democracy: Politicization and Participation in India* (New Delhi: Manohar, 1980), p. 347.

11. Yogendra K. Malik, "Attitudinal and Political Implications of Diffusion of Technology: The Case of North Indian Youth," in Yogendra K. Malik (ed.), *Politics, Technology and Bureaucracy in South Asia* (Leiden, Holland: E. J. Brill, 1983), pp. 45–73.

12. Rajni Kothari, "The Political Change of 1967," *Economic and Political Weekly,* vol. 6 (annual number, January 1971), p. 250.

13. A. H. Somjee, *Democratic Process in a Developing Society* (New York: St. Martin's Press, 1979), p. 8.

14. Yogendra K. Malik, *North Indian Intellectuals: An Attitudinal Profile* (Leiden, Holland: E. J. Brill, 1979), p. 139.

15. Ibid.

16. Yogendra K. Malik, "Determinants of Attitude Toward the Political System: The Case of North Indian Youths," *Asian Profile,* vol. 10, no. 5 (October 1982), p. 474.

17. Ashis Nandy, "The Culture of Indian Politics: A Stock Taking," *Journal of Asian Studies,* vol. 30, no. 1 (November 1970), p. 72.

18. Ibid., pp. 57–78.

19. W. H. Morris-Jones, *The Government and Politics of India* (Garden City, N.Y.: Doubleday and Co., 1967), p. 47.

20. Arun Shourie, "The State as Private Property," *Economic and Political Weekly* (March 1980), p. 508.

21. Ibid.

22. James C. Scott, "Corruption, Machine Politics and Political Change," *American Political Science Review* (December 1969), p. 1151.

Suggested Readings

Basham, A. L. (ed.). *A Cultural History of India* (London: Clarendon Press-Oxford, 1975).

Brass, Paul. *Language, Religion and Politics in North India* (London: Cambridge University Press, 1974).

Brown, D. Mackenzie. *The Nationalist Movement: Indian Political Thought from Ranade to Bhave* (Berkeley: University of California Press, 1965).

Brown, Judith M. *Modern India: The Origins of an Asian Democracy* (Oxford: Oxford University Press, 1985).

Freitag, Sandria B. *Collective Action and Community: Public Arenas and Emergence of Communalism in North India* (Berkeley: University of California Press, 1989).

Khare, R. S. *Culture and Democracy: Anthropological Reflections on Modern India* (Leham: University Press of America, 1985).

Kohli, Atul (ed.). *India's Democracy: An Analysis of Changing State-Society Relations* (Princeton: Princeton University Press, 1988).

Kothari, Rajni. "The Indian Enterprise Today," *Daedalus* (Fall 1989), pp. 51–67.

Mason, Philip (ed.). *India and Ceylon: Unity and Diversity* (London: Oxford University Press, 1967).

Nandy, Ashis. "The Culture of Indian Politics: A Stock Taking," *Journal of Asian Studies,* vol. 30, no. 1 (November 1970), pp. 57–78.

―――― . *At the Edge of Psychology: Essays in Politics and Culture* (New Delhi: Oxford University Press, 1980).

―――― . "The Political Culture of the Indian State," *Daedalus* (Fall 1989), pp. 1–21.

O'Connell, Joseph, Milton Israel, and W. Oxtoby (eds.). *Sikh History and Religion in the Twentieth Century* (Toronto: Toronto University Press, 1988).

Radhakrishn, S. *The Hindu View of Life* (New York: Macmillan Company, 1962).

Rudolph, Susanne H. "Consensus and Conflict in Indian Politics," *World Politics* vol. 31, no. 3 (April 1981), pp. 385–399.

Smith, Donald E. *Politics and Religion in South Asia* (Princeton, N.J.: Princeton University Press, 1966).

Srinivas, M. N. *Caste in Modern India and Other Essays* (Bombay: Asia Publishing House, 1962).

Weiner, Myron. "India: Two Political Cultures," in Lucian W. Pye and S. Verba (eds.), *Political Culture and Political Development* (Princeton, N.J.: Princeton University Press, 1965).

4
LEADERS AND SUCCESSIONS

Among the countries of South Asia only India and Sri Lanka have developed stable procedures for orderly succession of political leadership. And only in these two countries have there been no coup d'états or violent overthrows of the governments. Part of the explanation for this orderly transfer of power may be found in the institutional setup created by the political systems of these countries; but another important factor is the informal rules and procedures developed by leaders to resolve the succession struggle and to settle intra-elite conflicts. In this chaper we shall focus on the role of the personalities involved in setting the style of the political process and the informal norms of political behavior that influence the resolution of intra-elite conflict (see Chapter 5 for a discussion of the institutional structure itself).

India's regional and cultural diversities have resulted in the development of two sets of leaders, one representing the national aspirations of the people and another representing the regional aspirations. Whereas some of the leaders of national stature have a broad-based national following, others build their support base by establishing informal alliances with regional leaders, who have independent power bases.

Founders of Independent India

Mahatma Gandhi (1869–1948), Jawaharlal Nehru (1889–1964), and Vallabhbhai Patel (1875–1950), were leaders who dominated the independence movement. Their unique personalities, political behavior, and styles of leadership led each of them to make distinctive contributions to the politics and policies of the new India.

Mahatma Gandhi: Moralization of Politics

Mahatma Gandhi was a charismatic leader with a nationwide following. He pursued a style of leadership and set up certain institutional structures and norms of political behavior that still carry considerable weight in national politics. Gandhi's approach to politics was highly moralistic.

Some of the differences in the political processes of Pakistan and India and the political behavior of their leaders can be traced to the styles of their early leaders. What distinguishes Gandhi from Muhammad Ali Jinnah, the founder of Pakistan, is that Gandhi spiritualized politics in India. In the process he not only identified himself with the common man but also adopted a style of leadership that was rooted in the culture of India, especially in its Hindu religion. Following Hindu ideals of renunciation, he did not seek wealth or political power for personal gratification but rather devoted himself to the service of his countrymen. This approach to politics gave Gandhi the image of a saintly politician. In contrast, Jinnah did not develop contact with the Muslim masses but stayed aloof. His appeal to the religious sentiment of Muslims was to mobilize support for Pakistan, but he had little familiarity with the economic and political needs of the common man. In his appearance and life-style he was closer to the British rulers than to the average Indian.

Gandhi was a great organizer who perceived the enormous value of institutional structure in the political process. In 1920, when he took over the presidency of the Indian National Congress, he streamlined its organizational structure. Not only did he introduce the electoral process within the Congress, but he clearly defined the functions of different agencies, including its top decision-making bodies, called the Congress Working Committee (the executive), and its mass wing (the legislative branch), called the All India Congress Committee (AICC). The holding of regular elections of the Congress party president and the delegates to the AICC as well as officials at the provincial, district, and local party levels made the Congress party one of the most democratic organizations in the country.

Along the way, Gandhi consistently encouraged discussion and never stifled opposition. He thus contributed to the building of a powerful organization that has helped maintain stability in India's transition from a British dependency to a sovereign democratic polity. With its roots extending to far-flung villages of the country, the Congress party machine after independence became a powerful tool that the political elites successfully used to mobilize the voters.

In contrast, the Muslim League under Jinnah had no democratic organization; by the middle of the 1930s Jinnah had become its president for life. There was little discussion or debate within the leadership circles of the Muslim League. As a result, the Pakistani leaders had little experience in the operation of a democratic organization.

In the course of policy differences in India, Gandhi encouraged the disputing political elites to seek accommodation and compromise with each other. In subsequent years, this policy of accommodation and compromise became one of the main characteristics of India's democratic polity.

Jawaharlal Nehru: Charismatic Idealist and Modernist

Whereas Gandhi is called the Father of the Indian nation, Nehru (1889–1964) should be credited with building India's modern political institutions and with laying the foundations of its economic and foreign policies. In 1947, Nehru became independent India's first prime minister, and he held this position and dominated the Indian political scene until his death on May 24, 1964. He has been described as a

> master builder, one of the few great architects in the delicate and uncommon art of nation building. But he was not an isolated creation. He was a product of a half a century of freedom struggle molded by men like Gandhi, by imperial Britain, by a galaxy of life long comrades. And, he was made by countless Indians who gave him their affection.[1]

Nehru's commitment to democratic institutions and norms of behavior, his unbounded faith in science, technology, and the industrialization of the country, his emphasis on planned economic development in India, his concern for the poor, the downtrodden, and the minorities all deeply influenced political developments in India. He valued individual freedom and believed that only in a democratic system can an individual realize his or her full potential. Although the introduction of a parliamentary system in India based upon the British model may be attributed to the collective efforts of Western-educated elites, it was Nehru, as the first prime minister and the most powerful leader of the country, who put it into practice.

Not only did he adhere to the practice of holding elections for parliament on the basis of universal suffrage, an unusual practice in a Third World country, but he also respected the autonomy of the Election Commission and never intervened in its affairs.

Continuing a pre-independence practice, he held regular elections of party officials at all levels and thus maintained interparty democracy. To be sure, there were occasions on which Nehru was unwilling to tolerate dissent within the Congress party, as in 1951 when he forced Purushottam Das Tandon out of the party presidency because of the latter's commitment to Hindu chauvinistic ideology. But he respected the popular electoral verdict even when it went in favor of his ideological opponents. Nehru, like Gandhi, adhered to constitutional procedures and norms of behavior.

Nehru also permitted the democratic process to operate in the states. He was willing to accommodate the Congress party chief ministers, even when they disagreed with him. He rarely intervened in their affairs as long as they broadly followed the party platform. And he was willing to accommodate the demands of the regional leaders even if they did not belong to his party.

In addition, Nehru withstood pressure from the right wing of the Congress, which, after the creation of Pakistan, was less willing to treat Indian Muslims as equals of the Hindu majority. This right-wing faction wanted to modify Nehru's vision of a secular state in favor of Hindus. Ultimately, however, Nehru prevailed, granting Muslims and other minorities equal rights in the constitution of India. Nehru, like Mahatma Gandhi, had a national support base. He never appealed to regional or religious sentiments to keep himself in power. In addition to his authority based on the constitution, which Jinnah's successors in Pakistan lacked, Nehru had charisma and soon became a folk hero. He enjoyed the support of the masses, but he also had a very large following among intellectuals, especially among the English-educated and westernized intelligentsia who were committed to his ideals of religious tolerance and secular political culture.

As a modernist, Nehru considered science-based technology the key to the future prosperity and transformation of Indian society. He thus initiated policies that resulted in the establishment of a score of scientific institutions in India. For him, the industrialization of the country and scientific and technological development were interrelated goals to achieve economic independence of the country—hence his great emphasis on planned economic development.

Vallabhbhai Patel: Consolidator and Pragmatist

Sardar Vallabhbhai Patel (1875–1950), Nehru's contemporary and political rival, was a person of enormous organizational abilities and a pragmatic politician. He was also a "master of machine politics who revelled in political maneuvers. Nehru was the voice of the Congress, Patel its organizer."[2]

In their backgrounds, Nehru and Patel were very different from each other. Born on October 31, 1875, into a peasant family in a small town in Gujarat state, Patel was brought up in an environment dominated by orthodox Hindu values. It was no surprise that "Nehru and Patel differed on almost all public issues—yet they worked together for over forty years."[3] But their loyalty to Gandhi and the long association between these two giants of the freedom movement helped them to overcome their differences and to work together to set the new nation on a firm footing. Despite their differences, both Nehru and Patel were committed to democratic principles.

In addition to his appointment as deputy prime minister, Patel was in charge of the Home Ministry, which looked after domestic affairs. He also handled the Ministry of States, which oversaw the new government's relations with the princely states of India. Although almost two-thirds of India and three-fourths of the population had been ruled directly by the British, the other one-third of the territory and one-fourth of the population had been ruled by the princes (known as maharajas, rajas, nawabs, nizams, khans, and so forth). There were almost six hundred such princely states, some very tiny principalities, others as large as France. With the termination of British rule in India on August 15, 1947, legally all these native states could declare their independence and ask for international recognition. They therefore posed a serious threat to India's territorial integrity. But Patel, as a master strategist, succeeded in persuading the princes to join the Indian Union, and their territories were integrated into India.

Patel also recognized the importance of the highly skilled and well-trained members of the civil and administrative services, who had so well served the raj. As home minister he was able to win the loyalty of these elite services, ensuring continuity in civil administration. In this way Patel laid the foundation for the present-day administrative setup of India.

Unlike Nehru, however, Patel was not enamored with socialism; he had a conservative approach to economic issues. It was mainly through his efforts that, along with the public sector, the private sector came to occupy a vital place in India's economy.

Patel had a very strong power base in the Congress party machine among the Hindu nationalists and the landowning, business, and industrial elites of the country. It was only the ability of Nehru and Patel to work out their policy differences through discussion and deliberations that kept the Congress party organization intact. And it was the party organization that provided the vehicle for peaceful succession of leadership.

Nehru's Successors:
Rise of a Political Dynasty

The men who succeeded Nehru in the Congress party, as well as in the government, differed from him in their leadership styles, political behavior, and public policies. Rarely were they men of vision. They ensured a peaceful change of leadership, but their actions directly or indirectly contributed to the elevation of members of the Nehru dynasty to the center stage of Indian politics. The following party leaders and prime ministers played dominant roles in the post-Nehru era.

Kamaraj Nadar: Man of the Masses, Machine Politician, and King-Maker

Kumaraswami Kamaraj Nadar (1903–1975) rose to national prominence by building an alliance of powerful regional leaders. As the president of the Congress party he was able to resolve interparty struggles in the transfer of power from an older to a younger generation of leaders.

A man of the masses, Kamaraj had a humble origin, thus demonstrating that India is "indeed an open political system" in which a person could rise to the top position "no matter how low he starts."[4] The son of a village coconut seller from a low caste with no Western educational background, he became a powerful party boss in his native state of Tamilnadu. Displacing the Brahmin leadership of the Congress party in his state, Kamaraj became the chief minister of Tamilnadu and held that position from 1954 to 1963. As one scholar has noted: "Kamaraj was rather a rare phenomenon in a sense; he did not let political success change his ways of life or his common touch. A bachelor, he promoted no personal interests, built no fortune."[5] His unassuming manner, simple personal life, pragmatic political orientation, and enormous personal popularity in the south established him as a powerful regional leader.

Kamaraj was brought into national prominence when on June 2, 1964, with the assistance of prominent regional party leaders, he successfully managed the unanimous election of Lal Bahadur Shastri as the leader of the Congress parliamentary party. Shastri succeeded Nehru as prime minister. Subsequently, in February 1964, Kamaraj was elected to the presidency of the Congress party. Kamaraj became the center force of the "syndicate," an informal party organization consisting of such powerful regional party leaders as Atulya Ghosh of West Bengal, Sanjiva Reddy of Andhra Pradesh, S. K. Patil of Bombay, and S. Nijalingappa of Karnataka. As president of the Congress party, as kingpin of the syndicate, and with the informal support of the Congress state chief ministers, Kamaraj was able to reestablish the prominence of the organizational wing of the Congress in national politics.

In early 1966, following the sudden death of Lal Bahadur Shastri, Kamaraj put the weight of his office behind the candidacy of Indira Gandhi, and she was elected the leader of the Congress parliamentary party and prime minister by overwhelmingly defeating Morarji Desai. Such an institutionalized method of succession, promoted by leaders like Kamaraj, ensured for India not only continuous but also legitimate leadership.

Lal Bahadur Shastri: Consensus Builder

On June 2, 1964, Lal Bahadur Shastri (1904–1966) succeeded Nehru as the second prime minister of India. Unlike Nehru, Shastri was neither charismatic nor domineering. Born of humble social origin on October 2, 1904, in a Kayashta family of Uttar Pradesh, he was brought up in deprivation and poverty. Through sheer determination, hard work, and self-sacrifice he rose through the ranks of the Congress party and in 1950 became its general secretary, at a time when Nehru himself had taken over the party presidency. Shastri was a self-effacing person who demonstrated his organizational abilities in the 1952 elections. He was a compromiser, a person of even temperament, who could bring different factions of his party together. Even though he might not have been strongly committed to Nehru's ideology of socialism, he favored Nehru's policy of planned economic development.

Shastri held the position of prime minister from June 2, 1964, to January 11, 1966. During this short period he faced enormous problems, but he was remarkably firm yet flexible in handling them. He delicately handled the strained center-state relations, accommodating the demands of the state chief ministers. He demonstrated remarkable flexibility in agreeing to the indefinite continuation of English along with Hindi as the official language of the country, as demanded by the southern states. In addition, he showed his mettle in August 1965, when Pakistan attacked Kashmir, by ordering counterattacks on Pakistani territory in the Punjab. Although the war ended in a stalemate, he was nevertheless able to protect India's basic interests in Kashmir. Shastri died of a heart attack on January 11, 1966, hours after signing the Tashkent peace agreement terminating hostilities between India and Pakistan. As prime minister of the country, he had adhered to the rules and procedures initiated during the Nehru period.

Indira Gandhi: Dynamic, Controversial, and Authoritarian

The period of Indira Gandhi's dominance of Indian politics, from 1966 to 1984, put enormous strain on the country's political institutions as well as on the informal rules used to settle inter-elite conflicts. Unlike her father, Jawaharlal Nehru, Indira Gandhi (1917–1984) had little regard for established procedure and norms of democratic politics. In 1966 she was brought to power as the prime minister by the party bosses; by 1969 she had become embroiled in a power struggle with the same group of leaders. This power struggle evolved into a conflict between the "young turks" represented by Indira Gandhi and the older, conservative party bosses represented by the syndicate. Gandhi's progressive image resulted from the introduction of her mildly radical program of nationalization of banks, abolition of privy purses (pensions) for the rulers of the former native states, liberal loan terms for the poor sector of the society, and strong denouncement of the monopoly of business and industrial establishments in India. This progressive strategy paid her rich dividends. She earned the support of most of the intellectual establishment in India, particularly the leftists and the Marxists. She was quite successful in projecting the image of a dynamic leader seeking the establishment of an egalitarian social order in an ancient society traditionally dominated by ascriptive values and rigid social stratification. These progressive projects also helped her to ward off any threat to her authority from the Communist or socialist parties, which claimed to be champions of the poor. Having conducted herself as an accomplished politician, she surprised nobody when she won a massive majority in the 1971 parliamentary elections.

Riding on the wave of popularity generated by India's victory in the war with Pakistan over the issue of the creation of an independent nation of Bangladesh, she carried her Congress party to victory in the 1972 state elections. With these electoral victories she became not only the dominant force within the Congress party but also the undisputed leader of the country. She refused to seek accommodation and compromise with the discredited party bosses who had brought her to power. Instead she followed her own independent course of action, created a new party known as the Congress (I)—that is, I for Indira—and thereby provided herself a new power base.

Indira Gandhi's departure from the established constitutional practices that had been in operation since independence came as a shock, however. One of the most dramatic developments in the post-independence period was her declaration of national emergency. This provision is included in the constitution of India for cases in which the country's security is threatened by internal insurrection or external aggression. Only twice previously had such an emergency been declared, and for external reasons: once in 1962, when India and the People's Republic of China fought a brief war over a border dispute, and again in 1971, when the Indo-Pakistani War broke out over the liberation of Bangladesh. In 1975, however, India witnessed widespread discontent over the failure of Indira Gandhi's economic policies. She was unable to reduce unemployment, control inflation, or curb widespread corruption. The opposition leaders organized mass rallies and protest marches, some demanding the resignation of the state governments led by her party.

Ultimately, it was a crucial court decision against her that led to the declaration of internal emergency. On June 12, 1975, on the basis of an election petition, a judge of the High Court in Allahabad convicted Gandhi of breach of election laws. She lost her seat in parliament and was barred from holding any elective office for six years. As the violations were based upon minor technicalities of the law, however, she appealed the conviction to the Supreme Court of India, which reversed the decision of the lower court and allowed her to stay in power. But the lower court's verdict had undermined the legitimacy of her office, and it was the fear of losing her office that forced her to declare a national emergency. When the opposition leaders demanded her resignation, she feared widespread disruption and nationwide protests. The declaration of emergency on June 26, 1975, enabled her to arrest all her political opponents, including Jaya Prakash Narayan, a venerable Gandhian leader; Morarji Desai, a former deputy prime minister; Charan Singh, a prominent opposition leader; and thousands of other opposition leaders and party workers.

Indira Gandhi's decision to declare emergency was made with the support of her family and some of her close associates, rather than in consultation with the cabinet as required by constitutional law. The declaration has been criticized as a violation both of the spirit of the constitution and of the democratic policies in practice since independence.

The eighteen-month period of emergency was the first authoritarian rule experienced by India since the country had attained independence. Indira Gandhi enforced rigid press censorship. Numerous organizations were banned. Furthermore, paramilitary and police organization became arbitrary, creating an atmosphere of widespread oppression and fear.

Gandhi also successfully amended the constitution to free the prime minister from judicial control. In the future, electoral disputes involving such high public officials as the president, vice-president, and prime minister would not be referred to the courts. She also postponed a parliamentary election.

During this period her younger son, Sanjay, became a center of extra-constitutional authority. Even though he was not a member of the government, he launched a Five-Point Program that included, among other projects, forced sterilization—a stipulation limiting families to only two children. His arbitrary and arrogant exercise of political power created widespread dis-content and alienation, even among the members of the Congress party and India's widely respected bureaucrats. He arbitrarily transferred many civil servants and even dismissed chief ministers of the states who opposed his policies.

In short, Indira Gandhi not only differed from her predecessors in her style of leadership but also drastically changed even the substance of Indian politics. She sought to exercise state power on a personal level, sometimes disregarding constitutional norms and practices—as when she groomed her son Sanjay Gandhi to be her successor. In March 1977 she called parliamentary elections to legitimatize her authority and the constitutional changes made during the period of her emergency rule, but she miscalculated: Her party lost the election, and she could not even get herself elected to parliament. Such a humiliating defeat for Nehru's daughter demonstrated that India's illiterate voters had come to value the rules and procedures of a democratic polity. They resented the arbitrary exercise of political power by men such as Sanjay and the members of India's police administration. They also resented the loss of the links with the administration that they had enjoyed earlier through their representatives. Gandhi was brought back into power in the 1980 elections when her opponents could not hold together. She was assassinated on October 31, 1984.

Indira Gandhi was a complex and a dynamic personality. During her long term as prime minister she provided political stability in India. During this period India was able to make considerable economic progress, increase its technically skilled manpower, and establish itself as the dominant military power in the region. Despite the drawbacks of her leadership, Indira Gandhi's dedication to a strong and united India could not be questioned.

Morarji Desai: Promoter of Conservatism

On March 24, 1977, Morarji Desai (1896–), a Gujarati Brahmin and long-time political rival of Lal Bahadur Shastri and Indira Gandhi, was unanimously elected leader of the Janata parliamentary party, which had captured the majority of the seats in a national parliamentary election by defeating Indira Gandhi's Congress party. He thus became the fourth prime minister of India.

This orderly transfer of power from one leader to another as well as from the ruling party to the party in opposition demonstrated the sophistication of the Indian political elites. Even though the Janata government organized a couple of inquiry commissions to investigate the abuse of power by Indira Gandhi, her son, and some of her close associates during the emergency, Morarji Desai treated her with considerable respect and civility. By contrast to the political situations of its neighbors in South Asia, India's change of government did not result in political executions.

Morarji Desai is a product of the Congress culture. He does not differ much in background from the leaders who supported Indira Gandhi. Like them, Morarji Desai was a prominent member of the Congress party and held several cabinet positions, including that of finance minister and deputy prime minister in the cabinets of Jawaharlal Nehru and Indira Gandhi. After the 1969 split within the Congress party he joined with the members of the syndicate, which consisted of state party bosses. Morarji opposed Indira Gandhi's style of leadership, her excessive reliance on police force, and her economic policies. Along with Jaya Prakash Narayan and several other prominent opposition leaders, he was jailed during Indira Gandhi's emergency rule of 1975–1977.

A self-righteous, proud, and inflexible politician, Morarji Desai is the custodian of conservative policies in Indian politics. He is supported by India's powerful business and industrial community as well as by large-scale landowners. A Gandhian by ideological orientation, he was a close associate of Sardar Patel and became a leader of the right wing of the Congress party after Patel's death. Although he generally upholds the Congress party's commitment to secularism, his worldview has been strongly influenced by Hinduism.

As prime minister of the first non-Congress government of the country, Morarji Desai reestablished civil liberties and restored press freedom and the rule of law, which had been severely restricted during the emergency. He also promised to restore the pre-emergency balance existing among the executive, judicial, and legislative branches of the government.

Yet despite these significant changes, Morarji Desai's government lost direction. Soon it became overwhelmed by internal crises. The prevailing law and order deteriorated. In rural areas the members of the low castes were even subjected to atrocities perpetrated against them by higher caste people. In many places police and paramilitary forces revolted and had to be disarmed. Desai's government was also unable to check the rising prices. Consequently, protests and strikes became common. The Janata party itself became divided, forcing Morarji in 1979 to resign his position as the prime minister of the country.

Charan Singh: A Regional Leader with National Political Ambitions

Charan Singh (1902–1987), the fifth prime minister of India from July 1979 to January 1980, was a prominent fixture of Indian politics. Born in 1902 in a Jat (peasant farmer) subcaste family of western Uttar Pradesh, Charan Singh was very successful in organizing not only the members of his own subcaste but also such middle-level or backward agricultural subcastes as the Yadavs, Ahirs, Bhumihars, and Kurmis. Throughout most of his political career Singh was a champion of agrarian interests in Uttar Pradesh. He was the only member of the Congress party in the Uttar Pradesh cabinet who stood up against Nehru's farm policies. He was known for being stubborn and very ambitious, though not a team player, and he quite often found himself out of tune with most of his colleagues in the cabinet and the party. Like Morarji, Singh was another product of the Congress party who bolted the party in 1967 and formed his own party, eventually named the Bhartiya Lok Dal (BLD), or Indian People's party, to realize his own personal ambitions.

By causing a split in the Janata party, Singh was able to realize his ambition of becoming the prime minister of India. In 1977 when the Janata party captured a majority of seats in parliament, both Morarji and Singh were candidates for the office of the prime minister. Both leaders had only regional support, with no national following. The Janata party itself was a loose coalition of groups and powerful personalities. In order to avoid a split within the party, Jaya Prakash Narayan, a venerable Gandhian leader and the force behind the formation of the Janata party, successfully persuaded the party members to elect Morarji unanimously as the leader of the party. This election assured Morarji the office of the prime minister. The process itself did not satisfy Singh, however. He held that if an open contest for the position had taken place, he would have won. He continued to be a disgruntled member of the Janata government. Constant tensions within and among the different factions of the party enabled him and his supporters to defect from the party. It was only through the support of Indira Gandhi's Congress (I) party that he was able to demonstrate his majority in parliament and become the prime minister of the country in 1979. He could not, however, hold on to his position for long. The Congress (I) soon withdrew its support, leaving Singh without a majority in the lower house of parliament.

Indira Gandhi had extended her support to Singh only to cause a split within the Janata party, the main rival of her party. In such a situation Singh was forced to call the 1980 parliamentary elections, which his party lost.

Both the split within the Janata party and the rise of Singh to the position of prime minister illustrate the openness of the Indian political system as well as its capacity to absorb the shocks of unresolved interelite conflicts.

Rajiv Gandhi: The End of Dynastic Rule?

Rajiv Gandhi (1944–) became the sixth prime minister of India following Indira Gandhi's assassination on October 31, 1984. His elevation to the position of prime minister followed the established procedure of succession, and his appointment to this position by the president of India was subsequently confirmed by his unanimous election as party leader by 497 Congress (I) members of parliament.[6] Nevertheless, Rajiv is the first person to become the prime minister of this vast land without having held any ministerial position at either the national or state level. He was elevated to the high office of prime minister over the protests of many senior cabinet members and party men. Many of these persons had had far more administrative and political experience than Rajiv, whose political experience was limited to two years of organizational work within the Congress (I). A former airline pilot, he was brought into politics by his mother after the accidental death on June 23, 1980, of his younger brother, Sanjay. In 1981 he was elected to the lower house of parliament in a special election to fill the vacancy caused by the death of his brother. Rajiv entered politics reluctantly, his main incentive being to help his mother, Indira Gandhi, who had ceased to trust almost everybody except the members of her immediate family. He kept working under the shadow of his mother until he became prime minister.

There were certainly some cold calculations on the part of the Congress (I) members when they elected Rajiv as the leader of the party. None of the members of Indira Gandhi's cabinet were leaders of national standing. They would have been little help to the party in winning the forthcoming parliamentary elections. However, as a grandson of Jawaharlal Nehru and an heir to the Nehru dynasty, Rajiv had national recognition.[7] In addition, the sympathy generated by the brutal assassination of Indira Gandhi ultimately helped the party, when it was led by Rajiv, to win the election. Furthermore, Indira Gandhi had been grooming Rajiv for succession; by electing him as the leader of the party, her party men were fulfilling the slain leader's wishes. But Rajiv legitimized his elevation to the position of prime minister when he led his party to a massive victory in the parliamentary elections of 1984.

At the outset of his administration in 1984, the people of India had high expectations of Nehru's grandson. Unlike many of the old guard of

Indian politics, Rajiv was blessed with a clean public image, expectations of a new style of management, and a pragmatic approach to politics. Very shortly these high hopes were dashed as Rajiv developed an imperial and arrogant style of governance, becoming inaccessible not only to the people but also to high government and party officials. He lacked consistency and stability in his administrative organization at both the national and state levels. For instance, Rajiv reshuffled his cabinet twenty-seven times during his five-year term of office, and between 1985 and 1989 he changed Congress (I) party chief ministers in the states twenty times. In addition he surrounded himself with a small number of advisers, primarily civil servants, media experts, and foreign-trained technocrats who did not have roots in traditional Indian society.

Instead of eradicating corruption from the Indian body politic and distancing himself from the Congress (I) party's manipulators, powerbrokers, and influence peddlers, Rajiv's administration became identified in the minds of the public with the pursuit of amoral politics and corrupt politicians. Following the pattern set by his mother, he tended to centralize power in the prime minister's office, both in the party and the government. Although Rajiv liberalized the economy, leading to unprecedented economic and industrial growth, the benefits of such growth were unevenly distributed. The tendency toward arrogance, corruption, and the unequal distribution of new wealth led to public disenchantment with Rajiv, resulting in his electoral defeat in 1989.

It is too early to say whether electoral defeat will lead to a permanent decline in the political fortunes of Rajiv Gandhi and the end of the political dynasty he represents. Rajiv still remains the best-known leader of the Congress (I) party and in recent elections his party made a surprising comeback in south India.

V. P. Singh: A Political Crusader or a Political Opportunist?

With the inauguration of Vishwanath Pratap Singh (1931–) as the seventh prime minister of India in December 1989, a new era in Indian politics began. He is the third non-Congress prime minister. For the first time since independence India has a minority government. Another remarkable feature of this government is that it is supported in parliament by the Communists and the right-wing Hindu nationalists, the Bharatiya Janata Party (BJP). Singh's government, a coalition of centrist parties known as the National Front, if successful, is likely to be a unique experiment in the politics of the country.

V. P. Singh, as he is popularly known, is a mild-mannered, soft-spoken, and modest person. In 1987, Singh resigned as defense minister in the Rajiv government over the issue of corruption. He was subsequently expelled from the party for his outspoken criticism of corruption in the upper circles of the party and government. Although V. P. Singh organized his own group, known as the Jan Morcha (People's Front), he did not have any grass roots organizational support in the countryside. Very few politicians thought that he would be able to unite India's fractured opposition parties and defeat Rajiv Gandhi and his formidable electoral organization.

With more than a decade of administrative and political experience, Singh, who is well known for his personal integrity, discipline, and self-confidence, proved to be not only a skillful consensus builder but also an astute campaigner. Within a short period of time he was able to bring together powerful factional and party leaders and work out a common platform. In his campaign he was able to focus on the issues of political corruption, lack of accountability on the part of elected public officials, inefficiency in the government, and the imperial manner of Rajiv and his elite establishment. He was able to establish rapport with the common man and prove himself a deft communicator.

V. P. Singh's style of politics and administration is likely to be a contrast to Rajiv's. His government is not only likely to be more open to the people, but it may also change India's development strategies by channelling more resources to rural areas.

Although originating from a princely family of Uttar Pradesh, V. P. Singh neither leads a princely life nor displays aristocratic mannerisms. A law graduate of Allahabad University, Singh never practiced law, spending most of his youth in public service. Lal Bahadur Shastri, India's second prime minister, became Singh's mentor when he entered politics. Early on he demonstrated a high degree of moral stature and a disinterest in high public office, a trait that seems to have endeared him to his countrymen. His critics and political rivals term such behavior *political opportunism.* Whatever the realities, V. P. Singh, as the seventh prime minister of India, is likely to terminate the rule of the current political dynasty, if he is able to stay in power. To do this he must maintain cohesion within his party and lead his country at least through a full five years in office. (See Table 4.1 for a list of India's prime ministers.)

Regional Leaders:
Spokespersons of Subnationalism

Given the vast size of the country and the existence of strong subnational identities, the emergence of regional or subnational leaders in India as spokespersons for the interests of their people is not an unusual development. Maintenance of political stability in a multiethnic society is, however, dependent on the skills of the national leaders in dealing with the aspirations

TABLE 4.1 Prime Ministers of India: 1947–1990

Prime Minister	Party Affiliation	Year of Birth	Year of Death	Leadership Dates	Caste/ Subcaste (Religion)	Language/ Region
Jawaharlal Nehru	Congress	1889	1964	Aug. 1947–May 1964	Brahmin (Hindu)	Hindi-Speaking North (U.P.)
Lal Bahadur Shastri	Congress	1904	1966	June 1964–Jan. 1966	Kayastha (Hindu)	Hindi-Speaking North (U.P.)
Indira Gandhi	Congress Congress (I)	1917	1984	Jan. 1966–Mar. 1977 Jan. 1980–Oct. 1984	Brahmin (Hindu)	Hindi-Speaking North (U.P.)
Morarji Desai	Janata	1896		Mar. 1977–July 1979	Brahmin (Hindu)	Gujarati West (Gujarat)
Charan Singh	Janata (Secular)	1902	1980	July 1979–Jan. 1980	Jat (Hindu)	Hindi-Speaking North (U.P.)
Rajiv Gandhi	Congress (I)	1944	1989	Nov. 1984–Dec. 1989	Parsi- Brahmin (Hindu)	Hindi-Speaking North (U.P.)
V. P. Singh	Janata Dal	1931		Dec. 1989–	Rajput (Hindu)	Hindi-Speaking North (U.P.)

of the regional political elites. Unlike the political elites of immediate neighbors, those in India have shown greater flexibility in accommodating the aspirations of these regional leaders. So long as the territorial unity and integrity of the country are not threatened, the regional leaders have been allowed to pursue their goals through peaceful means. This is not to say, however, that no tension has existed between the two. On several occasions the agitation and protest movements led by regional leaders have resulted in political violence, the arrests of these leaders, and suspension of civil liberties in their areas. Eventually, however, it has been the politics of compromise and conciliation that have prevailed.

The following three case studies demonstrate the patterns of interaction between the national leaders and the regional elites.

M. G. Ramchandran: The Spokesperson for Tamil Nationalism

Emphasizing the linguistic and cultural heritage of the Tamil people in south India, the Dravida Munnetra Kazhagam (DMK), or Dravidian Progressive Federation, arose in 1949 as a political party projecting the cultural and subnational interests of the people of the state of Tamilnadu. The party resisted the Hindi chauvinism of the north as well as the Brahmin domination of politics in the south. Occasionally Tamil nationalists turned violent, expressing their strong opposition to the imposition of Hindi as the sole official language of the country. A radical faction among them even became secessionist and sought the creation of a sovereign state called Dravidistan, consisting of the Dravidian-speaking states of South India. But such a move was opposed by C. N. Annadurai, the founder of the DMK, who was content when his party captured power in the state. Finally, the national leaders' pledge not to impose Hindi on the south further undercut the separatist sentiments. At no stage did the Tamil nationalists actually mount a challenge to the integrity of the country.

In the late 1970s, M. G. Ramchandran (MGR) became the spokesperson of the Tamil nationalists. A close associate and follower of the towering Tamil nationalist leader C. N. Annadurai, MGR was one of the most popular film actors of south India. Presenting a populist program and capitalizing on his charisma, MGR became a powerful Tamil political leader with mass appeal.[8]

From 1977 until his death in 1988, MGR and his party were the dominant force in the politics of Tamilnadu. As a popular chief minister of his state, he was actively courted by leaders of national stature, including the leaders of the opposition and the leaders of the Congress (I). He brought the Tamil nationalist movement into the mainstream of Indian politics and used his skill and regional popularity to gain benefits for his state. He was an ardent supporter of greater state autonomy. After MGR's death in 1988, his rival

and the leader of the DMK, M. Karunanidhi, became the leader of the Tamil
nationalists.

Sheikh Mohammad Abdullah: The Lion of Kashmir

Among the several regional leaders of India, none was more durable or
flexible than Sheikh Mohammad Abdullah (1905–1982). A towering personality, the charismatic Kashmiri nationalist leader dominated state politics for
fifty years until his death in September 1982. Sheikh Abdullah not only
succeeded in securing special status for his people within the Indian Union;
he also gave a distinct subnational identity and a sense of pride to Kashmiris.
Though a devout Muslim he identified himself with the secular forces of
Indian politics, and until 1953 he worked in close association with Jawaharlal
Nehru.

After 1953 Sheikh Abdullah sought the creation of an independent
Kashmir. The result was that for a long time he was at odds with the
government of India; he was even imprisoned on several occasions. Ultimately,
however, he was able to reach an agreement with Indira Gandhi. The return
of Abdullah as head of the Kashmir government in March 1975 and the
recognition of him as the sole leader of his people paved the way for the
reconciliation between Kashmiri nationalists and the national political elites
of India. In addition, Abdullah's continuous adherence to secularism and his
constitutional approach to politics proved successful in preserving Kashmir's
autonomy. After his death in 1982 Sheikh Abdullah was succeeded by his
son Farooq Abdullah as the leader of Kashmir National Conference. Farooq,
unlike his father, has not been very successful in maintaining the autonomy
of Kashmir.

Harcharan Singh Longowal:
Spokesperson for Sikh Subnationalism

The Sikhs have used both agitational and constitutional means to achieve
concessions from the government of India. Mass civil disobedience has been
the primary tool of the Sikh leaders to achieve their political goals. In
response to this method, a Punjabi-speaking state was created in 1966 in
northwest India, in which Sikhs were a majority. Before its creation, they
did not constitute a majority in any state.

In 1982 the Akali Dal, a Sikh political party, launched a massive civil
disobedience movement seeking certain religious concessions and greater
political autonomy for the Punjab, where Sikhs are a majority. Sant Harcharan
Singh Longowal led the civil disobedience movement. The movement was
soon captured, however, by the religious fundamentalist and fanatic Sikh
country preacher, Jarnail Singh Bhindranwale. Often termed "Khomeini of

the Punjab," Bhindranwale became not only a threat to the territorial integrity of India and to its democratic structure but also a political rival of Longowal. Bhindranwale was able to attract alienated, rootless, and educated unemployed youth to his secessionist movement. His followers unleashed violence and terror in the region and challenged the authority of the Indian state. The result was an Indian army action against him that resulted in his death and the deaths of hundreds of his followers. Meanwhile, Longowal was arrested, along with many of his moderate associates. For the first time in the history of independent India, the country faced a dire threat to its unity.

Negotiations toward an accommodation of the Sikh grievances were begun in March 1985 when Longowal and his associates were released. Longowal disassociated himself and his party from the secessionist movement. He declared that Punjab, the Sikh-majority state, could not exist separate from India. In July 1985, when an eleven-point settlement was signed between Longowal (as president of the Akali Dal) and Rajiv Gandhi, the agitation against the national government was terminated. In the following month Longowal was assassinated by Sikh extremists. In the September 1985 election, however, Sikh voters endorsed the Longowal-Rajiv agreement; more specifically, 60% of them turned out to vote despite the extremists' call to boycott the election. The landslide victory of Longowal's Akali party demonstrated the success of the strategy of negotiated settlement over violent confrontation. Failure to implement the Longowal-Rajiv accord, however, has resulted in the rise of more militant Sikh leaders who have come to question the political legacy of moderate Sikh leadership.

*   *   *

In sum, the political leaders of India value the formal and informal rules for the peaceful transfer of political power as well as the negotiated resolution of interelite conflicts. With the exception of Bhindranwale in the Punjab and a few tribal leaders in the northeast of India, an overwhelming majority of national and regional leaders in Indian politics have come to accept certain rules of the political game—rules that involve the use of constitutional means as well as agitational approaches. The political leaders of India are able to maintain a high degree of civility at personal levels despite their political differences and occasional imprisonment. Political rivalry has rarely been transformed into personal enmity. Unlike the leaders in many other countries of the Third World, the political leaders of India are frequently willing to sit across a table to resolve conflicts through negotiation. It has been these norms of political behavior and the style of the leadership that have helped ensure the stability and continuity of the democratic system in India.

Notes

1. "Jawaharlal Nehru: A Troubled Legacy," *India Today*, June 15, 1984, p. 32.
2. Michael Brecher, *Nehru: A Political Biography* (London: Oxford University Press, 1959), p. 390.
3. D. V. Tahmakar, *Sardar Patel* (London: George Allen and Unwin, 1970), p. 266.
4. *Economic and Political Weekly*, vol. 10, (October 4, 1975), p. 1556.
5. Ibid.
6. *India Today*, November 30, 1984, p. 42.
7. Rajiv Gandhi's father, Feroze Gandhi, was a Parsi and not a Hindu; moreover, neither Indira nor Rajiv Gandhi is related to Mahatma Gandhi.
8. Robert L. Hardgrave, "The Celluloid God: MGR and The Tamil Film," *South Asian Review*, vol. 4, no. 4 (July 1971), pp. 307–312.

Suggested Readings

Akbar, M. J. *Nehru: The Making of India* (New York: Viking, 1988).

Brass, Paul, and F. Robinson (eds.). *Indian National Congress, 1885–1985, Ideology, Social Structure and Political Dominance* (Delhi: Chanakya, 1987).

Bhatia, Krishan. *Indira: A Biography of Prime Minister Gandhi* (New York: Praeger Publishers, 1974).

Brecher, Michael. *Nehru's Mantle: The Politics of Succession in India* (New York: Praeger Publishers, 1966).

Brown, Judith. *Gandhi and Civil Disobedience: The Mahatma in Indian Politics 1928–1934* (Cambridge: Cambridge University Press, 1977).

————. *Gandhi's Rise to Power: Indian Politics 1915–1922* (Cambridge: Cambridge University Press, 1972).

Carras, Mary C. *Indira Gandhi: In the Crucible of Leadership* (Boston: Beacon Press, 1979).

Desai, Morarji. *The Story of My Life* (New York: Pergamon Press, 1979), vols. 1, 2, and 3.

Fisher, Louis. *The Life of Mahatma Gandhi* (New York: Harper and Row, 1983).

Gopal, Sarvepalli. *Jawaharlal Nehru: A Biography* (Cambridge, Mass.: Harvard University Press, 1976), vol. 1.

————. *Jawaharlal Nehru: A Biography* (Cambridge, Mass.: Harvard University Press, 1979), vol. 2.

————. *Jawaharlal Nehru: A Biography* (Calcutta: Oxford University Press, 1984), vol. 3.

Hart, Henry C. (ed.). *Indira Gandhi's India: A Political System Reappraised* (Boulder, Colo.: Westview Press, 1976).

Malhotra, Inder. *Indira Gandhi: A Personal and Political Biography* (London: Hodder and Stoughton, 1989).

Malik, Yogendra K., and Dhirendra K. Vajpeyi (eds.). *India: The Years of Indira Gandhi* (Leiden, Holland: E. J. Brill, 1988).

Nehru, Jawaharlal. *Toward Freedom* (New York: John Day Company, 1942).

Rudolph, Lloyd I., and Susanne Rudolph. *The Modernity of Tradition* (Chicago: University of Chicago Press, 1967), part 2.

Sen Gupta, Bhabani. *Rajiv Gandhi: A Political Study* (Delhi: Konark, 1989).

Tahmankar, D. V. *Sardar Patel* (London: George Allan and Unwin, 1970).

Vasudeva, Uma. *Indira Gandhi: Revolution in Restraint* (Delhi: Vikas Publisher, 1974).

5
POLITICAL INSTITUTIONS AND GOVERNMENTAL PROCESSES

One of the major problems facing the leaderships in the countries of the Third World has been the creation of stable political institutions capable of governing the societies effectively, accomplishing sociopolitical changes peacefully, and providing a smooth transition of power. Events preceding the granting of independence and the widespread religious rioting that accompanied the division of the country had convinced the leaders of the Indian National Congress, who inherited the power from the British government, that India needed a powerful and effective set of political institutions at the national level to provide stability in a vast land. Sardar Patel summed up their position when he said that "the first requirement of any progressive country is internal and external security. . . . It is impossible to make progress unless you first restore order in the country."[1]

The assembly that deliberated the institutional structure for the new nation and undertook the task of framing a new constitution was created by the British government. An overwhelming majority of its members were elected indirectly by the legislative bodies existing in the provinces of British India. Although elections to the provincial legislative bodies, before the creation of a constituent assembly, were not held on the basis of universal suffrage, as many as 46 million voters participated in the 1946 elections. The constituent assembly was thus a representative body of Indians. It was convened in December 1946. Its membership was dominated by the Indian National Congress. It was a body consisting of intellectuals, lawyers, constitutional experts, and administrators as well as ideologues. In short, it was a representative body from which emanated the different shades of opinion to be found in the India of the 1940s.[2] Three years of discussion, debate, and deliberation on the draft of the constitution were required before it was adopted in November 1949. The new constitution, which came into effect on January 26, 1950, when India became a republic, is a lengthy and

78

complex document consisting of 395 articles and schedules. Despite some shortcomings, it has provided India with a stable system of government.

The Nature of the Constitutional System

The new constitution of the country represents a triumph of the modernists over the neotraditionalist element. It represents the viewpoint of those nationalist leaders who envisioned India as a modern nation-state. Such leaders drew freely from the U.S. and British constitutional systems and were deeply influenced by the experience of the liberal democratic societies of Canada and Western Europe. They also drew heavily from the Government of India Act of 1935.

The neotraditionalists represented by hardcore followers of Mahatma Gandhi idealized the creation of a highly decentralized, partyless system of government based upon the village *panchayats* (councils). Not seeing much wisdom in building a modern state system based upon a Western model, they had suggested that the village, where direct election was to prevail, should constitute the core of the system. The rest of the political institutions were to be elected indirectly. The neotraditionalists, however, lost out to the modernists.

During the colonial period, when they had waged a war against the arbitrary exercise of power by British rulers, Indian leaders had learned to value civil liberties. The incorporation of a detailed list of fundamental rights into the constitution reflected their eagerness to safeguard the civil rights and individual freedom of the common man. This list includes the rights to equality, to freedom of religion, to constitutional remedies, and against exploitation. The list also includes certain cultural and educational rights.

The constitution, with its impressive list of rights, seeks to alter the traditional Indian system of social stratification based upon ascriptive assignment of status. Its various articles abolish untouchability, provide equality of opportunities for jobs, and ensure equality in the eyes of the law. Realizing the impossibility of the operation of a democratic polity without freedoms, Articles 19 through 22 provide such basic rights as the freedom of speech and expression, the freedom to form associations, the freedom of movement, and the freedom to assemble peacefully without arms. The division of the country on the basis of religion had created a sense of insecurity among the minorities, especially the Muslims. To assuage their feelings and to guarantee their security, the constitution provides for freedom of religion and worship and prohibits discrimination in administrative, political, and social life on the basis of caste, creed, sex, or social origins.

All of these rights are protected by the courts, and judicial procedures are provided to ensure their enforcement. The Indian judiciary, especially the Supreme Court, has been active in protecting the basic rights of citizens.

These rights are not absolute or unlimited, however. The founders of the Indian constitution, though committed to fundamental rights and freedoms of citizens, were also concerned about the unity and territorial integrity of the country. Strong centrifugal tendencies have always been present in India. Many great subcontinental empires were broken up in the past as a result of the divisive forces existing within the region. The most recent experience that reinforced the fears about the breakup of the country was the creation of Pakistan. In keeping with these fears, the founders incorporated certain emergency provisions into the constitution to safeguard the unity of India. During periods of emergencies caused by foreign aggression and internal civil disorders, the enjoyment of these rights can be suspended. Through such laws as the Preventive Detention Act (1950), the Defense of Internal Security of India Act (1971), and the Maintenance of Internal Security Act, or MISA (1971), great authority has been left in the hands of the executive and administrative branches of the government. Under these acts the government can limit personal freedom to maintain civil order, and persons can be arrested without specification of the charges. Such limitations on individual rights have often been criticized by the advocates of civil liberty. Despite the occasional misuse of the emergency powers, such as that by Indira Gandhi in 1975–1977, Indians enjoy far greater freedom than their neighbors in Pakistan and Bangladesh.

The Directive Principles of State Policy, another distinguishing feature of the Indian constitutional system, is a statement of certain principles, goals, and ideals to be pursued by the state and the national governments in their policy formulations. The declaration was borrowed from the constitution of the Irish Republic. Many of the goals and principles therein constitute the wishes and various shades of ideologies and opinions represented in the constituent assembly, which could not be incorporated into either the fundamental rights section or other parts of the constitution. The Principles of State Policy directs the state to provide satisfactory means for people to earn their living, to obtain proper distribution of material resources of the community, to protect children and youth against exploitation, to promote the interest of the weaker sections of the society, and to introduce prohibition and ban cow slaughter. As they have no force of law, however, they cannot be enforced by the courts.

For purposes of amendment, the constitution has been divided into three sections. The section that deals with such important matters as the creation of new states out of the existing states and the creation and abolition of the second chambers for the state legislatures can be amended by a simple parliamentary majority. A second section, dealing primarily with fundamental rights, can be amended by two-thirds majority vote in parliament. Amendment of the last section of the constitution, which deals with the fundamentals of government such as the offices of the president or prime

Figure 5.1   Organization of the central government (India)

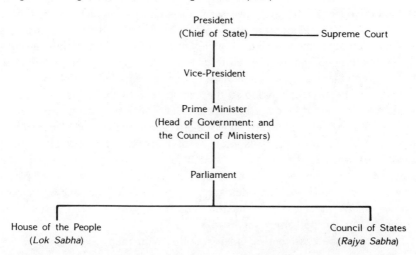

minister and the powers of the Supreme Court, requires not only a two-thirds majority of parliament but also ratification by a majority of the state legislative assemblies.[3]

The President, the Prime Minister, and the Cabinet

The institutional setup in India is headed by the president, the executive by the prime minister, and the judiciary by the Supreme Court, while the parliament is entrusted with the exercise of legislative power (see Figure 5.1). Before turning to the powers and functions of the officials listed in the figure, however, we should note that India has adopted the British system of parliamentary democracy. Unlike the United States, where the president is the chief of state as well as the head of government, Indians make a distinction between the two. The president in India, like the queen in the United Kingdom, is a ceremonial chief of state. The executive powers lie with the prime minister, who heads the government. The prime minister is closely linked to the lower house of parliament, to which he or she is held responsible. It is through the members of parliament that people exercise control over the prime minister. The Indian prime minister, unlike the U.S. president, does not have a fixed term of office. The prime minister can be removed from office by the lower house of parliament by a vote of no confidence.

The President. Though endowed with many executive powers, the president is, in fact, the chief of state rather than the head of government. He or she is elected for a term of five years, with no restriction on reelection (although no president of India has ever been elected for a third consecutive term). The president is chosen by an electoral college consisting of all elected members of the legislative assemblies existing in each one of India's twenty-two states, along with the elected members of the two chambers of the Indian parliament. A single transferable ballot is used, and the members of the electoral college are allowed to give their first and second preferences. In the event that no candidate is able to win a clear majority of the votes, the second preferences relating to the candidate with the lowest number of votes are transferred to other candidates. Such vote transferences continue until a person secures an absolute majority of votes and is declared the president of the country. This process of election, while complex, gives substantial voice to the states in the choice of the person who will be the chief of state. As the presidential election is conducted by an electoral college, there is no popular participation, and the event is not one of national excitement. A president may be removed by a process of impeachment conducted in the parliament of India.

Although the president of India is vested with many executive powers, in actual practice he or she acts only at the advice of the prime minister and the cabinet. During periods of national crisis, such as an attack on the country by a foreign power, internal insurrection, or acute financial crisis, the president may declare a state of emergency. In such situations, the powers of the national government are enormously enlarged. Fundamental rights and freedoms may even be suspended, and the country may be brought under a kind of authoritarian rule. The president may also declare a state of emergency in a particular state, where a failure of the constitutional machinery has occurred, and take over its administration for a limited period. However, the exercise of such drastic powers by the president is subject to control by both the cabinet and parliament.

The president of India has powers normally exercised by the ceremonial chiefs of state in other countries, such as the right of addressing the joint sessions of parliament, the right of signing bills with a limited veto, the right to appoint the justices of the Supreme Court and other high public officials, the right to receive ambassadors from other countries, and the right to grant pardon. He or she also serves as the head of the nation's armed forces. All of these powers are exercised only at the advice of the prime minister, however.

A majority of the seven persons elected to the president's office were drawn from active politics. The backgrounds of these seven have been diverse (see Table 5.1). Rajendra Prasad, the first president of India and a stalwart of the freedom movement, held the position from 1952 to 1962. A person with strong views on sociopolitical issues and a strong base in the conservative sector of the Congress party, he had constant political differences with Jawaharlal Nehru, the first prime minister of the country,

TABLE 5.1 Presidents of India

Year of Election	Name of the President	Religion	Party	Region/State	Native Language
1952	Rajendra Prasad	Hindu	Congress	North (Bihar)	Hindi
1957	Rajendra Prasad	Hindu	Congress	North (Bihar)	Hindi
1962	S. Radhakrishnan	Hindu	Congress	South (Tamilnadu)	Tamil
1967	Zakir Hussain (died in office)	Muslim	Congress	North (U.P.)	Urdu/Hindi
1969	V. V. Giri	Hindu	Independent (supported by Indira Gandhi)	South (Andhra Pradesh)	Kannada
1974	Fakhruddin Ali Ahmad (died in office)	Muslim	Congress (I)	Northeast (Assam)	Assamese/Urdu
1977	N. Sanjiva Reddy	Hindu	Janata Party	South (Andhra Pradesh)	Telugu
1982	Zail Singh	Sikh	Congress (I)	Northwest (Punjab)	Punjabi
1987	R. Venkataraman	Hindu	Congress (I)	South (Tamilnadu)	Tamil

although these differences were rarely made public. Nehru, however, treated him as the constitutional head of the state.

Prasad was succeeded by Sarvapalli Radhakrishnan (1962–1967), an academician and philosopher of international stature. Although Radhakrishnan had no independent power base in national politics, he did not hesitate to express his disagreement with Nehru's policies. Both Prasad and Radhakrishnan were elected as the nominees of the Congress party, but they were able to rise above party politics and meet frequently with the leaders of the opposition parties.

In 1967 Zakir Hussain, another academician, a Muslim, and a favorite of Indira Gandhi, was elected to the presidency as a nominee of the Congress party. With the election of Zakir Hussain, the presidency became more partisan than it had been in previous years. In 1969 Hussain died of a heart attack. Indira Gandhi supported V. V. Giri, an independent trade union leader, in opposition to the official Congress party candidate Neelam Sanjiva Reddy. (The latter was a nominee of the syndicate, an informal body of party bosses.) V. V. Giri was elected, defeating the official Congress party nominee. Even though Giri rarely showed any nonpartisanship and always acted on the advice of the prime minister, he never looked upon himself as the protégé of Indira Gandhi. After the 1969 presidential election, therefore, Gandhi became very careful in the selection of candidates to the presidency and sought to elevate only those persons to the office who would not defy her and would not show even nominal independence.

When V. V. Giri's term expired in 1974, Fakhruddin Ali Ahmad, a member of the cabinet and a staunch supporter of Indira Gandhi, was elected. It was Fakhruddin who signed the 1975 declaration of emergency proposed by Indira Gandhi that resulted in the suspension of democracy and virtually established an authoritarian system in India. Indira Gandhi's manipulation of the presidency made it evident that the occupant of this high office could play a key role in the operation of the country's institutional structure, as in the selection of the prime minister and the declaration of an emergency. This implication was further reinforced by the actions of Neelam Sanjiva Reddy, who in 1977 succeeded Ahmad when the latter died and the Janata party captured power by defeating the Congress party at the polls. Even though Reddy was a member of the Janata party, he was elected as a consensus candidate. During his term (1977–1982), he played a controversial role in the selection of the prime minister, especially when the Janata party lost its majority and no party had an absolute majority in parliament. Generally outspoken on public issues, he was not hesitant in giving polite criticism of a prime minister when he felt it was needed.

In 1982, when Reddy's term expired, Indira Gandhi, who had won the parliamentary election in 1980, successfully installed Giani Zail Singh, a Sikh, as the seventh president of India, instead of asking Reddy to seek a second term. As Zail Singh had neither the educational background nor the intellectual stature of his predecessors, his elevation to the presidency was not acclaimed by the country's upper-class establishment. He was looked upon as an unabashed Indira loyalist who would faithfully carry out her bidding to prove his loyalty. Singh remained loyal to Indira and helped in the smooth succession of Rajiv Gandhi to the position of prime minister after his mother's assassination. Nevertheless, Singh brought his high office close to the people. He was termed the people's president because he was one of the most easily accessible presidents of the country. The current president, R. Venkataraman, a senior statesman and an experienced administrator, has proven to be more impartial and nonpartisan in his behavior than his immediate predecessor.

The Vice-President. India's vice-presidency is not much different from its counterpart in the United States. Though elected by the two chambers of parliament in a joint session rather than by an electoral college, the vice-president performs some of the same functions as those of a U.S. vice-president. In addition to presiding over the sessions of the Council of States, the upper house of Indian parliament, the vice-president succeeds the president in the event of the latter's resignation, death, or incapacity. Unlike the U.S. vice-president, however, the Indian vice-president does not complete his predecessor's term. He acts as president only until a new president is elected—an event that must take place within six months. Under normal circumstances, the vice-president is elected for a term of five years. Some of the vice-presidents (such as Radhakrishnan, Zakir Hussain, and Giri) were subsequently elevated to the office of the presidency. The president and vice-president are traditionally expected to come from different regions of the country.

The Prime Minister and the Cabinet. The real executive of the country is made up of the prime minister and the cabinet. Despite the constitutional provision of the Westminster model of cabinet government in India, the prime minister has emerged as the undisputed chief of the executive. The personality of the prime minister determines the nature of the authority that he or she is likely to exercise. Such prime ministers as Lal Bahadur Shastri and Morarji Desai served as firsts among equals, but this was not the case with Jawaharlal Nehru and his daughter Indira Gandhi. Long-time domination of government by charismatic and powerful personalities such as Nehru and Indira Gandhi, and particularly the centralization of political power by Gandhi in her office, have rendered the Indian executive a prime ministerial government rather than a cabinet government.

Theoretically, the prime minister is selected by the president of India. In reality, the president invites the leader of the majority party in parliament to form the council of ministers. Usually political parties go to the parliamentary polls with a clear choice of their leaders. For the most part, the voters know, if and when a particular party wins a majority in the lower house of parliament, who is likely to be the prime minister. The Congress party has always entered the parliamentary election with a nationally known leader as its head—a strategy that has often given an opportunity to the voters to elect the prime minister of the country. In the 1984 and 1989 parliamentary elections, for instance, the Congress (I) went to the polls with Rajiv Gandhi as its leader.

The president can exercise some discretion in the selection of the prime minister when no party commands a clear majority in the lower house of parliament. When a party leader has a clear majority support in the lower house of parliament, the president has no choice but to call upon him to form the council of ministers.

If the voters are not satisfied with the performance of a prime minister and his or her government, they can vote the party out of power in the next parliamentary elections. In 1977, the voters defeated Indira Gandhi and her party for the excesses committed during her emergency rule. Instead, they gave a majority of seats to the Janata party in the lower house of parliament. When the Janata party leaders were unable to maintain unity within their ranks, however, they were replaced by the voters in the 1980 parliamentary elections and Indira Gandhi was brought back to the position of prime minister of the country. In 1989 Rajiv Gandhi was ousted from office for his nonperformance.

The prime minister determines the composition of the council of ministers as well as its inner core, the cabinet. Members of the cabinet occupy the highest position within the council of ministers, and they meet regularly under the chairmanship of the prime minister. The prime minister also distributes the portfolios, deciding who should get which department.

Members of the council of ministers are generally appointed from the prime minister's own party, and they must be or become members of parliament. The council of ministers represents a cross section of India's different states, regions, religions, and language groups. The nature and composition of the council of ministers also varies according to the prime minister in power.

Ever present in the cabinet have been organizations and committees, both informal and formal, that serve as the prime minister's inner core of advisers. According to Michael Brecher, in the early period of Nehru's prime ministership major policy decisions were made by an informal supercabinet consisting of Nehru and Patel, the two stalwarts of the freedom movement. Such decisions were subsequently submitted to the regular cabinet for its approval.[5] After Patel's death in 1950, an informal kitchen cabinet consisting of Maulana Abdul Kalam Azad and Rafi Ahmad Kidwai, later joined by Govind Ballabh Pant, became Nehru's main advisory body.

Since Nehru's time the cabinet has always contained many subcommittees consisting of important cabinet members. Indira Gandhi chaired a small cabinet subcommittee called the Political Affairs Committee, which consisted of senior members of the cabinet. This committee came to be known as a cabinet within a cabinet.

The prime minister's dominance of the executive in India has been reflected in the rise and expansion of the prime minister's secretariat, a body consisting of more than two hundred persons and headed by a principal secretary, a top-ranking bureaucrat. The principal secretary is assisted by six members of the Indian Administrative Services (IAS), the elite bureaucratic organization of India. This top echelon of the prime minister's secretariat also includes technocrats, economists, politicians, and personal assistants.[6] In some ways the prime minister's secretariat resembles the U.S. president's executive office. It is entrusted not only with preparation of the agenda for cabinet meetings and maintenance of the records of cabinet proceedings but also with coordination of the administration of different departments of the government headed by the members of the council of ministers. The prime minister and his or her secretariat also stay in close touch with the chief ministers of the states and with the members of the Planning Commission and the National Development Council, the two bodies entrusted with the job of shaping the economic and development policies for the country.

Parliament and the Legislation

The Indian parliament, entrusted with the power of legislation, consists of two houses, the *Lok Sabha* (House of the People) and the *Rajya Sabha* (Council of the States). The first is the lower house and the second the upper house of India's national legislature.

The Lok Sabha consists of 542 members elected from state and union territories on the basis of population. Each state is divided into several electoral districts, and each member of parliament (MP) represents around 1.5 million people. Voting rights are granted on the basis of universal adult suffrage; all eighteen-year-old citizens are eligible to vote. In 1989, there were 475 million voters. There has been a constant increase in voter participation over the years (see Table 5.2). The qualifying age for seeking election to the Lok Sabha is twenty-five years. Elections are conducted by an autonomous agency, the Election Commission, headed by a chief election commissioner who enjoys the status and power equivalent to that of a Supreme Court judge. He or she is not subject to political pressure and governmental interference.

Each MP is elected for a term of five years, although that span can be extended for one year during a period of emergency. Election to the Lok Sabha must be held within six months after the termination of such

TABLE 5.2   Voter Participation in Indian Parliamentary Elections, 1952–1984

Year	Electorate (in millions)	Votes Polled (in millions)	Turnout (percent)
1952	173.2	80.7	46.6
1957	193.7	91.3	47.1
1962	217.7	119.9	55.1
1967	250.1	152.7	61.1
1971	274.1	151.5	55.3
1977	321.2	194.3	60.5
1980	355.6	202.3	56.9
1984	375.8	238.4	63.4

Source: Based on data in Francis Robinson, ed., The Cambridge Encyclopedia of India, Pakistan, Bangladesh and Sri Lanka (Cambridge: Cambridge University Press, 1989).

an emergency. Elections are called by the president at the advice of the prime minister, who may ask for the dissolution of the Lok Sabha and call for elections well before the expiration of its term, provided that he or she feels confident that the election can be won by the ruling party.

As India does not enforce the residency requirement for the candidate, a person is free to seek elections to the Lok Sabha from any part of the country, even though he or she may not be residing in that constituency. In practice, however, most of the members seek election from the areas in which they reside. Quite frequently their choice of an electoral district is influenced by the composition of its population. People tend to vote along caste, community, religious, ethnic, and linguistic lines; therefore, even the Communist party of India puts up candidates of the caste or religion that is dominant in the district.

Elections to the Lok Sabha are vigorously contested. In the 1989 elections, there were 6,084 candidates to fill only 525 Lok Sabha seats.[7] Moreover, a substantial amount of money is spent during elections. Even though the limit on campaign spending is around 125,000 rupees (the ceiling fixed by the Election Commission), actual expenses may run much higher than that.[8] The cost of elections has been going up every year (see Table 5.3). Political parties select the candidates; there are no party primaries. Parties also try to meet a substantial part of the campaign expenses.

Voters vote more for the parties than for individual candidates, although, as noted above, the caste affiliation, religion, and personality of a candidate tend to influence voters' choices. As a large majority of the voters are illiterate, all of the political parties and independent candidates are allocated visual symbols by the Election Commission, for identification purposes. For example, a hand is the symbol of the Congress (I), while a hammer and sickle and a wheel are the symbols of the Communist party of India and the Janata Dal, respectively. It is for this reason that the candidates and the parties both give extensive exposure to these symbols while campaigning.

TABLE 5.3 Poll Expenditure for the Lok Sabha Elections

Year	Rs (in crores)	Rs (in millions)
1952	10.45	104.5
1957	6.90	69.0
1962	7.32	73.2
1967	10.95	109.5
1971	14.43	144.3
1977	30.00	300.0
1980	56.00	560.0
1984	800.00	8,000.0
1989	1,000.00	10,000.0 (expected)

Sources: Hindustan Times, January 4, 1984; Report on the Second General Elections 1957, vol. 1; Report on the Third General Elections in India 1962, vol. 1; Report on the Fifth General Elections in India 1971–72; Statesman Weekly, December 2, 1979; and India Today, December 15, 1989, p. 68.

Election campaigns run from four to six weeks. The campaign period is colorful, festive, and noisy. Parades, torchlight processions, mass rallies, and public square meetings addressed by the candidates and the nationally known leaders are common. Quite frequently, popular entertainers, folk singers, and film stars join in to promote a party or a candidate. Gaudy billboards and posters with the pictures of nationally known party leaders are prominently displayed, and much door-to-door canvassing occurs, especially in urban areas.

Although the political parties issue election manifestoes or party platforms, the parliamentary elections have been dominated since 1971 by one or two national issues rather than by a particular party platform. For instance, Indira Gandhi's garabi hatao (remove poverty) in 1971, her emergency rule and suppression of civil rights in 1977, her call for effective national government and political stability in 1980, Rajiv Gandhi's call for territorial integrity and the unity of the country in 1984 and V. P. Singh's pledge to remove corruption in 1989, were major focuses of the elections in those years.

The constituencies from which the candidates are returned to the Lok Sabha are single-member districts. The outcome of each election is determined by simple plurality, as in the United States and United Kingdom, rather than by an absolute majority. Thus a party may receive 44% of the votes and yet bag 73% of the seats, as happened in the case of the Congress party in the first three elections of India. In the 1984 parliamentary elections, the Congress (I) party, under the youthful leadership of Rajiv Gandhi, won 80% of the seats even though it received only 50% of the votes. Such a lopsided outcome results from multiple contests for the Lok Sabha seats.

The organization, powers, and functions of Lok Sabha are analogous to the ones existing within the House of Commons in the United Kingdom.

The Lok Sabha's meetings are presided over by the speaker, who, though elected on a party basis, tries to exercise considerable impartiality and to project a nonpartisan profile. He or she maintains order in the house and conducts its proceedings. The office of the speaker may have considerable influence, but the position is much weaker than that of the speaker in the U.S. government system.

The majority party is headed by a leader who is assisted by whips responsible for maintaining discipline within the party. As there are several small parties in the Lok Sabha, only the leader of a party with more than fifty seats is recognized as the leader of the opposition. Members and the leaders of the minor opposition parties, however, are provided the facilities to perform their role effectively.

The Lok Sabha meets at least twice in a year, with no more than six months between its two sessions. Although the MPs can address the house in any of the recognized languages of the country, a majority of the members speak in English or Hindi. When a member insists on speaking in another native language, English and Hindi translations of the speech are provided.

Votes on bills or other issues in the Lok Sabha are made strictly along party lines. Frequently, however, even the members of the ruling party become critical of their government's policies and programs. An individual MP tries to promote the interests of his constituents. But the district he represents in the Lok Sabha may be large and the voters unorganized. A member will tend to give priority to the powerful groups or better organized interests of his district over the average voter. On specific policy issues, each member is expected to follow the party lines.

Of the two houses of parliament, the Lok Sabha is far more powerful than the Rajya Sabha (Council of the States). The Lok Sabha has effective control over both ordinary legislation and money bills. If a deadlock develops between the two houses over an ordinary bill, a joint session of the two chambers is convened and a decision is made by a majority vote. Money bills can be initiated only in the Lok Sabha. The Rajya Sabha may scrutinize such bills, but it has no power to veto them. Similarly, it is the Lok Sabha that exercises ultimate control over the prime minister and the council of ministers, as only the Lok Sabha can pass a vote of no confidence.[9] The Rajya Sabha has no such power.

Following the British practice, the Lok Sabha devotes the first hour of its business to addressing questions to the ministers. The "question hour," as it is known, gives the MPs an opportunity to seek information from the government, put the ministers on the spot, and cause embarrassment to the government. Such a process keeps the ministers on their toes.

The Rajya Sabha is a much smaller body than the lower house, consisting of 250 members. Of that total, 238 are elected from the states roughly on the basis of population, although the smaller states are given slightly higher representation than their population would warrant. Like the U.S. Senate, the Rajya Sabha is a permanent body. Its members are elected for a period of six years, and one-third of them return every two years. The members of the Rajya Sabha are elected indirectly by the state legislative assemblies, to fill the vacancies caused by the retirement of the members. The Rajya Sabha, also referred to as the "house of the elders," is thus a representative body of the states. The remaining 12 members are appointed to the upper house by the president to give representation to citizens who have performed distinctive service in the areas of art, sciences, literature and social work.

The Rajya Sabha plays a role secondary to that of the Lok Sabha in that it has no control over the executive. Nevertheless, during emergencies, if the latter house is under suspension, it can become a forum to voice public concerns and serve to exercise modest checks on any exercise of arbitrary power by the executive.

Assessment of Parliament

Many Indian intellectuals bemoan the "decline" of the powers of parliament, of the quality of its members, and of the high standards of its debate since the glorious days of the Nehru period. Others criticize it for its lack of initiative in the areas of legislation or policy formulation. A third group of critics is dismayed by the election of a motley group of MPs in place of the gentleman politicians of the early years of independence. A part of this criticism seems to be misplaced; another part may be based upon the misconception of the role of parliaments in modern democratic societies.

Nehru was always deferential toward parliament and encouraged debate, whereas Indira Gandhi had reservations about the functioning of parliament and often stayed away when it was in session. But parliamentarians also responded with deference toward Nehru, whereas they subjected Indira Gandhi to considerable criticism. Between 1963 and 1982, twenty-one no confidence motions were made against different prime ministers: Lal Bahadur Shastri faced three during his eighteen months of administration, and Indira Gandhi faced sixteen during her thirteen years of leadership. Nehru faced only one such motion during his seventeen years of office. Moreover, whereas Shastri was called upon to defend his performance every six months and Indira Gandhi was so called upon almost every year, Nehru was asked to defend his record only once in seventeen years.[10] Whenever a no confidence motion was made against Indira Gandhi, the prime minister was forced to bring out her best speaker to defend her performance and to face the onslaught of outstanding opposition leaders and experienced parliamentarians.

Unlike the U.S. Congress, the parliament in India is a rather ineffective legislative body. Legislative initiative belongs to the cabinet. The ruling party's overwhelming majority in parliament generally enables it to get its legislative agenda through the Lok Sabha without much difficulty. Nevertheless, 68% of parliament's time is spent on "financial and non-legislative matters like calling attention notices, short discussions, zero hours, no confidence motions and adjournment motions."[11] There are several parliamentary committees, some of which, like the public accounts committee and committee on estimates, are active and able to influence public policies. Commenting on the roles of various committees dealing with financial matters, W. H. Morris-Jones has stated that such committees serve as a very important "check against the oppressive and arbitrary executive," adding that they become "as a substitute for a real opposition."[12]

A gradual change in the socioeconomic background of the members of parliament has taken place. English-speaking, Western-educated, urbane parliamentarians have been replaced by a vernacular-speaking, less educated, rural-born group of MPs. Since 1952, the domination of parliament by lawyers has declined, whereas the number of persons with an agricultural background has risen.[13] In a sense, parliament has become more representative of the Indian society. India is, after all, primarily an agricultural society. Parliamentary debates are widely reported in the press and the media, and considerable attention is paid to its proceedings.

Supreme Court: The Guardian of the Constitution and Law

The Supreme Court is the highest judicial tribunal of India. It consists of a chief justice and twenty-five associate justices, who are appointed by the president in consultation with the judges of the high courts and the prime minister. India has a unified judicial system. There are no separate state courts. Each state has a high court subordinate to the Supreme Court, and, at the national level, the Supreme Court sits at the head of an integrated judiciary. The Supreme Court has original as well as appellate jurisdiction. Following the practice existing in most federations, the original jurisdiction of the Supreme Court covers the disputes arising between the national government and the state governments, as well as cases involving two or more states. In significant civil and criminal cases, the Supreme Court serves as the final court of appeal.

Like the Supreme Court of the United States, India's Supreme Court enjoys the right of judicial review, even though its rights are not as extensive as those of the U.S. counterpart. The Indian Supreme Court has been the primary protector of civil liberties and fundamental rights, especially the right to private property. There has been constant conflict between the Supreme Court's right to judicial review and the parliament's claim to legislative sovereignty. The Supreme Court has denied parliament the absolute right to amend the constitution so as to limit the citizens' fundamental rights and civil liberties, particularly where the arbitrary takeover of private property is involved. The Congress party–dominated and Indira Gandhi–led parliament in 1976 passed the forty-second amendment asserting parliament's ultimate power to amend the constitution. Gandhi also tried to pack and politicize the court. A balance between the Supreme Court's power of judicial review and parliamentary authority was restored during the rule of the Janata party government (1977–1979) through the provision of the forty-fourth constitutional amendment, which partially modified the absolute power granted to parliament under the forty-second amendment.[14] Potential for conflict between the two branches of government persists, however.

Role of the State Governments

The Indian constitution provides for a federal system of government, with a division of powers between the national and the state governments. Unlike the state governments in the United States, however, those in India have only limited powers. Not only a majority of the powers, but all the residual powers as well, have been vested in the union government. Despite the existence of a powerful central government, the state governments have control over such important subjects as public order, police, administration of justice, agriculture, water supply and irrigation, education, public health, land rights, industries, and mineral development. They have also been given the right to levy taxes to raise revenue for the administration and to determine policies related to land use and land distribution as well as agricultural and industrial development within the states. In short, by capturing political power at the state level, a party or a group of political leaders can exercise control over the distribution of vital goods and services within its area. Because state government is an important source of patronage, there is intense intra-elite competition to capture elective positions at the state level.

Several important implications are related to the operation of India's federal system. This system provides institutional structures that grant self-government to its diverse people. It also provides the means to satisfy the political ambitions of regional elites as well as regional parties. State-level politics serves as a training ground for the politicians who may subsequently assume important roles in national politics. Many of India's able administrators, and some of its prime ministers, held important elective positions at the state level before they became prominent in national politics. Such former prime ministers as Lal Bahadur Shastri, Morarji Desai, and Charan Singh were elected to state legislative bodies and served in the state cabinets or were the state chief ministers beforehand. Even in the present cabinet of Prime Minister V. P. Singh are many ministers who held elective positions at the state level before being elevated to cabinet positions in the national government.

There are considerable differences in attitudes, orientations, and behavior between the national political leaders and the state-level politicians. Politicians at the state or regional level have close ties with caste and community leaders. Often they become intertwined with powerful local interests that are eager to maintain the status quo. Many state governments become dominated by the landowning classes that originated in the upper or the middle castes. As a result, they are unwilling to implement the social and economic reforms likely to benefit the poorer segments of society to which the lower castes belong. This brings them into conflict with the national political leaders, who are committed to the creation of greater social equality. The state political leaders keep themselves in power by appealing to the primordial loyalties of caste and religion. Many of them use their positions to benefit the members of their kinship group or community. The following fictional description of a state minister gives a very realistic picture of many state politicians:

> The minister's hometown was situated in the district of Bangaon. Thousands of people of his caste were settled in the area. Due to his kindness, scores of the young men of his caste got jobs to work for social welfare. It is true that many of them had to bribe the head clerk, before they could get a position. Whenever the people complained against the head clerk, the minister would protect him. What will you do against poor Mundrika? He is helpless. He has five daughters to marry [and due to worries and pressure] only a few hairs are left on his scalp. From where will the poor man get twenty-five thousand rupees [to marry off his daughters]? I am helpless whenever Mundrika appears before me, the kindness of my heart overwhelms my sense of justice.[15]

National leaders, on the other hand, seek to build national cohesion by playing down the traditional divisions existing within the society. Often the differences of approach and orientation between the two sets of politicians aggravate the tension between the state and central governments, especially if they belong to different parties.

There are twenty-two states in India. The organization of each of the state governments is presented in Figure 5.2.

1. The Governor is appointed by the president for a term of five years and holds office for as long as he or she enjoys the president's confidence. He or she is a representative of the national government in the state and exercises more powers in the state than the president does at the national level. Although the governor was intended to be the constitutional figure in the governmental setup of a state and to act in nonpartisan ways, the office has become politicized in recent years. Many of the governors had become embroiled in state politics, especially in those states in which non–Congress party governments were in power. It has been observed that "with the

Figure 5.2   Organization of the state government (India)

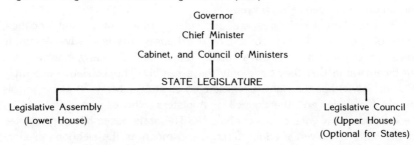

Governor
|
Chief Minister
|
Cabinet, and Council of Ministers
|
STATE LEGISLATURE

Legislative Assembly   Legislative Council
(Lower House)   (Upper House)
                                                        (Optional for States)

Congress (I) in power at the Center and the variety of homespun regional parties ruling in the states it has suddenly dawned on everyone that the governor may be a Trojan Horse sent by the Union Government."[16] Governors invite the leaders of the majority party in a state legislative assembly to form the government and to assume the office of chief minister. In the event that no party is in majority in assembly, which happens more frequently at the state level than at the national level, the governors become actively involved in the formation of a state government. The governor also has the power to dismiss a popularly elected state government. He or she can recommend instituting the "president's rule" in a state, thus enabling the national government temporarily to take over the administration of a state. These practices go against both the principles of a federation and the spirit of the representative government. Recently, therefore, the office of the governor has come under attack from the leaders of the opposition parties.

2. The Chief Minister, the Cabinet, and the Council of Ministers are vested with the exercise of executive power in a state. The institutional setup at the state level is normally under the effective control of the chief minister, who is the most powerful person in state politics. The chief minister also commands a majority in the state legislative assembly, determines the size of his or her council of ministers, distributes portfolios among these ministers, and presides over the meeting of his or her cabinet. During Nehru's prime ministership many state chief ministers became powerful regional leaders with considerable influence in national politics. W. H. Morris-Jones has described this stage of the operation of the Indian polity as a "bargaining federalism." In such a federation, he points out, "neither centre nor states can impose decisions on others" in which "hard competitive bargaining" would take place in such federally instituted agencies as the Finance Commission and Planning Commissions.[17] Chief ministers played a crucial role in the bargaining process until Indira Gandhi, after her 1972 landslide victory, undercut the power of most of the Congress party chief ministers. However, with the rise of many regional parties once again such chief ministers as M. Karunanidhi in Tamilnadu and Jyoti Basu in West

Bengal, the office of state chief minister has emerged as an independent and autonomous center of power.

3. The State legislatures are particularly important to state politics. Some of these legislatures consist of two houses, the legislative assembly (lower house) and the legislative council (upper house); many, however, are not bicameral in that they have only the assembly. The legislative assembly (*Vidhan Sabha*) has the right to legislate on all state subjects. It also controls the chief minister and the council of ministers, who can be dismissed by the adoption of a vote of no confidence. The state assemblies are elected on the basis of universal adult suffrage. Inasmuch as the elections of state assemblies have generally been separated from the parliamentary elections, elections to the Vidhan Sabhas are dominated by local and state issues.

The legislative councils are elected in part directly and in part indirectly, and some of the members are appointed by the governors on the advice of the chief ministers. The legislative council (*Vidhan Parishad*) plays a role secondary to that of the legislative assembly. The state legislative bodies work under almost the same rules of procedure as those followed in the national parliament.

The elections to the state legislative bodies are contested vigorously. On average, there are about five candidates for each seat. People show higher interest in assembly elections than in the elections of national parliament. It is through their representatives in the state legislative assembly that ordinary people are able to make political statements. The status of a candidate in the local community, his or her financial resources, and his or her party affiliations are all important factors contributing to a successful election to the state legislature.

On the whole, as noted above, the state legislative bodies have come to be dominated by the landowning members of the upper castes. The members of the legislative assembly (called MLAs) are generally less interested in legislative business or policy formulation than in securing benefits for their constituents or serving as power brokers between the bureaucrats and powerful interests in their constituencies. The services of an MLA are in great demand. It appears that ordinary citizens are constantly seeking the help of MLAs to intercede with the administration on their behalf. But their easy accessibility makes them an invaluable link between the people, the administration, and the state government.

Local Governments: The Roots of India's Democracy

There are a host of self-governing institutions in India's thousands of villages, towns, and cities. Local self-government in urban areas was, of course, introduced by the British government. Through several acts it established various types of local bodies, town committees, municipalities, and municipal corporations, all endowed with different levels of autonomy and financial power. Whereas corporations exist in the metropolitan areas or large cities, notified area committees with only very limited powers are present in small towns.

Even though the powers of the city government are limited, it is the only representative body that exists in a city. The members of a municipal committee, or a municipal corporation, and its presiding officials are included among the politically influential members of the community. They develop vital links with the MLAs, especially if they belong to the same party. Through various channels they are able to influence the allocation of resources at the state capital.

In rural areas the self-governing institutions are known as the *panchayats* (village councils), *panchayat samithis* (association of village councils), and *zila parishads* (district councils), existing at the village, block, and district levels, respectively. Like the city councils, these rural self-governing institutions are elected on the basis of universal adult suffrage. The *zila parishads* are the highest self-governing institutions existing in rural India. Over the years the powers, functions, and financial resources of these institutions have varied greatly. However, with the notable exception of the *zila parishads* in the states of Karnataka, Maharashtra, and Gujarat, they were never given the powers with which to play an effective role in the development of rural areas.

During the last few years, the positions and powers of the *panchayats* have been declining. A decline has also occurred in the elite support for evolving democratic institutions in rural areas. Contrary to the expectations of national leaders, these institutions have come to be dominated by the well-to-do segments of the upper castes. Consequently, the *panchayats* have become instrumental in perpetuating the traditional system of social stratification existing in rural India; indeed, the *panchayat* system seems not to have benefitted the landless labor and lower castes.

Local politicians who are elected to these self-governing institutions are able to build horizontal and vertical links with community organizations, based upon ascriptive and kinship ties, and with state-level politicians, who belong to different political parties. It is through this kind of informal network of power and influence that local politicians and political notables can not only mobilize the voters for the political leaders but can also serve to distribute patronage among their clients and supporters. This kind of institutional network, existing as it does at the different levels of Indian society, has been quite successful in integrating diverse elements of its population into a working political order.

Center-State Relations

The fathers of the Indian constitution created a powerful center. They believed that a strong center should help in maintaining the unity of the country. Nevertheless, in view of India's cultural diversities, they preferred a federal system of government over a unitary one. For various reasons since the adoption of the constitution, however, certain important changes have occurred, resulting in greater centralization of political power than the fathers of the constitution had envisioned.

Although no constitutional change took place in India's federal system, Indira Gandhi frequently resorted to its subversion. She made dubious use of some of the constitutional means to undermine the federal structure, especially the authority of the opposition-run state governments.

The office of the state governor, for instance, is a carryover from the days of the Raj. It was left in the post-independence constitutional structure, perhaps with the understanding that the state governor would perform only ceremonial functions and would not play any political role. In recent years, however, the office of the governor has become increasingly politicized. Both the Congress and the Janata party governments have appointed their party men as state governors. After her 1980 return to power, Indira Gandhi frequently appointed discredited state politicians and her loyalists as governors of the opposition-run state governments. She also transferred those governors of the states who refused to carry out her instructions. The governor of Jammu and Kashmir, B. K. Nehru, an able administrator and former member of the ICS, refused to dismiss Farooq Abdullah's government in Kashmir as demanded by the Congress (I) supporters of Gandhi on the grounds that such a move would not be in the national interest.[18] He was replaced soon afterward by Jagmohan, a Gandhi loyalist. Jagmohan carried out Indira Gandhi's instruction by dismissing Abdullah's government, disregarding established constitutional practices.

The governors of the opposition-run state governments of West Bengal, Karnataka, Sikkim, and Tamilnadu in the past had frequently behaved in partisan ways, involving themselves either in dismissing a popularly elected state government or in stalling the implementation of important cabinet decisions.

Nehru was extremely reluctant to impose president's rule (basically a takeover of the state administration by the national government) in the states. In 1949 he is reported to have observed that "so far as I am concerned, I do not propose, nor intend, nor look forward to, nor expect governments falling apart except through a democratic process."[19] The evidence suggests that he never started or encouraged any efforts at toppling the opposition-run state government. Under Indira Gandhi, however, the toppling of state governments by encouraging defection from the ranks of the opposition parties became a standard practice. The leaders of the opposition parties alleged that either by outright bribe or by a promise of a cabinet position in the state government, or both, Gandhi encouraged her Congress (I) party leaders to engineer defection and toppling of the opposition-run governments in the states.

This undermining of the federal structure and state autonomy and the frequent toppling of state governments controlled by the regional parties led to an increase in regional discontent and frustration, which found expression in periodic outbursts of violence and disorder.

The national government has far greater financial resources at its disposal than the states have. In fact, through grants-in-aid, budgetary provisions, and financial institutions, the center has been making inroads into many of the subjects allocated to the state governments.[20] Such encroachments by the national government on state rights and responsibilities have caused considerable strains in center-state relations.

Center-state relationships and the extent of state autonomy are issues that are likely to be debated in the coming years. Pressure is likely to increase for greater state autonomy.

The chief ministers from several states have already asked for greater legislative and administrative autonomy and have demanded that the "provisions in the Constitution would have to be changed to accommodate and give full play to the new definition of (a) center-state relationships and (b) relationships between the states."[21]

There seem to be three shades of opinion reflecting the position of different groups on the nature of the Indian federation. One group led by the Sikh party, the Akali Dal of the Punjab, makes the maximalist demand for the transfer of all powers to the states, with the exception of defense, foreign affairs, communications, railways, and currency. Such a demand, however, does not have countrywide support. Another group led by moderate regional leaders hopes to maintain a distance from the political control of New Delhi and seeks a reassertion of the spirit of federalism as embodied in the constitution of India. The third group, led by M. Karunanidhi of Tamilnadu and Jyoti Basu of West Bengal, seeks an extensive revision of center-state relations in the light of political experience gained during the last forty-two years during which the Indian constitution has been in effect. All three groups, no doubt, seek the revision of these relations within the framework of the Indian constitution. A one-man commission headed by a retired Supreme Court justice, Ranjit Singh Sarkaria, was appointed in March 1983 to look into the issue. In particular, the commission was authorized to examine the center-state relationship and to make recommendations to meet the new demands coming from the non-Congress-run state governments.

*   *   *

Political leaders in India, such as the Sri Lankan elites, have been successful in building and operating an effective and complex institutional structure. Unlike the systems in neighboring Pakistan and Bangladesh, that in India provides its citizens with ample opportunities to become involved in the political process. Indeed, the citizens of India have frequently used the constitutional process to change the government. The federal system of government, furthermore, provides enough opportunities to state and local politicians to protect their regional interests and to preserve their subnational identities. Even though occasional tensions arise between the national and state governments, the political institutions overall have shown considerable flexibility in diffusing these tensions without leading to any breakdown of the system.

Notes

1. Quoted in Granville Austin, *The Indian Constitution: Cornerstone of a Nation* (London: Oxford University Press, 1966), p. 45.

2. Ibid., p. 13.

3. M. V. Pylee, *Constitutional Government in India,* 3rd ed. (Bombay: Asia Publishing House, 1977), pp. 761–762.

4. *India Today,* April 15, 1984, pp. 22–23.

5. Michael Brecher, *Nehru: A Political Biography* (London: Oxford University Press, 1959), p. 395.

6. *India Today,* January 31, 1985, pp. 8–17.

7. *The Hindu: International Edition,* December 8, 1984.

8. *The Tribune,* November 1, 1979, p. 1.

9. Pylee, *Constitutional Government in India,* p. 403.

10. *India Today,* September 15, 1982, p. 11.

11. Ibid., p. 10.

12. W. H. Morris-Jones, *Parliament in India* (London: Longmans Green, 1957), p. 308.

13. A. Rahman and Nirmal Haritash, *The Role of Parliament in the Formulation of National Science and Technology Policy* (New Delhi: National Institute of Science, Technology and Development Studies, n.d.), p. 43.

14. Lloyd I. Rudolph and Susanne Hoeber Rudolph, "Judicial Review *versus* Parliamentary Sovereignty: The Struggle over Stateness in India," *Journal of Commonwealth & Comparative Politics,* vol. 19, no. 3 (November 1981), pp. 231–255.

15. Quoted in Yogendra K. Malik, "Contemporary Political Novels in Hindi," in Yogendra K. Malik (ed.), *Politics and the Novel in India* (New Delhi: Orient Longmans, 1978), p. 23.

16. *India Today,* February 15, 1984, p. 74.

17. W. H. Morris-Jones, *The Government and Politics of India,* 3rd ed. (London: Hutchinson University Library, 1971), p. 152.

18. *Economic and Political Weekly,* March 31, 1985, p. 231.

19. Quoted in Henry C. Hart, "Indira Gandhi: Determined Not to be Hurt," in Henry C. Hart (ed.), *Indira Gandhi's India: A Political System Reappraised* (Boulder, Colo.: Westview Press, 1976), p. 256.

20. K. K. George and I. S. Gulati, "Central Inroads into State Subjects: An Analysis of Economic Services," *Economic and Political Weekly*, April 6, 1985, pp. 592–602.

21. *India Today*, April 15, 1983, p. 9.

Suggested Readings

Austin, Granville. *The Indian Constitution: Cornerstone of a Nation* (New York: Oxford University Press, 1966).

Basu, Durga Das. *Introduction to the Indian Constitution*, 9th ed. (New Delhi: Prentice-Hall, 1984).

Baxi, Upendra. *The Supreme Court and Politics* (Lucknow: Eastern Book, 1980).

Chanda, Asok. *Federalism in India* (London: Allen and Unwin, 1965).

Maheshwari, S. R. *Local Government in India* (New Delhi: Orient Longman, 1971).

_____. *State Governments in India* (Delhi: Macmillan, 1979).

Malik, Yogendra K. "Political Finance in India," *Political Quarterly*, vol. 60, no. 1 (January 1989), pp. 75–94.

Morris-Jones, W. H. *Parliament in India* (Philadelphia: University of Pennsylvania Press, 1957).

_____. *The Government and Politics of India* (Garden City, N.Y.: Doubleday and Company, 1967).

Pal, R. N. *The Office of the Prime Minister of India* (New Delhi: Ghanshyam Publishers, 1983).

Pylee, M. V. *Constitutional Government in India*, 4th ed. (Bombay: Asia Publishing House, 1984).

Shukla, J. D. *State and District Administration in India* (New Delhi: National Publications, 1976).

Venkateswaran, R. J. *Cabinet Government in India* (London: Allen and Unwin, 1967).

6
POLITICAL PARTIES

Characteristics of the Indian Party System

The Recent Rise of Political Parties

Some parties and political factions were present in India before independence, but it was the Indian National Congress that dominated the political scene. As an umbrella organization leading the freedom movement, it was able to attract persons of diverse ideological persuasions and political goals who were willing to work toward achieving independence for the country. Whereas the Muslim League in Pakistan disintegrated soon after the creation of a Muslim majority state, it was fortunate for India that the Congress not only survived but was converted from a loosely organized freedom movement into a cadre-based mass party. In 1948, at the urging of Sardar Vallabhbhai Patel, the Congress party Working Committee (the party's top executive organization) passed a resolution banning factions that had their own constitutions or organizational structure and had previously been allowed to operate within the Indian National Congress. This action led to the exit of various factions, which then converted themselves into new political parties. When the Congress became the ruling party of India, for many dissidents the only other course left open was to form opposition parties.

The Common Socioeconomic Background of Party Leaders

There is a remarkable similarity in the socioeconomic background of the leaders of the various political parties of India. Most of the leaders of the opposition parties who left the Indian National Congress originated from the same strata of the society, had the same type of educational background, and shared the experience of the freedom movement. Most of them originated in the upper or upper-middle classes. Most were educated in the West, or in schools in India that followed a Western curriculum. This was true for the leadership of both the Congress and the parties of the ideological left and right. The middle class and the landowning upper and middle castes still dominate the parties, although an English language education may no longer be the common background.

Reliance on Powerful Personalities

Although the parties have been able to build organizational structures, they rely heavily on certain charismatic and powerful personalities or community and religious leaders. But this tradition has its disadvantages. For example, a party that is entirely dependent on one leader tends to disappear with his or her demise. In addition, influential persons sometimes change parties in search of power and position and carry their followers into the party of their choice. Domination of parties by small oligarchies is common. In the parties that have captured power at the national or state level, parliamentary wings under these strong leaders become dominant and organizational or mass wings are relegated to a secondary position, used primarily for the mobilization of the voters.

Factions Within the Parties

All political parties tend to be factionalized. In non-Communist parties the faction leaders tend to be community caste or religious leaders who have skillfully built patron-client relationships among the members of different castes or communities. Such factional leaders vie among themselves for political influence within the party and the government, entering into political alliances with one another in order to keep their political rivals out of power. Most of these factional alliances are nonideological; they also tend to shift a good deal, thus keeping the parties in a state of flux. In rural areas, moreover, traditional hostilities based upon caste and kinship are transformed into factional fights that lead to inter-party power struggles. In order to maintain unity, party leaders must constantly try to balance the interests of different factions.

In the communist or socialist parties, on the other hand, ideological considerations frequently lead to faction formation, although personality, caste, or regional affiliations can also play divisive roles despite the adherence of these parties to a common ideology.

Political parties have also created various auxiliary organizations in an effort to mobilize different sectors of the society. More specifically, most of the prominent parties have organized youth wings, student unions, women's organizations, and peasant and labor groups. In addition, parties with the necessary strength and resources hold camps, seminars, and conferences for the different wings of the party.

The Use of Nonparliamentary Means to Power

Although electioneering and campaigning in an effort to capture a maximum number of seats in public offices are said to be the main functions of the parties, very few parties are able to make a respectable showing using only these legitimate methods. As a result, political parties of all ideological persuasions frequently try to exploit political or social discontent to their advantage. They do not hesitate to use such nonparliamentary means as civil disobedience, mass demonstrations, strikes, and protest rallies to embarrass the party in power, and some of these tactics may become violent.

A Multiparty System

Since the disintegration of the consensus-based Congress system in 1967, the Indian parties have fit the category of a multiparty system. The Congress party itself is a coalition of diverse interests, factions, groups, and individuals. It has rarely been able to capture more than 50% of the votes, the remainder of which have been won by the opposition parties and independents. In the 1989 elections, no political party was able to win a majority in the lower house of parliament (see Table 6.1). At the state level the dominance of the Congress party is frequently contested by regional and local parties.

Indian parties are divided into four major groups:

1. All-India political parties have been officially defined as those national parties with broad-based national support and able to win a minimum of 4% of votes or more than 3% of the seats in at least four state legislative assemblies. Also defined as All-India political parties are those able to win 4% of votes or 4% of seats in the Lok Sabha. These parties present national platforms and emphasize national issues in the parliamentary elections. Based on the results of the 1984 and 1985 elections, the following parties are classified as All-India parties: the Congress (I), the Bharatiya Janata party (BJP), the Janata Dal, the Communist party of India (Marxist), and the Communist party of India. These parties draw support from different segments of the society and put up their candidates across state lines.

2. The second group consists of regional parties, which clearly represent subregional nationalism based upon the common languages, culture, and history of a region. Given the pluralistic nature of Indian society, the rise of such parties is not surprising. These parties try to aggregate regional interests regardless of the caste and religious affiliations of their members. Their power base and voting strength are confined to a particular geographic area. The following are the best-known regional parties: the Dravida Munnetra Kazhagam (DMK) and All-India Anna-DMK of Tamilnadu, the Telugu Desam of Andhra Pradesh, the National Conference of Jammu and Kashmir, and Assom Gana Parishad (AGP) of Assam.

3. The third group includes those parties and organizations that are exclusive in their membership; that is, they accept as members only those inhabitants of a particular religious or ethnic community. They seek to protect and promote the interests of that particular community alone, are

TABLE 6.1   1989 Lok Sabha Election by State and Union Territory

Seats contested: 525   *Results Declared: 525*

Seats Won by Parties

Number of Seats	State	Congress (I)	Janata Dal	BJP	CPI	CPM	Others
42	Andhra Pradesh	39	–	–			3
2	Arunachal Pradesh	2	–	–	–	–	–
54	Bihar	4	31	9	4	1	5
1	Goa	–	–	–	–	–	1
26	Gujarat	3	11	12	–	–	–
10	Haryana	4	6	–	–	–	–
4	Himachal Pradesh	1	–	3	–	–	–
6	Jammu & Kashmir	2	–	–	–	–	4
28	Karnataka	27	1	–	–	–	–
20	Kerala	14	–	–	–	2	4
39	Madhya Pradesh	8	3	27			1
48	Maharashtra	28	5	10	1		4
2	Manipar	2	–	–	–	–	–
2	Meghalaya	2	–	–	–	–	–
1	Mizoram	1	–	–	–	–	–
1	Nagaland	1	–	–	–	–	–
21	Oriss	3	16		1	1	–
13	Punjab	2	1				10
25	Rajasthan	–	11	13	–	1	
38	Tamilnadu	24	–	–	1	–	13
2	Tripura	2	–	–	–	–	–
1	Sikkim	–	–	–	–	–	1
85	Uttar Pradesh	15	54	8	2	1	5
41	West Bengal	4			3	26	8
Union Territories							
7	Delhi	2	1	4	–	–	–
1	Chandigarh	–	1	–	–	–	–
1	Lakshadweep	1	–	–	–	–	–
1	Dadar & Nagar Haveli	–	–	–	–	–	1
1	Daman-Diu	–	–	–	–	–	1
1	Pondicherry	1	–	–	–	–	–
1	Andaman	1	–	–	–	–	–
525		**193**	**141**	**86**	**12**	**32**	**61**

Source: Based on data in *Hindu: International Edition,* December 9, 1989.

basically nonaggregative in their nature, and generally mobilize their supporters by appealing to their particularist sentiments. The following parties fall into this category: the Shiromani Akali Dal of the Punjab, the Muslim League in Kerala, and the Shiva Sena in Bombay.

4. The last group of parties consists of those organized around powerful persons or local and state issues. Such parties may not survive very long; some may appear only for a short period and then disappear completely or merge into other parties. There are currently several such parties existing in various states.

The Congress System and the Congress (I)

The Congress system emerged after the country had attained independence. From 1947 until it broke down in 1967, this system was at the center of Indian politics, spanning three distinct stages in its post-independence development. The first phase (1947–1967) was the period of the Congress system; the second phase (1967–1977) was characterized by the decline and disintegration of the Congress system and the consolidation of power by a small oligarchy; and the third and current phase (from 1977 on) witnessed the development of a new system, which because of its domination by Indira Gandhi became known as the Indira Congress or Congress (I).

Rajni Kothari, who developed the model of the Congress system, asserts that the Congress party, based upon a broad consensus, was able to accommodate diverse interests and factions within its fold. These factions competed with each other but usually reached compromises without creating any breakdown of the system. The opposition parties worked outside the system and used the factional leaders of the Congress party to influence its policy decisions. These parties acted as pressure groups and frequently created informal alliances with the factional leaders of the ruling party.[1] The Congress system showed remarkable flexibility and accommodation in withstanding the pressure from within its own ranks as well as from the opposition groups. Often the programs, policies, and even personnel of the opposition parties were absorbed by the Congress system, thus leading to the strengthening of the one-party system in India.[2] This system operated during Nehru's leadership of the Congress party.[3]

The second phase in the development of the Congress party started with the critical elections of 1967, when it lost its predominant position at both the state and national levels. The social and political mobilization resulting from two decades of independence had increased subgroup awareness in the Indian society. Many new groups were brought into politics, and there was an increase in the polarization among different castes, communities, and religious minorities. In addition, several dissident groups became active, leading to increased competition at the state level for power and prestige within the Congress party. When the party became incapable of satisfying their aspirations, factional leaders sought to form alliances with the leaders of the opposition parties, thus contributing to the disintegration of local and state Congress party organizations.

At the national level, the death of Nehru and the rise of Kamaraj Nadar as the president of the organizational wing of the party led to the weakening of its parliamentary wing. The renewed conflict between the two sides was ultimately settled by the 1969 split within the party. Indira Gandhi, who was the leader of the parliamentary wing and the prime minister of the country, defied and defeated the party bosses by successfully supporting the election of V. V. Giri to the presidency of the country. She thus became the dominant force within the party. The Congress was no longer a party based upon broad consensus. Instead, it became dependent upon the charismatic personality and populist policies of Indira Gandhi for electoral victories. The parliamentary victories in the 1971 elections and subsequent party sweep of the state legislative assembly elections in 1972 not only made Indira Gandhi the undisputed leader of the party but also transformed the nature of the party. The new members recruited into the parliament and state legislative assemblies were not always part of the local party organizations and often lacked an independent power base. Moreover, the autonomy of the state party units was subverted by Indira Gandhi's policy of creating divisions between the organizational and legislative wings of the party. In general, the central leadership became highly oligarchic and autocratic. But in 1975, unable to contain the unrest caused by economic and social discontent and challenged by the opposition leader and total collapse of the party organizations in various states, Indira Gandhi declared a state of emergency and suspended democratic activities. With this period of emergency ended the second phase of the Congress party's history.

The third phase of the Congress party commenced after Indira Gandhi's defeat in the 1977 election, which was held following the termination of her emergency rule. In this election for the Lok Sabha, the Congress won 34.5% of the votes and 153 seats, in contrast to the 43.6% of the votes and 352 seats it had won in the 1971 elections. Indira Gandhi even lost her own seat in parliament. This defeat resulted in another split within the party, leading to the emergence of the Congress (I). Many of the old and experienced leaders left the party, blaming her for its humiliating defeat in the elections. As a result, the new Congress (I) became completely identified with her personality. Many of the party's top decision-making agencies, such as the Congress Working Committee and the All-India Congress Committee, lost their powers. Similarly, state party organizations were brought under her direct control, as was the presidency of the Congress party, given that she hand-picked the top functionaries. She built a pyramid-like organization that was run by her or her henchmen.[4] When the 1980 elections were held following the collapse of the Janata government, the Congress (I) led by Indira Gandhi returned to power by winning a massive majority. Assisted by her son Sanjay Gandhi, she selected only persons of proven loyalty to the Nehru/Gandhi family to run for parliament. She especially sought to reward those political cronies who had stood by her during the period in which she had been out of power; administrative experience and parliamentary skill did not matter. In the 1980 Lok Sabha elections, the Congress (I) polled 43% of the votes and won 351 out of 539 seats.[5] In June of the same year, Gandhi called elections to state legislatures, and the Congress (I) captured power in fifteen out of twenty-two states.

The return of the Congress (I) to power in 1980 was attributed to the failure and eventual disintegration of the Janata party coalition that had captured power in 1977. In the 1980 elections the opposition leaders who had become discredited failed either to put up a joint front against the Congress or to build electoral alliances to give it a tough fight.

Starting in 1971 a dramatic change in the composition of the Congress party elites took place. In that year a large number of political careerists and opportunists joined the party. In 1980, in addition to these elements, many persons of dubious character and criminal backgrounds entered into the Congress party.[6] Under Indira's leadership the Congress party simply became an instrument of personal power. She also sought to use the organization for dynastic succession. First she groomed Sanjay, her younger son, to take over the leadership of the party, but after his accidental death in June 1980, she brought in her elder son, Rajiv.[7]

In the 1984 parliamentary elections following the assassination of Indira Gandhi, the Congress (I) won with a record-setting vote, capturing around 50% of the popular vote and 396 Lok Sabha seats—a feat unmatched in the history of free India. The relentless campaign mounted soon after Rajiv's mother's assassination brought him a great many sympathy votes. His victory was made easier by a fragmented opposition led by old-guard politicians who had failed to establish their credibility with the masses.

The key issue in the 1984 election was the threat to national unity. The events in the Punjab and the separatist movement led by the Sikh extremists were alarming enough to persuade the people to vote for the Congress (I), a party that truly possessed a national image. The election result was perceived as the "clearest mandate possible on the central issue of national unity, [and] the rejection of Janata, DMKP and BJP opposition."[8] The Congress (I) under the leadership of Rajiv Gandhi swept all the states in the country except Andhra Pradesh, Jammu and Kashmir, and Sikkim.

In the 1989 parliamentary elections, the Congress (I) was, however, able to capture only 193 out of 525 seats, losing power at the center. The party was routed in the densely populated Hindi-speaking states of north India (see Table 6.1). In the 1990 elections held for the state legislative bodies, once again, the Congress (I) suffered humiliating defeat at the hands of the Janata Dal and Bharatiya Janata Party (BJP) and lost power in important states like Madhya Pradesh Bihar, Rajasthan, Gujarat, Orissa, Himachal Pradesh and others.

The constitution of the Congress party provides for an elaborate organization headed by a president, assisted by a Working Committee (the executive of the party), and supplemented by the All-India Congress Committee (AICC), the deliberative branch of the party. Its central office, located in New Delhi, supervises the work of the Pradesh (state) Congress committees (PCC) as well as other subordinate organizations. However, during her control of the party, Indira Gandhi stifled interparty democracy and did not hold party elections from 1972. Thus the party's organizational structure has been reduced to a machine that is held together by political notables who possess power and are able to distribute patronage.

The Congress party's program and policies have been generally moderate and reform oriented rather than radical, seeking to bring about gradual changes in the basic structure of Indian society. The party professes its commitment to democratic socialism and places special emphasis on the planned economic development of the country in which the government is expected to play a key role. For example, it stresses the need to place key industries such as steel, power, heavy chemicals, and capital goods industries under government control. Yet it also leaves room for free enterprise; for instance, agriculture, which constitutes the largest sector of the Indian economy, is left under private ownership. With the rise of Rajiv Gandhi and his associates, the Congress party moved closer to the centrist position and adopted even more pragmatic and flexible economic policies. In foreign relations the Congress party has been strongly committed to a policy of nonalignment, trying to keep equal distance from both the superpowers. Under the leadership of Indira Gandhi, however, the party became more pro-Soviet, and in 1971, the Congress party–led Indian government signed a treaty of friendship with the Soviet Union. Any change in the party's foreign policy position is unlikely, even under the new leadership.

The Janata Dal and the National Front:
A Centrist Alternative to the Congress (I)?

The Janata Dal was founded in October 1988 as a result of the merger of the following political groups and parties:

1. The Jan Morcha (People's Front) is led by V. P. Singh, a former defense minister in the Rajiv government. He and his close associates were expelled from the Congress (I) in 1987. The Jan Morcha stressed

value-based politics with a goal to reform the election process and
party finances, and pledged to restore secular and democratic principles in the political life of the country. The group had several
nationally known leaders but no organizational base.

2. The Janata party was formed on May 1, 1977, as a result of the
electoral alliance of various groups that had made Indira Gandhi and
her authoritarian rule of 1975–1977 the central electoral issue. Janata
came to power in 1977 after defeating Indira Gandhi and Congress.
Owing to the conflicting political ambitions of its factional leaders,
however, the Janata party was unable to maintain its internal cohesion.
Consequently, in 1979 the party split into various factions leading
to the collapse of the Janata government. In the 1980 and 1984
elections, Janata party support declined, being able to poll only 19
and 7 percent of the votes in the respective elections.

   In the 1985 state elections, the party improved its electoral
performance, capturing the majority of seats in Karanataka, an
important southern state. Nevertheless, the Janata party had little
chance of capturing power at the national level on its own. Since
many of its leaders, like the leaders of the Jan Morcha, were former
members of the Congress party, who had left Congress in disagreement
with Indira Gandhi on policy or personal issues, it was reasonable
for them to merge with groups having similar backgrounds.

3. The Bharatiya Lok Dal was founded and led by the late Charan
Singh, a Congress party maverick who left the party in 1967 and
became the non-Congress chief minister of Uttar Pradesh. By absorbing
many of the anti-Congress parties and some PSP and Swatantra
party members, the Lok Dal, under Charan Singh's leadership became
a major political force in north India. Although Lok Dal underwent
various name changes, its policies and program remained committed
to the interests of the well-to-do class of farmers who have reaped
the benefits of the Green Revolution.

After the death of Charan Singh in 1987, the party split into various
factions, one of which was led by Ajit Singh, son of Charan Singh, and
another by Devi Lal, the powerful chief minister of the state of Haryana.
Both factions drew support from the Jats and the members of backward
castes of U.P., Haryana, Rajasthan, and Bihar. In 1988, V. P. Singh was able
to persuade the leaders and the followers of both factions to merge into
the Janata Dal. The Lok Dal faction of the Janata Dal serves as an important
and powerful lobby for the farmers within the new party.

   Like the Congress party, the Janata Dal is an umbrella organization,
containing many anti-Nehru-Gandhi-dynasty groups opposed to the urban-
oriented development strategies of the Congress (I). Despite the factional

nature of the party and its organizational weaknesses, under the charismatic leadership of V. P. Singh, the party was able to capture 144 seats in the 1989 elections. It successfully defeated the Congress (I) in the Hindi-heartland of north India. In the 1990 state elections the Janata Dal improved its electoral performance by defeating the Congress (I) party in several important states including Orissa and Bihar.

In its public policies and programs, the Janata Dal occupies a centrist position, placing greater emphasis on rural development, decentralization of power both in the economy and politics, restoration of civil liberties, and accommodation of the demands of India's various religious and linguistic minorities.

In foreign policy, the Janata Dal seeks understanding and accommodation with India's neighbors rather than confrontation, as the Rajiv-led Congress (I) government did. In relations with superpowers the Janata Dal will adhere to the traditional policy of nonalignment.

The National Front is a loose coalition of national and regional parties that was formed in August 1988 under the chairmanship of N. T. Rama Rao. It consists of Janata Dal, Congress (S), and regional parties like the Telugu Desam of Andhra Pradesh, DMK of Tamilnadu and Asom Gana Parishad of Assam. V. P. Singh of the Janata Dal was elected the convener of the Front.

The primary goal of the National Front was to defeat the Congress (I) by way of avoiding multi-candidate electoral contests and through seat adjustments among its constituents. Although the Front adopted a 71-point platform pledging to root out corruption, seek political solutions to various communal and ethnic conflicts, grant greater state autonomy, and withdraw the Indian Peace Keeping Force from Sri Lanka, among others, its primary function was to provide India's opposition parties a degree of cohesion that they usually lacked at the time of election.

In the 1989 elections, while the Janata Dal concentrated its efforts in the north Indian states, it allocated a majority of the seats to Telugu Dasam and DMK in Andhra Pradesh, and Tamilnadu, respectively. Contrary to expectations the Telugu Desam and DMK were routed by the Congress (I) and its allies in the southern states, leaving them with only three seats.

At present the National Front government is dominated at the center by the Janata Dal, the regional parties functioning as junior partners in the coalition.

The Bharatiya Janata Party: Hindu Nationalist or an Alternate to the Congress?

The Bharatiya Janata party is a reincarnation of the Jana Sangh, the militant Hindu nationalist party founded in 1951 by Shyama Prasad Mookerjee.

Mookerjee and his associates advocated the building of a modern India on the concept of Hindu *rashtra* (nation), which is based upon democratic principles but derives its inspiration from rich *Bharatiya* (Indian) *samskriti* (culture) and *maryada* (traditions).[10] The party adopted four fundamentals: one country, one nation, one culture, and a rule of law that would determine Jana Sangh's future course of action.[11] The Jana Sangh was closely associated with a Hindu organization called the Rashtriya Swayamsevak Sangh (RSS), or National Volunteer Organization, which was opposed not only to the creation of Pakistan but also to the so-called appeasement policy of the Congress party toward Indian Muslims. The party supported a unitary government led by a strong center, the adoption of Hindi as the national language of the country, and a powerful military capable of ensuring India's dominance of the South Asian subcontinent. Most of the Jana Sangh's electoral support came from the Hindi-speaking states of north India, especially the upper caste urban commercial classes of the Punjab, Harayana, Himachal Pradesh, Delhi, Uttar Pradesh, and Madhya Pradesh.

In its economic policies, even though it favored central planning and consolidation of the public sector, the Jana Sangh has opposed extensive government control of the economy.

The Jana Sangh's experience as a unit of the Janata party, the trials and tribulations of its leadership during the emergency rule of 1975, its administrative experience in the national government, and its close association with J. P. Narayan brought about considerable transformation of its ideologies. From an ideology of Hindu chauvinism with an emphasis on Bharatiya culture, Hindi language and militant anti-Pakistan foreign policy, it moved to noncommunal and pragmatic political and economic policies. In foreign policy, for example, it sought an accommodation with Pakistan. The party also demonstrated a healthy civil libertarian and prodemocratic stand. But its efforts to become a more aggregative and broad-based party caused considerable confusion within its ranks and soured its relations with the RSS, an organization that formerly provided it considerable electoral support.

The traumatic events of 1984 and the emotional turmoil resulting from the assassination of Indira Gandhi at the hands of her two Sikh bodyguards caused a Hindu backlash that helped the Congress (I) win a landslide; but it also hurt the BJP, which had tried to strike an electoral deal with the moderate section of the Sikh leadership. Its plight was evident from the fact that it could win only 2 seats although it contested 226 seats of the Lok Sabha. After its poor performance in the 1984 elections, the BJP, under the leadership of L. K. Advani, reoriented its policies and programs. It reverted to its original ideology of Hindu nationalism and adopted an anti-Muslim public posture. Helped by the rising tide of Hindu militancy, BJP was able to capture 86 seats in the 1989 elections (see Table 6.1) and it emerged as the third largest party in the Lok Sabha. In the 1990 state elections the BJP won a majority of seats in Madhya Pradesh and Himachal Pradesh and emerged as a strong contender for sharing power in important states like Gujarat and Rajasthan.

The Bharatiya Janata party, which is cadre based and well disciplined, possesses one of the best organizational networks of the non-Communist parties. Its leadership has high goals, and it looks upon itself as an alternate to the Congress (I).

The Communist Party of India (CPI)

The Communist movement in India has undergone various strategic and ideological transformations. It has always been plagued with factional conflicts and has experienced several splits. The Communist party of India, which held its first all-India session in 1927, faced serious problems in its effort to create a suitable balance between the political realities existing in India and the foreign policy goals of the Soviet Union. Its leadership's ideological subservience to Moscow frequently led it into conflicts with the nationalist aspirations of the people of India. Thus, in 1942, when the Indian National Congress under the leadership of Mahatma Gandhi launched the Quit India movement and sought freedom from British rule in exchange for India's support for British war efforts, the CPI decided to join with the British government and denounced Gandhi's movement. Britain and the Soviet Union had formed a common front against Nazi Germany, so the Communists supported the "people's war" while ignoring the dominant national aspirations. Similarly, in 1947 they supported the Muslim League on the issue of Pakistan and thus alienated the majority of Indians who were opposed to the division of the country on a religious basis.

After the independence of the country in 1947, the CPI followed the Stalinist line by denouncing the Congress party leaders as being the slaves of imperialist interests. Under the leftist leadership of B. T. Ranadive, the CPI launched a movement of terrorism and incited peasant uprisings, which, however, were suppressed by the national government. But with the new political leadership in the Soviet Union and the ongoing process of de-Stalinization under Khrushchev, the Soviets decided to befriend the Nehru government. This change in Soviet foreign policy forced the CPI to alter its course of action. In 1958, therefore, it adopted the Amritsar resolution and pledged to seek power and social change through parliamentary means. The dominant faction within the party supported Nehru's "progressive" policies, especially his foreign policy.

During the 1969 split in the Congress party, and later during the national emergency, the CPI consistently supported Indira Gandhi and her government. Only after the 1977 defeat did it try to chart an independent course of action. The more radical Marxists in India look upon the CPI as primarily a "revisionist" party that has lost its revolutionary direction and always follows the policy lines dictated by Moscow.

The CPI has pockets of support in different parts of the country, primarily Andhra Pradesh, Bihar, eastern Uttar Pradesh, Kerala, and West Bengal. In the 1989 elections, the CPI was able to capture 12 seats, a doubling of its 1984 performance when it won only 6 seats (see Table 6.1).

The Communist Party (Marxist):
An Indian Road to Marxism-Leninism?

A 1964 split in the CPI led to the founding of India's second Communist party, called the Communist party (Marxist). The split resulted from a clash of ideologies between the pro-Moscow faction led by S. A. Dange and the alleged pro-Chinese faction headed by Jyoti Basu, Hare Krishna Konar, and E.M.S. Namboodiripad. Subsequently, however, the new party modified its pro-Chinese stance and sought to direct the Communist movement in accordance with the political and historical realities existing in India. Under the able leadership of Jyoti Basu and E.M.S. Namboodiripad, the party adopted an independent course for Indian Communists, maintaining distance from both the Chinese and Soviet Communist parties. For example, it staunchly opposed Indira Gandhi's emergency rule as well as her subversion of the federal system in India. At the same time it favored the formation of selective electoral alliances with ideologically similar parties, excluding such rightist parties as the BJP.

At present, the CPM is in power in West Bengal, where it commands a considerable following among the intellectuals, students, industrial workers, landless labor, and poor farmers. Since 1967, when it first contested the elections, it has been able to maintain steady support among voters, receiving around 6% of popular votes. In the 1989 elections, CPM supported anti-Congress parties, capturing 32 seats in contrast to 22 seats it won in 1984. The CPI and CPM support the National Front government led by V. P. Singh.

Both of the Communist parties have strong cadre-based organizations and provide considerable regional autonomy to their party units.

The Communist Party (Marxist-Leninist)

When the Communist movement in India became involved in electoral politics, a portion of the young generation of Communists became disenchanted with the older generation of leadership. Renouncing the parliamentary methods of their elders and following the Maoist line of radicalization of the peasantry, they launched a peasant revolution in the Naxalbari area of rural northern West Bengal. In 1969, under the leadership of such young and idealistic persons as Kanu Sanyal and Charu Mazumdar, the third

Communist party of India (Marxist-Leninist) was founded. The party immediately called for an armed uprising.[12] The Communist party of China not only extended recognition to the new party; it also provided considerable propaganda support. But the leftist state government led by the Marxists in West Bengal, with the support of the national government, was able to suppress the revolt and contain the peasant uprising.

Although the CPI (ML) is still left with some pockets of support among youth groups, many of its leaders have either given up political activity or started flirting with electoral politics![13] The "Naxalites," as most of the left-wing radicals and the extremists were formerly called, are now split into several small factions and splinter groups.

Regional Parties

1. The Dravida Munnetra Kazhagam (DMK) and the All-India Anna DMK represent the cultural nationalism of the people of Tamilnadu, who speak the Tamil language and take pride in their Dravidian (non-Aryan) heritage. The Dravidian cultural revival movement and the DMK are closely intertwined.[14] C. N. Annadurai, the charismatic leader of the DMK, transformed this social-cultural revival movement into a political party. Initially the party sought the creation of a sovereign state in the south; later on, however, it gave up its separatist demand. Now the DMK seeks only greater state autonomy and an end to the domination of the south by the Hindi-speaking north.

In the 1967 election the DMK defeated the Congress party at the polls and became the ruling party in Madras, a state that the DMK renamed as Tamilnadu (meaning "a country of Tamils"). After the death of Annadurai in 1969, a power struggle developed between M. Kurananidhi and M. G. Ramchandran (MGR), leading to the formation of the All-India Anna DMK (AIADMK) by the latter in 1972. Soon thereafter the AIADMK came to dominate the state politics; its success in the elections of 1977 resulted in MGR's assumption of the chief ministership. In national politics MGR's party has become allied with the Congress (I). And in the 1984 state elections, the AIADMK again captured the majority in the Tamilnadu legislature. In the 1989 state elections, however, the DMK, under the leadership of M. Karunanidhi, a rival of the late MGR, won a massive majority, defeating both the Congress (I) and AIADMK.

2. The Telugu Desam is a comparatively new political phenomenon that in 1982 gained dominance in Andhra Pradesh's politics under the leadership of N. T. Rama Rao, a matinee idol (just as M. G. Ramchandran is in Tamilnadu). The party originated in reaction to Indira Gandhi's frequent imposition of unpopular Congress party chief ministers on the people of Andhra Pradesh. Most of these chief ministers did not last very long, and

the faction-ridden state Congress party failed to deliver on its promises. N. T. Rama Rao had only to appeal to the subnational pride of the Telugu people; the Telugu Desam denounced the New Delhi domination of the state politics and in 1983 won an impressive majority in the state election, defeating the Congress party. Since its formation, the Telugu Desam has faced various challenges from the Congress party. In both the 1984 parliamentary election and the 1985 state election, however, it routed the Congress (I) at the polls: For the Lok Sabha it won 28 out of 49 seats, and in the March 1985 state elections it won 202 out of 287 seats. In the 1989 parliamentary and state elections, the Telugu Desam suffered a humiliating defeat at the hands of the Congress (I), losing control of the state government. N. T. Rama Rao and his party are strong advocates of greater state autonomy.

3. The Jammu and Kashmir National Conference was founded by Sheikh Mohammad Abdullah, a Kashmiri freedom fighter. His efforts resulted in the development of Kashmiri self-respect and a strong sense of subnational identity. The National Conference under his leadership was able to secure for Jammu and Kashmir a special status in the Indian union not given to any other Indian state. After the death of the sheikh in 1982, however, the party became divided into two factions—one led by his son, Farooq Abdullah, and the other by the sheikh's son-in-law, G. M. Shah. Abdullah's government, which won a clear majority in the 1982 state election, was dismissed through Congress (I) manipulation. In its place Indira Gandhi installed a government led by G. M. Shah's faction of the National Conference, which was supported by the Congress (I) members. However, in the 1984 elections the Farooq-led National Conference once again swept the parliamentary election in Kashmir Valley. Although in the 1989 parliamentary elections the National Conference, under the leadership of Dr. Abdullah, captured 3 out of 6 seats, recent violent demonstrations against his government indicate that his party is losing touch with the Kashmiri nationalists.

In addition to the major regional parties are such minor regional parties as Jharkhand Mukti Morcha in Bihar, Sikkim Sangram Parishad (SSP) led by N. B. Bhandari, and Asom Gana Parishad, led by Prafulla Mahanta, in Assam.

Communal or Sectarian Parties

Of all the sectarian and communal parties in India in the post-independence period, the most successful in promoting the cause of a particular religious community has been the Shiromani Akali Dal.

The Akali Dal is a militant political organization with religious appeal; it claims to be the exclusive representative of the Sikhs, who constitute a majority in the state of Punjab. The Akali Dal is closely associated with the educational, cultural, and religious life of the Sikhs. For example, it is

the Akali party that has a monopoly over the Shiromani Gurudwara Prabhandak Committee (SGPC), the management body for the Sikh temples.
The SGPC not only exercises control over the Sikh temples, it also possesses
huge revenues in the form of offerings made by Sikh devotees. Through
its skillful use of SGPC funds, the Akali Dal manages several Sikh educational,
cultural, and religious institutions. Thus, the Sikh denominational schools,
colleges, and other societies not only employ Sikh intellectuals and party
workers but also try to create a distinct subnational identity among the
Sikhs.[15]

From time to time the Akali party has been in power in the Punjab,
but until the 1985 election it was able to maintain itself in power only in
coalition with other parties. As such coalitions are usually unstable, the
Akali party governments collapsed frequently. Akalis have therefore often
resorted to agitation in seeking their political goals. One such instance
occurred in 1982, when the Akalis launched a mass agitation against the
national government, seeking, along with certain religious concessions, greater
autonomy for the Sikh-dominated state of Punjab. When the party lost
control of the agitation to the religious fundamentalists and Sikh extremists,
a bloody confrontation with the national government resulted. In 1985 the
majority faction of the Akali party led by Harcharan Singh Longowal reached
an agreement with the national government and terminated its agitation.
Subsequently, it won elections in the state and was brought back to power
in the Punjab.[16] As the Akali party is divided into several factions, however,
its leadership finds it hard to maintain internal cohesion. In the 1989 Lok
Sabha elections, it was the radical faction of the Akali party, led by Simranjit
Singh Mann, that won 6 out of 13 seats in Punjab. His faction of the Akali
party defeated the moderate Akali factions led by Prakash Singh Badal and
Surjit Singh Barnala, former chief ministers of the state. The Akali party
also faces a serious challenge from the Sikh extremists, who seek to establish
a sovereign Sikh state called Khalistan.

*   *   *

In sum, the larger political parties in India, as in Sri Lanka, are able to
bring different segments of society together. At the same time, the political
system allows the operation of other parties representing mainly ethnic,
regional, and religious interests. Both the Indian and the Sri Lankan systems,
unlike those of Pakistan and Bangladesh, give opportunities to politicians
and political parties to grow, to participate freely in the political process,
and to deepen their political experience. Both countries' systems enable the
political parties to mobilize voters and to capture political power through
the electoral process.

Notes

1. Rajni Kothari, "Congress 'System' in India," *Asian Survey,* vol. 4, no. 12 (December 1964), pp. 1–18.

2. W. H. Morris-Jones, "Parliament and Dominant Party: Indian Experience," *Parliamentary Affairs,* vol. 17 (Summer 1964), pp. 296–307; and Gopal Krishna, "One Party Dominance—Development and Trends," in Rajni Kothari (ed.), *Party Systems and Election Studies: Occasional Papers of the Centre for the Study of Developing Societies,* no. 1 (Bombay: Allied Publishers, 1967), pp. 19–98.

3. Bhagwan D. Dua, "India: A Study in the Pathology of a Federal System," *Journal of Commonwealth and Comparative Politics,* vol. 19, no. 3 (November 1981), p. 261.

4. Stanley A. Kochanek, "Mrs. Gandhi's Pyramid: The New Congress," in Henry C. Hart (ed.), *Indira Gandhi's India: A Political System Reappraised* (Boulder, Colo.: Westview Press, 1967), pp. 93–124.

5. Richard Sisson and William Vanderbock, "Mapping the Indian Electorate: Trends in Party Support in Seven National Elections," *Asian Survey,* vol. 23, no. 10 (October 1983), p. 1142; and Javed Alam, "The Vote for Political Stability and the Implications: An Analysis of 1980 Election Results," *Political Science Review,* vol. 21, no. 4 (1983), p. 313.

6. Paul R. Brass, "National Power and Local Politics in India: A Twenty-Year Perspective," *Modern Asian Studies,* vol. 18, no. 1 (1984), pp. 89–118; and James Manor, "Anomie in Indian Politics: Origins and Potential Impact," *Economic and Political Weekly,* Annual Number (May 1983), pp. 225–234.

7. Robert L. Hardgrave, Jr., "India on the Eve of Elections: Congress and the Opposition," *Pacific Affairs,* vol. 57, no. 3 (Fall 1984), pp. 404–428.

8. Gopal Krishna, "A Nation State to Defend," *Times of India,* January 7, 1985.

9. *India Today,* January 15, 1985, p. 18.

10. Craig Baxter, "The Jana Sangh: A Brief History," in Donald E. Smith (ed.), *South Asian Politics and Religion* (Princeton, N.J.: Princeton University Press, 1966), p. 81.

11. Ibid. See also Craig Baxter, *The Jana Sangh: A Biography of Indian Political Party* (Philadelphia: University of Pennsylvania Press, 1969).

12. Marcus F. Franda, "India's Third Communist Party," *Asian Survey,* vol. 9, no. 11 (November 1969), pp. 797–818.

13. *India Today,* January 13, 1985, p. 28.

14. Marguerite Ross Barnett, *The Politics of Cultural Nationalism in South India* (Princeton, N.J.: Princeton University Press, 1976).

15. Baldev Raj Nayar, *Minority Politics in the Punjab* (Princeton, N.J.: Princeton University Press, 1966); and Paul R. Brass, "Ethnic Cleavages and the Punjab Party System 1952–1972," in Myron Weiner and John Osgood Field (eds.), *Electoral Politics in the Indian States,* vol. 4 (New Delhi: Manohar Book Service, 1974), pp. 7–61.

16. Gopal Singh, "Socio-Economic Basis of Punjab Crisis," *Economic and Political Weekly,* vol. 19 (January 1984), pp. 42–507; Sucha Singh Gill and K. C. Singhal, "The Punjab Problem: Its Historical Roots," *Economic and Political Weekly,* vol. 19 (April 1984), pp. 603–608; and Yogendra K. Malik, "Sikh Militancy and the

Akali Party in Punjab: Move for Secessionism or Greater Autonomy?" *Asian Survey,* vol. 26, no. 3 (March 1986), pp. 344–362.

Suggested Readings

Barnett, Marguerite Ross. *The Politics of Cultural Nationalism in South India* (Princeton, N.J.: Princeton University Press, 1976).

Baxter, Craig. *The Jana Sangh: A Biography of an Indian Political Party* (Philadelphia: University of Pennsylvania Press, 1969).

Bhambri, C. P. *The Janata Party: A Profile* (New Delhi: National, 1982).

Brass, Paul R. *Factional Politics in an Indian State: The Congress Party in Uttar Pradesh* (Berkeley: University of California Press, 1966).

Brass, Paul R. and Marcus Franda (eds.). *Radical Politics in South Asia* (Cambridge, Mass.: The MIT Press, 1973).

Dasgupta, B. *The Naxalite Movement* (Bombay: Allied Publishers, 1974).

Erdman, Howard. *The Swatantra Party and Indian Conservatism* (Cambridge: Cambridge University Press, 1967).

Fickett, Lewis P., Jr. *The Major Socialist Parties of India: A Study in Leftist Fragmentation* (Syracuse, N.Y.: Maxwell School, Syracuse University, 1970).

Hardgrave, Robert L., Jr. *The Dravidian Movement* (Bombay: Popular Prakashna, 1965).

Hartmann, Horst. *Political Parties in India* (New Delhi: Meenakshi Prakashan, 1982).

Kochanek, Stanley A. *The Congress Party of India: The Dynamics of One-Party Democracy* (Princeton, N.J.: Princeton University Press, 1968).

Naik, J. A. *The Opposition in India and the Future of Democracy* (New Delhi: S. Chand, 1983).

Nayar, Baldev Raj. *Minority Politics in the Punjab* (Princeton, N.J.: Princeton University Press, 1966).

Ram, Mohan. *Indian Communism: Split Within Split* (Delhi: Vikas Publishers, 1969).

Sen Gupta, Bhabani. *Communism in Indian Politics* (New York: Columbia University Press, 1972).

Weiner, Myron. *Party Politics in India: The Development of a Multi-Party System* (Princeton, N.J.: Princeton University Press, 1957).

———. *Party Building in a New Nation: The Indian National Congress* (Chicago: University of Chicago Press, 1967).

7
GROUPS AND INTEREST ARTICULATION

The segmented nature of Indian society tends to stimulate diverse group activity. Before India came under British control, traditional and ascriptive ties based upon kinship and community provided easy avenues for the organization of individuals to protect their common interests. Then, during the British rule, competition for jobs and the need to obtain economic and business concessions encouraged Indians to organize themselves. It was not surprising, therefore, that in the early stages of British rule in India, "in every province, at every level and inside every category, political associations were formed as the expression of claims and counter-claims, of group and counter-group, of competitors vying for the favor of the Raj by playing politics and couched in its own formulae."[1] The subsequent introduction of representative institutions and electoral politics after independence provided incentive to politically ambitious persons to organize all kinds of groups and associations.

Group Activity

Group activity was encouraged by the leadership of the Indian National Congress, which led the nationalist movement. With the blessings of such nationally known leaders as Nehru and Patel, peasants' organizations, trade unions, women's associations, student unions, youth organizations, associations promoting the spread of literacy in native languages, and various other nonascriptive associations sprang up all over the country.[2] These groups became important links between the Western-educated English-speaking elites and the illiterate or semiliterate masses. They became, in effect, vital tools of mass mobilization. The group leaders, in turn, gradually became aware of the potential of group activity. They often used their group strength to promote their own interests and organizations by influencing first the policies of the Indian National Congress and subsequently the decisions of the state and national governments.

The complex post-independence institutional network created by the new constitution of India provided a new focus for interest groups. Multiple centers of power have emerged. The village councils, municipal governments, district administrations, state legislative bodies, council of ministers, and a host of bureaucratic organizations and administrative agencies have become open to various kinds of pressure, thus intensifying group activity.

For example, the national government is engaged in making policy decisions affecting the sociocultural life of persons belonging to a wide variety of communities, regions, and language groups. Thus the government has become the focus of attention of all types of pressure groups.

The competition for power and influence among rival groups is both a divisive and an integrative process. On the one hand, the activities of religious minorities such as the Muslims, Sikhs, and Christians evoke protest from the members of the majority religion and tend to aggravate intercommunal tension and reinforce the religious divisions. On the other hand, many nontraditional economic groups such as the Chamber of Commerce and Industry, the trade unions, and the peasants and farmers organizations tend to play an integrative role. These are open groups that draw their membership from people of all segments of Indian society engaged in the same trade.

Interest groups in India do not enjoy much autonomy. Quite frequently they are dominated by political parties, which use them to advance their partisan goals rather than to promote the interests of group members. Such manipulation of groups by parties or politicians, especially groups based upon community and common religious affiliations, actually tends to hurt the interests of their members.

All varieties of interest groups, including the institutional, associational, community, and anomic, frequent the landscape of Indian politics. Several promotional groups advocating cultural, economic, and social causes also exist.

Pressure groups in India seem to get a better response from the politicians than from the members of the bureaucracy. Many politicians, in fact, become openly associated with a particular interest group and intervene in the administration on behalf of their clients. Frequent consultations also take place between the leaders of groups and the heads of departments. Occasionally the government appoints the representatives of specialized interests such as the educationists, labor leaders, business people, religious leaders, social workers, journalists, and lawyers to various advisory bodies and commissions.

The positions and the level of political activities of some of the prominent groups operating in Indian politics are described as follows.

Business

Business and commercial classes, like their organizations, have serious image problems. Traditionally, business people have not been accorded a high status in society. In the Hindu social system, the trading and commercial classes represented by the Vaishya caste occupy a lower status than the Brahmins, the carriers of sacred knowledge, and the Kshatriyas, the administrators and the warriors. The low level of the first social position is further reinforced by the poor image of the Banias and the Marwaris,[3] the leading members of the trading communities. They are often depicted as mean, ruthless, and dishonest misers. As Stanley Kochanek has pointed out, modern political ideologies such as Marxism and Gandhism, to which many Indian leaders subscribe, also tend to depict business people as exploiters.[4] By the late 1980s, this situation seemed to be changing: A new breed of enterprising businessmen, with considerable sophistication, had risen in both established and new business groups, and the political parties, in order to meet the escalating cost of electioneering, had become dependent on business donations. These developments have given the world of business a respectability not previously enjoyed.

In order to promote their interests, industrial and business elites have made several successful efforts to organize themselves. Many of these organizations came into existence during the British period, while others were organized after independence. More recent associations have been organized on an industry-wide basis, seeking to protect the newly established industries against foreign competition.

The following are the three business organizations of national standing: the Federation of Indian Chambers of Commerce and Industry (FICCI), the Associated Chamber of Commerce and Industry of India (Assocham), and the All-India Manufacturers Organization (AIMO).

Today FICCI is the largest and the most influential business organization in India; it represents more than 100,000 business firms, including 200 business and industrial units.[5] In recent years various business and industrial houses have competed with each other to control this powerful organization. In 1983 an extensive membership drive was undertaken by comparatively newer business and industrial proprietors to bring the FICCI under their leadership. In 1980 it had fewer than 600 voting members; by 1983 the voting membership had increased to 1,450. These new members were recruited by rival business groups from Uttar Pradesh and Bihar. The membership elects its top policy-making body, the executive committee, which in turn elects a vice-president who after one year becomes the president of the organization. Intensive efforts have been directed at the control of these two agencies.[6] The representatives of the organizations freely meet with the important officials of the government.

The other major business organizations, the Associated Chamber of Commerce and Industry in India (Assocham) and the All-India Manufacturers Organizations (AIMO), are smaller in size and have a different type of clientele. The Assocham represents foreign, especially British, industrial and trading interests in India, whereas the AIMO serves to protect and promote the interests of medium-sized manufacturers in and around Bombay.[7]

Aside from their efforts to lobby the prime minister, the members of the cabinet, and the top bureaucrats, the business organizations have become interested in influencing the parties' programs, policies and selection of candidates for parliament and the state legislatures.

The two well-established top industrial houses, the Birlas and the Tatas, vie with each other to influence the government policies as well as public opinion to enlarge their industrial empires and strengthen their business interests. The Birlas have always been close to the ruling party—first to the Congress party and now to the Congress (I). The Tatas, however, have maintained a distance from the Congress (I) and instead have supported the opposition parties, especially those advocating free enterprise and less government regulation of the economy. Both business houses constantly try to improve their public image by donating large sums of money to religious and humanitarian causes: The Birlas tend to promote the Hindu religious organizations whereas the Tatas have established research foundations, hospitals, and scholary institutions.

The rise of a well-educated new generation of managerial elites along with the Western-educated young generation of industrial proprietors has produced a considerably higher degree of self-confidence and assertiveness in today's business world of India.

Labor

Labor organizations in India, unlike the business organizations, are highly politicized and lack organizational autonomy. India's major trade unions, as the subsequent discussion makes evident, are divided along party lines: (1) The Indian National Trade Union Congress (INTUC), with a membership of 2.4 million, is the country's largest trade union organization and is affiliated with the Congress (I). (2) The Bharatiya Mazdoor Sabha (BMS), with a membership of 1.8 million, receives its organizational and political inspiration from the Bharatiya Janata party. (3) The Centre of Indian Trade Unions (CITU), claiming 1.7 million members, is controlled by the Communist party (Marxists). (4) The All-India Trade Union Congress (AITUC), with its 1.7 million members, is dominated by the Communist party of India.

Datta Samant, a medical practitioner and political maverick, recently emerged as a major trade union leader. Samant is an independent and does not have any party affiliation. He currently represents around 500 trade unions with a 1.6 million membership.[8]

The labor unions are strongly influenced by the political parties. Observing this close relationship between the parties and the labor union, R. D. Agarawal has commented that

> union leaders set up rival unions or defect from one party to another along with their union following. In doing this, they never consult or seek approval of the constituent members. The latter naturally find little interest in the ideological predilections or shifting political loyalties of their leaders. They often feel bewildered or even confused at the political acrobatics of their leaders.[9]

The history of the labor movement as well as the unions' recent operations in India lead to the conclusion that "the unions were not organizations of workers, but organizations for workers run by political leaders and social workers."[10]

The leaders of the trade unions do not come from the ranks of the working classes. Instead, most of their top leaders are wealthy English-speaking intellectuals or professionals. Under this leadership, the unions frequently go on strike, either to harass the proprietors or to demonstrate the organizational power of their union bosses. In addition, they often make excessive demands and resort to the use of physical coercion.

Farm Groups

There are three basic types of agricultural interests existing in India: (1) large-scale landowners, (2) medium-scale farm owners and small-scale peasant proprietors, and (3) sharecroppers and landless labor. The large-scale landowning class, which consists of absentee landlords known as *zamindars,* became intertwined with the bureaucracy and state-level Congress party organizations. By successfully influencing the formulation and imple-mentation of the land reform policies of the Congress party–run state governments, they were able to block land reforms, which they opposed. It was only after pressure was exerted by the central government that the state governments undertook some significant land reforms. The influence of large-scale landowners is now on the decline.

It is the medium-scale landowners and the small peasant proprietors of the middle castes who have emerged as the most influential rural group. Because of their large number they are able to capture power at the local level and sometimes even at the state level. Most of the members of this group in north India are now associated with major political parties, including the Congress (I), the Janata Dal, and the Akali Dal. Chaudhary Devi Lal, the leader of the Lok Dal, which has now merged into the Janata Dal, and the deputy prime minister in the National Front government, has been the most articulate spokesperson of this agricultural group. Its members have consistently opposed increases in land taxation and the introduction of an agricultural income tax. They also seek high prices for farm products and lower prices for agricultural supplies.

By contrast, the rural poor, who comprise the sharecroppers and landless labor, lack money, organization, and influence. Even though they constitute the largest segment of the farm population, they have not been able to articulate their demands effectively. The largest peasant organization, All-India Kisan Sabha (Farmers Association), was founded in 1936 by the Indian National Congress to mobilize farm support for the independence movement. Soon, however, the organization came under the control of the Communist party of India. The Congress party subsequently organized Bharat Sevak Samaj (Indian Service Association) and the Farmers' Forum to mobilize peasants, but without much success.

In addition to the efforts they have made through the Kisan Sabha, the Communist and leftist parties have occasionally organized regional peasant uprisings to occupy land forcibly. One such Communist-inspired uprising, the Telengana uprising in Hyderabad, took place in the late 1940s; another occurred in Naxalbari, West Bengal, in the late 1960s. These uprisings did not, however, accomplish much for the rural poor, who continue to have little influence on agricultural policies.

Students

Students constitute one of the most politicized segments of Indian society. The political development of the student community is attributed partly to the freedom movement and partly to the behavior of the political leaders in the post-independence period. Before India achieved its independence, the leaders of the Indian National Congress frequently called upon the students to give up their studies to participate in the civil disobedience movement. Since independence, the leaders and the political parties have vied with each other both to capture the student unions existing on the campuses of the 105 universities and the thousands of colleges, and to recruit the student leaders into political parties. Many students are ready to use even minor grievances as reasons to stage protests, strikes, and demonstrations against unresponsive school administrations. Moreover, political leaders and parties alike have used the students' demands to help gain their partisan interests. The opposition political parties, for example, have often mobilized the students either to embarrass a state government or to dislodge a government from power if it suits their political designs to do so. The ruling parties, on the other hand, have tried to win the support of the student leaders by granting them business permits, while well-connected campus leaders have wielded political power and distributed patronage and money.

Only a small minority of more than a half–million university graduates each year are able to obtain gainful employment. With few or no job possibilities, many ambitious students look to parties and political leaders to advance their careers. For this reason, student politics in India tends to be special interest and issue oriented rather than ideologically oriented.[11] It is not surprising, therefore, that students have become an influential pressure group in Indian politics.

The Military

India's military establishment has not become as politicized as those of Pakistan and Bangladesh. It is subordinate to and controlled by the country's civilian rulers. This is not to say that India's military establishment is devoid of influence, however. On the contrary, as the military is under civilian control, it must exert pressure to influence the government's budgetary allocations and defense policies. India's security needs are enormous. It has long land borders and sea coasts and since independence has fought four wars with its neighbors: three with Pakistan (in 1947–1948 and 1965 over Kashmir, and in 1971 over Bangladesh) and one with China (in 1962 over Sino-Indian borders). Thus the military has earned the respect of both Indian politicians and the masses in recent years.

At present, India maintains the fourth largest army in the world, with almost 1 million men in uniform.[12] It is a well-disciplined and thoroughly professional body. But for the last ten years, India's total spending on its military establishment has averaged only between 3.5 and 3.9% of its GNP,[13] compared to 6% of the GNP in Pakistan and 10% of that in China.[14] For this reason, the military establishment seeks to influence governmental allocation of India's scarce financial resources. Since 1962 the Indian defense ministry has been headed by politicians with national stature and distinguished administrative abilities who have been very effective in advancing the needs of India's military establishment. Now the chiefs of staff of the three armed forces have been granted both a voice in defense policy formulation as well as easy access to the higher echelon of political decision-making agencies. The three service chiefs are now occasionally invited to participate in the deliberation of the Defense Committee of the cabinet, the highest civilian agency dealing with the needs of India's armed forces.

In recent years the Indian military establishment has maintained strict neutrality in Indian politics, yet the army has frequently been called upon to restore civil order. Such frequent use of the army for civilian purposes does not bode well for its resolve to maintain a nonpolitical role.

The Intelligentsia

India possesses a well-established and articulate intelligentsia[15] as well as a large pool of highly technically trained manpower. India's technocrats include engineers, doctors, agronomists, scientists, and agriculture experts.

This group could be called the general intelligentsia in that it provides highly skilled technical services but does not play the role of opinion maker. The strength of India's technically qualified manpower is estimated at 2.5 million, the third largest in the world.[16] More than 2,000 research units, operating in different departments of governments, research councils, and universities, employ thousands of scientists and researchers. Even though these people play only marginal roles in the general policy formulations of the country, they nevertheless exert pressure in terms of the allocation of financial resources for their institutions. A few key scientific persons heading such organizations as the Atomic Energy Commission and India's space program do, however, have direct access to country's top decision makers.

A more influential part of India's intelligentsia are those journalists, editors, authors, columnists, and opinion leaders who criticize, evaluate, and pronounce moral judgments on the activities of the political elites and bureaucrats, and on the general direction of sociopolitical changes taking place within the society. Most of these intellectuals have adopted an anti-establishment posture. Some independent periodicals such as *Seminar* and *The Economic and Political Weekly,* as well as opinionated magazines such as *Mainstream, Thought,* and *Link,* which deal with critical socioeconomic issues and provide in-depth analysis of political subjects, have only limited circulation; nevertheless, they draw considerable attention from the top echelon of the political elites.

The English-speaking intellectuals who write in India's newspapers enjoy a high status within Indian society. India's national newspapers, such as *The Times of India, Indian Express, Hindustan Times, The Statesman,* and *The Hindu* have high standards and are considered high-quality newspapers. In recent years such English fortnightlies as *Sunday, Frontline,* and *India Today* have also emerged as major sources of information. The investigative news reporting in *India Today,* in particular, has earned widespread acclaim. Many young reporters and journalists have successfully exposed scandals involving politicians and public officials. For example, the resignation and subsequent prosecution of A. R. Antulay, the former chief minister of the state of Maharashtra, resulted from this new style of investigative journalism. Compared to its counterpart in the United States, the Indian press still plays only a limited role in public life, but its influence is growing.

The vernacular intellectual establishment occupies a less prestigious position than its English counterpart, but it has a larger readership. Although their impact at the national level is limited, vernacular-speaking intellectuals exercise considerable influence in the state capitals. And even though writings in regional languages (with few exceptions) have yet to develop the national press tradition of cogent analysis of political and economic issues, the regional press has frequently demonstrated the courage to withstand heavy political pressure.

Caste and Religious Groups

Indian groups organized on the basis of social origin or groups whose membership is "drawn from the community in which individuals are born" have been referred to as community associations.[17] Such community associations date back to nineteenth-century British India. It was the English-educated Indians who took the initiative to form these organizations. As Anil Seal has point out, "the membership of these bodies was restricted to one caste or community. Their sole reason for existence was to better the lot of these members."[18] In the pre-independence period such associations were often created to promote social reform and modernization of communities through the establishment of educational institutions.[19] Since independence they have become important vehicles of political mobilization and articulation of interests: "The caste provides channels of communication and bases of leadership and organization which enable those still submerged in the traditional society and culture to transcend the technical political illiteracy which would otherwise handicap their ability to participate in democratic politics."[20] Castes articulate their demands through politics in several ways. The relationship between caste groups and politics can be summarized as follows:

1. The people of the same caste are organized on an associational basis to seek political concessions.
2. Persons of the same caste may line up support behind a particular party and try to use it to seek political influence.
3. A caste group may organize a party of its own. For example, B. R. Amdedkar, a well-known leader of the untouchables, organized the Republican party of India.[21]
4. A group of castes may come together to form a common organization or federation to protect their interests and to advance the political fortunes of their leaders.[22]
5. Political parties may select a candidate for an electoral office at the local or state level who belongs to the dominant caste. If elected he or she may serve to advance its members' interests.
6. Caste-based alliances may be formed between powerful leaders within the same party.

It should be noted, however, that caste associations carry more political influence at the local or state level than across the state lines.

In contrast to caste associations, India's various religious groups tend to organize on an all-India basis. Although the castes constitute an integral part of Hindu religious society, religious groups in general are broad-based organizations, often claiming distinct political or subnational identities.

Hindu Groups. Many Hindus feel they have grievances to protest. In the first place, they have long felt that even though Hindus constitute an overwhelming majority in the country, their interests have been ignored by the politicians. The Western-educated political elites who led the independence movement and subsequently became the ruling elites have always placated the minorities. Some Hindus blame the Congress party's leadership for the division of their "motherland" by the creation of the Muslim state of Pakistan on the western borders of India. In addition, some Hindus object to their treatment by Muslims: They point out that in neighboring Pakistan the majority's religion, Islam, has become the state religion and the Hindus have been driven out. In Bangladesh, another neighboring country in which Muslims are a majority even though Islam has not been declared a state religion, Hindus have little representation and feel they are treated as second-class citizens. The ruling classes of India, they assert, have put the interests of religious minorities before those of the majority in order to win elections.

There are several Hindu sectarian organizations. The most active and articulate organization promoting the political interests of Hindus has been the Rashtriya Swayamsevak Sangh (RSS), which provides an important channel for the assertion of militant Hindu nationalism. The RSS was founded in 1925 by a Maharashtrian Brahmin, Keshav Baliram Hedgewar, in Nagpur, where it still maintains its headquarters. Slowly and steadily it established its branches in all parts of India, although its largest following is in the Hindi heartland of north India. M. S. Golwalkar, another Maharashtrian Brahmin who became its chief organizer in 1940 after the death of Hedgewar, led the organization through various crises and transformed it into a militant political force after the partition of the country. Golwalkar summed up the ideology of this organization when he declared:

> The non-Hindu peoples in Hindustan must either adopt the Hindu culture and language, must learn to respect and hold in reverence Hindu religion, must entertain no idea but those of glorification of the Hindu race and culture, i.e. they must not only give up their attitude of intolerance and ungratefulness towards this land and its age-long traditions but must also cultivate the positive attitude of love and devotion instead—in a word they must cease to be foreigners, or may stay in this country, wholly subordinated to the Hindu nation, claiming nothing, deserving no privilege, far less any preferential treatment—not even citizens' rights.[23]

The RSS has built an effective paramilitary organization and possesses a large, active, and well-disciplined membership. Although it claims to be a cultural rather than political organization, the RSS became a major force behind the Jana Sangh, a militant Hindu nationalist party. Since 1979, with the formation of the Bharatiya Janata party (BJP), the RSS seemed to have achieved a degree of autonomy, and it supports the parties and candidates that it believes are committed to the promotion of interests of Hindus. It has maintained a militant anti-Muslim posture, and its workers are frequently blamed for inciting anti-Muslim rioting in urban areas.

Muslim Groups. The creation of a Muslim majority state out of British India against the strong opposition of the Hindu majority left India's more than 100 million Muslims in a state of confusion. A large number of the educated, well-to-do, and politically conscious Muslim elites went to Pakistan, leaving behind millions of their co-religionists without either leaders or a well-knit political organization. The present day Muslim population in India consists mostly of "smaller peasantry, landless, laborers, the artisans in the villages and lower middle class in the cities."[24] At present, Muslims do not constitute a majority of the population in any state of India except Jammu and Kashmir. Of the 356 districts of India into which the country is divided for administrative purposes, there are only 3 (2 in West Bengal and 1 in Kerala) in which the Muslims form a majority, outside of Jammu and Kashmir. Almost half of the Muslim population lives in the large states of Uttar Pradesh, Bihar, and West Bengal. In only 30 districts do Muslims constitute more than 30% of the population. Moreover, Muslims are under-represented in India's prestigious civil services, armed forces, and large economic concerns owned by government or private companies.[25]

But the shock of partition is now over, and the Muslim community has come out of its post-partition daze. A whole generation of young Muslims has grown up looking upon India as the land of their birth; they are no longer saddled with guilt feelings over partitioning the country. Furthermore, in 1971 the Muslim Bengalis in the eastern wing of Pakistan actually fought for their independence. Their efforts resulted in the creation of Bangladesh, founded on linguistic and cultural similarities. So it has become evident to many Indian Muslims that even a common religion and national identity do not always go together.

After independence the Muslims faced many alternatives to safeguard their interests, such as organizing a party of their own, working through the existing secular parties, or simply forming pressure groups and lobbying for their causes.[26] Although most of them attempted to work through the Congress party, the Muslim League in the south, as a particularist party, and the Jamaat-i-Islami, as a sociocultural pressure group in the north, have emerged to speak on their behalf. The Muslim League has been partly successful in Kerala and to a lesser extent in Tamilnadu in forming political alliances and sharing power in coalition governments. Nonparty organizations such as the Jamaat-i-Islami and the Majlis Tamir-i-Millat of Hyderabad have focused mostly on such issues as Muslim personal law, instruction in Islam in educational institutions, promotion and recognition of Urdu (a language closely associated with the Muslim culture in the north) as one of the state languages in Uttar Pradesh and Bihar, and the protection of religious identity. Because of the traditional orientation of their leadership and their orthodox religious approach, Muslim pressure groups have not been able to focus on economic issues. The Muslims' primary concern is still government protection for physical security, personal property, and Islamic law. (India does not enforce a uniform civil law; rather, it allows such important minorities as the Muslims to practice their own religious laws.)

Other Religious Groups. A host of smaller religious groups continually exert pressure on the system. In particular, the Sikhs, a group comprising one of India's most innovative and enterprising religious minorities, use the Shiromani Gurudwara Prabhandak Committee (SGPC), the Akali Dal, the Chief Khalsa Diwan, the All-India Sikhs Students Federation, and the recently founded Sikh Forum, among many others, to advance their religious, economic, and political interests.

Tribal Groups. These interest groups are strongly based upon community and kinship ties. There are various estimates of India's tribal population, ranging from 7 to 30 million.[27] Some of the tribes have embraced Hinduism, some have been converted to Christianity, and many of them practice their own animistic religions. Considered by many Indians to be rather dangerous and strange people, they live in India's forests and hills in different parts of the country. The states of West Bengal, Madhya Pradesh, Orissa, Bihar, Assam, and Rajasthan each contain more than 2 million tribal people. And in northeast India, bordering on Assam, there is a large concentration of tribal people including the Nagas and Mizos, who are now organized into their own states called Nagaland and Mizoram.

In recent years many tribal associations have emerged, seeking to enhance employment opportunities for their members. Another of their objectives is to resist the encroachment on their lands by India's ever-increasing nontribal population. Some large tribal groups also seek to capture political power through the electoral process on their own or in alliance with other political parties.

Styles of Articulation

The interest groups in India employ a variety of methods and styles in making their demands on the system. The wealthier and better-educated groups may use quiet persuasion; they may also work through the existing institutional network. Common practices include submission of petitions and memoranda, waiting in delegations on ministers and top party officials, litigation, and publication of propaganda through the news media. But case studies demonstrate that the government is often not responsive to quiet and peaceful styles of articulation. When the group leaders resort to street politics, the government becomes alert. It seems to act only when the situation becomes explosive. Regarding the interaction between the group leaders and government officials, M. N. Srinivas has observed that in India "a grievance has to mature into a street riot in order to attract the attention of those in power. It would not be an exaggeration to say that all classes of Indians everywhere have come to realize that the only way they can convince the rulers of the strength of their feeling is by resorting to the politics of street violence."[28]

*   *   *

In sum, the Indian political system provides considerable freedom to different sectors of the society to make demands upon the system. As in other South Asian countries, political elites in India are easily accessible. The interest groups are both modern and traditional. Along with occupational and economic groups, there are groups based upon caste, religious, and tribal affiliations. Interest groups frequently lobby the members of parliament, the council of ministers, the bureaucracy, and the party leaders, resorting to agitation if constitutional methods are unsuccessful. Indeed, agitational methods have become an accepted part of the political process. Tension generated by the use of such agitational methods is often diffused by the politics of accommodation practiced by Indian political elites.

Notes

1. Anil Seal, "Imperialism and Nationalism in India," in John Gallagher, Gordon Johnson, and Anil Seal (eds.), *Locality, Province and Nation: Essays on Indian Politics 1870 to 1940* (London: Cambridge University Press, 1973), p. 21.

2. Myron Weiner, *The Politics of Scarcity: Public Pressure and Political Response in India* (Chicago: University of Chicago Press, 1962), pp. 22–23.

3. The Banias and Marwaris are important subcastes among the Vaishyas. They are well known for their enterprising skills. In fact, India's largest industrialist family, Birla, is Marwari.

4. Stanley A. Kochanek, "The Federation of Indian Chambers of Commerce and Industry and Indian Politics," *Asian Survey,* vol. 11, no. 9 (September 1971), pp. 866–885; and *Business and Politics in India* (Berkeley: University of California Press, 1974).

5. Kochanek, "The Federation of Indian Chambers of Commerce and Industry and Indian Politics," pp. 869–870.

6. *India Today,* April 30, 1983, p. 77.

7. Kochanek, "The Federation of Indian Chambers of Commerce and Industry and Indian Politics," p. 869.

8. *India Today,* February 28, 1982, pp. 50–59.

9. R. D. Agarwal, "Political Dimensions of Trade Unions," in R. D. Agarwal (ed.), *Dynamics of Labor Relations in India* (New Delhi: Tata McGraw Hill Publishing Company, 1972), p. 64.

10. E. A. Ramaswamy, "Politics and Organized Labor in India," *Asian Survey,* vol. 13, no. 10 (October 1973), p. 914.

11. Lloyd I. Rudolph, Susanne H. Rudolph, and Karuna Ahmed, "Student Politics and National Politics in India," in Joseph Di Bona (ed.), *The Context of Education in Indian Development* (Durham, N.C.: Program in Comparative Studies on Southern Asia, 1974), p. 206.

12. Srikant Dutt, *India and the Third World: Altruism or Hegemony?* (London: Zed Books, 1984), p. 72.

13. Stephen P. Cohen and Richard L. Park, *India: Emergent Power?* (New York: Crane, Russak and Co., 1978), p. 17.

14. Raju G. C. Thomas, "The Armed Services and the Indian Defense Budget," *Asian Survey,* vol. 20, no. 3 (March 1980), p. 282.

15. Edward Shils, *The Intellectuals Between Traditions and Modernity: The Indian Situation, Supplement I, Comparative Studies in Society and History* (The Hague: Mouton, 1961).

16. Government of India, *Sixth Five Year Plan* (Delhi: Government of India Press, 1981), p. 318.

17. Weiner, *The Politics of Scarcity,* p. 36.

18. Anil Seal, *The Emergence of Indian Nationalism* (London: Cambridge University Press, 1968), p. 15.

19. T. N. Madan and B. G. Halbar, "Caste and Community in the Private and Public Education of Mysore State," in Susanne H. Rudolph and Lloyd I. Rudolph (eds.), *Education and Politics in India* (Cambridge, Mass.: Harvard University Press, 1972), pp. 121–147.

20. Lloyd I. Rudolph and Susanne H. Rudolph, "The Political Role of India's Caste Associations," *Pacific Affairs,* vol. 33, no. 2 (March 1960), p. 5.

21. Eleanor Zelliot, "Learning the Use of Political Means: The Mahars of Maharashtra," in Rajni Kothari (ed.), *Caste in Indian Politics* (New Delhi: Orient Longman Ltd., 1970), pp. 29–69.

22. Rajni Kothari and Rushikesh Maru, "Federating for Political Interests: The Kshatriyas of Gujarat," in Rajni Kothari, *Caste in Indian Politics,* pp. 70–101.

23. Quoted in Craig Baxter, *The Jana Sangh: A Biography of an Indian Political Party* (Philadelphia: University of Pennsylvania Press, 1969), p. 31.

24. M. J. Akbar, *India: The Siege Within* (New York: Viking Penguin Inc., 1985), p. 309.

25. Akbar, *India: The Siege Within,* p. 310.

26. Theodore P. Wright, Jr., "The Muslim League in South India Since Independence: A Study in Minority Group Political Strategies," vol. 60, no. 3 (September 1966), p. 579.

27. Christoph Von Furer-Hamendorf, "The Position of Tribal Population in Modern India," in Philip Mason (ed.), *India and Ceylon: Unity and Diversity* (London: Oxford University Press, 1967), p. 187.

28. Quoted in Yogendra K. Malik, "Conflict Over Chandigarh: A Case Study of Inter-State Dispute in India," *Contributions to Asian Studies*, vol. 3 (1973), p. 62.

Suggested Readings

Altbach, Philip (ed.). *Turmoil and Transition: Higher Education and Student Politics in India* (New York: Basic Books, 1968).

Calman, Leslie. *Protest in Democratic India: Authority's Response to Challenge* (Boulder, Colo.: Westview Press, 1985).

Chatterji, R. *Union Politics and the State: A Study of Indian Labor Politics* (New Delhi: South Indian Publishers, 1980).

Cohen, Steven P. *The Indian Army: Its Contributions to the Development of a Nation* (Berkeley: University of California Press, 1971).

Crouch, Harold. *Trade Union and Politics in India* (Bombay: Manaktalas, 1966).

Das Gupta, Jyotirindra. *Language Conflict and National Development: Group Politics and National Language Policy in India* (Berkeley: University of California Press, 1970).

Engineer, A. Ali (ed.). *Communal Riots in Post-Independence India* (Hyderabad, A.P.: Sangram Books, 1984).

Erdman, Howard L. *Political Attitudes of Indian Industry* (London: Athlove Press, 1971).

Giri, V. V. *Labor Problems in Indian Industry*, 3rd ed. (New York: Asia Publishing House, 1972).

Hardgrave, Robert L., Jr. *The Nadars of Tamilnad: Political Culture of a Community in Change* (Berkeley: University of California Press, 1960).

Kochanek, Stanley A. *Business and Politics in India* (Berkeley: University of California Press, 1974).

———. "Briefcase Politics in India: The Congress Party and the Business Elite," *Asian Survey*, vol. 27, no. 12 (December 1987), pp. 1278–1301.

Kothari, Rajni (ed.). *Caste in Indian Politics* (New Delhi: Orient Longman Ltd., 1970).

Rao, M.S.A. *Social Movements in India* (New Delhi: Manohar Publications, 1979).

Rao, A. V. Raman. *Indian Trade Unions* (Honolulu: University of Hawaii, 1967).

Weiner, Myron. *The Politics of Scarcity: Public Pressure and Political Response in India* (Chicago: University of Chicago Press, 1962).

8
THE EXECUTIVE AND THE BUREAUCRACY: POLICY FORMULATION AND IMPLEMENTATION

Along with political institutions and political parties, bureaucracy is an important element in that it helps ensure stability and administrative continuity. The bureaucracy of India consists of tenured civil servants who remain in their administrative posts even when the political bosses lose their elective positions. The members of a bureaucracy are expected to make decisions on a rational rather than political basis. In addition, they must observe certain rules and procedures that are essential for an orderly conduct of administration.

Like other South Asian states, India inherited well-developed traditions of administration from the British raj. On the other hand, whereas in Pakistan and Bangladesh the civil servants and the members of the armed forces have taken over the government, in India the elected politicians are the top decision makers.

Cabinet and Bureaucracy:
Policy Formulation and Implementation

The government of India is a complex network of departments, bureaus, regulatory agencies, boards, and a host of commissions and autonomous organizations. Politicians head the departments; bureaucrats assist them in the administration of these departments. Key policy decisions are made by the members of the cabinet, which is also responsible for the coordination of the work of various departments of the government. On the other hand, bureaus, regulatory agencies, and state-run industrial corporations are headed by the members of the bureaucracy, whose work is overseen by the ministers.

135

The Indian bureaucracy is a legacy from the British. During the British rule, however, it served primarily as a regulatory agency, whose primary responsibility was to raise revenue and maintain law and order so as to serve the interests of the colonial rulers. Its functions remained limited even when the British government adopted certain benevolent policies directed toward expansion of educational and other public service–related activities. The British did not use the government and bureaucracy as agents of social change. Following independence from the British and with the rise of the welfare state in India, however, the government became actively involved in shaping the social and economic life of the country. Today the state has the primary responsibility for rapid development through the democratic process. Accordingly, the members of parliament and the council of ministers have set development goals. These individuals are not experts, however; it is the bureaucrats who make recommendations for the introduction of appropriate legislation to help achieve those goals.

Under these conditions the responsibilities of the bureaucracy have increased enormously. The actions of the civil servants are expected to reflect the aspirations of elected representatives, and the bureaucrats themselves are expected to mobilize human and material resources to help modernize the society. As a consequence, "thanks to the growth of the governmental activities resulting from the logic of modern nationalism and the increasing complexity of the modern life, the bureaucracy has emerged as the major locus of political power in the central government."[1] Despite their key administrative positions, however, the bureaucrats are no longer the "masters" that they had been during the British period. The real power lies with the ministers, who often remind the members of the bureaucracy that they are public servants.

Organization and Tradition of Indian Bureaucracy

Broadly speaking, the civil services in India can be grouped into three major categories: all-India services, central (union) services, and state civil services.

1. The top echelon of all-India services consists of the Indian Administrative Service (IAS) and the Indian Police Service (IPS), both of which have their roots in the British period of Indian history. The Indian Administrative Service is the successor of the British-designed elite Indian Civil Service (ICS), which is frequently referred to as being "heaven born" because of the high prestige and status bestowed upon it by the society and the ruling classes. Contemporary members of the Indian Administrative Service claim to have inherited the traditions of their predecessor. The Indian Police Service and other all-India services originating during the British period also carry the glamour inherited from that period. In a country where the

unemployment rate is very high among university graduates, a government job not only provides security but also pays well and offers a good retirement system. Entry into Indian service jobs is all the more desirable because they command the highest status among government jobs.

It was the ICS that ruled India for a century and, assisted by the IPS, provided the well-known "steel frame" that enabled the British to govern India so effectively for such a long period. Both the ICS and the IPS were originally staffed by the British, although even before India had achieved its independence considerable Indianization of these services had occurred. Because of the services' close association with British rule, there were many Indian nationalists who sought their abolition after independence. It was Sardar Patel, however, who defended the services and very wisely perceived them as institutions of enormous value for the effective administration of a country as vast as India.

After independence, India kept only two all-India services, the IAS and the IPS; but later on the number of such services increased, to include engineering, health, medicine, agriculture, education, and other services necessary for the development of the country. The Rajya Sabha (the Council of States) can create a new all-India service by two-thirds majority.

The members of the Indian Administrative Service, the elite component of the bureaucratic system in the country, look upon themselves as the guardians of the national interests, unity, and territorial integrity of the country. They claim to stand above the linguistic and communal cleavages within Indian society. In this respect, they are the representatives of what Myron Weiner has termed the "elite political culture" of the country.[2] The members of both the IAS and the IPS are very conscious of their high status within Indian society, and the traditions have fostered an *esprit de corps* among them. This spirit and pride create a sense of professional independence that may help them to withstand political pressure. The Indian Administrative Service and other all-India services are genuinely national organizations and are able to reach every part of the country.

2. The central services include such divisions as the Indian Revenue Service, the Postal Service, the Indian Audit and Account Service, the Indian Railways Account Service, and the Indian Customs and Excise Service.

3. Finally, there are the cadres of civil services created by the states, which perform similar functions at the state level. It is the national IAS and the IPS that occupy positions of power and status, however; the state bureaucracies are assigned mostly to subordinate positions.

Recruitment and Training of the Bureaucrats

Recruitment to the services is based upon merit, and there is considerable objectivity in the selection process. The Union Public Service Commission,

an autonomous body, is entrusted with the job of holding examinations for
the applicants seeking entry into the top echelon of Indian bureaucracy.
The examinations, with slight variations for each service, place emphasis
on the applicant's proficiency in English and background in humanities and
social sciences. Personality tests, through extensive interviewing conducted
by the members of the Union Public Service Commission, constitute a vital
part of the selection process. No candidate is allowed to join the services
without being interviewed. Both the tests and the interviews are based on
the values and orientations of the upper and the middle classes. The recruits
are fairly young (21–24 years old), and only college graduates are allowed
to take the test. Every year more than 12,000 college graduates from all
parts of the country compete for the 200 or so positions to be filled.

The young recruits are first given one year of extensive training in the
National Academy of Administration located in the hill town of Mussoorie.
The new entrants study economics, public administration and government
organization, the constitution of India, and Indian criminal law, among other
subjects. In recent years the Indian Institute of Public Administration in
New Delhi has begun to offer short courses and seminars designed to expose
the senior members of the Indian Administrative Service to the newest
methods of management and empirical research. However, training on the
job is still considered the highest priority.

Each state in India designs its own rules and procedures regarding the
recruitment of state-level bureaucrats; most are modeled on the procedures
established at the national level. All states maintain their own public service
commissions and use objective criteria to fill positions in the civil services.

The members of both the IAS and the state civil services are trained
as "generalists" on the basis of British traditions.[3] As generalists they are
expected to be equipped with the knowledge, skills, values, and attitudes
to make policy recommendations not only in the areas of administration
but also in scientific, technical, and educational matters as well. Upward
career mobility, enhancement of status, and increased material rewards are
dependent upon their performance as well as their obedience to and loyalty
toward their immediate superiors.

Administrative Responsibilities and Upward Mobility

Upon the completion of his or her training, an IAS or IPS officer is
assigned to a state cadre. According to established practice, no more than
50% of the recruits of India's elite services will serve in the states of their
origin. These officers, then, are recruited and trained on the national level,
and a substantial number of them will serve outside of their own states.
Through this process they develop a national orientation and become
instruments of national integration. The uniformity of values and training

of these civil servants is unmatched by any other organization except the armed forces.

New IAS officers usually start their careers at the district level (for administrative purposes each one of India's twenty-two states are divided into several districts). IAS officers are put in charge of district administration with the title of collector, district officer, or deputy commissioner. During the British period such officers were given almost full responsibility for the administration of the district; in fact, they were chief magistrates. Not only were they responsible for maintaining law and order, inasmuch as they had control over the police, but they also supervised the administration of local self-government, public health, education, agriculture, irrigation, and other activities. In the post-independence period, IAS officers have also been assigned duties related to economic and industrial development of the district. Each officer is assisted by several junior officers who belong to the state civil service cadre. It is during this field assignment that an IAS officer's administrative abilities are tested with respect to "generalism." Many IAS officers spend their entire careers at the district level; others move on to the state secretariat. In the state secretariat, situated in the state capital, the members of the Indian Administrative Service hold important positions. As secretaries of the departments, they assist state ministers in the performance of their functions. In addition, they make recommendations leading to the formulation of departmental policies. The highest position an IAS officer can hold in the state is that of chief secretary. A chief secretary is responsible for the coordination of the many departments. He may also influence the postings of younger and junior IAS officers to different positions.

In India the states are required to contribute officers to the central secretariat, which stands at the apex of the national bureaucratic structure. At this level the final policy decisions are made. Positions in the central secretariat carry a great deal of prestige and are therefore desirable to the members of the Indian Administrative Service. Each state prepares a list of those IAS officers it is willing to spare, from which the central government can make its selection. Most of these officers go on deputation to New Delhi, some for a specific number of years, others on a permanent basis. In the central secretariat they start as undersecretaries or deputy secretaries, become joint secretaries, move on to the senior positions of additional secretaries, and then finally become the secretaries of departments. Most serve as the chief administrative aides of the ministers. The brightest and best officers are placed in the prime minister's secretariat, or in such key ministries as home, defense, finance, foreign affairs, industries, and commerce. Frequently a state and the central government will compete with each other over the services of intelligent and talented administrators.

The national and state governments have set up several corporations that engage in economic and business activities. The managing heads, who require specialized training, are normally recruited from the private sector. Occasionally, however, an IAS officer may be put in charge of such a corporation. In that case he would be required to make business decisions and to act as an executive rather than as an administrator. Such a position may not help him in his upward mobility, however.

Social Origins and Value Orientations

Despite their key position within the institutional structure of India, the members of India's elite services have a very narrow social base. Because of a quota system, almost 20% of the new entrants to the Indian Administrative Service since independence have been members of the low or backward castes; nevertheless, an analysis of the bureaucrats' class origin demonstrates that "the middle and upper middle classes of urban origin have continued to grab the lion's share of the most powerful positions within the society."[4] Evidence collected by another observer shows that the members of these elite organizations "come from relatively high income families, with family income often exceeding Rs 15,000 a year; the father and often both parents are highly educated and enjoy high status in society."[5] The children of "the businessmen and business employees are less well represented than civil servants and professionals [and] . . . outside the middle class, the farmers and agricultural labourers forming the bulk of the work force are grossly underrepresented in all services even more than the artisans and the industrial workers."[6] Just as the Indian Administrative Service is dominated by the middle class, there are numerous landowners belonging to the Jat subcaste in the Indian Police Service.

During the British rule, the Indian Civil Service was often criticized as being India's new caste system created to maintain the elitist nature of the colonial system of administration. Today it is not uncommon to hear the Indian Administrative Service referred to as the continuation of the ICS under a new name. As elitist organizations, "the services are allowed to restrict their intake and keep their monopoly over strategic positions in the bureaucracy."[7] Despite the elitist nature of Indian bureaucracy, however, it would be hard to deny that its highly intelligent and skilled members stand committed to the goals of modernization and industrialization of the country.

The Bureaucracy and the Changing Political Culture

The bureaucracy in India has been under pressure from various directions. The introduction of representative government has generated tension between the elected representatives and the bureaucrats. These strains result from the differences between the cultures to which the groups belong. Unlike the career of a member of the administrative services, an elective representative's career is dependent on his ability to be responsive to the needs of his constituents. He is guided by what has been termed political rather than administrative rationality. Unlike the administrator, the politician has no tenure; his reelection is dependent upon the results he is able to obtain for his clientele. Hence the more services he is able to provide the electorates, the better his chances for reelection. Bureaucrats, on the other hand, as they are not dependent on voters, are more concerned with rules, regulations, and procedures. The contrast creates tensions between the result-oriented politician and the rule-bound civil servant.

Until 1947 bureaucrats were unaccustomed to taking orders from the popular representatives. Now the situation is dramatically different. Civil servants face far greater pressure at the state and local levels than at the national level. Before independence, for instance, a district officer was not subject to any local control, and his administrative powers were almost unrestrained. Now a local MLA (Member of the Legislative Assembly of a state) represents a major restraint on the district officer's administrative authority. An influential MLA of the ruling party frequently intervenes in the administration on behalf of his supporters and allies. And an MLA's easy access to the state chief minister makes him a powerful person in a district and forces the district officials to yield to his pressure. Despite the tenured position and the protection enjoyed under the civil service regulations, the district officer and his associates can be transferred to undesirable locations or to supervisory positions without much power and glamor, if they refuse to cooperate with an influential MLA.

The tension between the administrators and elected representatives has been aggravated by the increasing role of the state in the expansion of social services and the economic and agricultural development of the country. The government has set up numerous elective bodies at the village, town, city, and state levels so that the popular representatives can become involved in the process of economic development. Under these conditions, the cooperation between elective representatives and civil servants becomes important in the mobilization of the masses necessary in the course of achieving the goals set by the planners.

Many recent studies of the interaction between bureaucrats and representatives illustrate the distrust and tension between the two groups. It is believed that "insofar as interrelationships between officials and political leaders were concerned, the former were largely inclined to consult the latter, but only a few were willing to be guided by their advice."[8] The bureaucrats generally look upon the political leaders as irrelevant to the achievement of nationally desirable development goals. They believe that most of the politicians seek benefits only for the supporters who belong primarily to their caste or community. Indeed, such an assumption on the part of the administrators is not entirely incorrect.

At the national level, the bureaucracy is free from this pressure of parochial interests. Nevertheless, in the post-Nehru era the civil servants and the central secretariat have been constantly subjected to political pressure. Both the Congress (I) and the opposition party ministers have tried to politicize the bureaucracy inasmuch as the more pliant and politically loyal bureaucrats have occasionally been rewarded by promotion and choice appointments. Of course, such efforts undermine the traditional nonpartisan and independent nature of Indian administrative services.

The bureaucrats of India also feel threatened by the rise of the new class of technocrats. The realization of the economic and industrial development goals of the government has required the services of a host of engineers, scientists, economists, agricultural experts, planners, and other specialists; and the government has accordingly hired thousands of technocrats. But these experts not only demand equal status with the administrators; they also seek to share power with them. As a result, the new class of technocrats has further undercut the powers of the Indian civil bureaucracy.

Bureaucratic Corruption

Corruption among the bureaucrats and among the members of the law enforcement agencies, though it occurred even during the British period, was never as widespread as it is today. Traditionally, status within the society was assigned on an ascriptive basis, social mobility was limited, and social stratification was rigid. Even though these ascriptive principles persist, money and material wealth are now becoming the basis on which one can achieve higher status. The far greater social acceptance of corruption today than in previous periods can be attributed to the decline in the Indian value system. Among the middle classes illegal income has even become a social qualification; it often adds to the status of a person within the community.

At the same time, wide disparities have developed since independence in the incomes of bureaucrats, business people, and manufacturers. The existence of a sheltered market as well as the growing middle-class demand for consumer goods account for the tremendous rise in income of business people and manufacturers of consumer goods. By contrast, the pay scales of the top-level bureaucrats have not correspondingly increased; indeed, the bureaucrats are presently being paid far less than their counterparts in the private industries and businesses. Moreover, the often excessive and vulgar displays of wealth on the part of the business people may in part account for the civil servants' vulnerability to accepting bribes.

The chances for bureaucratic corruption are further aggravated by the multiplicity of rules and regulations dealing with economic and industrial expansion and granting of licenses.[9] Alleged widespread corruption in the civil services has led to many a cynical attitude toward the integrity and honesty of the bureaucrats.[10]

Assessment

Despite increased political pressure, the relations between the members of the civil services and the representatives and ministers have been improving. Both groups are learning to respect each other's contributions to the governance of the country. Moreover, there is now a far smaller social gap between a minister and a civil servant than existed at the time of independence in 1947. In most cases both the civil servant and the minister have originated in the middle classes. Unlike their counterparts in Pakistan and Bangladesh the members of the administrative services are also adapting themselves to the democratic setup of the country. District officers now value the local politician as an important link with the masses. During periods of emergency they seek the help of local representatives to mobilize the people so as to achieve administrative goals.

As noted, bureaucratic corruption is a known fact of political life. Many analysts feel, however, that the degree of corruption has been overstated. There are more checks on bureaucratic corruption than on the ministerial or political variety. An Administrative Vigilance Division now exists in the Home Ministry to register complaints of corruption against the members of the bureaucracy. Many such cases are investigated, and guilty officials are punished. In addition, efforts have been made in recent years to lift the ceiling on salaries of bureaucrats, thus raising morale and discouraging bribery. Moreover in training and educational background, the members of the Indian Administrative Service are in no way inferior to the members of the Indian Civil Service, which served the British rulers of India so well. Despite a certain amount of corruption, then, a well-organized and well-staffed bureaucratic institutional structure currently serves as the mainstay of India's political stability.

*　　*　　*

In sum, India, like other South Asian states, has inherited some well-nurtured bureaucratic institutions from the British. The civil services, however, have undergone a subtle transformation. In addition to performing its basic administrative functions, the Indian bureaucracy has become an important tool for achieving the developmental goals set by elected representatives. Unlike the civil servants in Pakistan and Bangladesh, Indian bureaucrats have become responsive to democratic institutions and norms of behavior. Efforts to politicize the bureaucracy have been only partly successful, however. Indeed, its organizational solidarity has made possible a considerable autonomy and professional independence.

Notes

1. Dennis Encarnation, "The Indian Central Bureaucracy: Responsive to Whom?" *Asian Survey,* vol. 19, no. 11 (November 1979), p. 1126.

2. Myron Weiner, "India: Two Political Cultures," in Lucian W. Pye and S. Verba (eds.), *Political Culture and Political Development* (Princeton, N.J.: Princeton University Press, 1965), pp. 199–244.

3. Asok Chanda, *Indian Administration* (London: George Allen and Unwin, 1967), pp. 97–134; and Richard P. Taub, *Bureaucrats Under Stress* (Berkeley: University of California Press, 1969), p. 191.

4. Ram D. R. Sharma, "Selection of Civil Services," *Economic and Political Weekly,* January 27, 1979, p. 141.

5. Shreekant Garg and Palin K. Garg, "Brave New World of Young Indian Decision-Making Elite," *Economic and Political Weekly,* vol. 14, no. 34 (August 25, 1979), p. M-95.

6. V. Subramaniam, *Social Background of India's Administrators* (New Delhi: Public Division, Ministry of Information Broadcasting, 1971), p. 124.

7. Harry W. Blair, "Mrs. Indira Gandhi's Emergency—The Indian Election of 1977, Pluralism and Marxism: Problems and Paradigms," *Modern Asian Studies,* vol. 4, no. 2 (April 1980), p. 280.

8. H. R. Chaturvedi, *Bureaucracy and the Local Community* (Columbia, Mo.: South Asia Books, 1977), p. 149.

9. Surjit Singh, "Political and Bureaucratic Corruption in India," *Journal of Government and Political Studies,* vols. 2 and 3, nos. 1 and 2 (September–March 1978–1979), p. 65.

10. Samuel J. Eldessveld, V. Jagannadham, and A. P. Barnabas, *The Citizens and the Administrator in a Developing Democracy* (Glenview, Ill.: Scott, Foresman and Company, 1968), pp. 29–30.

Suggested Readings

Bhambhri, C. P. *Bureaucracy and Politics in India* (Delhi: Vikas Publications, 1971).

Bayley, David H. *The Police and Political Development in India* (Princeton, N.J.: Princeton University Press, 1969).

Braibanti, Ralph (ed.). *Asian Bureaucratic Systems Emergent from the British Imperial Tradition* (Durham, N.C.: Duke University Press, 1966).

Chanda, Asok. *Indian Administration* (London: George Allen and Unwin, 1967).

Dwivedi, O. P., and R. B. Jain. *India's Administrative State* (New Delhi: Geetanjali Publishing, 1985).

Heginbothan, Stanley. *Cultures in Conflict: The Four Faces of Indian Bureaucracy* (Berkeley: University of California Press, 1975).

Jain, R. B. (ed.) *Public Services in Democratic Context* (New Delhi: Indian Institute of Public Administration, 1983).

Maheshwari, S. R. *Indian Administration* (New Delhi: Orient Longman, 1974).
Potter, D. C. *India's Administrators 1919–1983* (Oxford: Oxford University Press, 1986).
Weidner, Edward W. (ed.). *Development Administration in India* (Durham, N.C.: Duke University Press, 1970).

9
MODERNIZATION AND DEVELOPMENT: PROSPECTS AND PROBLEMS

Traditionalism and Modernism: Coexistence and Conflict

Since the end of World War II, societies such as that of India have been engaged in trying to achieve the various interrelated goals associated with modernization and development. Modernization is perceived here as the assertion of secular rather than sacred, rational rather than mythical, universal rather than parochial, and achievement-oriented rather than as-criptive norms.[1] In a modern society, then, the individual, no longer of the parochial world, is inducted into the larger world of state and national society.

India's political elite looked upon institution building as a part of the developmental process that would enable the society to govern itself effectively, provide for citizens' participation in the political process to ensure legitimacy of the system, and create political stability to achieve economic growth and social justice.

To bring about a transformation in the organizational structure of a traditional society based upon ascriptive norms and values, then, the Indian elites have chosen the path of moderation rather than that of radicalism, and conciliation rather than confrontation. Unlike the People's Republic of China, India decided to avoid a frontal assault on the values and institutions inherited from its past. But India's record of modernization has been a mixed one at best. Although the granting of voting rights to all citizens has ensured equal political participation, the electoral process and right to vote have also revitalized the caste system, thus enabling the traditionally dominant castes to consolidate their hold on both economic and political power, especially in rural India. By capturing political power at the local and state levels, these upper castes have successfully sabotaged efforts at land reform, leaving the rural poor even poorer. At the same time, however,

participatory politics has created a new group identity and sense of assertiveness among the members of the lower castes.

Each national election since 1971 has demonstrated that voters are well
aware of national issues. The right to vote seems to have integrated the
average Indian into the mainstream of national life, leading to the assertion
by one political analyst that "we have now a national electorate which is
responsive to national concerns. In the slow and uncertain process of nation-
building the development of a national electorate represents a great achievement."[2] Empirical evidence leaves little doubt that Indians are as "supportive
of their system as people in any Western society."[3] Indeed, the voters'
political awareness is evident in the election results. In 1971 the voters gave
a massive mandate to Indira Gandhi when she presented herself as a
progressive politician fighting against discredited party bosses, but in 1977
they voted her out for denying their democratic rights during her authoritarian
rule (June 1975–March 1977). In the 1980 elections they dislodged the
leaders of the Janata party–led government for their failure to maintain
order within their ranks, and in 1984 they gave a massive majority to Rajiv
Gandhi to preserve the national unity against the secessionist movement
launched by the Sikh extremists in the state of Punjab. Four decades of
democracy in India have led observers to conclude that "it is now hard to
envision India breaking apart as some predicted 35 years ago."[4] Nevertheless,
frequent outbreaks of communal rioting, violent expressions of linguistic
subnationalism, and territorial claims made by regional elites against one
another amply demonstrate the strength of the primordial loyalties and
continuing conflict between the traditional and modern elements in Indian
society.

Institutional Stability

As noted, Indian leaders, in contrast to those of its neighbors and many
other Third World countries, drafted, adopted, and implemented a constitution
with considerable speed. Under the guidance of its charismatic leaders, the
Indian political system has developed an institutional structure capable of
facilitating the peaceful resolution of conflicts. The three key institutions—
the Congress party, the federal structure of the government, and an apolitical
bureaucracy—have aided the smooth transition of India from its colonial
stage to political maturity. Despite its domination for a time by the towering
personalities of Patel and Nehru, the Congress party continued to function
as a federal organization, with a consistent accommodative interplay of
power politics between the regional and national elites. Moreover, the regional
political leaders, especially after the reorganization of the states along linguistic
lines, were able to get the regional demands conceded at the national level.

This situation, however, underwent a dramatic change with the slow, steady rise of Indira Gandhi to a dominant position in national politics. Even if one does not agree with James Manor that a complete disintegration of the Congress party organization occurred,[5] one must concede that Gandhi transformed the Congress party beyond recognition. She stripped such party agencies as the Congress Working Committee, the parliamentary board, and the All-India Congress Committee (AICC) of much of their power and reduced them to nonentities. She also reduced the state party organizations to an ineffectual position, such that they no longer played an independent role in the regions they were supposed to represent. In addition, Gandhi tried to subvert federalism in India by undermining the authority of state governments.

Indira Gandhi demanded personal and not institutional loyalty. As a result, there was considerable politicization of the Indian civil services once famed for their professional independence and integrity.

Yet despite Gandhi's efforts to manipulate the country's political institutions to achieve her personal and partisan goals, the constitutional system has remained intact. Political institutions have already started to reassert themselves. The Congress party, though held together by "opportunism— by the power, patronage, and money that public office can command"[6]— is still the only organization with a nationwide following.

India's civil service, too, still attracts highly qualified, intelligent, and talented young persons from all parts of the country, and the bureaucracy still possesses the organizational structure to reassert its autonomy.

The stability and strength of India's system have been tested by the peaceful transition of power not only from one leader to another but also from one political party to another. Even in October 1984, when Indira Gandhi's assassination led to widespread rioting in Delhi and other parts of India, Rajiv Gandhi was sworn in as the prime minister of the country speedily and smoothly and with no constitutional crisis. He then legitimized the change of leadership by holding a nationwide election, thus ensuring continuity and institutional stability.

Finally, the operation of an independent judiciary headed by the Supreme Court of India, the administrative workings at the district, local, and village levels, and the operation of several autonomous commissions and agencies also point to the strength of India's institutional structure.

Planning for Development:
Industrial and Agricultural

The consolidation of the state through territorial integration and the establishment of effective political institutions were perceived by the leaders as preconditions for steady economic growth. India's leaders also realized that the country needed industrial and agricultural revolutions if it was to enter the twentieth century. In particular, the key to the removal of the mass poverty existing in India was believed to be the application of science and technology to the utilization of the material and human resources of the country. At the initiative of Jawaharlal Nehru, a Planning Commission was created in 1950. The Commission is basically an advisory body consisting of economists, technocrats, statisticians, and ministers for planning and finance. Chaired by the prime minister, it draws up India's Five Year Plans for effective and balanced utilization of its resources in both the agricultural and industrial sectors of its economy. It also makes frequent assessments of the country's progress and recommends changes in its development strategies. The Five Year Plans are submitted to the National Development Council, which, in addition to the prime minister and the union cabinet staff, includes the state chief ministers as members. Both the Commission and the Council direct the economic development of the country, first through the mobilization of the country's internal resources by means of taxation and later on through the investment of funds in specific projects.

India's planned economic development has been directed toward (1) achieving a high economic growth rate, (2) building the country's industrial and technological self-reliance, (3) creating full employment, and (4) achieving social justice by removing the gross inequalities existing within the society.

Economists differ in their assessment of India's economic performance. Within the framework of India's pluralistic social structure and democratic polity, they generally consider India's development efforts to be quite impressive. The economic performance of India is often compared to that of the People's Republic of China. Both countries are large in size, both have huge populations, both exhibit a great degree of social diversity, and both started with the same level of economic development. John Mellor, a respected economist, has observed that "overall growth rates have been within a half percentage of each other with the edge to India." In addition, "India's food grain production trend has been some 30 percent faster than China's and has gradually accelerated over time. Industrial growth in the two countries has been surprisingly similar: 6.7 percent for China and 6.1 percent for India. China has boosted its large-scale heavy-industry sector (e.g., steel) considerably more rapidly than India, as would be expected of a centrally planned and organized nation."[7] Although India has received more than $14 billion in foreign aid in absolute terms, its per capita level is low given the size of the population.[8] India's development efforts have been funded primarily through internal sources, soft loans, and grants, although foreign aid has also played a vital role in providing goods and services critical to its economic growth.

Today India is self-sufficient in almost all sectors of its economy. Through various systems of controls, inducements, and import substitutions, the country is now able to produce all of its consumer goods and almost all of its capital goods. Only a few of its industries remain dependent upon imports for equipment and parts. Given that India has the world's third largest technically trained manpower, and given the recent liberalization of government control of the economy and the tax incentives for industrial and business expansion, economists look forward to future growth with considerable optimism.

In the areas of social justice, full employment, and the removal of poverty and economic disparities, however, the Indian economy does not have much to boast about. The society of India is socialistic; it aims at the establishment of a mixed economy with social justice based upon redistribution of goods and services. But India's private sector currently produces far more goods than the public sector, which suffers from both waste and inefficiency. More important, after nearly four decades of planned economic development, the Planning Commission admitted in 1981 that "improvement in the consumption expenditure of the poorest in rural areas though significant has not been large enough to lead to any substantial reduction in the percentage of population below the poverty line."[9] The social developmental goals—that is, increased economic productivity, satisfaction of the basic needs for essential goods and services, and provision of adequate shelter, nutrition, public transportation, and health and educational facilities for the masses—are still far from realized. For example, in 1977–1978 it was estimated that 48% of the Indian population in rural areas and 41% in urban areas still lived below the poverty level, with the total number living in abject poverty close to 300 million. Recent observations of the government's spending for development-related policies have revealed that "an unduly large share of resources is . . . absorbed in production which relates directly or indirectly to maintaining or improving the living standards of higher income groups."[10] Thus the main beneficiaries of economic growth have been India's growing middle class, consisting of urban-educated groups and business people, as well as the well-to-do rural farmers.

The growing middle class is both a strength and a weakness of the political system. A substantial part of this class is living off the state. It does provide strategic and political support for the ruling elite by accepting the legitimacy of the system. But its growing capacity for luxury goods has resulted in its securing a larger share of scarce resources than its number would warrant.

Furthermore, India's economic planners have failed to reduce unemployment. The industrial sector of the Indian economy provides jobs for 26.5 million workers, barely 9% of the national work force. An overwhelming majority of its population (230 million out of a total labor force of 285 million) is still dependent upon agriculture for its living. But in rural India the estimated number of unemployed or underemployed people is about 25 million. Agricultural employment is seasonal, leaving a very large number of people out of work when the harvesting season is over.[11]

To keep pace with its population growth and to provide jobs for the 30 million new entrants in the job market each year, India requires an economic expansion that, unfortunately, is beyond its reach. In the urban areas alone, 2.5 million new jobs are needed every year, but the country has been unable to provide more than three-quarters of a million such jobs.[12] Even the Green Revolution in agriculture, which was accomplished through the introduction of high-yield seeds, chemical fertilizers, pesticides, increased irrigation, and advanced farm techniques, has touched only a small sector of India's rural population.

Stresses and Strains — *Exam Question*

The ongoing process of sociopolitical change in India and the increased competition for scarce resources are placing enormous pressure on the political system. Moreover, increased mass expectations as well as enhanced caste/class consciousness are creating stresses on the society that hitherto have not been experienced. The main areas of concern are as follows:

1. Caste/class-based conflicts are not only more frequent of late; they are erupting into ghastly violence as well. Earlier, the landowning dominant castes in the rural areas had been able to mobilize the low-caste voters for the Congress party in addition to the voters of their own castes; in other words, the low castes followed the leadership of the dominant castes. But this relationship in the countryside has changed; the low-caste voters are no longer willing to submit to the dictates of traditional rural leaders.[13] Younger, better-educated low-caste leaders seem determined now to assert their independence. The assertion of independence, however, has not always brought them positive results; on the contrary, such actions have invited retaliation by the landowning castes. Supported by the middle castes, the upper castes have resorted to brute force to teach their former subordinates a "lesson." Uttar Pradesh and Bihar have witnessed some of the worst incidents of caste violence in recent years.

Caste riots in urban areas have been directed against both the quota system used for government jobs and the practice of reserving seats in professional colleges for the members of backward castes. This system of "reverse discrimination" has been resented by upper caste Hindus.

In addition, the uneven distribution of the gains from the Green Revolution in such states as the Punjab and Haryana has increased the tension between the landowning and landless castes. Unwilling to work on the wages offered to them by the landowning castes, the landless labor groups have increasingly resorted to the organization of unions. As there is a seasonal shortage of labor, and, more important, as unionization on the part of the low castes is looked upon as an affront to the dominant castes, the latter have frequently resorted to the use of force against the members of scheduled castes.

2. The introduction of criminal elements into politics has paralleled the rise of a new breed of politicians who find enormous opportunities for social mobility in democratic politics: "Unlike the gentlemen politicians of earlier years, they know that the difference between being and not being in power is vital in their lives."[14] Because these politicians are entirely dependent on politics for their social status as well as for their earnings, in urban areas they are often willing to form alliances with criminals, smugglers, and other antisocial elements, as well as with the police establishment, to stay in power.

Similarly, in rural areas the politicians, the landowning castes, and the police establishment often work together openly to suppress the landless labor.[15] In 1980 Sanjay Gandhi, the younger son of Indira Gandhi who was put in charge of the party organization in Uttar Pradesh, India's most populous state, recruited many young men with criminal records for the youth wing of the Congress party.[16]

3. The intensification of communal divisions has resulted in increased religious rioting. Religious fundamentalism verging on fanaticism is on the rise because the modernization process has eroded traditional values and religious identities. To counter this trend, religious minorities are increasingly turning to their scriptures, reasserting their symbols, and organizing themselves on a communal basis. The result has been an increase in religious hostility among different communal groups. The number of violent clashes between Hindus and Muslims, for example, rose from 238 in 1975 to 500 in 1983, and the number of those killed increased from 110 in 1978 to 278 in 1980, when a total of 427 communal clashes were reported.[17] Most of the victims have been Muslims. The worst cases of sectarian violence in the post-partition history of India were the 1983 widespread rioting in Assam against the "aliens" (the Bangladeshi migrants), in which 1,200 were killed, and the unprecedented violence against the Sikhs in Delhi and other parts of India following the assassination of Indira Gandhi by her two Sikh bodyguards in October 1984, resulting in the death of more than 2,000 people.

Communal violence springs not only from religious conflict but from political and sociological problems as well. Gangs of unemployed, rootless, and alienated youth often roam the streets of towns and cities that have experienced an influx of migrants from the rural areas and other parts of the country. These migrants do not have any neighborhood ties or kinship bonds. Frequently divided along religious or caste lines, the gang leaders are on the lookout for opportunities to indulge in violence. They often enjoy the protection of local party bosses or communal leaders who use them for political purposes.

4. Ethnic unrest has resulted from the mobilization of small ethnic or tribal groups. Until recently, such groups were only marginally relevant to national politics. Now, however, they are becoming increasingly fearful of losing their subgroup identity as well as their land and ways of life—losses that have forced them to use violent methods to protect themselves against outsiders. The continuation of ethnic and tribal unrest in the northeastern hill states of Nagaland, Meghalaya, Mizoram, and Tripura is a testament to the unresolved issue of subnational and regional autonomy in that part of the country.

5. Regional competition for scarce resources has emerged as another major source of national concern in states with non-Congress (I) governments. Disparities in the distribution of natural resources are inevitable in a country the size of India. However, the ongoing process of industrialization and modernization has further accentuated these disparities, resulting in gross man-made regional imbalances in wealth, living standards, and general prosperity. Whereas the Punjab and Haryana have reaped enormous benefits from the Green Revolution and have become granaries of the country, other states such as Uttar Pradesh, particularly eastern Uttar Pradesh, and Bihar and Orissa, have hardly been touched by the prosperity. Thus, in contrast to the farmers and peasants in the Punjab and Haryana, an overwhelming majority of the population of Uttar Pradesh, Bihar, and Orissa still live in abject poverty.

Despite government efforts to achieve a balance, regional inequalities have become even more pronounced. W. Kirk, after carefully analyzing the subject, has concluded that "if one examines what has happened in India in the thirty-four years of independence as opposed to what has been planned there is little evidence of the reduction of spatial inequalities."[18] Yet, although the reasons for which development efforts have succeeded in one region and failed in others may be cause for further debate, it cannot be denied that one of the reasons for the present unrest in the Punjab is its reluctance to share its river water with the neighboring states of Haryana and Rajasthan.

Constitutional distribution of financial resources between the state and national governments has made the state governments dependent on the national government for both financial survival and economic development. Yet a national government motivated by partisan interests may not only kill the development plans of an opposition-run state government; it can virtually squeeze it out of office. In addition, interregional competition and antagonism have been accentuated by skillful political manipulation of industrial projects, material resources, and financial institutions to deprive the opposition-run state governments of their rightful share of development funds.

The Need for Technology

It is not unusual for a country of subcontinental size such as India, given its substantial natural resources, manpower, and geographic location, to seek technological self-reliance and a dominant place among the nations of South Asia. India's political leaders and economic planners have consistently emphasized the interrelationship between the viability of national independence and technological self-reliance. But the direct importation of technology and the purchase of turn-key industries have never been considered sufficient to guarantee national independence. Even though technological self-reliance has been emphasized in most of the Five Year Plans, it was only after the Bangladesh War that political leaders such as Indira Gandhi started recognizing it as a critical element for India's survival. At the same time, the National Committee on Science and Technology stressed that for national survival it "becomes imperative that a developing country should have an indigenous science and technology capacity of its own."[19] The Committee added that "in the absence of such a capability a developing country is placed in a position of perpetual dependence *vis-à-vis* the suppliers of technology, be they the governments of the advanced countries or the large international corporations" and correctly recognized that "technology . . . becomes an agent of foreign dominance rather than the vehicle for international development."[20] It was in the quest for national self-reliance immediately after independence that the need for capital goods industries became clear.

What also became clear was the fact that the science-based industries of the post–World War II era required greater technological capabilities. And only through sophisticated research and development activities undertaken by the native scientific community can progress toward technological refinement be sustained. Accordingly, India has established many research and development-related institutions manned by the country's best scientists. Indian scientists and technocrats have demonstrated their strength and abilities in agriculture, in the design and development of atomic plants, in the launching of weather and communication satellites, and in some defense-related industries. They have also directed substantial energies toward the development of appropriate rural technology, including the use of animal waste to produce energy (biogas) and the production of trees with high yields of wood suited to conditions in India.

In view of the fact that almost 90% of India's scientific and technological research is conducted under the aegis of the government of India, one might assume that India has been able to achieve a high degree of technological self-reliance. Unfortunately, however, evidence suggests that "there are no takers of Indian research, especially industrial research. Prospective users of industrial research either do not know or deliberately ignore it in favor of foreign technology, experience, risk coverage, prestige and other economic and cultural reasons."[21] Even in the public-sector industries, where large projects in fertilizers and power generation are undertaken with the approval of union ministers, Indian technological know-how and indigenous capabilities have been ignored in favor of foreign collaboration.

In short, India's native scientific manpower is underutilized. The government can hire only a limited number of technocrats, and private industries are unwilling to invest in research and development. Industry's view is that with its small industrial output it has no hope of matching the research and development of industrial countries. Therefore, native industrial and business organizations "in their haste to service a newly growing middle class market . . . have simply bought off the shelf technology from developed countries and concentrated on marketing and selling. They, for reasons of profit or otherwise, may have failed to invest in the research and development that would enable the products to remain current with world standards."[22] In auto manufacturing, for instance, Indian industrialists have collaborated with their British and Italian counterparts; but unlike the Japanese, who by collaborating with the United States developed their own technology, Indian industrialists have done little to improve upon borrowed technology.

Hence, although India is recognized today as the preeminent military power in South Asia,[23] it has yet to achieve technological self-reliance. Despite its considerable economic achievements and increased industrial production, India is dependent on the advanced industrialized world for both the latest technology and scarce capital.

*   *   *

In sum, the existence of stable and complex political institutions has enabled India to achieve a degree of modernization. Traditional institutions and values, however, still survive. Indians are proud of the achievements of their political system; nevertheless, the system faces severe internal stresses and strains. The revival of regional and religious conflicts has placed strains on the country's internal resources. The founders of the Indian system planned to raise the standard of living of its people through economic planning, but despite industrial and agricultural developments, Indian elites have not been able to remove the economic disparities. India's democratic institutions have thus been undermined, as their success is dependent not only on the system's ability to achieve economic and technological self-reliance but also on its efforts to reduce the growing gap between the small but influential middle class and the mass of its poor.

Notes

1. Lloyd I. Rudolph and Susanne H. Rudolph, *The Modernity of Traditions* (Chicago: University of Chicago Press, 1967), p. 3.

2. Gopal Krishna, "A Nation-State to Defend," *Times of India,* January 7, 1985.

3. Samuel J. Eldersveld and Bashiruddin Ahmed, *Citizens and Politics: Mass Political Behavior in India* (Chicago: University of Chicago Press, 1978), p. 292.

4. Paul H. Kreisberg, "India's Inside Threat," *New York Times,* November 4, 1984.

5. James J. Manor, "Anomie in Indian Politics: Origins and Potential Wider Impact," *Economic and Political Weekly,* vol. 18, nos. 1 and 2 (Annual Number, 1983), p. 725; and "Party Decay and Political Crisis in India," *Washington Quarterly* (Summer 1981), pp. 24–40.

6. Robert L. Hardgrave, Jr., "India on the Eve of Elections: Congress and Opposition," *Pacific Affairs,* vol. 57, no. 3 (Fall 1984), p. 409.

7. John W. Mellor, "The Indian Economy: Objectives, Performance and Prospects," in John W. Mellor (ed.), *India: A Rising Middle Power* (Boulder, Colo.: Westview Press, 1979), p. 86.

8. Ibid., pp. 87–88.

9. Government of India, *Sixth Five Year Plan* (New Delhi: Government of India Press, 1981), p. 7.

10. *Economic and Political Weekly,* vol. 14, nos. 30–32 (August 1979), p. 1220.

11. *India Today,* September 30, 1983, pp. 54–55.

12. *New York Times,* September 12, 1980, sec. A, p. 11.

13. Duncan B. Forrester, "Electoral Politics and Social Change," *Economic and Political Weekly,* vol. 3, nos. 26–28 (July 1968), p. 1079; and P. Lyon and James Manor (eds.), *Transfer and Transformation: Political Institutions in the New Commonwealth* (Leicester: Leicester University Press, 1983).

14. Ashis Nandy, "Myths, Persons and Politics," *Seminar* (October 1979), p. 19.

15. Paul R. Brass, "National Power and Local Politics in India: A Twenty-Year Perspective," *Modern Asian Studies,* vol. 18, no. 1 (1984), p. 93; *Political Weekly,* vol. 3, nos. 26–28 (July 1968), p. 1079; and P. Lyon and James Manor (eds.), *Transfer and Transformation: Political Institutions in the New Commonwealth* (Leicester: Leicester University Press, 1983).

16. D. K. Joshi, "Indira Gives Priority to Image Problem in U. P.," *India Abroad* (New York), October 19, 1984, p. 2.

17. Kuldip Nayar, "In Six Years Sectarian Clashes Have Intensified," *India Abroad* (New York), June 15, 1984, p. 2.

18. W. Kirk, "Core and Peripheries: The Problems of Regional Inequality in the Development of Southern Asia," *Geography,* vol. 66, p. 188.

19. "Reports and Documents," *Minerva,* vol. 11, no. 4 (1973), p. 539.

20. Ibid.

21. Aqueil Ahmad, "Science and Technology in Development: Policy Options for India and China," *Economic and Political Weekly* (December 1978), p. 2085.

22. William K. Stevens, "India: Once a Giant in Science: Tries to Rekindle the Creative Fire," *New York Times,* November 9, 1982, pp. 17–18.

23. Stephen P. Cohen and Richard L. Park, *India: Emergent Power* (New York: Crane, Russak and Co., 1978), p. 6.

Suggested Readings

Akbar, M. J. *India: The Siege Within* (New York: Viking Penguin Books, 1985).

Barddhan, Pranab. *The Political Economy of Development in India* (New York: Basil Blackwell, 1984).

Bjorkman, James (ed.). *Fundamentalism, Revivalists and Violence in South Asia* (Riverdale, Md.: Riverdale Publishing Co., 1988).

Eldersveld, Samuel J., and Bashiruddin Ahmed. *Citizens and Politics: Mass Political Behavior in India* (Chicago: University of Chicago Press, 1978).

Frankel, Francine R. *India's Political Economy 1947-1977* (Princeton, N.J.: Princeton University Press, 1978).

Hardgrave, Robert L., Jr. *India Under Pressure: Prospects for Political Stability* (Boulder, Colo.: Westview Press, 1984).

Kohli, Atul (ed.). *India's Democracy: An Analysis of Changing State-Society Relations* (Princeton, N.J.: Princeton University Press, 1988).

Manor, James. "Anomie in Indian Politics: Origins and Potential Wider Impact," *Economic and Political Weekly,* vol. 18, nos. 1 and 2 (Annual Number, 1983), pp. 725-734.

Mellor, John W. (ed.). *India: A Rising Middle Power* (Boulder, Colo.: Westview Press, 1979).

Nayar, Baldev Raj. *India's Quest for Technological Independence* vol. 1 and 2 (New Delhi: Lancers Publishers, 1983).

————. *India's Mixed Economy: The Role of Ideology and Interests in its Development* (Bombay: Popular Prakashan, 1989).

Rosen, George. *Industrial Change in India: 1970-2000* (Riverdale, Md.: Riverdale Publishing Co., 1986).

Rudolph, Lloyd, and Susanne H. Rudolph. *In Pursuit of Lakshmi: The Political Economy of Indian State* (Chicago: University of Chicago Press, 1987).

Shah, Ghanshyam. *Protest Movements in Two Indian States: A Study of Gujarat and Bihar Movement* (Delhi: Ajanta Publications, 1977).

Thomas, Raju. *India's Security Policy* (Princeton, N.J.: Princeton University Press, 1986).

Vajpeyi, Dhirendra K., and Yogendra K. Malik (eds.). *Religious and Ethnic Minority Politics in South Asia* (New Delhi: Manohar Publications, 1989).

Weiner, Myron. *Sons of the Soil: Migration and Ethnic Conflict in India* (Princeton, N.J.: Princeton University Press, 1978).

Wilson, A. Jayaratnan and Dennis Dalton (eds.). *The States of South Asia: Problems of National Integration* (London: C. Hunt and Company, 1982).

Wood, J. R. *State Politics in Contemporary India: Crisis or Continuity?* (Boulder, Colo.: Westview Press, 1985).

PART 2

PAKISTAN

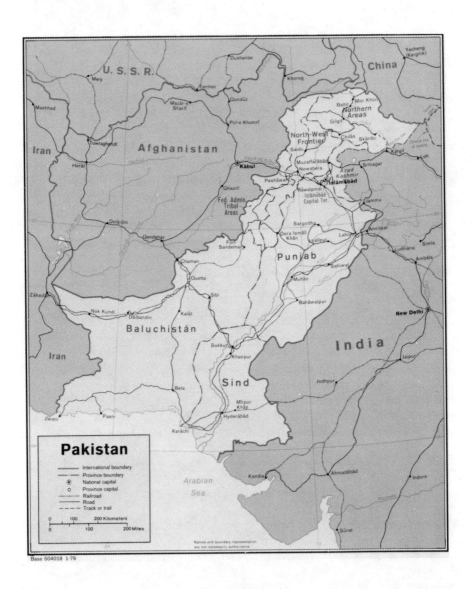

Pakistan

International boundary
Province boundary
⊛ National capital
○ Province capital
Railroad
Road
Track or trail

0   100   200 Kilometers
0   100   200 Miles

Names and boundary representation
are not necessarily authoritative

Base 504018 1-79

10
SOCIETY'S HERITAGE
AND ITS MEANING
FOR THE PRESENT

Pakistan came into existence as fulfillment of the dream to create a Muslim homeland in South Asia. Forty years later that dream, though tarnished, persists. This chapter serves as an introduction to the complex and perplexing political environment of the state.

The Land: A River and Its Region

Pakistan possesses one of the most varied geographical settings in the world. Sindh, the southernmost province of the state, boasts the fine white sand beaches of the Arabian Sea and Karachi, a large natural port and the largest city in the country. Inland Sindh is a semi-desert region, in which the population is clustered along the winding banks of the Indus River. Balochistan, Pakistan's largest province, presents a startlingly forbidding landscape. Eastern Balochistan is dominated by the Sindhi Desert, and the western part of the province is composed of surreal mountains. Except for the area surrounding Quetta, Balochistan is very sparsely settled. The Punjab, fed by five major rivers (the Indus and its four tributaries—the Jhelum, Chenab, Ravi, and Sutlej), is the breadbasket of Pakistan. It is also the most densely populated province in the state. Depending upon the availability of water, the Punjab varies from the semi-arid regions in the south to the lush irrigated plains near Lahore and the foothills surrounding Islamabad and Rawalpindi. The North-West Frontier Province (NWFP) presents the most varied landscape of all. In the south the NWFP is indistinguishable from the plains of Sindh or Balochistan, and in the west the mountains, particularly in the Khyber Pass region, are reminiscent of Balochistan's mountains. In the north, however, the North-West Frontier Province features some of the highest mountains in the world; depending upon the annual rainfall and local ecology, they vary from arid forbidding mounds to lush deciduous or alpine slopes.

Pakistan is predominantly an agricultural state. Agriculture accounts for 21% of the gross domestic product (GDP) and employs 49% of the labor force.[1] Given such dependency on agriculture, the availability of water becomes extraordinarily critical. The main source of such water is the Indus and its tributaries, as well as the Kabul, which enters from Afghanistan. The British, during the period of colonial rule, constructed an extensive system of irrigation canals in the Punjab that have been maintained and expanded since partition. The state of Pakistan has also built an extensive system of dams, barrages, and canals that includes the largest earth-filled dam in the world, the Tarbela Dam on the Indus, as well as the massive Mangla (Jhelum) and Warsak (Kabul) dams. Despite such efforts, however, agricultural production still depends to a great extent on the weather. During periods of abundant and balanced rainfall, times are good; during periods of drought or overabundant rainfall, times are bad.

The People: Ethnic and Linguistic Diversity

Since the separation of Bangladesh in 1971, truncated Pakistan has contained five major ethnic groups: Punjabis, Sindhis, Pathans, *muhajirs* (refugees), and Baloch. Each of these groups is defined by an admixture of linguistic and regional attributes. Generally speaking, the Punjabis are centered in the Punjab and their ostensible mother language is Punjabi; the Sindhis are domiciled in Sindh and speak Sindhi; the Pathans live in the North-West Frontier Province and speak Pushto; the muhajirs live in the urban areas of Pakistan (particularly Karachi and Hyderabad) and are usually native speakers of Urdu; and the Baloch live in Balochistan and speak Baloch or Brohi.

There is significant slippage in these definitions of ethnic identity, however. Pakistan's ethnic composition has been deeply affected by external and internal migration. Most obvious is the case of the muhajirs—the Indian Muslims or their descendants who opted for Pakistan during partition, settling for the most part in Karachi and other urban areas. Furthermore, subsequent to partition significant in-migration has occurred, primarily from India and Bangladesh. The 1981 census estimates that this movement has accounted for 4 million migrants to Pakistan since 1948.[2] Not included in the census data are an additional 2.5–3 million "temporary migrants" or "refugees" from Afghanistan. Most such individuals are Pushto speaking and are close ethnic relatives of the Pathans. Accordingly, most have taken residence in border communities or refugee camps in the NWFP and northern Balochistan.

In addition to such international migration, interprovincial and intra-provincial migration has taken place. Two patterns deserve note. One has

TABLE 10.1   Pakistan: Population by Province, 1981

Area	Population (1,000's)	% Change 1973–1981	% Total 1981	% Urban 1981
Punjab	47,116	26.3	56.2	27.5
Islamabad	335	42.6	.4	60.2
MWFP	10,885	29.8	13.0	15.2
FATA	2,175	−12.7	2.6	–
Sindh (excluding Karachi)	13,863	30.3	16.5	22.5
Karachi	5,103	45.2	6.1	100.0
Balochistan	4,305	77.2	5.1	15.6
Pakistan	83,782	28.3	100.0	28.3

Source: Adapted from Government of Pakistan, Census Organization, *Main Findings of the 1981 Census* (Islamabad: Manager, Printing Corporation of Pakistan Press, 1983).

been the phenomenon of rural to urban migration, spurred by brighter employment opportunities in the cities. The urban population of Pakistan grew by 7.25 million (31%) from 1972 to 1981 (see Table 10.1).[3] A second phenomenon, also largely fueled by employment prospects, has been the interprovincial shifting of population from the Punjab, NWFP, and the Federally Administered Tribal Areas (FATA) to Balochistan and Sindh. These phenomena have had two major consequences: The major urban areas of Pakistan—Karachi, Lahore, and Rawalpindi/Islamabad—have become far more ethnically diverse, and the indigenous population of the smaller provinces, particularly Balochistan and Sindh, have become threatened by the prospect of outside domination. For instance, Quetta, the capital of Balochistan, has more Pathan residents than local Baloch;[4] and in Sindh only 52% of the population are native speakers of Sindhi.[5]

Problems of definition also exist in regard to linguistic determinants of ethnicity. Pakistan has a national language, Urdu, and perhaps 90% of the population can speak it or at least understand it. Less than 5% of the population can speak or understand English, yet it has remained the predominant medium of higher education, the courts, and government since partition. Although numerous attempts have been made to enhance the significance of Urdu in the national life of Pakistan, along with parallel attempts to limit the importance of English, such efforts have been blunted from two directions. Some have argued, on the one hand, that increasing the use of Urdu will detract from the importance of provincial languages, particularly Sindhi and Pushto. On the other, many argue that discarding English would limit the international prospects of Pakistani graduates, and that such a policy would favor native speakers of Urdu and closely related Punjabi at the expense of other linguistic communities. Underlying the debate regarding the enhancement of Urdu in Pakistan is the fact that Urdu, though the link language of the state, is the primary language of only a small minority of the population. The 1981 census disclosed that Urdu was "usually spoken" by only 7.6% of the households in Pakistan (mostly muhajirs or children of muhajirs and primarily in Karachi or Islamabad), compared to the percentages for other languages (see Table 10.2). A further complicating factor is that such linguistic diversity is not related exclusively to provincial domicile. For instance, only 79% of those domiciled in the Punjab speak Punjabi in their homes; 68% of those domiciled in the NWFP speak Pushto; 57% of Balochistan-domiciled people speak Balochi or Brohi; and only 52% of those domiciled in Sindh speak Sindhi.

Given the diversity of communities, ethnic stereotypes are plentiful and widely held in Pakistan. Punjabis view themselves as civilized heirs of the martial tradition (see Chapter 1), providing the society with fine soldiers, efficient administrators, yeoman agriculturalists, and pious Muslims. Outside communities view Punjabis as arrogant, deceitful, and domineering—and resist their "dominance" of the society. Muhajirs, at least those who live in urban areas, consider themselves the intellectual leaders of the society—and indeed they are disproportionately represented in the universities, professions, administration, and big business. Other communities view the muhajirs as an effete and somewhat illicit commercial class, doubting both their sincerity as "true" Muslims and their patriotism, owing to their former ties to India. The Pathans consider themselves a pure tribe of consummate warriors following the ancient and manly path of the *Pakhtunwali* (way of the Pathan—hospitality, honor, and revenge). Outside communities view the Pathans as lawless, rough, and anti-intellectual. Sindhis take great pride in the antiquity of their culture and the purity and beauty of their language. They also claim a connection to the font of mystical Islam and Sufi orders. Outside communities view the Sindhis as country bumpkins, dominated by perverse feudal chieftains. Finally, the Baloch trace their ancestry to Aleppo and are proud of their accomplishments as warriors and independent survivors of their harsh environment. Outside communities view the Baloch as the archetypical stumbling, backward provincials.

The Religion: Islam as the Sine Qua Non

The cement that holds Pakistan together is Islam. Pakistan's existence was predicated on the belief that the Muslims, a prospective minority, would be dominated and discriminated against by the Hindu majority in an undivided, independent India (see Chapter 11). This belief provided the impetus for Muslim nationalism in the subcontinent and eventually led to British and Congress party acceptance of a plan that assigned contiguous Muslim-majority districts to Pakistan and all other districts to India (see Chapter 1). One consequence of the mass transfer of people at the time of partition

TABLE 10.2 Pakistan: Language Usually Spoken in the Household, 1981 (in percentages)

Area	Urdu	Punjabi	Pushto	Sindhi	Balochi	Brohi	Hindko [a]	Siraiki [b]	Others
					Languages				
Punjab	4.3	78.7	0.8	0.1	0.6	–	–	14.9	0.7
Islamabad	11.2	81.7	4.2	0.2	0.2	–	–	0.6	1.8
NWFP	0.8	1.1	68.3	0.1	–	–	18.1	4.0	7.6
FATA	–	0.1	99.7	0.1	–	–	–	–	0.1
Sindh (including Karachi)	22.6	7.7	3.1	52.4	4.5	1.1	0.4	2.3	6.0
Balochistan	1.4	2.2	25.1	8.3	36.3	20.7	0.1	3.1	2.8
Pakistan	7.6	48.2	13.1	11.8	3.0	1.2	2.4	9.8	2.8

[a] Hindko is spoken primarily in the Hazara division of the NWFP.
[b] Siraiki is spoken in Southern Punjab, particularly in the urban centers of Multan and Bahawalpur. Depending on political perspective, it is considered a variant of Punjabi or Sindhi.

Source: Adapted from Government of Pakistan, Census Organization, *Main Findings of the 1981 Census* (Islamabad: Manager, Printing Corporation of Pakistan Press, 1983).

TABLE 10.3   Pakistan: Religion by Province, 1982

	Religions (1,000's)					
Area	Muslim	Percentage Muslims	Ahmadiyya[a]	Christian	Hindu	Others[b]
Punjab	46,110	98	64	1,061	29	28
Islamabad	331	97	1	8	–	–
NWFP	11,003	99	11	39	4	3
FATA	2,190	99	1	6	1	–
Sindh (including Karachi)	17,557	92	21	177	1,221	52
Balochistan	4,258	98	6	20	20	–
Pakistan	81,450	97	104	1,310	1,276	113

[a]The data probably underestimate the size of the Ahmadiyya community.
[b]The category of "others" includes Parsi, Sikh, Buddhist, and unspecified others.

Source: Adapted from unpublished data, Census Organization of Pakistan (1984).

(Hindus and Sikhs to India, Muslims to Pakistan) was the increase in the percentage of Muslims in the new state. Owing to a number of factors, not the least of which was the greater ethnic violence occasioned by partition in undivided Punjab, the transfer of ethnic communities was far more complete in West Pakistan than in East Pakistan. By 1948 the percentage of Muslims in West Pakistan exceeded 97%;[6] this predominance has increased in the years that have followed (see Table 10.3).

Pakistan's existence, therefore, is predicated on Islam, and its population is composed of a predominant majority of Muslims. Given this confluence of factors, Pakistan has possessed what can be termed an "Islamic mandate"—that is, the motivation and capability to create an Islamic state. This mandate is given great emphasis in Pakistan owing to the nature of Islam itself. Islam does not accept the separation of church and state. Indeed, to Muslims Islam is a complete code of life—religious, political, and moral. Accordingly, there is no contradiction involved in seeking an Islamic solution to the "secular" ills of society. This fact, as we shall see, is a crucial key to understanding Pakistan's development.

Muslim Nationalism and the Demand for Partition

An early proposal for a separate state based on the principle of Muslim nationalism was made by Muhammad Iqbal (1876–1938), Pakistan's most renowned poet and philosopher. In December 1930 he stated: "I would like to see the Punjab, North West Frontier Province, Sind and Baluchistan amalgamated into a single state. Self-government within the British Empire or without the British Empire, the formation of a consolidated North-West Indian state appears to me to be the final destiny of the Muslims of at least North-West India."[7] Chaudhury Rehmat Ali (1897–1951) is credited with having coined the word *Pakistan* as an acronym created from the names of the territories proposed to be included in the new state: *P*unjab, *A*fghania (North-West Frontier Province), *K*ashmir, *I*ran, *S*indh, *T*ukharistan, Afghanistan, and Balochis*tan*.[8] As *Pakistan* also literally translates as "land of the pure," the selection of the acronym was doubly meaningful.

Despite the yearnings for a separate Muslim state, the mainstream of Muslim opinion, represented by the Muslim League and its leader Muhammad Ali Jinnah (1876–1948), pursued a policy of cooperation with the Congress party and favored a loose federal relationship among provinces within a united India, once independence was achieved. By 1937, however, Jinnah and the Muslim League had begun to experience a change of heart. Two explanations are usually given for this volte-face: (1) Jinnah and his colleagues were growing increasingly impatient with Congress's insistence on a strong central government (prospectively dominated by Hindus) at the expense of minority community (i.e., Muslim) interests. This development, the Muslim League argued, ran counter to the intent of the Government of India Act of 1935. Therefore, the demand for a separate state was portrayed as essentially a defensive strategy to preserve the rights of minority Muslims. (2) In 1937 the Muslim League, running on the platform of an undivided India in the elections to the provincial assemblies sanctioned by the Government of India Act of 1935, was handed an unexpected and over-whelming defeat. Of the 489 Muslim seats, only 104 were won by the Muslim League.[9] Given this rebuff at the polls, the Muslim League was forced to change tactics. The strategy eventually adopted was to invoke the specter of Hindu domination in an undivided India by stressing the theme of "Islam in Danger" and the consequent "solution" of a separate Muslim state.

Accordingly, the Muslim League adopted a resolution at its annual meeting on March 23, 1940—the so-called Lahore Resolution—calling for the creation of a separate Muslim state. The substantive passage reads:

> . . . geographically contiguous units (of British India) are (to be) demarcated into regions which should be so constituted, with such territorial adjustments as may be necessary, that the areas in which the Muslims are numerically in a majority as in the North-Western and Eastern zones of India should be grouped to constitute *Independent States* in which the constituent units shall be autonomous and sovereign.[10]

Subsequent to the Lahore Resolution, the sentiment for a divided India grew rapidly. The popularity of the Muslim League and Jinnah soared now that they represented an easily identifiable platform, and the time of partition neared.[11]

The Failures of Independence

Pakistan's record as an independent nation-state is anything but happy. The litany of failures includes the following: the inability to compose a constitution until nine years after independence; the abrogation of that constitution and two others during the next twenty years; three wars with India, one of which was a clear defeat for Pakistan; the failure to gain Kashmir; the inability to form stable democratic institutions; the failure either to sustain economic development or to effect meaningful redistribution of wealth to the impoverished masses; the separation of a majority of the population when the state of Bangladesh was formed; the inability to silence regional and sectarian disputes; and, finally, the inability to sustain a clear concept of and direction to Pakistan's nationalism.

It must also be stressed that Pakistan has faced a unique confluence of problems since partition, problems that would have taxed the capabilities of any state.

The Disabilities of Partition

Pakistan was born in bloodshed. The partition of India in 1947 resulted in a mass exodus of refugees unparalleled in human history. Perhaps as many as 12 million refugees were created as a consequence of the partition plan, and as many as 2 million lost their lives in the communal bloodbath that accompanied the mass transfer of populations. Partition disrupted virtually all aspects of life within the new state of Pakistan. First, there was the problem of the refugees themselves; many penniless, all landless. A second problem concerned the division of records and assets. Official assets (money, property, equipment, etc.) were divided up according to an 82.5% to 17.5% ratio favoring the larger state of India; furthermore, such assets were not made available to Pakistan immediately at partition. Third, there was a dearth of managerial and administrative talent inherited by Pakistan. In the civilian bureaucracy only 146 officers (including 50 British officers) opted for service in Pakistan—and fewer than 20 of these had had more than fifteen years of experience.[12] In the military the highest-ranking Muslim officer was a colonel, and only a total of 100 officers with rank of captain or above opted for Pakistan.[13] Fourth, the new state was born with little concern for ethnic homogeneity or geographical contiguity. The largest single ethnic group, the Bengalis, were separated from West Pakistan by 1,000 miles of Indian territory. We have already discussed the ethnic and linguistic cleavages among the communities of West Pakistan—but the differences between Bengali and West Pakistani were even more divisive (see Chapter 16).

Relations with India

In addition to such disabilities, Pakistan has had to contend throughout its history with an often hostile neighbor, India. Pakistan has fought three wars with India, in 1948, 1965, and 1971. The grievances between the two states are many, including, but not limited to the atrocities committed by both sides during partition, the claims concerning the disputed territory of Kashmir, ideological and religious differences, and competition over regional dominance in South Asia. Such continual disputes with India have undoubtedly weakened Pakistan in several ways—economically, ideologically, militarily, and perhaps territorially. It is generally assumed in Pakistan that the secession of Bangladesh would not have been successful without the intervention of the Indian Army on the side of the Bengalis. (The regional relationships are discussed in Chapter 31.)

National Leadership

Pakistan was also unfortunate in losing its two most able statesmen soon after partition. Muhammad Ali Jinnah, the motive force behind the Pakistan Movement and Pakistan's first governor general, died on September 11, 1948, barely a year after independence was granted. Liaquat Ali Khan, Jinnah's most able lieutenant, was assassinated three years later on October 16, 1951. No subsequent leader has ever been able to command the unchallenged support of all communities and regions of the state.

Considering the confluence of these factors, what is even more surprising than the "failures of independence" of the new state is the fact that Pakistan has continued to exist at all.

Economic Limitations

The economic performance of Pakistan since 1977 has been very impressive. The gross national product has grown at an average annual rate of approximately 6%, domestic savings have increased at an even higher rate, and the availability of consumer goods has soared. On the whole, however, the economy has had to "run very fast to stay in the same place." Despite its remarkable performance, Pakistan remains a relatively poor state.

The limitations preventing the rapid turnaround of Pakistan's economy are demographic, political, and geographical in nature. First, Pakistan suffers the effects of very rapid population growth; indeed, the rate is conservatively estimated at 2.87% per year.[14] Such rapid growth exerts extreme pressures on the social services (health, education, transportation); it also swells the ranks of the underemployed labor force. Similar demographic problems have been incurred by the influx of the 2.5 to 3 million Afghan refugees since 1979. Such problems are particularly severe in the NWFP, where Afghans constitute approximately 30% of the labor force. Second, there are limitations imposed by the government. In 1981, for instance, the Pakistani government spent 6.9% of its GNP on defense (28.1% of total government spending).[15] And given Pakistan's difficult security situation, such expenditures are not likely to decrease in the near future. Pakistan also suffers from geographical bad luck: Despite the discovery and exploitation of significant natural gas reserves, Pakistan continues to import a considerable amount of its energy requirements.

*   *   *

In sum, the problems facing Pakistan are severe and promise no easy solution. In the chapters that follow we shall look at various dimensions of Pakistan's political history. Chapter 11 explores the integrative effects of Islam; Chapter 12 reveals the disintegrative effects of regionalism; Chapters 13 and 14 describe Pakistan's political institutions, policy process, and elite group interaction, respectively; and Chapter 15 concludes with an assessment of Pakistan's future.

Notes

1. Federal Bureau of Statistics, *Pakistan Statistical Yearbook, 1988* (Karachi: Manager, Printing Corporation of Pakistan Press [hereinafter referred to as MPCPP], 1988), pp. 111; 473.

2. Calculated from GOP, Census Organization of Pakistan, *Main Findings of the 1981 Census of Pakistan* (Islamabad: MPCPP, 1984).

3. Calculated from Ibid.

4. According to the 1981 census, Quetta Division had 136,000 native Pushto speakers and only 33,000 native Baluchi or Brohi speakers. See GOP, Population Census Organization, *1981 Census Report of Baluchistan Province* (Islamabad: Population Census Organization Printing Press, 1984), p. 107.

5. GOP, Population Census Organization, *1981 Census Report of Sind Province* (Islamabad: Population Census Organization Printing Press, 1984), p. 104.

6. Rounaq Jahan, *Pakistan: Failure in National Integration* (New York: Columbia University Press, 1972), p. 11.

7. Khalid bin Sayeed, *Pakistan: The Formative Phase, 1857–1948* (Karachi: Oxford University Press, 1968), pp. 103–104.

8. Ibid., p. 104.

9. Ibid., p. 83.

10. Quoted in Muhammed A. Quddus, *Pakistan: A Case Study of a Plural Society* (Columbia, Mo.: South Asia Books, 1982), p. 24.

11. See David Gilmartin, *Empire and Islam: Punjab and the Making of Pakistan* (Berkeley: University of California Press, 1988).

12. Ralph Braibanti, *Research on the Bureaucracy of Pakistan* (Durham, N.C.: Duke University Press, 1966), p. 116.

13. bin Sayeed, *Pakistan: The Formative Phase*, p. 305.

14. GOP, Planning Commission, *Sixth Five Year Plan* (Islamabad: MPCPP, 1984), p. 406.

15. Stephen P. Cohen, *The Pakistan Army* (Berkeley: University of California Press, 1984), p. 15.

Suggested Readings

Burki, Shahid Javed. *Pakistan: A Nation in the Making* (Boulder, Colo.: Westview Press, 1985).

Gilmartin, David. *Empire and Islam: Punjab and the Making of Pakistan* (Berkeley: University of California Press, 1988).

Kureshy, K. U. *A Geography of Pakistan* (Karachi: Oxford University Press, 1978).

Qureshi, Ishtiaq Hussain. *The Struggle For Pakistan* (Karachi: University of Karachi, 1965).

Sayeed, Khalid bin. *Pakistan: The Formative Phase, 1857–1948* (Karachi: Oxford University Press, 1968).

———. *Politics in Pakistan: The Nature and Direction of Change* (New York: Praeger Publishers, 1980).

Syed, Anwar Hussain. *Pakistan: Islam, Politics, and National Solidarity* (New York: Praeger Publishers, 1982).

Wolpert, Stanley. *Jinnah of Pakistan* (New York: Oxford University Press, 1984).

Ziring, Lawrence. *Pakistan: The Enigma of Political Development* (London: Dawson, 1980).

11
ISLAM AND THE POLITICAL CULTURE OF PAKISTAN

Islam is one of the world's most significant religions. It is based on the teachings and life experiences of the warrior-statesman, the Prophet Muhammad. The basic teachings of Islam were revealed to Muhammad through divine inspiration and are found in the *Quran*. The life experiences of the Prophet (*Sunnah*) were compiled by his early followers and are codified in the books of traditions (*Hadith*). Both the *Quran* and the *Sunnah* are inseparably linked components of the corpus of Islam. Accordingly, Islam is both a religious doctrine and a code of social and political organization.

Before we embark on a discussion of the interaction of Islam and Pakistan's political culture, two critical factors of such interaction must be emphasized. First, Islam does not accept the separation of church and state. To Muslims, Islam is a complete code of life that encompasses religious, legal, moral, social, and political practices. Therefore, it is meaningful to speak of an "Islamic political system," an "Islamic economic system," or an "Islamic legal system." Second, the concept of Muslim nationhood encompasses the concept that Islam is both an ethical ideal and a polity. The entire Islamic world may be regarded as one nation or community (*umma*), which, ideally, should constitute a unified "Islamic state." The acceptance of Islamic law— rather than ethnic, linguistic, regional, or historical factors—is the basis for organizing the Islamic polity. The coexistence of these two principles helps explain the interaction of Islam and politics in Pakistan. The concept of Pakistan was rooted in the demands for the creation of a Muslim homeland state, and subsequent policies of the independent state have been legitimized as expressions or reassertions of Islamic ideology. Despite widespread consensus on the ideal of Pakistan, however, there has been little, if any, consensus on the means to achieve such an ideal.

Islam in the Constitutions

Since the formation of the state of Pakistan, the society has been divided ideologically into two loosely defined groups: "fundamentalists" and "modernists." Members of the former favor the expansion of Islamic law in various spheres of Pakistani national life. They may also favor the adoption of Islamic law—in regard to punishments and the style of dispensing justice or as the source of provisions of law, the method of training judges, or the final arbiter of legislation. They may favor the expansion of Islamic practices such as the abolition of bank interest (*riba*), prohibition of alcohol, gender segregation, establishment of Islamic taxation, and so forth. Finally, they may favor a severing of ties with Western social mores and culture. The basic thrust of such fundamentalist thought is not conservative, in the sense of preservation of institutions; rather it is activist. The goal is to restructure Pakistan in a form more in accord with perceptions of what an Islamic state should be. Conversely, modernists take a more restrictive view of the scope of the Islamic mandate. They may be opposed to the expansion of Islamic law and the enforcement of Islamic practices, or they may favor development along the secularist lines of the West.

It took Pakistan nine years to adopt its first constitution. One major reason for the delay was contention over prospective Islamic provisions in the document. The first task of the Constituent Assembly was to define the basic directive principles of the new state, and in March 1949 the fruit of this exercise, the Objectives Resolution, was passed. It contained the following provisions dealing with Islam:

> The Government of Pakistan will be a state. . . .
> Wherein the principle of democracy, freedom, equality, tolerance and social justice, as enunciated by Islam, shall be fully observed;
> Wherein the Muslims of Pakistan shall be enabled individually and collectively to order their lives in accordance with teachings and requirements of Islam, as set out in the Holy Quran and Sunnah;
> Wherein adequate provision shall be made for the minorities freely to profess and practice their religion and develop their culture.[1]

Once established, these provisions have remained virtually unchanged in the otherwise quite fluid environment of constitutional law that has characterized Pakistan's statehood. Indeed, in 1985, the Objectives Resolution was incorporated into Pakistan's constitution.

Once objectives were established, the more difficult task of framing the basic principles to implement them faced the Constituent Assembly. The report of the Basic Principles Committee took nearly three years to complete. Regarding Islam it recommended at the urging of the *ulema* (religious scholars—singular *alim*) that the head of state constitute a Board of Ulema consisting of not more than five persons "well-versed in Islamic law" to review all provisions passed by the national legislature. If it was the unanimous opinion of this board that any pending legislation was "repugnant to the Holy Quran or Sunnah," the legislation would be referred back to the legislature for requisite amendments. Excluded from the purview of such a board would be all fiscal legislation.[2] This recommendation received a cold response when it was released to the general public, and the final *Basic Principles Report* eventually adopted by the Constituent Assembly in 1955 deleted mention of the board.[3]

Provisions for the establishment of such an institution were also not included in the final draft of the 1956 constitution. In its place the president was empowered to appoint a committee that would look into the question of "[bringing] existing law into conformity with the Holy Quran and Sunnah." Other Islamic provisions of the 1956 constitution were similarly without teeth. The preamble adopted the vague wording of the Objectives Resolution. The "directive principles of state policy" provided that the "state shall endeavor . . . to make the teaching of the Holy Quran compulsory [for Muslims]; to promote the unity and observance of Islamic moral standards; and to secure the proper organization of *zakat* [charitable tax], *wakfs* [religious endowments], and mosques." The state was also to "endeavor" to "prevent prostitution, gambling, the taking of injurious drugs: and . . . the consumption of alcoholic liquor other than for medicinal . . . purposes." The preamble also called upon the state to "eliminate *riba* [literally usury, but generally applied to all interest] as soon as possible."[4] Obviously, then, one outcome of the nine-year process of constitution formation in Pakistan was a dilution of the fundamentalist position. Pakistan was designed to be a Muslim state, but the mechanisms to implement such a vision were intentionally weak, vague, or ill defined.

The 1956 constitution was short lived. It was abrogated two and a half years after its adoption as a consequence of the military coup that brought General Ayub Khan to power in 1958. During the discussion preceding the adoption of the 1962 constitution, the issue of the status of Islam in Pakistan was again debated. Once again the modernists prevailed. And when it came time to write the 1973 constitution (the 1962 constitution was suspended in 1969 and abrogated in 1972), a similar outcome resulted. Each of Pakistan's constitutions had defined Pakistan as an "Islamic state," but the determination of what that meant in terms of law or practice was left for later, after a time-consuming evolutionary process. As events have indicated since 1977, Pakistan is still undergoing such evolution.

An Islamic State? Zia's Reforms

General Zia-ul-Haq assumed power following a military coup in July 1977. Eighteen months later he announced a series of reforms termed *nizam-*

i-Mustafa (Islamic political system—literally, rule of the Prophet), proclaimed to be designed to bring all laws into conformity with Islamic tenets and values. The reforms were aimed at three aspects of secular life: judicial and legal, economic, and educational.

Judicial and Legal Reforms

Consequent with the announcement of the reforms, President Zia promulgated four *hudood* ordinances (singular *hadd*) outlining Islamic punishments and standards of evidence for theft, *zina* (sex-related crimes), consumption of intoxicants, and *qazf* (the wrongful imputation of immodesty to a woman).[5] The hadd punishments (punishments with an express sanction in the *Quran* and *Sunnah*) are the amputation of the left hand for theft, stoning to death for adultery, and eighty lashes for *qazf* or the consumption of alcohol. Several other Islamic laws have also been introduced or are pending introduction.[6]

In order to implement these legal reforms, new judicial institutions were also established. The busiest and most important of these is the Federal Shariat Court (FSC), or Islamic law court. The FSC has heard thousands of appeals against conviction under the hudood ordinances, has addressed hundreds of "Shariat petitions" (petitions challenging the validity of laws on the basis of Islam), and has completed a monumental review of all civil and criminal laws in Pakistan, testing for "repugnancy" to Islam. Indeed, the FSC has assumed many of the functions envisaged by the Basic Principles Committee for the Board of Ulema. Appeals from the FSC are heard by the Shariat Appellate Bench of the Supreme Court.

Despite such hectic activity, however, the cumulative effect of such decisions on the legal system has been modest, for two reasons. First, the courts have been banned from the consideration of laws dealing with constitutional principles, fiscal matters, and martial law regulations.[7] Second, the courts have been staffed, for the most part, by jurists who are "Islamic moderates," falling somewhere in the middle of the continuum of fundamentalists and modernists.

Economic Reforms

In 1980, provisions for the compulsory collection of *zakat* (a tax assessed against capital assets) and *ushr* (agricultural tax) were introduced.[8] These taxes are traditional Islamic methods of collecting and distributing welfare. Zakat is assessed at 2.5% of cash value of financial assets, ushr at 5% of the profits from agricultural land. Monies collected through this process are made available to local zakat committees for distribution to poor Muslims and to charities. The zakat system, as implemented, has been opposed by the minority Shia sect of Islam whose legal system is at variance with that of the majority Sunnis on a number of points. Accordingly, Shias have been made exempt from the compulsory payment of zakat. Also, under the regime of President Zia (1977–1988), Islamic banking practices were introduced to eliminate bank interest (riba).

Educational Reforms

A new educational policy introduced in 1981 has established compulsory courses in Quranic and Islamic studies throughout the educational system, introduced Arabic as a compulsory foreign language requirement, and proposed the establishment of separate women's colleges. Despite extensive publicity, such reforms have had only a marginal impact on the educational system of Pakistan.[9] Moreover, like other Islamic reforms, they have been decried both by those who think that the reforms have gone too far and by those who think they have not gone far enough.

The future of nizam-i-Mustafa remains in doubt. Neither modernists nor fundamentalists were particularly happy with Zia's system. Indeed, Prime Minister Benazir Bhutto (1952–) promised to dismantle Zia's Islamic policies during the course of her 1988 election campaign, claiming that Zia's nizam-i-Mustafa was barbaric, reactionary, undemocratic, and discriminatory toward women. But she was unable to deliver on this promise. Pakistan's Islamic mandate makes it difficult, if not impossible, to pursue policies that may be perceived as anti-Islamic. It seems certain, therefore, that the question of the form Islam should take in the Islamic state is likely to remain problematical for the foreseeable future.

Divisions Within and Outside Islam

Sunni and Shia

Sectarian differences within Islam have widened the gulf between fundamentalists and modernists in Pakistan. Most Muslims in Pakistan are Sunni followers of the Hanafi legal system. But there are significant numbers of Shias as well—both Ithna Asharis (so-called Twelvers, the branch of Shiism dominant in Iran) and Ismailis (followers of the Aga Khan). Census data does not exist on the size of each group, although it is generally acknowledged that Ithna Asharis constitute 10–15%, and Ismailis 2–3% of the population.

This division has been politically significant to Pakistan in two regards. First, the Sunni-Shia rift has resulted in numerous communal disturbances throughout Pakistan's history. The intensity and frequency of such disturbances have increased since the 1979 revolution in Iran, which installed a chauvinistic Shiite regime. Second, the presence of the large minority community has helped to curb the power and influence of the Sunni majority, particularly that of the fundamentalist religious elite. One consequence of the latter circumstance has been to reinforce the tendency of Pakistan's leaders to move slowly on the pace of Islamization.

The Ahmadiyya: Who Is a Muslim?

The Ahmadiyya are members of a religious sect who follow the teachings of the late nineteenth-century religious leader and self-proclaimed "prophet," Mirza Ghulam Ahmad (c. 1840–1908). Ahmad was a prolific polemicist, the author of hundreds of pamphlets and religious tracts. The targets of his writing were primarily Christian missionaries, but he often ran afoul of orthodox Islamic groups as well. Heretical to such latter groups were a confusing and contradictory set of claims made by Ghulam Ahmad between 1892 and 1906, interpreted by his followers as constituting proof of Ahmad's prophethood. Such claims, argued orthodox Muslims, violated a central tenet of Islam that Muhammad was the final prophet.[10]

Consequently, clashes between the Ahmadiyya community and the politico-religious groups of ulema have been frequent. The most violent confrontation occurred in 1953.[11] One outcome of these disturbances was the discrediting of the ulema (who were blamed by the inquiry commission as being responsible for instigating the violence) and, by implication, their demands for an "Islamic constitution." Indeed, with many of their leaders in jail, opposition to the secular nature of the proposed 1956 constitution evaporated.[12] In 1973, the issue was resurrected and in the aftermath of the resultant bloodbath, an amendment was made to the 1973 constitution that designated the Ahmadiyya as a "non-Muslim minority" community.[13] Similarly, President Zia, reacting in 1984 to threats of potential violence against the Ahmadiyya by disaffected ulema, placed further legal restrictions on the community.[14] It is likely that the Ahmadiyya question will continue to haunt decision makers in Pakistan for the foreseeable future. In an Islamic state the question of who is a Muslim is of crucial importance, and as Pakistan's experience has demonstrated, the determination of that fact is not always easy.

*   *   *

In sum, three facts are of indisputable significance to the interaction of Islam and politics in Pakistan. First, the formation of Pakistan was predicated on the demand for the establishment of a Muslim homeland. Second, a majority of Pakistan's population are Muslims. Third, there is a consensus among Pakistan's population that Islam should influence the development of Pakistan's institutions and political process. However, the task of translating such a consensus into stable political institutions has proven very difficult for Pakistan's decision makers. It took Pakistan nine years to draft its first constitution, a delay that was largely a consequence of disagreement over the Islamic components of the new state. Unfortunately, the adoption of the short-lived 1956 constitution did not settle the issue of the relationship between Islam and Pakistan's political system. As we have seen, Pakistan has suffered through an enduring crisis relative to the definition of who is a Muslim. Zia's nizam-i-Mustafa, designed in part to settle such issues, raised more questions than it answered. Ironically, Pakistan was born as the embodiment of Islamic ideology, but forty-three years later Pakistan is still struggling with the definition of what that legacy entails.

Notes

1. Adapted from GOP, Ministry of Justice and Parliamentary Affairs, *The Constitution of the Islamic Republic of Pakistan as Modified up to 19th March 1985* (Islamabad: MPCPP, 1985), article 2(a).

2. GOP, *Report of the Basic Principles Committee* (Karachi: Government of Pakistan Press [hereinafter referred to as GOP Press], 1952), chapter 3, nos. 3–8.

3. GOP, *Report of the Basic Principles Committee as Adopted by the Constituent Assembly of Pakistan on the 21st September 1954* (Karachi: GOP Press, 1954). A detailed account of the formation of the 1956 constitution is found in Herbert Feldman, *A Constitution for Pakistan* (Karachi: Oxford University Press, 1956), and in Leonard Binder, *Religion and Politics in Pakistan* (Berkeley: University of California Press, 1961).

4. *The Constitution of the Islamic Republic of Pakistan (1956)*, articles 25, 28, 29, and 198.

5. See the Offences Against Property (Enforcement of Hudood) Ordinance 1979, the Offense of Zina (Enforcement of Hudood) Ordinance 1979, the Offense of Qazf (Enforcement of Hudood) Ordinance 1979, and the Prohibition (Enforcement of Hudood) Ordinance 1979 found in *The Major Acts* (Lahore: Khyber Law Publishers, 1984), pp. 1–30. For details regarding the implementation of these laws, see C. H. Kennedy, "Islamization in Pakistan: Implementation of the Hudood Ordinances," *Asian Survey*, vol. 28, no. 3 (March 1988), pp. 307–316.

6. For instance, the Law of Evidence was redrafted in 1984 as the Qanoon-i-Shahadat Order, 1984 (Act X of 1984). Pending legislation includes a revision of laws relating to bodily hurt (murder, manslaughter, assault, and so forth) made incumbent by the Supreme Court's December 1989 decision to affirm Federation of Pakistan v. Gul Hasan Khan *All-Pakistan Legal Decisions (PLD)* 1980 Peshawar 1, a case that had declared relevant provisions of Pakistan's Penal Code "repugnant to Islam." For further discussion see C. H. Kennedy, "Islamization and Legal Reform in Pakistan, 1979–1989," *Pacific Affairs*, vol. 61, no. 4 (Spring 1990).

7. These provisions have been challenged on several occasions. The proposed 9th Amendment to the Constitution, pending before the Senate since 1986, calls for the lifting of such jurisdictional restrictions. Similarly, Zia's short-lived Enforcement of Shariah Ordinance, 1988 *PLD* 1988 Central Statutes 29, removed such restrictions. Failing to gain the necessary support of the National Assembly, the latter ordinance

became defunct with no legal effect in early 1989. For details see C. H. Kennedy (1990).

8. Zakat and Ushr Ordinance, *PLD*, 1980 Central Statutes, 97–124.

9. See Louis Hayes, *The Crisis of Education in Pakistan* (Lahore: Vanguard Books, 1987), esp. pp. 99–111.

10. See Yohanan Friedmann, *Prophecy Continuous: Aspects of Ahmadi Religious Thought and its Medieval Background* (Berkeley: University of California Press, 1989); Spencer Lavan, *The Ahmadiyya Movement: A History and Perspective* (Delhi: Manohar, 1974); and C. H. Kennedy, "Towards the Definition of a Muslim in an Islamic State: The Case of the Ahmadiyya in Pakistan," in Dhirendra Vajpeyi and Yogendra Malik, eds., *Religious and Ethnic Minorities in South Asia* (Riverdale, Md.: Riverdale Press, 1989), pp. 71–108.

11. See Government of Punjab, *Report of the Court of Inquiry constituted Under Punjab Act II of 1954 to enquire into the Punjab Disturbances of 1953*, Muhammad Munir, chairman (Lahore: Superintendent Government Printing, 1954).

12. This argument is convincingly made in Sayed Riaz Ahmad, *Maulana Maududi and the Islamic State* (Lahore: People's Publishing House, 1976), pp. 68–74.

13. Articles 106(3) and 260.

14. Anti-Islamic activities of the Qadiani Group, Lahori Group and Ahmadis (Prohibition and Punishment) Ordinance, 1984, *PLD* 1984 Central Statutes, 102.

Suggested Readings

Ahmad, Sayed Riaz. *Maulana Maududi and the Islamic State* (Lahore: People's Publishing House, 1976).

Binder, Leonard. *Religion and Politics in Pakistan* (Berkeley: University of California Press, 1961).

Feldman, Herbert. *A Constitution for Pakistan* (Karachi: Oxford University Press, 1956).

Government of Pakistan, Cabinet Division. *Ansari Commission's Report on Forms of Government 4th August 1983* (Islamabad: Printing Corporation of Pakistan Press, 1984).

Iqbal, Muhammed. *The Reconstruction of Religious Thought in Islam* (Lahore: Ashraf Publications, 1962).

Kennedy, Charles H. "Islamization and Legal Reform in Pakistan, 1979–1989," *Pacific Affairs,* vol. 61, no. 4 (Spring 1990).

———. "Islamization in Pakistan: Implementation of the Hudood Ordinances," *Asian Survey* vol. 28, no. 3 (March 1988), pp. 307–316.

Maududi, Syed Abul. *The Islamic Law and Constitution,* 7th ed. (Lahore: Islamic Publications Ltd., 1980).

Mumtaz, Khawar, and Farida Shaheed, eds. *Women of Pakistan: Two Steps Forward and One Step Back?* (London: Zed Books, 1987).

Munir, Muhammed. *From Jinnah to Zia* (Lahore: Vanguard Press, 1979).

Patel, Rashida. *Islamisation of Laws in Pakistan* (Karachi: Faiza Publications, 1986).

Sayeed, Khalid bin. *Pakistan: The Formative Phase, 1857–1948* (Karachi: Oxford University Press, 1978).

Syed, Anwar Hussain. *Pakistan: Islam, Politics, and National Solidarity* (New York: Praeger Publishers, 1982).

Weiss, Anita, ed. *Islamic Reassertion in Pakistan* (Syracuse: Syracuse University Press, 1986).

12
REGIONALISM

Ethnoregional Identifications

As we have seen, the homeland for the Muslims of South Asia was formed with little concern for the ethnic homogeneity of its peoples. Currently, Pakistan encompasses five major ethnic groups (see Chapter 10), and eight major languages are spoken by its population. Ethnoregional identifications roughly correspond with the provincial domiciles, but the fit is imperfect owing to the effects of partition and internal migration. Perhaps more important than the objective differences between peoples, however, are the *perceptions* of ethnoregional differences held by Pakistan's population. Indeed, the perception of ethnic discrimination against Bengalis that resulted in the eventual secession of Bangladesh was spawned in the contentious ethnoregional environment of Pakistan (see Chapter 16).[1] Unfortunately, Pakistan is still beset with such perceptions of ethnoregional grievances and the potential for additional "Bangladeshes."

Punjabi Dominance

At the heart of ethnoregional sentiment in Pakistan is the perception by Punjabis and non-Punjabis alike that the Punjabi community dominates the politics and society of the state. There is considerable objective support for this perception. First, Punjabis constitute a majority of the population, approximately 60%.[2] Second, Punjabis dominate membership in the civil bureaucracy[3] and the military.[4] Third, the Punjab is by far the wealthiest and most developed province in the state. Indicators of such advantage include differentials in per capita income, life expectancy, levels of industrialization, urbanization, and literacy.[5] In the face of such facts, nationals of the smaller provinces perceive themselves as underrepresented or even dominated by the larger ethnoregional group. As we will see, this latter perception is ironically fueled by governmental policies designed to assuage such perceptions.

Sindhi Regionalism

Sindh to a greater extent than any other province in Pakistan has experienced an extensive influx of inhabitants, first from India (the *muhajirs*, or refugees) and, after partition, from the other provinces of Pakistan. More often than not, these non-Sindhis have continued to cling to their native province's culture and language, ignoring the local traditions and often failing to learn the Sindhi language. Exacerbating the tensions occasioned by this "alien" intrusion has been the fact that such newcomers were often better educated, wealthier, more cosmopolitan, and better able to compete in a modernizing state than the Sindhi sons of the soil.[6] Particularly galling to the indigenous Sindhis has been the rapid commercial growth of Karachi fueled by refugees and later by Punjabi money and talent with relatively little corresponding benefits to the indigenous Sindhis. Indeed, the rural areas of Sindh have remained largely unaffected by the rapid growth of Karachi, and the social patterns that have prevailed in Sindh for centuries have remained largely unchanged. Rural Sindh is still largely dominated by a semifeudal system in which rich landlords, who often hold hereditary religious offices as well, control numerous near-destitute peasants. Exacerbating the perception of Sindhi subordination in the rural areas have been governmental policies that award tracts of reclaimed agricultural land in Sindh to retired civil and military officers, the majority of whom are Punjabi or Pathan.

Originally the demand for "Sindhu Desh" (Sindhi homeland) was directed primarily at the muhajir community, which controlled the commercial and industrial life of Karachi. Aggravating such sentiments in the early years of Pakistan's statehood were the successive attempts by Muhammad Ali Jinnah and Liaquat Ali Khan to make Urdu the national language of Pakistan. Also aggravating Sindhi grievances was the One Unit Plan (1955–1970), which integrated Pakistan's four western provinces into one administrative unit with its capital in the Punjab at Lahore.[7] Sindh was further isolated when the federal capital was moved from Karachi to Islamabad.

But the greatest impetus for Sindhi regionalism is inextricably linked with the career and demise of the late Prime Minister Zulfiqar Ali Bhutto (1927–1979). Bhutto was the scion of a very prominent landholding family based in Larkana, Sindh. During his regime he encouraged Sindhi sentiments by empathizing with the grievances of the Sindhis and by promising to rectify past injustices. Among the policies pursued by his government were land reforms, the purposes of which were both to weaken the power of the landlords in Sindh and to end non-Sindhi ownership of Sindhi agricultural land. Bhutto also nationalized heavy industry, banks, and insurance. Each of these actions was perceived in the Sindh as a challenge to the interests of the muhajirs; similarly, Bhutto's civil and military reforms were perceived as detrimental to non-Sindhi interests. In the aftermath of Bhutto's overthrow by a military coup and his eventual execution, Sindhi regionalism gained a focal point, perhaps even a martyr, and has correspondingly proliferated.[8]

During President Zia-ul-Haq's regime (1977–1988), Sindh became the most disaffected of all of Pakistan's provinces. Many Sindhis perceived Zia's government as Punjabi inspired—at best oblivious to the grievances of Sindhis, at worst conspiring to strengthen further the position of Punjabis at the expense of the Sindhis. Perhaps the most serious challenge to Zia's rule was the Movement for the Restoration of Democracy (MRD), which inspired the disturbances of 1983 that originated in, and for the most part remained confined to, rural Sind. At the heyday of the 1983 disturbances, Sindhi separatists voiced grievances reminiscent of Bengali leader Mujibur Rehman's Six Points (see Chapter 16). For instance, these dissidents called for increased provincial autonomy; insisted on reducing disparities in economic development; charged the federal government with inadequate allocation of federal government funds; claimed underrepresentation in the military, bureaucratic, entrepreneurial, and political elites of the state; and charged that Sindhis were treated as second-class citizens, even in their own province.[9] The airplane crash that killed President Zia in August 1988 and the subsequent election of Benazir Bhutto to the office of prime minister dramatically changed such perceptions. Sindhi grievances remained, but there was widespread confidence that Benazir's regime, led by a daughter of Sindh, would be more accommodative of Sindhi interests.

As the daughter of the late prime minister, Benazir inherited the mantle of Sindhi leadership. This was both a benefit and a liability. In the general election of 1988, Benazir's political party, the Pakistan People's Party (PPP), won every national assembly seat in rural Sindh; and the PPP was able to form a majority government in the Sindh provincial assembly. However, the widely held perception of Benazir's and the PPP's close affiliation with the Sindh played havoc with her government's attempts to forge national unity in the nation-state. Mian Nawaz Sharif (1948–), chief minister of Punjab, proved particularly adept at characterizing Benazir's policies as pro-Sindhi and anti-Punjabi. Indeed, such resultant "Punjabi nationalism" provided the cement that has held the disparate elements of the opposition Islamic Democratic Alliance (*Islami Jamhoori Ittehad*—IJI) together. Further, Benazir's close affiliation with Sindhi interests poisoned the short-lived PPP-MQM (Muhajir Qaumi Mahaz—Muhajir National Movement) accord, which in turn led to her downfall in August 1990.

Muhajir Assertiveness

For most of Pakistan's history, the political desires of Pakistan's Urdu-speaking muhajir community have remained dormant. Such dormancy was shattered following the Karachi communal riots of December 1986. At that time muhajirs, organized by the MQM and its leader Altaf Husain (1949–), participated in the mass bloodletting between indigenous Sindhis (defined in 1986 to include both ethnic Sindhis and muhajirs) and "outsiders" (Pathans, Punjabis, and Afghans). Muhajir militancy continued after the riots and resulted in the forceful expression of several demands by the MQM upon the federal government. Two demands are most salient. The first is the repeal or significant revision of Pakistan's ethnic quota system for government employment. According to the MQM, the size of the "urban Sindh" quota (7.6%) unfairly restricts muhajir entry into Pakistan's elites. Second, the MQM demands the repatriation of approximately one-half million "stranded Pakistanis" (popularly known as "Biharis") many of whom languish as stateless people in refugee camps in Bangladesh. Both of these demands are anathema to Sindhi interests. Sindhi leaders do not favor a revision of the ethnic quota as it currently disproportionately favors Sindhi candidates; nor does Sindhi leadership look with favor upon the repatriation of the "stranded Pakistanis," who they fear will take up residence in Karachi.

Despite such conflicts of interest, the MQM joined the PPP's coalition government following the national elections of 1988. It is generally acknowledged that the PPP promised to pursue the MQM's demands in exchange for the support of the MQM in the national assembly. Benazir's government, however, proved unable or unwilling to keep its promises. The immediate consequence was that the MQM left the coalition government and joined the opposition IJI. This switch precipitated a motion of no-confidence against Benazir's government on November 1, 1989, which narrowly failed. Benazir's position continued to deteriorate until she was removed from office on August 2, 1990.

Ominously, the sundering of the PPP-MQM alliance is closely related to the resumption of ethnic violence in urban Sindh (Karachi and Hyderabad) since late 1989. In February 1990, massive communal riots claimed the lives of dozens in Karachi. The main rift lies between Sindhis organized by the PPP's student wing, the Pakistan Student's Federation, and muhajirs who are linked to the MQM.[10]

Pathan Separatism

In the NWFP the call for an independent entity of "Pakhtunistan" predates independence. Pakhtunistan means different things to different people, ranging from the demand for the formation of a new state incorporating Pathan areas on both sides of the Afghanistan-Pakistan border to a mere change of nomenclature for the NWFP. In any event, the call for a Pathan entity stems from the perception of the common ethnic, cultural, and linguistic background of the Pathan communities on both sides of the border.

Before partition, the demand for a separate Muslim state was weaker in the frontier regions of Pakistan than in the more settled areas. Undoubtedly, one reason for such a distinction was the fact that few Hindus lived in the frontier. The grievances of the Pathans, therefore, were directed at the British and not at the confluence of British and Hindu domination as in Sindh or the Punjab. Consequently, the pre-partition sentiments of the Pathan leaders found a natural ally in the policies of the Indian National Congress party, and few took part in the Pakistan Movement. Indeed, Khan Abdul Ghaffar Khan, the most prominent pre-partition Pathan leader, was referred to as the "Frontier Gandhi" for his espousal of an undivided India and his use of nonviolent civil disobedience.

Subsequent to partition, development in the NWFP was slow and uneven. Building upon a similar foundation of grievances engendered by the status of a minority backward province that was eventually to result in Mujib's Six Points and the eventual secession of Bangladesh, Khan Abdul Ghaffar Khan formed the West Pakistan portion of what became in 1957 the National Awami party (NAP). This party never amounted to much in the Sindh or Punjab, but it took firm root in the NWFP and Balochistan. Indeed, in the 1970 election the NAP emerged as the most significant party in the NWFP; and with the cooperation of the Jamiat-ul-Ulema-i-Islam (JUI), it was able to form the provincial government. Khan Abdul Wali Khan (the leader of the NAP and son of Ghaffar Khan) and Bhutto were natural rivals; both were ambitious politicians who saw their rivalry in zero-sum terms. Between 1971 and 1974, relations between the two became increasingly acrimonious, and following the assassination of NWFP Minister and Pakistan People's party (PPP) member H. M. Sherpao, allegedly perpetrated by NAP sympathizers in early 1975, Bhutto arrested Wali Khan, dissolved the provincial government, and banned the NAP. A lengthy trial of Wali Khan on the charge of murder ensued, although Bhutto was ousted before a verdict could be reached.[11] The charges against Wali Khan were dropped in 1977 following Bhutto's overthrow.

The Afghanistan war has complicated issues relevant to Pathan separatism. Afghanistan has never accepted the validity of the Durand Line, which demarcates the Afghan/Pakistan border. Cross-border raids by Afghan airplanes, commonplace during the period of the Soviet occupation (1979–1989), highlighted this fact. A further complication is the status of the Afghan refugees who have taken up residence in the NWFP. Several sectarian clashes between Shias and Sunnis, particularly in the Kurram Agency, have been exacerbated by the influx of Afghans, most of whom are Sunnis. There is growing sentiment in the NWFP that the Afghans also constitute a drain on the already limited resources of the province. Since the Soviet withdrawal in 1989, these issues have been finessed by both the Zia and Benazir regimes through a combination of tacit noninterference in Pathan tribal affairs and extensive domestic and international financial subsidies to the refugee communities. If and when the Afghanistan war finally ends, such policy options will be closed to Pakistan's decision makers.

Baloch Nationalism

Balochistan is Pakistan's largest, poorest, and most sparsely settled province. It constitutes roughly 40% of Pakistan's landmass but only 5% of its population. Furthermore, a majority of Balochistan's population is non-Baloch. In the northern areas of the province, Pathans predominate; and in Las Bela and Sibi districts, Sindhi and Siraiki are spoken more frequently than Balochi or Brohi, whereas in Quetta District, Punjabi or Pustho is more often spoken. Only in the sparsely settled districts of Kalat and in the districts bordering Iran do Baloch languages predominate.[12] More Baloch actually live outside of Balochistan than within, and the largest concentration is in Karachi.

At the time of partition, Balochistan was only partially incorporated into Pakistan. British policy prior to independence had treated Balochistan as a large buffer zone and granted local Baloch leaders wide autonomy within their traditional sphere of influence. In 1955, Pakistan moved to incorporate the territories as part of the One Unit Plan and the tribal leaders in "merger agreements" ceded their territories to Pakistan. In return for the cession of control, the leaders were granted privy purses.[13] In practice, however, the Baloch tribal leaders maintained considerable autonomy over their former domains. But the merger sparked the expectations of the masses for major social change. Such incipient politicization found expression in the 1970 elections, and Balochistan, like the NWFP, elected the NAP to power; moreover, two Baloch nationalists—Mir Ghaus Baksh Bizenjo and Sardar Ataullah Khan Mengal—were installed as governor and chief minister of the province, respectively. Both were linked closely to the NWFP NAP and to Wali Khan. In addition, like Wali Khan, both eventually ran afoul of Bhutto's ego and his vision of a new Pakistan.

Tensions between the Baloch NAP government and the federal government came to a head on February 12, 1973, when a cache of arms allegedly destined for Baloch separatists was discovered in the residence of the Iraqi military attaché in Islamabad.[14] The government reacted by confiscating the arms, dismissing the Baloch government, and arresting its leaders. As a result of such "provocations," Baloch guerrillas began to ambush army convoys. The war rapidly escalated; at its peak between 80,000 and 100,000 Pakistani army personnel were in Balochistan. Despite considerable loss of life, the results of the conflict were inconclusive. Fighting continued intermittently until Bhutto was removed from government in 1977. Upon assuming power, General Zia released from 6,000 to 11,000 Baloch leaders from jails (the estimated number depends on the source) and declared amnesty for the guerrillas who had taken refuge in Afghanistan or Iran.[15]

Under Zia, a tenuous peace prevailed between the central government and Balochistan. This situation was shattered by the death of Zia and the subsequent election of Benazir. The PPP fared very poorly in Balochistan, winning only one seat in the national assembly and three in the Baloch provincial assembly. Consequently, a coalition of several Baloch-based regional parties formed the provincial government under the direction of the Chief Minister Nawab Akbar Bugti. Although not a separatist, Nawab Bugti advocates increased provincial autonomy and has called for "noncooperation" with the central government.

*   *   *

In sum, Pakistan, like India and Sri Lanka, was formed through the amalgamation of several "nations"—groups with distinctive languages, cultures, and ethnicity. For the states of South Asia such an outcome was partially a consequence of British colonial policy, which paid only slight attention to the ethnic homogeneity of its administrative units. But in Pakistan it was also the consequence of the ideological demand for an Islamic state. In the ideal of Pakistan was envisioned the creation of a state that would transcend the national particularism of its population. Pakistan was to form a community of Muslims. Unfortunately, the cement of Islam proved too weak to prevent the dismemberment of the state in 1971. Consequently, Pakistan has the dubious distinction of being the only state in the twentieth century that has suffered a successful violent separatist movement. Therefore, unlike its neighbors (although they, too, must contend with the deleterious effects of competing nationalisms), Pakistan carries the double burden of precedent: Pakistan has been the victim of a successful secessionist movement, and would-be opponents of the continued integrity of Pakistan are encouraged by their predecessors' success.

Notes

1. See, for instance, Rounaq Jahan, *Pakistan: Failure of National Integration* (New York: Columbia University Press, 1972); and Muhammad A. Quddus, *Pakistan: A Case Study of a Plural Society* (Columbia, Mo.: South Asian Books, 1982).

2. Punjab constitutes 56% of the population according to the 1981 census, but significant numbers of Punjabis also live in other provinces of Pakistan.

3. See C. H. Kennedy, "Policies of Redistributional Preference in Pakistan" in N. Nevitte and C. H. Kennedy, eds., *Ethnic Preference and Public Policy in Developing States* (Boulder, Colo.: Lynne Rienner Press, 1986). The approximate numbers of officers in the federal bureaucracy in 1981 break down as follows: Punjab, 51.6%; NWFP, 11.7%; Urban Sindh, 22.3%; Rural Sindh, 4.4%; Balochistan, 3.2%; Northern Areas and Federally Administered Tribal Areas, 5.0%; and Azad Kashmir, 1.7%.

4. Stephen P. Cohen, *The Pakistan Army* (Berkeley: University of California Press, 1984). According to Cohen (p. 45), 75% of all ex-servicemen come from only

three districts in the Punjab (Rawalpindi, Jhelum, and Campbellpur [Attock]) and from two adjoining districts in the NWFP (Kohat and Mardan).

5. Charles H. Kennedy, "Policies of Preference in Pakistan," *Asian Survey* (June 1984), p. 689.

6. For details, see Theodore P. Wright, "Indian Muslim Refugees in the Politics of Pakistan," *Journal of Commonwealth and Comparative Politics* vol. 12, no. 2 (1974), pp. 189–201; and Theodore P. Wright, "Center-Periphery Relations in Pakistan: Sindhis, Muhajirs, and Punjabis," *Comparative Politics* (forthcoming Spring 1991).

7. See Herbert Feldman, *The End and the Beginning: Pakistan 1969–1971* (Karachi: Oxford University Press, 1976), pp. 51–61.

8. For the most complete treatment of Bhutto's term in office, see Shahid Javed Burki, *Pakistan under Bhutto, 1971–1977* (New York: St. Martin's Press, 1980); for the most comprehensive treatment of the land reforms, see Ronald J. Herring, *Land to the Tiller: The Political Economy of Agrarian Reforms in South Asia* (New Haven, Conn.: Yale University Press, 1983).

9. See Ross Masud Husain, "The Sindh Question," *Viewpoint* (October 4, 1984), p. 34.

10. For details see "Bloodbath in Karachi," *Newsline* (Karachi: February 1990), pp. i–viii.

11. Lawrence Ziring, *Pakistan: The Enigma of Political Development* (London: Dawson, 1980), pp. 148–159; and Tahir Amin, *Ethno-National Movements of Pakistan: Domestic and International Factors* (Islamabad: Institute of Policy Sciences, 1988), pp. 88–92.

12. Derived from GOP, Population Census Organisation, *1981 Census Report of Baluchistan* (Islamabad: Population Census Organisation Press, 1989), p. 107.

13. Ziring, *Pakistan: Enigma of Political Development,* p. 160.

14. Selig Harrison, *In Afghanistan's Shadow: Baluch Nationalism and Soviet Temptations* (New York: Carnegie Endowment for International Peace, 1981), p. 35.

15. For a more complete description of the war, see Harrison, *In Afghanistan's Shadow,* pp. 35–40; Tariq Ali, *Can Pakistan Survive? The Death of a State* (London: Penguin, 1983), pp. 115–123.

Suggested Readings

Ali, Tariq. *Can Pakistan Survive? The Death of a State* (London: Penguin, 1983).

Amin, Tahir. *Ethno-National Movements in Pakistan: Domestic and International Factors* (Islamabad: Institute of Policy Sciences, 1988).

Feldman, Herbert. *The End and the Beginning: Pakistan 1969–1971* (Karachi: Oxford University Press, 1976).

Harrison, Selig. *In Afghanistan's Shadow: Baluch Nationalism and Soviet Temptations* (New York: Carnegie Endowment for International Peace, 1981).

Inayatullah. "Internal and External Factors in the Failure of National Integration in Pakistan," in Stephanie G. Neumann, ed., *Small States and Segmented Societies: National Political Integration in a Global Environment* (New York: Praeger Publishers, 1976).

Jahan, Rounaq. *Pakistan: Failure of National Integration* (New York: Columbia University Press, 1972).

Kennedy, Charles H. "Policies of Ethnic Preference in Pakistan," *Asian Survey,* vol. 24, no. 6 (June 1984), pp. 688–703.

————. "Policies of Redistributional Preference in Pakistan," in N. Nevitte and C. H. Kennedy, eds., *Ethnic Preference and Public Policy in Developing States* (Boulder, Colo.: Lynne Rienner Press, 1986).

Quddus, Muhammed A. *Pakistan: A Case Study of a Plural Society* (Columbia, Mo.: South Asian Books, 1982).

Sayeed, Khalid bin. *Politics in Pakistan: The Nature and Direction of Change* (New York: Praeger Publishers, 1980).

Syed, Aslam. "Political Parties and the Nationality Question in Pakistan," *Journal of South Asian and Middle Eastern Studies* vol. 12, no. 1 (Fall 1988), pp. 42–75.

Wirsing, Robert G. "Ethnicity and Political Reform in Pakistan," *Asian Affairs* vol. 6, no. 2 (Summer 1988).

Ziring, Lawrence. *Pakistan: The Enigma of Political Development* (London: Dawson, 1980).

13
PARTIES AND LEADERS

Thus far our analysis has centered on the underlying foundations of Pakistan's existence as a nation-state. We have noted that Islam is the raison d'être of Pakistan and that the effects of divisive regionalism are the primary threat to the continued vitality of the state. In the next two chapters we shall shift our focus of analysis to a discussion of Pakistan's political history. This chapter explores political parties and leadership; the next discusses Pakistan's fluid constitutional structures and the resultant content of public policy.

Political Parties: The Failure of Interest Aggregation

Political parties have not worked very well in Pakistan—though not for want of trying: Literally hundreds of political parties have existed during Pakistan's brief history. But, with few short-lived exceptions, such parties have been ineffective in performing the functions usually associated with such institutions—interest articulation, interest aggregation, and policy formulation. Of course, other institutions have taken up the slack; that is, the policy process in Pakistan has typically bypassed political parties, with effective power going to unelected advisers of heads of government and to civil and military bureaucrats.

There are four explanations for such ineffectiveness. The first is personalism. Pakistan's political parties (with the possible exception of the religious parties) have been both the creations and the vehicles of at most a few individuals. When such individuals have died, the parties associated with them have died as well. For instance, the Muslim League dispersed into warring factions after its leader and motive force, Muhammad Ali Jinnah, died in 1948; then it disintegrated following Liaquat Ali Khan's assassination three years later.

Second, political parties in Pakistan have often fallen prey to regionalism. An examination of Tables 13.1–13.3 reveals that political parties have derived most of their strength from limited regional constituencies: PPP—Sindh and

TABLE 13.1 Pakistan National Assembly Elections, 1970–1971

Party	Punjab	Sindh	NWFP	Balochistan	West Pakistan	East Pakistan	Total
AL	–	–	–	–	–	160	160
PPP	62	18	1	–	81	–	81
NAP	–	–	3	3	6	–	6
PML(Q)	1	1	7	–	9	–	9
PML(C)	2	–	–	–	2	–	2
CML	7	–	–	–	7	–	7
PDP	–	–	–	–	–	1	1
JUP	–	–	6	1	7	–	7
JUI	4	3	–	–	7	–	7
JI	1	2	1	–	4	–	4
IND	5	3	7	–	15	1	16
Total	82	27	25	4	138	162	300

For West Pakistan, the parties in this table are arranged according to their ideological positions. The Pakistan People's Party (PPP) under Bhutto and the National Awami Party (NAP) and Wali Khan were on the left of the political spectrum, whereas the three Muslim Leagues—PML(Q), PML(C), and CML, under Abdul Qayum Khan, Pir of Pagaro, and Daultana, respectively— belonged to the center. On the right were the three religious parties: Jamiat-ul-Ulema-i-Pakistan (JUP) under Maulana Hazarvi [JU(H)], Jamiat-ul-Ulema-i-Islam (JUI) under Maulana Mufti Mahmud, and Jamaat-i-Islami (JI) under Maulana Maududi.

Source: Adapted from Craig Baxter, "Pakistan Votes, 1970," Asian Survey, vol. 11, no. 3 (March 1971), p. 211.

to a lesser extent Punjab; Awami League—East Pakistan; National Awami Party (NAP)—Balochistan and NWFP; IJI—Punjab; MQM—urban Sindh.

A third explanation for the ineffectiveness of political parties in Pakistan is factionalism. This factor is primarily attributable to the operation of kinship (biradari) politics. In Pakistan politics is often viewed as a struggle between competing kinship groups for scarce resources and for prestige and honor. Political parties, then, become loose confederations of kinship groups; and political leaders are typically prominent members of important families. Loyalty to such parties, therefore, is generated by neither doctrinal nor ideological allegiance to a program, but rather by individuals within the party. When personal considerations or rivalries intervene (and they often do), leaders typically abandon the party and take their followers with them.

Finally, party politics in Pakistan has been subject to a history of repression. Martial law during civilian regimes (in which curbs are placed on political activities) and direct military government (in which political parties are typically banned) are the rules and not the exceptions of Pakistan's political process. Restrictions on political party activity were in effect during most of President Zia's regime. Such restrictions were lifted in March 1986.

TABLE 13.2 National Assembly Results, 1977

Provinces	Total Seats	PPP	PNA	QML
Punjab	116[a]	108[a]	8	–
Sindh	43	32 (17 + 15[b])	11	–
NWFP	34 (28 + 8[c])	8	17	1
Balochistan	7	7 (3 + 4[b])	–	–
Total	200	155	36	1

The parties composing the PNA were Tehrik-i-Istiqlal (Asghar Khan), Jamaat-i-Islami (Mian Tufail Muhammed), Jamiat-ul-Ulema-i-Islam (Mufti Mahmud), Jamiat-ul-Ulema-i-Pakistan (Shah Ahmed Noorani), Pakistan Muslim League (Pir Pagaro), National Democratic Party (Sardar Sherbaz Mazari), Pakistan Democratic Party (Nawabzada Nasrullah Khan), Khakzar Tehrik (Muhammed Ashraf Khan), and Azad Kashmir Muslim Conference (Sardar Abdul Qayyum).

[a]Includes Islamabad's one seat.
[b]Elected "unopposed."
[c]Tribal areas' seats that went to independents.

Source: Adapted from Sharif al Mujahid, "The 1977 Pakistani Elections: An Analysis," in Manzooruddin Ahmad, Contemporary Pakistan: Politics, Economy and Society (Karachi: Royal Book Company, 1982), p. 83.

Muslim League: One and Several

The Muslim League was the only major political party in existence in Pakistan at independence, and it possessed all of the advantages a party could wish for. Nearly every Muslim in Pakistan claimed allegiance to the party (62 of 76 members of the First Constituent Assembly were members of the Muslim League; most others were Hindus); the party was associated with the dynamic and exceedingly popular Muhammad Ali Jinnah, who was the governor general and president of the Constituent Assembly; and finally, the Muslim League had few institutional rivals. Yet fewer than ten years later the party had disintegrated into numerous warring factions. Why? First, the two individuals most closely associated with the party, Jinnah and Liaquat, died shortly after independence. With the death of these party stalwarts went the image of the Muslim League as the party of all of Pakistan. Second, the Muslim League was never able to develop a coherent ideology. The party had been formed in order to secure the independence of the Muslim state from British India. After independence, however, its task was much less clear. These difficulties were compounded by the party's continued attempts to be a party of national unity (a vestige of Jinnah's influence), integrating all shades of opinion under its mantle. Such attempts

TABLE 13.3   National Assembly Results, 1988

Party	Punjab	Sindh	NWFP	Balochistan	FATA[a]	Total
PPP	53	31	7	1	–	92
IJI[b]	44	–	8	2	–	54
MQM	–	13	–	–	–	13
JUI/F	–	–	3	4	–	7
PAI	3	–	–	–	–	3
ANP	–	–	3	–	–	3
BNA	–	–	–	2	–	2
NPP	2	–	–	–	–	2
JUI/D	–	–	1	–	–	1
Independents	11	2	3	2	8	26
Undeclared	3	–	1	–	–	4
Total	116	46	26	11	8	207

The full names of the parties are PPP–Pakistan People's Party; IJI–Islami Jamhoori Ittehad; MQM–Muhajir Qaumi Mahaz; JUI/F–Jamiat-ul-Ulema-i-Islam (Fazlur Rehman); PAI–Pakistan Awami Ittehad; ANP–Awami National Party; BNA—Balochistan National Alliance; NPP–National People's Party; JUI/D—Jamiat-ul-Ulema-i-Islam (Darkhwasti).

[a]Federally administered tribal areas.
[b]The IJI was a nine-party alliance. Its members were Pakistan Muslim League (Forward Bloc), Khakshar Party, JI, JUI/D, Markazi Jamiat ahle-Hadith, Azad Group, Nizam-i-Mustafa Group, Hizbe Jihad, and Jamiat Masheikh.

Source: Adapted from Yaseen Rizvi, Pakistan Elections '88 (Lahore: Print-Point, 1988), p. 76.

rendered the remnants of the Muslim League's platform vague and plati-
tudinous. Third, the constitutional impasse, peculiar to the formation of the
new state and caused by the unresolved issues of political representation
and the status of Islam, proved to be beyond the organizational capabilities
of the party.

Accordingly, in 1954, the Muslim League was routed in the East Pakistan
provincial election (see Chapter 18), winning only 10 of 309 seats; and in
1955 it lost its majority in the West Pakistan Legislative Assembly to the
landlord-dominated, Punjab-centered Republican party.[1] Between 1955 and
1958, the fortunes of the party continued to decline. In 1957 the Muslim
League lost control of the national government, and in 1958 Ayub Khan
(1907–1970) staged a bloodless military coup. Subsequent to 1958, the
Muslim League has remained largely defunct, although several parties have
borrowed its name, including the party of Muhammad Khan Junejo, Pakistan's
prime minister, 1985–1988.

Jamaat-i-Islami

Islamic parties have been the most ideologically consistent parties in
Pakistan; and the most articulate and largest of these has been the *Jamaat-*

i-Islami (JI), or Association of Islam. The JI was founded in 1941 in Lahore by Maulana Maududi. Its general aim, shared for the most part by all Islamic parties in Pakistan, has been to increase the significance of Islam in the state by promoting Islamic policies, practices, and politicians. Since the early 1950s the JI has campaigned on the platform of reorganizing the polity along lines suggested by the practices of the pious caliphate of Islam (A.D. 632–661). Accordingly, the JI has opposed westernization—for example by campaigning against capitalism, socialism, and party-based representative government. It has also opposed the adoption of "corrupt" Western social practices such as bank interest, birth control, relaxed sexual mores, and women's emancipation. In the place of Western institutions and practices it foresees the adoption of a state ruled by Shariah (Islamic law). In such a state a pious *amir* (nonhereditary king) will rule with the consent of learned Islamic legal scholars (i.e., ulema).[2] Members of the JI have been prominent in Pakistan's politics since independence. The JI was the dominant voice for ulema interests in the debates preceding the adoption of Pakistan's first constitution; it was active in the anti-Ahmadiyya communal disturbances of 1953; and it led the opposition to the Family Law Ordinance (1961) and participated in opposition politics from 1950 to 1977. The JI is highly structured, in that it is organized around party cells found in universities, and membership in the party is tightly controlled, based solely on selection by the leadership. Consequently, most of the JI's members are university educated, although socially they represent the urban lower-middle class. Despite its ideological prominence, the JI has enjoyed only limited electoral success in Pakistan.

Regional Parties

As previously noted, national parties in Pakistan have derived the bulk of their respective support from particular regions of the state, but their platforms have typically attempted to attract all of Pakistan's voters. The two most successful parties in Pakistan's history, the Muslim League (with strongholds in West Pakistan, particularly Punjab and Sindh) and the PPP (Sindh and Punjab), were no exceptions to this rule; neither were the Islamic parties: JI (Punjab and Karachi), Jamiat-ul-Ulema-i-Islam (JUI—NWFP and Balochistan), and Jamiat-ul-Ulema-i-Pakistan (JUP—Sindh). However, numerous other parties have made regional autonomy the focus of their appeal. The National Awami Party (NAP) and its successors, the National Democratic Party (NDP) and the Awami National Party (ANP), have derived the bulk of their strength from Pathan voters in the NWFP and Balochistan. Similarly, Baloch autonomist interests have been voiced by the Balochistan National Alliance (BNA); Sindhi separatist sentiments by the Jiye Sindh; and expatriate Punjab and Pathan community interests in Sindh and Balochistan by the

Punjabi Pushtun Ittehad (PPI—Punjab Pathan Alliance). But the most significant ethnoregionalist party to emerge from the 1988 elections was the MQM. The MQM represents the interests of Pakistan's muhajir community that resides for the most part in Karachi and Hyderabad. In the 1988 national assembly elections the MQM won 13 seats, making it the third largest party in Pakistan.

Islami Jamhoori Ittehad (IJI)

The Islamic Democratic Alliance is a composite party that formed in 1988 to contest the general elections. The IJI consists of nine parties, but two parties predominate—the Pakistan Muslim League (Forward Bloc) and the JI. The former is a faction of the PML that remained loyal to Zia after he dissolved the national assembly on May 29, 1988. Under the leadership of Mian Nawaz Sharif, the IJI won 32% of the votes in the national assembly election but, more significantly, won a plurality of seats in the Punjab provincial assembly election and accordingly formed the government. From his position as chief minister of the Punjab, Nawaz Sharif and his IJI emerged as the main opposition to Benazir's government. On November 1, 1989, Sharif led a no-confidence motion against Benazir's government in the national assembly. It failed by only 12 votes.[3] Nine months later, on August 2, 1990, this goal of the IJI was accomplished when President Ghulam Ishaq Khan dismissed Benazir's government and named Ghulam Mustapha Jatoi (1931–) as caretaker prime minister pending elections announced for October 1990.

Pakistan People's Party (PPP)

The PPP was largely the creation of one man, Zulfiqar Ali Bhutto. As such, the party was as enigmatic, complex, and full of contradictions as the man himself. On the one hand, the party represented a left-leaning populist movement in that Bhutto espoused the cause of "Islamic socialism," which attempted to blend the spirit of Islam with socialism. The resulting policies of such a blend included land reform, to favor the peasants; the nationalization of industries, to decrease the power of the industrialists; and administrative reforms, to limit the power of the unelected bureaucratic elite. Indeed, in its early days the PPP counted many leftist intellectuals among its members. On the other hand, the PPP was built upon the foundations of the old ruling class of Pakistan (the landed gentry), and the style of politics practiced by Bhutto was reminiscent of biradari factionalism, replete with personal vendettas and periodic purges of PPP members. Moreover, as many analysts of PPP policies have argued, the outcomes of the reforms contemplated by the party fell far short of its ambitious platform.

The PPP came to power by winning a majority of the West Pakistan seats in the 1970 election; it won with an even greater margin in 1977.

However, the nine-party alliance that merged to contest the 1977 election, the Pakistan National Alliance (PNA),[4] claimed that the election had been rigged. Civil unrest ensued during the spring and early summer, and General Zia staged a coup in July. Bhutto was eventually imprisoned on the charge of complicity in the attempted murder of a political rival (Ahmad Raza Kasuri, whose father was mistakenly murdered), and after a lengthy trial he was hanged on April 4, 1979.

Zia banned the PPP along with other parties in 1979, but after party restrictions were lifted in early 1986, the party reemerged as a potent political force under the dynamic leadership of Benazir Bhutto (1952–), Zulfiqar's daughter. Although the PPP was able to secure a plurality in the national assembly elections of 1988, the party's mandate was much narrower than it had been during the elder Bhutto's regime. The PPP entered into a coalition with the MQM and several independent MNAs to form the government in December 1988.

Leaders

It is beyond the scope of this chapter to present a detailed treatment of the political careers of Pakistan's leaders. We may find it useful, however, to look briefly at the political backgrounds of seven of Pakistan's most significant leaders: Muhammad Ali Jinnah, Liaquat Ali Khan, Maulana Maududi, Ayub Khan, Zulfiqar Ali Bhutto, Zia-ul-Haq, and Benazir Bhutto. Table 13.4 presents a list of Pakistan's heads of state and government since partition.

Muhammad Ali Jinnah: The Father of Pakistan

Jinnah (1876–1948) was the son of a wealthy Khoja Ishmaili Shiite merchant. His father, who expected the young Jinnah to take over the family business, sent him to London to study commerce. Jinnah found the study of law more congenial to his tastes, however, and in 1895 he was admitted to the bar at Lincoln's Inn. Already a member of the Congress party, Jinnah in 1913 also joined the Muslim League with the intention of merging the League with the programs of the larger and longer-established Indian National Congress. His efforts helped pave the way toward the Lucknow Pact (1916), a cooperative agreement between the Muslim League and the Congress that later led to the Government of India Act of 1919 (see Chapter 1). But Muslim League–Congress unity proved short-lived, and Jinnah resigned his Congress party membership in 1920 after disagreeing with Mahatma Gandhi's tactics of *satyagraha* (passive resistance). Between 1920 and 1937 Jinnah waged an increasingly difficult battle against the forces of Hindu-Muslim disunity, but his political strategy changed following the Muslim

TABLE 13.4   Heads of State and of Government

Leaders	Position	Dates
Muhammad Ali Jinnah	Governor General	August 1947–September 1948
Liaquat Ali Khan	Prime Minister	August 1947–October 1951
Khawaja Nazimuddin	Governor General	September 1948–October 1951
Ghulam Muhammad	Governor General	October 1951–August 1955
Khawaja Nazimuddin	Prime Minister	October 1951–April 1953
Muhammad Ali Bogra	Prime Minister	April 1953–August 1955
Iskander Mizra	Governor General/President	August 1955–October 1958
Chaudury Muhammad Ali	Prime Minister	August 1955–September 1956
H. S. Suhrawardy	Prime Minister	September 1956–October 1957
I. I. Chundrigar	Prime Minister	October 1957–December 1957
Firoz Khan Noon	Prime Minister	December 1957–October 1958
Muhammad Ayub Khan	Chief Martial Law Adm. (CMLA)/President	October 1958–March 1969
Muhammad Yahya Khan	President	March 1969–December 1971
Zulfiqar Ali Bhutto	President/Prime Minister	December 1971–July 1977
Muhammad Zia-ul-Haq	CMLA/President	July 1977–August 1988
Muhammad Khan Junejo	Prime Minister	March 1985–May 1988
Ghulam Ishaq Khan	President	August 1988–
Benazir Bhutto	Prime Minister	December 1988–August 1990
Ghulam Mustapha Jatoi	Prime Minister (caretaker)	August 1990–

League's humiliating defeat in the provincial elections of 1937. Accordingly, Jinnah came to espouse the Two Nation Theory and eventually sponsored the Lahore Resolution of 1940. His arguments were twofold: (1) In a united India, Muslim interests would be dominated by the majority community Hindus; and (2) the prospects of an Islamic state were in danger of subversion by such an outcome. Under this plank the Muslim League came to dominate Muslim politics in the subcontinent, and Jinnah, as president of the party (1934–1948), emerged as its unchallenged leader.

Jinnah was an unlikely figure to assume such a role. He was an aloof, haughty, elitist intellectual. He had never learned Urdu or Bengali, and his personal life was quite secular. However, Jinnah was brilliant and tireless, and his ability to deal with the British as well as with the legal complexities engendered by the prospects of partition made him an indispensable vehicle of Muslim nationalism.

The Quaid-i-Azam (great leader) died on September 11, 1948, within thirteen months of assuming the position of governor general of Pakistan. Although he had accomplished much during his lifetime, his legacy is mixed. His dominance of the Muslim League and his assumption of the governor generalship, perhaps necessary for pursuing the goal of Pakistan and preserving unity after independence, nevertheless retarded the growth of representative democracy in the state by providing a precedent for one-man rule. Similarly, Jinnah's Muslim League, crafted to secure its nationalist demands, proved ineffective as a political party after independence.

Liaquat Ali Khan: The Lieutenant

Liaquat's political career was mainly undertaken in the shadow of Jinnah. Liaquat (1895–1951) was born in Karnal, Punjab, the son of an important landlord. Like Jinnah, he was liberally educated at Aligarh, Allahabad, and finally Oxford; also like Jinnah, he was a lawyer. Unlike Jinnah, however, Liaquat lacked personal charisma, and his political constituency was small. A younger son, he pursued his political career in the United Provinces (now Uttar Pradesh) rather than in the Punjab.

The basis of Liaquat's power was his close relationship to Jinnah. The latter had selected the young inexperienced lawyer as general secretary of the Muslim League in 1936. The choice was propitious as Liaquat proved an astute organizer; perhaps more important, he was able to hold the disparate factions of the party together. In 1947, Liaquat became Pakistan's first prime minister, although he remained in the background as Jinnah effectively ran the government from the post of governor-general.

After Jinnah's death, Liaquat became the dominant personality of the government of Pakistan, but most analysts agree that Liaquat's performance in office was ineffectual. First, his leadership was challenged by the Bengali, Khwaja Nazimuddin, who served as governor general (1948–1951), and later as prime minister (see Chapter 18). Second, the unresolved issues of political representation and the status of Islam, muted as long as Jinnah lived, were joined during Liaquat's tenure. Finally, Liaquat could not accomplish the critical task of supervising the drafting of a constitution. Perhaps such issues would have been resolved if Liaquat had lived, but the Quaid-i-Millat (leader of the nation) was felled by an assassin's bullet in Rawalpindi, on October 16, 1951.

Maulana Syed Abul A'la Maududi: Advocate of an Islamic State

Of the leaders discussed in this section only Maulana Maududi (1903–1979) never held political office. Nevertheless, Maududi's contribution to politics in Pakistan is very significant. Maududi was born in Aurangabad (Maharashtra, India), the son of a lawyer who later abandoned the profession because it was "un-Islamic." Maududi studied at a *madrassah* (Islamic religious school) and later took matriculation in religious studies. His formal scholarly studies were cut short by his father's death, and Maududi entered on a career in journalism. Soon Maududi became the editor of a small politico-religious journal and, using this as a base, became well known for his writings. In 1937, Muhammad Iqbal sponsored Maududi's activities by establishing him in a *waqf* (religious endowment) near Lahore. It was here that Maududi wrote his most influential works and established the Jamaat-i-Islami.

Maududi was a prolific writer. He wrote in Urdu, but because JI party members served as his translators, his books and pamphlets gained a wide audience in English and Arabic as well. His primary vehicle was the hastily written, mass-distributed, topical, and propagandistic religious pamphlet. During his career, Maududi authored literally hundreds of such pamphlets, which, when collected and edited, formed his dozens of published books. His best-known book is *The Islamic Law and Constitution.*[5]

Maududi's goal was to increase the importance of Islam in Pakistan and, by the same token, to increase the influence of the JI. His active espousal of related causes often landed him in prison (1947, 1953, 1964 and 1967). To a certain extent such "persecution" increased the appeal of both Maududi and the JI; however, the appeal of the JI has always been limited to a relatively small number of committed believers. The JI received less than 3% of the vote in the 1970 elections, but the legacy of Maududi's writings belies such limited popular support.

Muhammad Ayub Khan: Soldier-Statesman

Ayub Khan (1907–1970) was the quintessential "British generation" military officer.[6] Ayub was born in the village of Rehana, fifty miles north of Rawalpindi; his father was a *subedar major* (noncommissioned officer) in the British Indian Army. Ayub was never a very good student (he stated in his autobiography that he failed the sixth grade),[7] but after diligent work he was eventually admitted to Aligarh. Ayub's teachers, impressed by his "sporting ability" and family background, encouraged him to undertake studies at Sandhurst (the British military academy), where he graduated with a commission in 1929. Ayub fought with British forces in Burma during the Second World War. After the war, as one of a handful of Muslim Sandhurst-trained graduates, his rise was meteoric. In 1951 he was selected by Liaquat as Pakistan's first Pakistani army commander-in-chief. (The post had previously been held by British officers under contract.)

From his background and training Ayub internalized two characteristics that were greatly to influence the course of Pakistan's history. First, Ayub was firmly wedded to the integrity of the Pakistan Army. Second, Ayub distrusted the "disloyalty" and vacillations of Pakistan's politicians. Therefore, when (according to Ayub) he was offered control of government in 1954 (by Governor General Ghulam Muhammad), he turned it down because it would damage the prestige of the armed forces. But four years later, in the midst of the civil unrest caused by "self-serving politicians, wrangling over portfolios," and Iskander Mirza's abrogation of the 1956 constitution, Ayub moved.[8] On October 5, 1958, through the strategic repositioning of two brigades of troops, and without a single shot being fired, Ayub became chief martial law administrator. Ayub remained the head of state and of government (after February 1960 as a "civilian" president) until his forced resignation on March 25, 1969.

Zulfiqar Ali Bhutto: Islamic Socialist and Champion of the Old Order

Bhutto (1927–1979) was perhaps the most enigmatic of all of Pakistan's leaders. He was the son of Sir Shahnawaz Bhutto, a wealthy and well-known landlord from central Sindh. Sir Shahnawaz was very active in politics, and he bequeathed to his son the task of looking after the landed interests of his family as well as those of other landed aristocrats in the province. This influence contrasted with Bhutto's earned status as a member of the urban intelligentsia. Bhutto attended Oxford University and the universities at Southern California and Berkeley. The tensions between these interests were to shape the political career of Pakistan's most skilled politician.[9]

At the age of thirty-one Bhutto was made minister of fuel and natural resources in Ayub's first cabinet; later he became foreign minister. Bhutto used these positions as a base for developing his own political constituency. In the process, he increasingly espoused a leftist position. Accordingly, as minister of fuels he worked out an oil exploration agreement with the Soviet Union, and as foreign minister he worked toward strengthening Pakistan-China relations. Following the 1965 war with India, and perhaps sensing that Ayub's hold on the government was slipping, Bhutto broke with Ayub and became openly critical of Ayub's foreign policy. He was subsequently dismissed from the cabinet in 1967. Outside of government at that point, Bhutto set about building a national following through extensive travel, speechmaking, and the publication of several books. Bhutto's support for Third World causes, his socialist rhetoric, and his outspoken criticism of the unpopular Ayub regime won him many followers, particularly among students and intellectuals in West Pakistan's urban areas. He also organized the Pakistan People's party (PPP).

Following the 1970 election and the civil war, Bhutto emerged in the anomalous position of civilian head of a military regime; his official title upon assuming office was president and chief martial law administrator. The termination of martial law and the promulgation of the 1973 constitution redefined his position as prime minister.

It must be stressed here that Bhutto's style of leadership was greatly influenced by his "feudal" background. Although he espoused a populist egalitarian domestic program and a liberal nonaligned foreign policy, Bhutto's approach to politics was autocratic. He perceived opposition to his policies as a personal affront, and the history of his rule is replete with the political repression of his rivals. Ironically perhaps, Bhutto fell victim to a comparatively minor gaffe (i.e., minor relative to the enormity of other alleged crimes)[10]— namely, complicity in the bungled assassination of a former member of the PPP turned political opponent. Bhutto was eventually convicted of murder, his appeal was rejected by a 4 to 3 decision of the Supreme Court, and he was hanged on April 4, 1979.

Mohammad Zia-ul-Haq: The "Reluctant" Leader

Like Ayub, Zia (1924–1988) was a career military officer serving with British Indian forces during World War II. He received his commission in 1945 from the Indian Military Academy at Dehra Dun. Zia was born in Jullundur, East Punjab (India). After twenty years in the lower ranks of Pakistan's officer corps, he was promoted to colonel in 1968, brigadier in 1969, and major general in 1972. In 1975, Zia was appointed lieutenant general and corps commander.[11] Up to this point, his military career was unexceptionable: He had a deserved reputation as a devout Muslim, he had avoided political intrigue, and on many occasions he had proven his loyalty to the state and to the chain of command. These characteristics attracted Bhutto (who since assuming office had feared another military coup), and he accordingly appointed Zia chief of army staff over the heads of several more senior generals in 1976.

Thus the military coup of 1977 headed by General Zia came as a surprise to Bhutto. Perhaps Zia was a reluctant participant in the coup, his hand forced by the military's long-standing grievances with the Bhutto regime and by the deteriorating law and order situation following the 1977 election.[12] Regardless of motive, Zia maintained power for over eleven years, first as chief martial law administrator (1977–1985) and as president (1979–1988). Zia died in a plane crash on August 17, 1988. Some believe he was assassinated.

Benazir Bhutto: Daughter of Destiny

Benazir Bhutto's life has been shaped greatly by her role as the daughter of Zulfiqar Ali Bhutto. At the insistence of her father, Benazir was educated abroad (Radcliffe College and Oxford University). He had entertained hopes that his daughter would undertake a career in the foreign service. Such plans were derailed, however, following Zia's military coup in 1977, and the eventual execution of Zulfiqar Bhutto in 1979. To Benazir, the military's actions were illegal, the execution of her father "murder," and her father's wrongful death had made him a martyr (*shaheed*). Accordingly, she became obsessed with avenging her father's death, restoring the PPP to power, and reestablishing her father's 1973 constitution.[13]

Through a series of propitious circumstances, including Zia's dissolution of the national assembly in May 1988 and the sudden deaths of Zia and several senior military officers before a new national assembly could be elected, she managed partially to accomplish her goals in December 1988. At that time Benazir led the PPP to a narrow victory in the national assembly elections and became prime minister. However, her task remains unfinished. During her administration (1988–1990), her policy options were constrained both by the corporate interests of the military and by the constitutional structure her government inherited.

*   *   *

In sum, perhaps nothing highlights the differences in the political fortunes of Pakistan and its South Asian neighbors (particularly India and Sri Lanka) more sharply than a discussion of political parties and leadership. Pakistan has suffered since partition from weak and ineffective political parties, as has Bangladesh since its independence in 1971. By contrast, India has benefited from the legacy and continuing resilience of the Congress party, and Sri Lanka is the better for the continued vitality of opposition between the long-established UNP and the SLFP. Similarly, Pakistan's political history has demonstrated a discontinuous pattern of successive periods of paternalistic leadership (as has that of Bangladesh). The Ayub regime was replaced by the Bhutto regime, which in turn was replaced by the Zia regime, which in turn was replaced by the Benazir regime, which in turn has been dismissed. Each of these transfers of power attempted to sever ties with the past, by reversing and discrediting the policies of predecessor regimes. By contrast, Indian leadership has demonstrated a remarkable degree of continuity, at least until the election of V. P. Singh, through the successive predominance of members of the Nehru family.

Notes

1. K. K. Aziz, *Party Politics in Pakistan 1947–1958* (Islamabad: National Commission on Historical and Cultural Research, 1976), pp. 105–110.

2. The best overview of Maududi's political beliefs is found in Sayed Riaz Ahmad, *Maulana Maududi and the Islamic State* (Lahore: People's Publishing House, 1976).

3. For details of the politics of the no-confidence motion, see Zaffar Abbas, "Win Some, Lose Some," *Herald* (Karachi: December 1988), pp. 25–43.

4. The Pakistan National Alliance (PNA) was a loose coalition of nine political parties formed to contest the 1977 general elections. (See Table 13.2 for its membership.)

5. Syed Abul A'la Maududi, *The Islamic Law and Constitution,* 7th ed. (Lahore: Islamic Publications, 1980).

6. This useful categorization is found in Stephen P. Cohen, *The Pakistan Army* (Berkeley: University of California Press, 1984), pp. 55–63.

7. Mohammed Ayub Khan, *Friends, Not Masters: A Political Autobiography* (Karachi: Oxford University Press, 1967), p. 4.

8. Ibid., pp. 52, 70–76.

9. This theme is developed fully in Shahid Javed Burki, *Pakistan Under Bhutto, 1971–1977* (New York: St. Martin's Press, 1980).

10. After Bhutto was removed from office, the Zia regime published a three-volume White Paper exposing in great detail Bhutto's alleged excesses. See Government of Pakistan, *White Paper of the Misuses of the Media; White Paper on the Conduct of the General Elections of 1977; White Paper on the Performance of the Bhutto Regime* (Islamabad: Manager, Printing Corporation of Pakistan Press, 1978).

11. Lawrence Ziring, *Pakistan: The Enigma of Political Development* (London: Dawson, 1980), p. 197.

12. See, for example, Cohen, *The Pakistan Army*, pp. 107–110.

13. See Benazir Bhutto, *Daughter of Destiny* (New York: Simon and Schuster, 1989).

Suggested Readings

Afzal, M. Rafique. *Political Parties in Pakistan 1947–1958* (Islamabad: National Commission on Historical and Cultural Research, 1976).

Ahmad, Sayed Riaz. *Maulana Maududi and the Islamic State* (Lahore: People's Publishing House, 1976).

Aziz, K. K. *Party Politics in Pakistan 1947–1958* (Islamabad: National Commission on Historical and Cultural Research, 1976).

Bhutto, Benazir. *Daughter of Destiny* (New York: Simon and Schuster, 1989).

Bhutto, Zulfikar Ali. *If I Am Assassinated* (Delhi: Vikas Press, 1979).

_____ . *Myth of Independence* (Karachi: Oxford University Press, 1969).

Burki, Shahid Javed. *Pakistan Under Bhutto, 1971–1977* (New York: St. Martin's Press, 1980).

Feldman, Herbert. *Revolution in Pakistan: A Study of the Martial Law Administration* (London: Oxford University Press, 1967).

_____ . *The End and the Beginning: Pakistan 1969–1971* (London: Oxford University Press, 1970).

Gallup Pakistan. *Pakistan at the Polls: Gallup Political Weather Report, November 1988* (Islamabad: Gallup Pakistan, 1988).

Khan, Mohammed Ayub. *Friends, Not Masters: A Political Autobiography* (Karachi: Oxford University Press, 1967).

Waseem, Mohammed. *Politics and the State in Pakistan* (Lahore: Progressive Publishers, 1989).

Wolpert, Stanley. *Jinnah of Pakistan* (New York: Oxford University Press, 1984).

Ziring, Lawrence. *Pakistan: The Enigma of Political Development* (London: Dawson, 1980).

_____ . *The Ayub Khan Era* (Syracuse, N.Y.: Syracuse University Press, 1971).

14
CONSTITUTIONAL STRUCTURES AND POLICY IMPLEMENTATION

This chapter has two purposes: to outline Pakistan's confusing and complex constitutional history and to discuss the policies implemented by Pakistan's three longest-standing leaders—Ayub Khan, Zulfiqar Ali Bhutto, and Zia-ul-Haq—and by its most recent leader, Benazir Bhutto. As we shall see, the fit between the constitutional structures of the state and the policies pursued by its leaders is an imperfect one.

The Structures of Government:
Pakistan's Constitutions

Constitutional government in Pakistan has been more sham than substance. Pakistan has had five constitutions in its brief history: one inherited at independence (Government of India Act, 1935, as modified by the India Independence Act, 1947 [see Chapter 1]) and four indigenous creations (1956, 1962, 1972, and 1973). Pakistan has also been governed at times without benefit of a written constitution (1958–1962, 1969–1971); under a suspended constitution (1977–1985); and under a "modified" though "restored" constitution (1985–). Ideally, a constitution is the framework of a government's intentions; it describes structural arrangements, allocates functional powers, and establishes limits to political authority. But constitutions, however artfully drafted, are always reflective of the state they represent. A state cannot overcome its problems solely through constitution making. Pakistan is a case in point. This section outlines the characteristics of Pakistan's seven constitutional phases since independence.

Phase One: 1947–1956

At partition (1947), Pakistan was declared a free sovereign dominion to be governed until a constitution could be formulated by the Constituent

Assembly acting under the Government of India Act 1935, as amended by the Indian Independence Act. Until the new constitution could be drafted, the Constituent Assembly (CA) doubled as a National Assembly; in its latter role the CA was empowered to enact legislation. Therefore, the combination of pre-partition enactments and CA legislation constituted the effective law of the state. The duties of the governor general, however, were ambiguous. At the crux of the ambiguity were these questions: whether the CA could pass laws without the consent of the governor general, and whether the governor general had the legal authority to disband the CA. This ambiguity remained unchallenged until 1954.

The task of constitution making (see Chapter 11) facing the CA proved to be very difficult. It was so difficult, in fact, that Ghulam Muhammad (governor general, 1951–1955) tested the aforementioned constitutional ambiguity by disbanding the CA on October 24, 1954. He argued that since the CA was unable to produce a constitution, it was prolonging its existence at the expense of the nation. Ghulam Muhammad's action was upheld by the Supreme Court of Pakistan in 1955. The court argued that the governor general had the power not only to disband the CA but also to veto any legislation passed by it. Therefore, when the second Constituent Assembly was convened, it could do little more than follow the framework established by the governor general. Instead of a decentralized legislature-dominated system, a form of presidential government emerged. The viceregal tradition of a strong executive set apart from and superior to other political machinery had been reestablished.

Phase Two: 1956–1958

Pakistan's first indigenous constitution was promulgated on March 23, 1956. It established Pakistan as an Islamic republic and replaced the governor general with a president. The constitution was described as "federal in form and parliamentary in composition," but objective circumstances in the state made both claims dubious. First, as a means of muting the question of representation for East Pakistan, the new governor general, Iskander Mirza, amalgamated the provinces of West Pakistan into "One Unit" in October 1955. This arrangement, which was to persist until 1970, negated any federal solution to Pakistan's regional problem. With only two units in the federation, and with one holding effective control, the possibility of meaningful federalism was nil. Second, by 1956, the prospects of parliamentary democracy had become bleak. The Muslim League, the only party of national unity, was in disarray. It commanded almost no support in East Pakistan, and its platform was virtually nonexistent. The only other significant party was the Awami League (its strength limited to East Pakistan), a party that ultimately repented its decision to support the 1956 constitution. Such party weakness led to extreme governmental instability. From August 1955 to October 1958, Pakistan had four separate governments. Under such circumstances, it is no wonder that the promised general elections to the National Assembly were never held, and that President Iskander Mirza (governor general, 1955–1956; president 1956–1958) was encouraged to suspend political activity, disband the legislative assembly, and declare martial law, thus abrogating the constitution less than three years after its promulgation.

Phase Three: 1958–1969

Pakistan was governed under martial law, without the benefit of a written constitution, from 1958 to 1962. General Ayub Khan, commander-in-chief of the army since 1951, staged a military coup in association with Iskander Mirza, but then forced Mirza out of the presidency and assumed the post himself in October 1958. Ayub's experience as a soldier had taught him that politicians had brought Pakistan to the brink of collapse. He therefore believed in a centralized government with strong leadership. These views were embodied in the institutions he created (see below); they were also embodied in Pakistan's second indigenous constitution, the latter largely a creation of Ayub.

Ayub's constitution was promulgated on March 1, 1962. The new constitution established a presidential form of government. Pakistan's president (Ayub) was to be both head of state and head of government. Essential decisions were to flow to and from his office, implemented by powerful civilian bureaucrats (members of the executive). The constitution also established the Basic Democrats (elected local officials) as an electoral college to select the president and members of the National Assembly and provincial legislatures. The 1962 constitution created a National Assembly, but its powers were weak; it was designed more to legitimize the decisions taken by the executive than to act as an independent legislature.

Phase Four: 1969–1971

Ayub resigned in March 1969. General Agha Muhammad Yahya Khan, his successor, suspended the 1962 constitution, ended the electoral role of the Basic Democrats, and reestablished martial law. Yahya also held national elections in December 1970. But the results of these elections proved unacceptable to Pakistan's ruling elite, and martial law, now termed "emergency rule," remained in force. Eventually General Yahya sent additional troops to East Pakistan, thereby precipitating the civil war and the dismemberment of the state.

Phase Five: 1972–1977

After the civil war, Pakistan's military was in a shambles and, accordingly, saw no choice but to hand over authority to the most successful candidate in West Pakistan in the 1970 election, Zulfiqar Ali Bhutto. Bhutto governed until 1973 under military-sponsored emergency legislation; indeed, Bhutto was originally installed as civilian chief martial law administrator (CMLA) and president.

Within four months Bhutto lifted martial law and institutionalized his regime within the context of an "interim constitution" in April 1972. Under the terms of this document, Bhutto as president was granted broad powers reminiscent of the powers granted viceroys under the British raj. For instance, the governors of the provinces were appointed by the president and were solely responsible to him, and the powers of the National Assembly were left weak and ineffective.

Once secure in office, Bhutto presided over the drafting of Pakistan's fourth constitution, which was promulgated on April 10, 1973. Unlike the interim constitution, the 1973 constitution called for the establishment of a parliamentary system. The prime minister, a post Bhutto assumed after resigning his position as president, would be the effective head of government, with the president reduced to merely a figurehead. Although the 1973 constitution established that the prime minister was to be elected by a majority of the National Assembly, many restrictions were placed upon this provision. For instance, votes of no confidence could not be passed unless the Assembly had already named the prospective successor to the prime minister, and for a no-confidence vote to be accepted, a majority of the prime minister's party had to cast votes of no confidence. Functionally, the powers granted Bhutto under the 1973 constitution were as broad as those delegated to Ayub under the 1962 constitution. Again, the viceregal tradition of Pakistan politics had prevailed.

Phase Six: 1977–1985

Bhutto was removed from office following mass disturbances led by the PNA, alleged voting irregularities, and a military coup on July 5, 1977. The successor regime under Zia-ul-Haq, however, chose not to abrogate the 1973 constitution. Rather, Zia's government suspended the operation of that constitution and governed directly through the promulgation of martial law regulations. Such regulations were defined by the courts as nonjusticiable and functionally equivalent to constitutional precepts. Between 1977 and 1981, Pakistan did not have legislative institutions. In 1981, Zia appointed the Majlis-i-Shura (Federal Council), but its functions were wholly advisory to the chief martial law administrator. In December 1984, Zia was elected through a referendum to the position of president. Nonpartisan elections (political parties were not allowed to compete although members of the "defunct" parties could do so as individuals) were held in February 1985 to choose members of the newly established national and provincial assemblies.

Phase Seven: 1985–

Before the newly elected assemblies could meet, President Zia announced long-expected modifications in Pakistan's constitution. Accordingly, on March 2, 1985, Zia promulgated the Revival of the Constitution of 1973 Order. This document ushered in the seventh phase of Pakistan's checkered constitutional history. Nominally a "revival" of the 1973 constitution, the presidential order fundamentally altered the terms of that constitution. Most important, the Revival Order dramatically increased the powers of the president. First, it reversed the lines of functional authority between the prime minister and the president. The president was given the power to appoint and dismiss the prime minister; and the prime minister's role was defined as largely advisory to the president. Second, it gave the president authority to appoint and dismiss the governors of the provinces and the federal ministers. Third, the president was given the functional authority to dissolve the National Assembly and the provincial assemblies.

In November 1985, the National Assembly passed the Constitution (Eighth Amendment) Act, which further legitimized Zia's constitutional order. Indeed, the Eighth Amendment protected actions taken during Zia's martial law regime with a retrospective constitutional justification. Article 270–A:2 states:

> All orders made, proceedings taken and acts done, by any authority or by any person, which were made, taken or done, or purported to have been made, taken or done, between the fifth day of July 1977, and the date on which this Article comes into force, in exercise of the powers derived from any Proclamation, President's Orders, Ordinances, Martial Law Regulations, Martial Law Orders, enactments, notifications, rules, orders, or bye-laws, or in execution of or in compliance with any order made or sentence passed by any authority in the exercise or purported exercise of powers as aforesaid, shall, notwithstanding any judgment of any Court, be deemed to be and always to have been validly made, taken or done and shall not be called in question in any Court on any ground whatsoever.[1]

In short, the Revival Order coupled with the Eighth Amendment substantially modified the 1973 constitution by concentrating predominant political authority in the hands of the president.

Despite such constitutional safeguards, the government under Prime Minister Muhammad Khan Junejo proved too independent for President Zia's liking and on May 29, 1988, Zia dissolved the national assembly and the provincial assemblies and promised to hold fresh elections by November. Before such elections could be held, however, Zia died in an airplane crash on August 17. Therefore, Zia's sudden death left Pakistan without a president, prime minister, national assembly, chief ministers, or provincial assemblies.

The chairman of the senate (not dissolved by Zia's order), Ghulam Ishaq Khan (1915–), became interim president. Under Ghulam Ishaq, elections were held in November that resulted in Benazir Bhutto's emergence as prime minister. In December, Ghulam Ishaq was elected to a five-year term in office as president.

The election of Benazir did not in itself change Zia's constitutional system. Although Benazir campaigned on a platform calling for the restoration of the 1973 constitution, her electoral mandate was too narrow to engineer the two-thirds majority needed to amend the constitution or to rescind the 8th Amendment. Moreover, Ghulam Ishaq has pursued policies that have served to protect the prerogatives of the office of the president. During 1989, Ghulam Ishaq won two much-publicized showdowns with Benazir that preserved intact the presidential powers of appointment of the senior judiciary and the military. Indeed, Ghulam Ishaq exercised his ultimate authority under the terms of the 1985 Constitution by dismissing Benazir's government and dissolving the national and provincial assemblies in August 1990. A diagram of Pakistan's government (1985–) is given in Figure 14.1.

Policies and Institutions

More important than the constitutional forms of government are the policies that Pakistan's leaders have pursued. This section traces the policies of four of Pakistan's most important leaders and the effects of their policies on the institutions of the state.

Ayub's Regime (1958–1969): The Military as Praetorians

Ayub believed in centralized authoritarian government. He was convinced that the people of Pakistan were too uneducated, divided, impoverished, and unsophisticated to form democratic institutions. He was also convinced that Pakistan's politicians were merely self-serving parasites on the body politic. The institutions established and the policies pursued by Ayub were reflective of these biases.

The system of government established by Ayub placed great reliance on Pakistan's civilian bureaucrats. To Ayub, bureaucrats were the ideal ruling elite: They were intelligent, well educated, loyal to the state, and experienced in administration. Therefore, the majority of Ayub's advisers and cabinet ministers were civilians with administrative, legal, financial, or agricultural experience. The most prominent group of such bureaucrats was the Civil Service of Pakistan (CSP), the lineal descendent of the Indian Civil Service (ICS) (see Chapter 1). During Ayub's regime the 400-odd members of the CSP came to dominate virtually every locus of authority in government.[2]

Figure 14.1   Structure of Pakistan's government

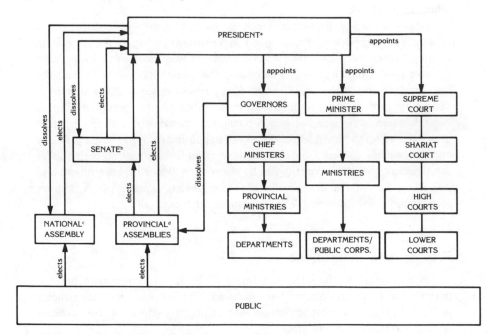

[a]President Zia-ul-Haq was elected directly by the public through a referendum for a five-year term commencing in March 1985. Subsequently, the president is to be selected by an "electoral college" consisting of members of the national assembly, senate, and provincial assemblies. Ghulam Ishaq Khan was elected by this method in December 1988.

[b]The Senate consists of 87 members. Fourteen are selected by each of the four provincial assemblies (56); 8 are elected from the Federal Tribal Areas; 3 are appointed by the President from the Federal Capital; and 5 are selected by each of the four provincial assemblies (20) to represent "ulema, technocrats, and other professionals."

[c]The National Assembly (Majlis-i-Shura) has a total of 237 members (207 Muslims, 10 non-Muslims, and 20 women).

[d]The Punjab Assembly consists of 260 members (240 Muslims, 12 women, and 8 non-Muslims); the Sindh Assembly has 114 members (100 Muslims, 5 women, and 9 non-Muslims); the NWFP Assembly has 87 members (80 Muslims, 4 women, 3 non-Muslims); and the Balochistan Assembly has 45 members (40 Muslims, 2 women, 3 non-Muslims).

Source: Government of Pakistan, Ministry of Justice and Parliamentary Affairs, The Constitution of the Islamic Republic of Pakistan (as modified up to 19th March 1985) (Islamabad: Manager, Printing Corporation of Pakistan Press, 1985).

Despite his military background, Ayub chose relatively few military officers to staff political or administrative posts.[3] The military served in Ayub's government (especially after 1962) as loyal "praetorians" (the emperor's loyal personal guards during the Roman Empire). Their role was to support the regime from the barracks. Ayub accordingly removed his military uniform shortly after taking office and otherwise consciously downplayed his military origins.

Given Ayub's distrust of politicians, it should come as no surprise that Ayub's regime limited the importance of the legislature, political parties, and elections. There was no National Assembly during the period of martial law, and the 1962 constitution established a very weak legislature. Although Ayub reluctantly allowed the operation of political parties, he placed restraints on the political activities of many politicians and restrictions on the freedom of the press. Ayub's own party, the Convention Muslim League, was a creation of its leader and never amounted to more than a label for Ayub's colleagues in government. Ayub did hold five national elections, but every one of them had a severely restricted franchise. In each case, the electors were the 80,000 Basic Democrats. During the first election, a referendum in 1960, this question was asked: "Do you have confidence in the President, Field Marshal Ayub Khan?" Of the total electorate, 96% answered "yes."[4] During the second, in 1962, members of the National Assembly and the provincial assemblies were elected by the Basic Democrats. The fourth, the 1965 presidential election, followed a new election for Basic Democrats and involved a contest between Ayub and the Combined Opposition party's candidate, Fatima Jinnah (Muhammad Ali Jinnah's sister). Given the nature of the franchise, Jinnah did surprisingly well, winning 34% of the total vote and 47% of the vote in East Pakistan.[5] The fifth, also in 1965, elected new assemblies at the national and provincial levels.

Ayub believed that Pakistan was not ready for democracy.[6] Therefore, in 1959 he established the Basic Democracies (BD) Scheme, a program designed to teach democracy from the "grass roots." Under the BD program, local councils were constituted at the union, tehsil (subdistrict), and district levels. Such councils were partially constituted by direct election, but above the union level a majority of each council's membership was appointed.[7] Functionally, the BD program was dominated by civilian bureaucrats. The functions performed by the councils were also severely constrained. Under Ayub, therefore, local government became increasingly dominated by bureaucrats, especially by the CSP. Ayub's government also introduced land reforms touted to reduce the power of landlords. The reforms placed ceilings on the individual holdings of agricultural land, but most analysts agree that they were ineffective.[8]

Ayub believed that capitalism would be the most direct path to economic development in Pakistan. Accordingly, he pursued industrial policies that favored business and capital-intensive investment. Indeed, Pakistan's gross domestic product grew at a very rapid rate (approximately 6% per year) during Ayub's regime. However, Ayub's policies also resulted in increased economic inequalities between East and West Pakistan, as most foreign aid and industrial investment were channeled to West Pakistan. His policies also increased the inequalities of income distribution within the population—the rich got richer, but the poor remained poor.[9]

The two most important accomplishments of Ayub's foreign policy were (1) the settlement in 1962 of the boundary dispute with the People's Republic of China, which paved the way for a lasting Sino-Pakistan friendship, and (2) the Indus Basin Treaty of 1960, which provided for the division of waters with India. Ayub's greatest failure was the 1965 war with India. At least before 1965, Ayub had cultivated the image of the United States' most trusted ally. However, during the 1965 war, the United States (Pakistan's only major arms supplier), in an effort to appear neutral, cut off military supplies to both Pakistan and India. This action, viewed as a betrayal of trust by Ayub, gravely damaged U.S.-Pakistan relations. In addition, the cut-off of arms forced Pakistan to the peace table. The Tashkent Agreement of 1966, negotiated by Ayub, ended the war but was viewed by many in Pakistan (including Foreign Minister Zulfiqar Ali Bhutto although he was a member of the negotiating party) as a sellout to India.

Many factors led to the resignation of Ayub in March 1969. Among them were Ayub's deteriorating health (he suffered a pulmonary embolism in 1968); the alleged corruption of his son, Capt. Gohar Ayub; Ayub Khan's increasing unpopularity in East Pakistan; and growing internal military disenchantment with his regime after the 1965 war. Pakistan's economy also suffered a downturn in the late 1960s. In any event, West Pakistan's urban masses took to the streets in 1968–1969 calling for the breakup of Ayub's system. The disturbances were spearheaded in West Pakistan by the gifted orator Zulfiqar Ali Bhutto. After some delay, East Pakistan joined the protests.

Bhutto and Reforms (1971–1977)

Bhutto had agitated since 1968 for the ending of Ayub's system of government. As a consequence, his task upon assuming office was to restructure institutions while increasing his personal authority.

One of the main targets of Bhutto's restructuring was the civil bureaucracy. Accordingly, in 1973, Bhutto purged 1,303 civil bureaucrats from the government and announced his administrative reforms. The reforms abolished all service cadres (semifunctional groups that had represented bureaucratic interests), including the CSP; modified the pay structure to weaken the advantage enjoyed by CSP officers; enlarged the Civil Service

Academy by forming the Academy for Administrative Training; eliminated reservation of administrative posts (a practice that favored CSP officers); and began a program of lateral recruitment (political appointment of administrators).[10] One consequence of the reforms was the dilution of the power of civil bureaucrats and their replacement with members of Bhutto's Pakistan Peoples Party (PPP) and with those personally loyal to Bhutto.

As has been the case with all the leaders of Pakistan, Bhutto ruled with the consent of the military. The civil war had left the military establishment weak and unpopular. In this context, Bhutto took the opportunity to dismiss some senior military officers and to promote others who were personally loyal to him. He also abolished the position of commander-in-chief, replacing it with the office of chief of staff (General Zia was appointed to this position in 1976). Ultimate authority, therefore, was transferred to the prime minister. In addition, a clause was inserted into the 1973 constitution stating that any abrogation of the constitution, as had happened in the 1958 coup, would constitute an act of "high treason" against the state.

Bhutto, as an elected civilian and as leader of the PPP, personally favored increasing the importance of the legislature and of political parties. However, his style of leadership was quite authoritarian, and his image of party politics allowed for little dissent from his positions. Accordingly, Bhutto placed restrictions on, and later banned, the principal opposition party, the National Awami party (NAP), and periodically purged his own party of members who did not agree with his policies (see Chapter 13). Bhutto had hundreds of political opponents arrested during his regime. And like Ayub, Bhutto placed restrictions on freedom of the press.

Yahya Khan, Bhutto's immediate successor, had abolished the electoral college aspect of the Basic Democracies program upon assuming office in 1969. Bhutto introduced a modified form of local government, the People's Works Program, which called for the establishment of four tiers of elected officials; like the BD program, however, such councils were functionally dominated by civil bureaucrats. The only significant change was that Bhutto had replaced some of the career bureaucrats with personally loyal party faithfuls.

More important than Bhutto's local government institutions were his land reforms. Bhutto, the self-styled champion of Pakistan's peasant masses, dubbed himself the Quaid-i-Awam (leader of the masses). He also campaigned on the slogan of *kapra, makaan, and roti* (clothing, housing, and food) for the rural and urban masses. Bhutto introduced two land reforms (1972 and 1977). Both, like Ayub's policy, placed ceilings on the ownership of agricultural land, although Bhutto's ceilings were lower than those of Ayub. In practice, however, Bhutto's land reforms were no more successful than Ayub's in curbing the power of the landlords or in distributing land to the landless.[11]

Whereas Ayub was a true believer in capitalism, Bhutto espoused Islamic socialism. Thus, in 1972, he nationalized insurance, banking, and a number of heavy industries. The performance of the economy during Bhutto's regime was poor; analysts disagree as to whether such performance was the result of Bhutto's economic policies or a combination of unfortunate circumstances (e.g., the increased price of oil after 1973, disastrous harvests, and floods).

Perhaps Bhutto's greatest achievements were in foreign policy. When Bhutto assumed office, Pakistan was a virtual international pariah. The cause of such ostracism was the highly publicized brutalities of the West Pakistan Army during the civil war. In this context, Bhutto's achievements are remarkable. Bhutto successfully negotiated for the return of Pakistan's prisoners of war from India and Bangladesh through the Simla Agreement with India of 1972; greatly strengthened relations with China; established stable detente with Pakistan's historic foes, India and the USSR; improved relations with the United States (the latter reestablished military aid agreements with Pakistan during Bhutto's regime); and in 1974 convened the Islamic summit, a meeting of the heads of the Islamic world.

But Bhutto's regime collapsed because his reforms made many enemies, the two most significant of which were the military and the opposition politicians. As earlier noted, Bhutto introduced several reforms that affected the military. The most important motives underlying the coup of 1977 were the establishment of the Federal Security Force (FSF) and the Balochistan War (see Chapter 13). The first of these, a para-military security organization, preempted the authority of the military. The undeclared civil war in Balochistan also proved very unpopular among Pakistan's military officers, particularly as it occurred on the heels of the debacle in East Pakistan.

In any case, following the 1977 election in which the PPP was returned in a landslide but tainted victory, the Pakistan National Alliance took its grievances to the streets. The military, led by General Zia-ul-Haq, intervened— ostensibly to maintain order.

Back to the Military with Zia (1977–1988)

General Zia promised to relinquish power and hold a general election within ninety days of the military coup that brought him to power. However, Zia held office for over eleven years, and only his death prevented him from continuing longer. Obviously, Zia's regime was a military regime; hence it demonstrated much in common with Pakistan's other military regimes (those of Ayub and Yahya), but there are important differences as well.

Like Ayub, Zia believed in centralized, authoritarian government. But while Ayub came to this conclusion reluctantly, aware as he was of the weakness of the state and its institutions, Zia justified his continued rule as a matter of accommodating the necessities of Islam (see Chapter 11).

Zia increasingly viewed his role as that of an Islamic head of state who legitimately holds power and deserves the loyalty and support of his subjects as long as he governs the state according to the precepts of Islam.[12] Central to his regime, therefore, was the establishment of a nizam-i-Mustafa (rule of the Prophet) (see Chapter 11).

The Zia regime took a position somewhere in between that of Ayub and Bhutto on the question of the significance and importance of the civilian bureaucracy. One of Zia's first acts after assuming office was to abolish the lateral recruitment program of his predecessor and to subject the bureaucratic appointees of Bhutto to review by the Federal Public Service Commission. In addition, Zia reappointed several former CSP officers and other senior bureaucrats who had been dismissed by Bhutto. Zia also appointed many civilian bureaucrats as close personal advisers. On the other hand, Zia did not reestablish the CSP, nor was the civilian bureaucracy as central to the decision-making process as it was under Ayub.[13]

Unlike Ayub or Bhutto, Zia relied greatly on the military to fill administrative posts. One reason for this was that Pakistan remained under martial law between 1977 and 1985. Under Zia's system of martial law, Pakistan was divided into several "zones," each of which was governed by a deputy chief martial law administrator drawn from the military and carrying the rank of lieutenant general. Further, Zia established martial law tribunals, which possessed jurisdiction parallel to Pakistan's civil courts. The latter were staffed by senior military officers. Finally, Zia established a 10% quota for retired military officers at all officer-level ranks in the civilian bureaucracy. As a consequence, many important posts in the bureaucracy were held by active and retired military officers.[14]

Zia's distrust of politicians was even greater than that of other Pakistani leaders. Accordingly, the Zia regime placed severe restraints on political activity. In 1979, a martial law regulation banned all political parties and prohibited the future electoral activity of any party that failed to register with the Election Commission. Most of Pakistan's parties failed to register. In addition, specially constituted Disqualification Tribunals (1970) barred hundreds of politicians on a · case-by-case basis from contesting future elections. Finally, amendments to the Political Parties Act (1962), in 1979 and in 1984, banned former national and provincial office bearers and former federal ministers who had held office during the Bhutto years (1971–1977) from contesting elections. Such restrictions were lifted shortly before the 1985 elections, although most of those barred chose not to participate. Most remaining restrictions on political party activity were lifted in 1986. Zia failed to hold national elections in Pakistan until December 1984. At that time, he held a referendum (reminiscent of Ayub's) asking the people of Pakistan whether they supported Zia's policies of Islamization and the ideology of Pakistan, with a "yes" vote interpreted as giving Zia an additional five-year term as president (March 1985–March 1990). Zia was said to have received a 98% affirmative vote. In February 1985, "party-less" elections for the national and provincial assemblies were held. Although many of the political restrictions were partially lifted for the election, few prominent politicians took part in the poll. However, campaigning for the elections was brisk and the turnout at the polls was surprisingly high (53%). Moreover, the conduct of the polls themselves may have been among the fairest in Pakistan's history. Nevertheless, the national and provincial assemblies that were elected remained weak; and they were dissolved by presidential fiat in May 1988.

Zia revived many aspects of Ayub's Basic Democracies (BD) through the establishment of local bodies programs in each of the provinces. Elections to local bodies (a four-tiered system of subprovincial government) were held in 1979, 1983, and 1987. Unlike the Basic Democracies, however, Zia did not use the local body representatives as an electoral college, nor were civilian bureaucrats as dominant in the system as during BD or under Bhutto's system. The elections were nonpartisan and the local bodies were dominated by rural notables (members of the landholding elite). Whatever their shortcomings, however, the local bodies institutions constituted the most representative and effective form of local government ever implemented in Pakistan.[15] Although Zia did not abolish the land reform legislation of his predecessors, he also took no steps to implement it.

Zia followed a capitalist line in economic policy, although he was reluctant to denationalize the industries that were nationalized by Bhutto. In fact, the number of "autonomous corporations" and "public enterprises" actually increased during the Zia regime. The performance of Pakistan's economy under Zia was very impressive, although it must also be stressed that the Pakistani economy benefited greatly from remittances from Pakistanis working abroad.

The foreign policy of the Zia regime centered on the Soviet presence in Afghanistan, and Zia's crowning achievement was the Soviet withdrawal in February 1989. Indeed, Pakistan's foreign policy was influenced by Afghanistan in several regards. First, the Soviet-Afghan War created many refugees (variously estimated at 2–3 million) who have taken sanctuary in Pakistan. The presence of the Afghan refugees and their sympathizers precipitated several Soviet-Afghan reprisals, including bombings, directed at refugee camps within Pakistan's border. Second, the Soviet presence in Afghanistan prompted the resumption of U.S. aid to Pakistan. In 1981, the United States signed a six-year $3.2 billion military aid and economic credits package with Pakistan. In addition, the United States sold Pakistan forty F-16 airplanes. Third, the combination of the foregoing factors moved Pakistan toward a de facto alignment with the United States. It also affected relations with India, although, on balance, these relations improved under Zia (see Chapter 31).

PPP Part Two: Benazir (1988–1990)

Those who anticipated rapid change under Pakistan's first democratically elected government since 1977 were disappointed by Benazir's term in office. First, Benazir's government was unable to restore the 1973 constitution nor did it rescind the 8th Amendment. Second, the PPP-led national assembly passed no new legislative bill during its tenure; in fact, only ten bills, all minor amendments to existing legislation, passed the assembly. Third, center-provincial relations deteriorated markedly during Benazir's tenure, as evidenced by the widening rift between the PPP and IJI in Punjab and by the proliferation of ethnic violence in the Sindh. Fourth, the Afghan war remains unresolved.

Of course, Benazir's government operated under severe disadvantages from the start. The PPP gained a very narrow plurality in the 1988 election; consequently, it was forced to enter into a shaky coalition with the MQM and several independent MNAs in order to form the government. As a result, much of the energy of the PPP leadership was expended in the attempt to maintain power. Such efforts were complicated by the decision of the MQM to withdraw from the government in October 1989. Moreover, Benazir's government, like all civilian regimes in Pakistan, served at the sufferance of the military.

Despite such disappointments and inherent weaknesses, the accomplishments of Benazir's government were not inconsiderable. Benazir's greatest accomplishment was to further democratize the society. Arguably, the political system of Pakistan was more open (e.g., greater press freedoms and political party activity) during Benazir's twenty months in office than at any other time in Pakistan's history. Also, Benazir was able to improve Pakistan's foreign relations with the United States, the Commonwealth nations, and, at least until the rekindling of the Kashmir dispute in February 1990, with India.

*   *   *

In sum, many states demonstrate a gap between constitutional structures and political practices. In Pakistan this gap has been chronic and wide. As we have seen, Pakistan has undergone seven separate constitutional phases. Further, Pakistan's leaders have not been averse to modifying existing constitutional structures to accommodate their political ends. Such phenomena have resulted in part from the inability of Pakistan to establish a constitutional structure that is acceptable to all people.

Forty-three years after independence, two basic problems remain un-resolved: the status of Islam, and the relations between the center and the provinces. Both have had a negative effect on the stability of Pakistan's constitutional structures. Indeed, unless and until such problems are adequately addressed, Pakistan's state institutions are likely to remain unstable and its constitutional structures fluid.

Notes

1. Act XVIII of 1985, Constitution (Eighth Amendment) Act, 1985–1986 *PLD* Central Statutes, p. 6.

2. For details see Charles H. Kennedy, *Bureaucracy in Pakistan* (Karachi: Oxford University Press, 1987), esp. pp. 213–214.

3. Lawrence Ziring, *Pakistan: The Enigma of Political Development* (London: Dawson, 1980), p. 88.

4. Altaf Gauhar, "Pakistan: Ayub Khan's Abdication," *Third World Quarterly*, vol. 7, no. 1 (January 1985), p. 108.

5. Asaf Hussain, *Elite Politics in an Ideological State: The Case of Pakistan* (London: Dawson, 1979), p. 137.

6. See for instance, Mohammad Ayub Khan, *Friends, Not Masters: A Political Autobiography* (Karachi: Oxford University Press, 1967).

7. For details see Inayatullah, *Basic Democracies, District Administration and Development* (Peshawar: Pakistan Academy for Rural Development, 1964).

8. For details see Ronald J. Herring, *Land to the Tiller: The Political Economy of Land Reform in South Asia* (New Haven: Yale University Press, 1983).

9. For details see Gustav F. Papanek, *Pakistan's Development: Social Goals and Private Incentives* (Cambridge: Harvard University Press, 1967).

10. For details see Kennedy, *Bureaucracy in Pakistan*, pp. 129–152.

11. Herring, *Land to the Tiller*, pp. 100–103, 117–125.

12. See Government of Pakistan, Cabinet Division, *Ansari Commission's Report on Form of Government 4th August 1983* (Islamabad: Manager, Printing Corporation of Pakistan Press, 1984).

13. Kennedy, *Bureaucracy in Pakistan*, pp. 122–125; 145–150.

14. Ibid., pp. 122–125.

15. G. Shabbir Cheema, *The Performance of Local Councils in Pakistan: Some Policy Implications* (Islamabad: United Nations Development Project Report, 1984).

Suggested Readings

Baxter, Craig, ed. *Zia's Pakistan: Politics and Stability in a Frontline State* (Boulder, Colo.: Westview, 1985).

Baxter, Craig and Razi Wasti, eds. *Pakistan: Emerging Democracy* (Lahore: Vanguard Press, 1990).

Burki, Shahid Javed. *Pakistan Under Bhutto, 1971–1977* (New York: St. Martin's Press, 1980).

Feldman, Herbert. *A Constitution for Pakistan* (Karachi: Oxford University Press, 1956).

Government of Pakistan, Cabinet Division. *Ansari Commission's Report on Form of Government 4th August 1983* (Islamabad: Manager, Printing Corporation of Pakistan Press, 1984).

Government of Pakistan, Ministry of Law. *The Constitution of the Islamic Republic of Pakistan as Modified 19 March 1985* (Islamabad: Manager, Printing Corporation of Pakistan Press, 1985).

Herring, Ronald. *Land to the Tiller: The Political Economy of Land Reform in South Asia* (New Haven, Conn.: Yale University Press, 1983).

Kennedy, Charles H. *Bureaucracy in Pakistan* (Karachi: Oxford University Press, 1987).

Kochanek, Stanley. *Interest Groups and Development: Business and Politics in Pakistan* (Karachi: Oxford University Press, 1983).

Sayeed, Khalid bin-. *Politics in Pakistan: The Nature and Direction of Change* (New York: Praeger Publishers, 1980).

Waseem, Mohammed. *Politics and the State in Pakistan* (Lahore: Progressive Publishers, 1989).

Ziring, Lawrence. *Pakistan: The Enigma of Political Development* (London: Dawson, 1980).

15
THE FUTURE OF PAKISTAN

Pakistan faces an uncertain future. Forty-three years after independence, it is still confronted with profound challenges to its integrity as an independent nation-state. Such challenges stem both from numerous domestic short-comings and from Pakistan's hazardous international security environment. This chapter serves as a summary of such challenges.

Modernization and Development:
Pakistan's Unresolved Dilemma

The years following World War II witnessed the emergence of the subdiscipline of development in the social sciences. With respect to eco-nomics, development concerns the process by which a society achieves self-sustaining growth; in sociological terms, the process is one of movement toward a more egalitarian class structure; in political terms, the process is one of movement toward more representative institutions. In each case, development places an emphasis on increasing the capabilities and complexity of institutions in order to create or prompt the desired social change.

Closely wedded to the concept of development is modernization. Mod-ernization theory argues that societies follow a unilinear process from traditional forms of social organization to more modern forms. For instance, as a society modernizes, "primordial attachments" (kin, caste, religion, ethnicity) weaken and are gradually replaced with modern forms of social organization (class, ideology, secularism). Indeed, modernization is both a cause and a consequence of the developmental process.

The catalyst for the sudden prominence of these theories was the emergence of the dozens of new nations carved from the breakup of colonial empires in Asia and Africa. Early (1955–1965) advocates of development and modernization held that with the right combination of assistance (money, human resources, organizational planning, and so forth) from the developed/ modern nations (the West), the transformation of the recipient nations would be rapid and inevitable. But subsequent events have proven the more enthusiastic claims of such advocates to be matters of mere wishful thinking.

Neither the development process nor the transformation to modernity has been easy for most new nations. Pakistan is a case in point.

Traditional and Modern Sectors

Largely unforeseen by the formulators of development and modernization theory were two processes that have influenced the pace of social change in most new states: (1) the uneven rate of social change within such states, and (2) resistance to change by powerful groups within the affected states.

Pakistan's population offers many contrasts. On the one hand, there is a relatively small segment of the population whose behavior is indistinguishable from counterparts found in New York or London. Such individuals are Western educated, belong to professions or perform occupations parallel to those of the West, contemplate global issues through the international mass media, live in Western-style houses, and are secular in customs and habits. The much larger segment of the population, on the other hand, is illiterate; its members belong to tradition-bound villages (with attendant networks of kin, caste, and ethnicity), perform occupations that have remained largely unchanged for millenia, and live in houses constructed from mud.

Of course, such distinctions are correlated with income and education. The distribution of both remains very unequal in Pakistan. In 1989, over 75% of the population was illiterate, and although the mean per capita income was $360 (high by South Asian standards), the median income was less than $100. Objectively speaking, therefore, Pakistan has two sectors of society—one modern and one traditional.

Pakistan's political system is dominated by elite groups. In the context of the traditional-modern dichotomy, two of these elites (religious and landholding) have been the most consistent advocates of traditional structures and processes. The great majority of members of other elite groups, particularly those in the civil bureaucracy and the professional elites, have been consistent champions of modernity. Indeed, it is useful to view the political history of Pakistan, at least in part, as a struggle between tradition and modernity. Both the tortuous process of constitution making and the still unresolved issue of the role of Islam in the state fit this model. We must also stress that Pakistan's decision makers (like those in most states of the Third World) have sought to formulate policies that do not exacerbate the modern-traditional rivalry. Bhutto's Islamic Socialism was one such attempt; Zia's nizam-i-Mustafa is another.

Institution Building

Pakistan's greatest shortcoming since partition has been its inability to establish stable and effective political institutions. The litany of its failures is long: unenforced constitutions, dormant legislatures, ineffective political parties, and persistent military rule. From the perspective of political development, Pakistan is a signal failure. Unfortunately, such difficulties are likely to continue into the foreseeable future.

First, there is the question of national unity. If a state is to build effective political institutions, a broad agreement on the fundamentals of the state is required. As demonstrated numerous times in Pakistan's history, however, such an agreement does not exist. Pakistan is divided by regionalism and language. Even the potential unifying effects of a shared religion, Islam, have constituted an additional source of ideological disunity throughout Pakistan's troubled history.

Second, Pakistan's failures of institution building have been both a cause and a consequence of additional failures. Pakistan's decision makers have often sought the quick-fix solution to problems of institution building, often scuttling existing programs or institutions when they encountered resistance. Pakistan's checkered history of local government is a case in point. None of the numerous local government programs established over the decades since partition have survived a change of regime; many have not lasted long enough for that.

Third, the stakes of politics in Pakistan have become quite high. The groups in control share the considerable perquisites of office; those out of power are often consigned to prison or exile. In such a setting, the emphasis is obviously not on creating long-lasting institutions but, rather, on maintaining power.

Finally, like many Third World states, Pakistan faces the dilemma of chronic military rule. It has become an axiom of political science that once the threshold of military involvement in civilian politics has been crossed, one finds it increasingly easy to cross the threshold on subsequent occasions. Indeed, Pakistani politics has been dominated by the military since 1958. The country has been under martial law for roughly half of that period, and military leaders have been the head of government for all but the two Bhutto regimes (1971–1977; 1988–1990). One could credibly argue that military governments benefit states insofar as they tend to maintain law and order (not an insignificant benefit), provide a consistent foreign policy, and (although this point is contested) promote economic development more effectively than their civilian counterparts.[1] However, military regimes are notoriously inept at creating representative political institutions, as Pakistan's experience with military regimes has clearly demonstrated.

External Threats

Obviously Pakistan does not exist in a vacuum. In fact, it faces one of the most difficult security environments of any state in the world. Pakistan is surrounded by perceived enemies. On the east is India; on the west is Soviet-dominated Afghanistan. India is Pakistan's longest and most troublesome opponent. Pakistan has fought three wars with India (1948, 1965, 1971), and many Pakistanis continue to view Indians as implacable foes. Moreover, Pakistan's difficulties with Afghanistan, also not of recent origin, were exacerbated by the Soviet occupation of the state (1979–1989). Complicating this already difficult situation is the fact that the Soviet Union supplies India with arms.

In this context one can readily understand why Pakistan's decision makers have been very concerned with the security of the state. One indicator of such concern has been military spending. Pakistan has a standing army of a half-million soldiers; it spends nearly 7% of its gross national product on defense; and its military expenditures of $21 per capita are greater than those of any other state in South Asia.[2] Despite such high spending, however, Pakistan's army is still less than one-half the size of India's.

A second consequence of uncertain security has been Pakistan's nuclear weapons program. After India exploded a nuclear device in 1974, Prime Minister Bhutto launched a heavily publicized nuclear development program in Pakistan. However, the international community, and particularly the United States, disapproved of Pakistan's attempt at nuclear proliferation, and the United States subsequently applied pressure on France (which had agreed in 1976 to sell a nuclear reprocessing plant to Pakistan) to withdraw from nuclear agreements with Pakistan. When Pakistan continued clandestinely to seek nuclear capabilities, the United States invoked provisions of the Symington amendment to the Foreign Assistance Act in 1977 and cut all assistance save food aid to Pakistan, although this amendment was interpreted in 1981 as permitting the provision of new economic and military assistance. Since that time, the question of whether Pakistan possesses nuclear weapons capabilities has generated much speculation. Both Zia's and Benazir's governments have consistently stated that Pakistan does not have the bomb but, rather, has sought nuclear capabilities solely for peaceful purposes.[3]

Also related to Pakistan's troubled security are the Afghan refugees. The Soviet invasion of Afghanistan caused more than 2 million potentially permanent refugees to flee to Pakistan. Their presence has placed severe demands on Pakistan's economy and significantly increased underemployment, particularly in the NWFP and Balochistan.

Pakistan-U.S. Relations

Pakistan's most important ally is the United States.[4] But the relationship can be likened to a stormy love affair in which one of the participants is serious and wants to settle down (Pakistan) while the other (the United

States) wants to keep its options open and play the field. Pakistan's initial foreign policy called for nonalignment, but that stance began to change in the mid-1950s as the United States sought allies to combat the spread of communism. The United States found its most ardent South Asian support in the person of Ayub Khan, and, until 1965, Pakistan was the United States' "most allied ally."[5] But this arrangement ended when the United States stopped arms shipments to Pakistan during the 1965 Pakistan-Indian war. Until such aid was discontinued, the United States had been Pakistan's dominant arms supplier, providing $1.2 billion in military aid from 1954 to 1965.[6] The United States viewed the stoppage of arms as conducive to peace in South Asia; Pakistan viewed it as a betrayal by an ally. Between 1965 and 1979, relations between the two states remained cordial and the United States periodically resumed limited arms sales to Pakistan, but never close to the levels prevailing before 1965. Indeed, during the 1971 war, the United States provided little material assistance to Pakistan despite the well-publicized "tilt toward Pakistan."[7] U.S.-Pakistan relations reached their nadir in 1979 when the American Embassy in Islamabad was burned by an angry mob instigated by the United States' alleged involvement in a plot to occupy the Ka'aba in Mecca. However, this trend of events was reversed when the Soviet Union launched its invasion of Afghanistan in December 1979. After a change of administration in Washington and over a year of negotiations, Pakistan emerged with a six-year $3.2 billion arms sale and economic assistance package in 1981. This agreement was renewed for a three-year period in 1988 at $600 million per year. These agreements made Pakistan the third largest recipient of U.S. security aid in the world (after Israel and Egypt).

The United States has also been Pakistan's largest supplier of foreign economic assistance. Since 1947, the United States has supplied bilateral grants totalling more than $2 billion and has provided bilateral loans in excess of $4.5 billion. These sums constitute more than one-third of the total assistance granted Pakistan by all sources since partition.[8]

*   *   *

Pakistan will soon enter its fifth decade of statehood. Unfortunately, many of the problems facing the newly formed state in 1947 are still unresolved. First, Pakistan remains a relatively poor country. Although its economy has expanded rapidly since partition, the population has grown at an almost equal rate. Furthermore, the inequalities in distribution of resources have remained largely unaffected by such economic growth. Second, Pakistan still struggles with the problems of choosing a structure of government acceptable to its people and of forming stable and effective institutions. Third, Pakistan faces an insecure international environment. Finally, Pakistan is still searching for a distinctive national identity.

Pakistan's survival into the twenty-first century will require a combination of luck, dynamic and skillful leadership, an acceptable settlement of Pakistan's long-standing constitutional and representational disabilities, and the cooperation of all of its people.

Notes

1. See, for instance, Eric Nordlinger, *Soldiers in Politics: Military Coups and Governments* (Englewood Cliffs, N.J.: Prentice-Hall, 1977); and Charles H. Kennedy and David Louscher, eds., *Civil-Military Interaction in Asia and Africa* (Leiden: E. J. Brill, forthcoming 1991).

2. Stephen P. Cohen, *The Pakistan Army* (Berkeley: University of California Press, 1984), p. 15.

3. For a more extensive treatment of the subject of regional nuclear proliferation and the specific role and capabilities of Pakistan, see Rodney W. Jones, ed., *Small Nuclear Forces and U.S. Security Policy: Threats and Potential Conflicts in the Middle East and South Asia* (Lexington, Mass.: Lexington Books, 1984); and Rodney W. Jones, *Nuclear Proliferation: Islam, the Bomb and South Asia,* Washington Papers no. 82 (Washington, D.C.: Center for Strategic and International Studies, Georgetown University, 1981).

4. Further readings on U.S.-Pakistan relations include: Shirin Tahir-Kheli, *The United States and Pakistan: The Evolution of an Influence Relationship* (New York: Praeger Publishers, 1982); Leo E. Rose and Noor A. Husain, eds., *United States-Pakistan Relations* (Berkeley: Institute of East Asian Studies, 1985); and Leo E. Rose and Kemal Matinuddin, eds., *Beyond Afghanistan: The Emerging US-Pakistan Relations* (Berkeley: Institute of East Asian Studies, 1989).

5. S. Tahir-Kheli, *The United States and Pakistan,* pp. 1–25.

6. Cohen, *The Pakistan Army,* p. 138.

7. See Henry Kissinger, *The White House Years* (Boston: Little, Brown, 1979); Christopher Van Hollen, "The Tilt Revisited," *Asian Survey,* vol. 20, no. 4 (April 1980); and Craig Baxter, "The United States and Pakistan: The Zia Era and the Afghan Connection," in Adam Garfinkle, ed., *Friendly Tyrants* (New York: St. Martin's Press, 1990).

8. Calculated from Government of Pakistan, *Pakistan Statistical Yearbook 1988* (Islamabad: Manager, Printing Corporation of Pakistan Press, 1988), pp. 610–651.

Suggested Readings

Ahmed, Viqar, and Rashid Amjad. *The Management of Pakistan's Economy: 1947–1982* (Karachi: Oxford University Press, 1984).

Baxter, Craig, ed. *Zia's Pakistan: Politics and Stability in a Frontline State* (Boulder, Colo.: Westview Press, 1985).

Baxter, Craig and Razi Wasti, eds. *Pakistan: Emerging Democracy* (Lahore: Vanguard Press, 1990).

Burke, S. M. *Pakistan's Foreign Policy* (London: Oxford University Press, 1973).

Burki, Shahid Javed, and Robert La Porte, eds. *Pakistan's Development Priorities: Choices for the Future* (Karachi: Oxford University Press, 1984).

Cohen, Stephen. *The Pakistan Army* (Berkeley: University of California Press, 1984).

Norman, Omar. *The Political Economy of Pakistan, 1947–1985* (London: Routledge and Kegan Paul, 1988).

Rose, Leo E., and Noor A. Husain, eds. *United States-Pakistan Relations* (Berkeley: Institute of East Asian Studies, 1985).

Rose, Leo E., and Kamal Matinuddin, eds. *Beyond Afghanistan: The Emerging US-Pakistan Relations* (Berkeley: Institute of East Asian Studies, 1989).

Tahir-Kheli, Shirin. *The United States and Pakistan: The Development of an Influence Relationship* (New York: Praeger Publishers, 1982).

Venkataramani, M. S. *The American Role in Pakistan* (Lahore: Vanguard Press, 1984).

Ziring, Lawrence, et al., eds. *Pakistan: The Long View* (Durham N.C.: Duke University Press, 1977).

PART 3

BANGLADESH

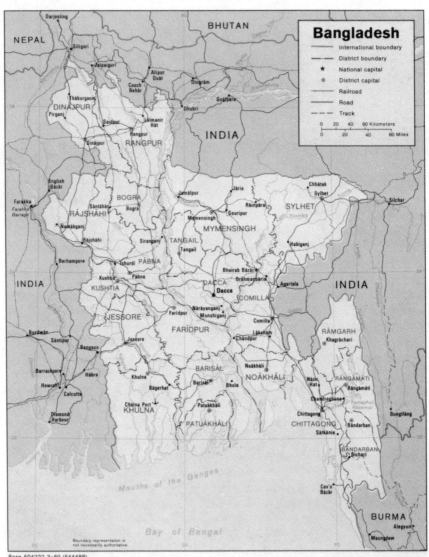

Bangladesh

	International boundary
	District boundary
★	National capital
⊙	District capital
	Railroad
	Road
	Track

0   20   40   60 Kilometers
0   20   40   60 Miles

NEPAL

BHUTAN

Darjeeling

Siliguri

Jalpaiguri

Alipur
Duār

Cooch
Behār

Dinārā

Goālpāra

Dhubri

INDIA

Thākurgaon

DINAJPUR

Pirganj

Saidpur

Lālmanir
Hāt

Lālmanir Hāt

Rangpur

Dinājpur

RANGPUR

English
Bāzār

Farakka

Farakka
Barrage

Santāhār

BOGRA

Bogra

Jamālpur

Jāria

Chhātak

Sylhet

SYLHET

Silchar

RĀJSHĀHI

Nawābganj

Rājshāhi

Berhampore

Mymensingh

Rāutpāra

Gouripur

MYMENSINGH

Habiganj

Sirānganj

TANGAIL

Tangail

Ishurdi

PĀBNA

Pābna

Kushtia

Bhairab Bāzār

Brāhmanbāria

DACCA

Dacca

COMILLA

Agartala

INDIA

KUSHTIA

JESSORE

Jessore

Nārāyanganj

Munshiganj

Farīdpur

FARĪDPUR

Comilla

Lākshām

Chāndpur

RĀMGARH

Khagrāchari

Bardwān

Sāntipur

Bangaon

Hābra

Barrackpore

Howrah

Calcutta

Khulna

BARISĀL

Barisāl

Bhola

Noākhāli

NOĀKHĀLI

Nazir
Hāt

RĀNGĀMATI

Rāngāmati

Bāgerhat

Chandraghona

Karnaphuli
Reservoir

Bungtlāng

Diamond
Harbour

Chālna Port

KHULNA

Patuākhāli

Chittagong

CHITTAGONG

Sārkānia

Bandarban

PATUĀKHĀLI

BANDARBAN

Bichari

Mouths of the Ganges

Cox's
Bāzār

BURMA

Alegyun

Bay of Bengal

Maungdaw

Boundary representation is
not necessarily authoritative.

Base 504222 3–80 (544488)

16
SOCIETY'S HERITAGE
AND ITS MEANING
FOR THE PRESENT

When Bangladesh became independent from Pakistan in 1971, the action was seen by many as the logical division of two disparate wings of a country united only by Islam, a mutual concern about India, and—partly facetiously— the routes of Pakistan International Airlines, but divided by language and social customs. Pakistan had fought to keep alive the fiction that all Muslims in the subcontinent belonged to a separate nation, distinct from the Hindus, that should be unified under a single government and had struggled to retain its unity, preserving the ties between East and West Pakistan in the face of vast cultural differences that could not be covered up by the common thread of Islam. To a few outsiders the Pakistani leadership seemed to be acting in 1971 as Abraham Lincoln had done in the 1860s to preserve the Union; to others, surely a majority, the leadership was seen as emulating George III, but in a singularly vicious manner. In this chapter and the next we will discuss the society of Bangladesh and the causes for its demand for separation from Pakistan. But first the land of Bangladesh must be described. As we shall discover, there are vast differences between Bangladesh and Pakistan that, in themselves, contribute to cultural differences.

Land and Water: Ecology and Economy of a Delta

Bangladesh is largely formed by the delta of two of the world's major river systems, the Ganges (called Padma in Bangladesh) and the Brahmaputra (Jamuna). Both rise in the Himalayas: the Brahmaputra on the northern slopes in Tibet and the Ganges in India on the southern side of the mountain range. They are joined by the Meghna, which rises in the Assam hills south of the Brahmaputra and drains areas that receive the highest amount of rainfall in the world. The interlacing streams that cover most of Bangladesh provide the country with a valuable network for boat transport of people

229

and goods, but they can be both a blessing and a curse during the flood season. Even though the silt deposited replenishes the fertile but overworked soil, the damage done by the torrents can often be substantial. The rivers are shallow and therefore rise very rapidly when excess water flows, so in a typical year about one-tenth of the land is severely flooded during the rainy season and the country gives the appearance of a series of islands in a sea.

The principal crops are rice and jute, both of which require substantial amounts of water. Jute is the major cash crop, but the market for this fiber is not growing. Rice is the staple foodgrain. Production has been expanded, especially since the Ziaur Rahman government took office, but Bangladesh must still import substantial amounts of foodgrains, often the less popular wheat. Imports in 1987 exceeded 1.7 million metric tons;[1] domestic production of rice was about 14.3 million metric tons in 1983–1984 and 13.4 millon tons in 1981–1982.[2] Wheat production was in excess of 1.1 million tons in 1983–1984.[3] Tea is grown in the hills of Sylhet Region (formerly a district) and provides another cash crop.

In 1976–1977, it was estimated that the average rural Bangladeshi consumed only 1,707 calories per day. In the urban areas the amount was 1,866 calories per day.[4] This total had improved to 1,927 calories (or 87% of the minimum requirement) in 1982, but no urban-rural breakdown is available.[5] It is generally estimated that at least 80% of the rural population and 70% of the urban is below the poverty line.[6] The effect of this factor on personal and national development is quite clearly negative.

There are few natural resources in Bangladesh aside from its fertile but overcrowded soil. Natural gas, a major exception, has been found in abundance. About 45% of the nation's electricity is generated by natural gas and another 25% by the country's only hydroelectric station, located at Kaptai on the Karnafuli River just where that stream emerges from the Chittagong Hill Tracts. Gas is also used for the manufacture of nitrogenous fertilizers. The search for oil continues, but none has been discovered so far.

Urbanization has been slower in Bangladesh than in the other countries of South Asia. About 87% of the population is rural,[7] despite a near doubling of the largest city, Dhaka (including its industrial suburb of Narayanganj), between 1974 and 1981, to a total of 3.4 million. Chittagong, the principal seaport and an industrial center, is the only other city of more than a million; its population is 1.5 million. Khulna, also an industrial center, had a population of 700,000 in 1981, but no other city exceeded a half-million people. Near Khulna is the second seaport, an anchorage at Chalna.

The People and the Pressures of Demography

Bangladesh (excluding such city-states as Hong Kong and Singapore) is the most densely populated nation in the world. In an area of 55,126 square miles (a bit smaller than Wisconsin), it contains a population of about 110 million, or almost 2,000 people per square mile. (At the same density, the United States would contain about 6.5 billion people.) The population, moreover, is growing at a rate of 2.8% per year, a rate that will double the population in about twenty-eight years if no significant lowering of the rate occurs. Population projections suggest that Bangladesh may have 144 million people by 2000.[8] Population growth and its relationship to food production is therefore one of the most important problems of Bangladesh.

The majority of the people are Bengalis, a branch of the Indo-Aryan people who migrated eastward from the main group that had entered the subcontinent during the second millenium B.C. The area was probably populated sparsely by Dravidian groups. The characteristics of the Dravidians can be seen in the mixed population that predominates today in Bangladesh. Bengalis tend to be shorter and darker in complexion than other Indo-Aryans, especially those who live in the area that is now Pakistan. Discrimination against Bengalis in East Pakistan for these reasons as well as for their presumed "nonmartial" attributes (see Chapter 1) was part of the discontent in Bangladesh when it was part of united Pakistan. A Mongoloid strain can also be noted, especially among Bangladeshis from Sylhet and Chittagong, which may indicate that the pre-Indo-Aryan population of the eastern districts of Bangladesh was at least partially Mongoloid rather than solely Dravidian.

A number of tribal groups remain within Bangladesh. Although they constitute only about 1% of the population, they are important for the political problems they have caused.[9] Those outside the Chittagong Hill Tracts Region are mainly parts of tribes, such as the Garos, whose main groups are located in India. These tribal groups are most often Christian and are intermingled with other Bangladeshis in the Mymensingh, Rajshahi, and Sylhet regions. In the Chittagong Hill Tracts Region there are tribal groups who are Buddhist or retain animist traditions, and who are opposed to the extension of central rule and particularly fear the migration of Bangladeshis from the plains into the hill areas. Almost constant fighting has occurred in the Hill Tracts since independence in 1947. Prior to that time, the British had maintained an "inner line" (that is, a line inside the international boundaries with India and Burma) beyond which property ownership and settlement was forbidden to nontribals. The nontribals from the plains have at times evaded this regulation, extending trade and de facto landownership into the hills. But the tribes have resisted this trend by means of guerrilla activities. The Bangladesh government, while resisting the military action, has taken steps to extend educational, health, and other social services to the hill areas, has included representatives of the tribes in the governmental structure and has extended a limited degree of autonomy.[10] Nevertheless the problem remains the country's only significant hindrance to full national integration. The region is adjacent to areas in India and Burma, where tribal dissidence is also endemic.

A small portion of the Bangladesh population, but one of political and economic importance, is descended from Muslims who migrated to Eastern Bengal during the period of Muslim rule in north India. This group has been described as a "national elite" especially because of its concern before independence with all-India Muslim matters rather than the problems of the Bengali Muslims. It is often distinguished by its use of Urdu rather than Bengali as the family language. This elite group was in control of the Bengal provincial branch of the Muslim League before independence and ruled in Dhaka for some time after 1947. The differences between the "national elite" and the "vernacular elite" will be discussed in Chapter 17.

Language and Culture: Differences in United Pakistan

There were clear ethnic differences between the peoples of East and West Pakistan, but the language difference was one that caused dispute almost from the day of independence. Both Bengali and Urdu are derived from Sanskrit. Urdu, the language Muhammad Ali Jinnah and others wished to have chosen as the national language of Pakistan, was predominently spoken in northern India, and Delhi and Lucknow were known as centers of literary activity. Urdu was not a language native to West Pakistan, although it is closely related to both Punjabi and Hindi. It was originally the language of the camp (*urdu* means camp in Turkish)—that is, of Muslim soldiers in India. It uses a modified Arabic script, and its vocabulary has assimilated a number of words from Persian and Arabic in addition to its Sanskritic syntax and vocabulary.

Bengali, however, has remained closer to its Sanskritic roots. It is descended from the eastern intermediate language (one of the *prakrits*) and is written in a script derived from that used in Sanskrit. There have been additions to the language from Arabic, Persian, and English sources as rulers using those languages and Urdu left their impact on the language, but Sanskritic roots predominate.

Bengalis, both in Bangladesh and in West Bengal, are proud of the literary tradition of their language. Although much of the writing is attributed to Hindus, it is honored by both Muslims and Hindus. The only Indian writer to win the Nobel prize, Rabindranath Tagore (1861–1941), is recognized in Bangladesh as well in India as the author of each country's national anthem. One of the ill-advised steps of the Pakistan government in the 1960s was to ban Tagore's poetry and songs from Radio Dhaka.

The initial Pakistani insistence on Urdu as the national language provided one of the principal grievances of the east wing against the west wing. In his only post-independence visit to East Pakistan in March 1948, Jinnah declared that Urdu would be the official language and added that anyone who opposed this decision was an "enemy of Pakistan." In February 1952, the anger in East Pakistan that had been simmering since Jinnah's visit boiled over into demonstrations on the language issue. In putting down the demonstration in Dhaka, the police killed several students. The anniversary of the date remains an important event in Bangladesh, and a monument has been erected on the spot where the killings took place.[11]

Support for Urdu was seen by the Bangladeshis as a plank in the Muslim League platform. The reaction to Muslim League support for Urdu was a sharp decline in that party's popularity. The party was also viewed as a tool of the national elite, rather than a proponent of the aspirations of the regional or vernacular elite. This and other factors contributed to the defeat of the Muslim League by the United Front in the 1954 provincial election. Later that same year, in September, the Pakistan Constituent Assembly decided that both Urdu and Bengali would be national languages of Pakistan. This move did not, however, defuse the animosity that had built up over the language issue and could now be diverted to other issues.

Language was the principal symbol of the cultural distinctness between East Pakistan and West Pakistan. There were other differences that were more subtle but nonetheless caused some straight-laced West Pakistanis to complain. Among these were such seemingly innocuous matters as wider use of music (usually of a secular nature), and lesser use of the veil by Bengali Muslim women. Some West Pakistanis went so far as to accuse Bengali Muslims of being false Muslims who wore Islam as only a thin veneer over the Hinduism of their past.

Religion: Secularism or Islamism?

Bangladesh is 86.6% Muslim. The balance of the population is mostly Hindu (12.1%), with small Christian (0.3%), Buddhist (0.6%), and animist groups.[12] The Muslims are almost all Sunnis; there are virtually no Shia of the Ithna Ashari ("Twelver," Iranian) sect and only a few followers of the Aga Khan ("Sevener," Ismaili) sect.

Bengal came under Muslim rule from Delhi in 1202, when the last Hindu ruler was expelled from his capital at Nadia, now in West Bengal. Conversion of lower-caste Hindus appears to have occurred rapidly. The instrument of conversion seems to have been *sufi* and other preachers who proclaimed a religious system that did not include the disabilities of the rigid caste system reinstated by the last Hindu dynasty. Some members of the upper castes also converted to Islam to secure their positions in the higher echelons of society, but these apparently were few in number, even though Bengal was an independent area under Muslim rulers from 1341 to 1541. The Muslim elite (*ashraf*) of the pre-independence period were principally drawn from the official migrants who were posted in Bengal and who were given grants of land in that province. As mentioned earlier, they formed the national elite.

Visitors to Bangladesh and Pakistan will notice the very personal nature of Islam in Bangladesh as contrasted to the attempts at statist or corporate enforcement of Islamic law and rules in Pakistan. By and large, such key elements of Islam as keeping the fast during the month of Ramadan are left to individual Muslims, who may do as they wish.

Sheikh Mujibur Rahman declared that a secular state was among the four pillars of what came to be known as Mujibism (the others being nationalism, democracy, and socialism, as will be discussed in Chapter 19). The constitutional provision incorporating these pillars was modified during the regime of Ziaur Rahman to state that Muslims would be facilitated in ordering their lives in accordance with the *Quran* and *Sunnah*, but further steps to implement this provision have not been taken and the rights of the minorities have not been limited. There was concern at the time that Islamic fundamentalist parties might become an important factor in politics, but this concern has proven unfounded. During the Ershad regime, a constitutional amendment made Islam the state religion, but, although there are evident psychological problems for the minorities, there have been no restrictions on them. Islam, then, is a key matter for individual Muslim Bangladeshis, but the fundamentalist demands common in many Muslim countries have not yet been prominently seen in Bangladesh.

The Hindu population comes largely from the Scheduled Castes, a legal term dating from the Government of India Act of 1935 to describe those formerly called "untouchables" or, in Gandhi's word, *Harijans* (Children of God). Many of the higher-caste Hindus took part in the migration of the early 1950s, and some of those who remained left in 1971 as refugees to India and did not return. The upper castes had controlled much of the commercial, financial, and intellectual life of eastern Bengal, and many of the larger landlords were Hindu. Land reform programs trimmed the wealth of the latter group, and other difficulties, including occasional communal riots, discouraged many of the former from remaining in East Pakistan.

The Buddhist groups are almost entirely tribal in origin, although some have settled in the nonhill districts, especially Chittagong. The few Christians present in Bangladesh have not been a significant political factor. The activities of Christian missionaries—activities largely devoted to education, health, and other social work—are monitored by the government, but there have been few conversions.

Notes

1. World Bank, *World Development Report, 1989* (New York: Oxford University Press, 1989), table 4, p. 170.

2. *Statistical Handbook of Bangladesh, 1984–85* (Dhaka: Ministry of Planning, 1985), p. 303.

3. Ibid., p. 310.

4. *Statistical Handbook, 1983*, p. 524.

5. World Bank, *World Development Report*, table 28, p. 218.

6. *Statistical Handbook, 1983*, p. 524.

7. *World Bank Development Report*, table 31, p. 224.

8. World Bank, *World Development Report*, table 26, p. 214.

9. *Statistical Handbook, 1983*, pp. 132–133.

10. See Peter J. Bertocci, "Resource Development and Ethnic Conflict in Bangladesh: The Case of the Chakmas in the Chittagong Hill Tracts," in Dhirendra Vajpayee and Yogendra K. Malik, eds., *Religious and Ethnic Minority Politics in South Asia* (New Delhi: Manohar, 1989).

11. Lawrence Ziring, "Politics and Language in Pakistan: A Prolegomena, 1947–1952," *Contributions to Asian Studies*, Vol. 1 (1971).

12. *Bangladesh Population Census, 1981: Analytical Findings and National Tables* (Dhaka: Bangladesh Bureau of Statistics, August 1984), p. 75.

Suggested Readings

Kamruddin Ahmad. *A Socio-Political History of Bengal* (Dhaka: Zahiruddin Ahmad, 1975).

Sufia Ahmad. *Muslim Community in Bengal, 1884–1912* (Dhaka: University Press, 1974).

Craig Baxter. *Bangladesh: A New Nation in an Old Setting* (Boulder, Colo.: Westview Press, 1984).

A.K. Nazmul Karim. *The Dynamics of Bangladesh Society* (New Delhi: Vikas, 1980).

Charles Peter O'Donnell. *Bangladesh: Biography of a Muslim Nation* (Boulder, Colo.: Westview Press, 1984).

17
SOCIALIZATION AND POLITICAL CULTURE

At independence, Bangladesh was frequently and grimly described by foreign observers as an "international basket case."[1] This phrase came about as a reflection not only of the destruction of the nation during the civil war but also of the very poor economic conditions that prevailed in East Pakistan before independence. Indeed, eastern and predominantly Muslim Bengal had for perhaps a century been the poorest or very nearly the poorest of all of the territories in British India. In this chapter, we will look at the grievances held by East Pakistanis against West Pakistanis before 1971, which led to the 1966 demand, generally known as the Six Points, by Sheikh Mujibur Rahman for a reordering of the political, economic, and military arrangements in a united Pakistan. The political culture of Bangladesh is closely tied to the history of mistreatment by West Pakistanis, as seen by Bangladeshis; for many Bangladeshis, participation, directly or indirectly, in conflict with West Pakistan has served as a very real means of political socialization.

Grievances in United Pakistan

In the preceding chapter, the vast cultural and linguistic differences between the east and west wings of Pakistan were outlined. Also noted were the demonstrations and political actions of the Bengalis against the initial demand from the central government that Urdu be made the sole national language of Pakistan. Language comes close to the very core of human beings; a denial that one's language can be used for one's relations with the government is a blow that will often be resisted. As mentioned earlier, the eventual victory of the Bengalis regarding the equal status of Bengali and Urdu (which included the continued use of English as a link language so long as it was needed) did not end the grievances but merely permitted the Bengalis to concentrate on others that were also important to them. These grievances took three forms: political, administrative (both civil and military), and economic.

236

Political Grievances

The political grievances of the Bengalis are rooted in the East Pakistanis' feeling that they were being denied a voice in the governing of Pakistan commensurate with their population (about 54% of the total of Pakistan). In considering the phrase "independent states" in the Lahore resolution of 1940 (see Chapter 10), they felt that each area of Muslim concentration— the east and the northwest of India—should have been recognized separately at independence. They objected to the 1946 amendment of the resolution in which it was declared that a single state of Pakistan should be formed, and felt that within this arrangement a system similar to that of the cabinet mission plan should be set up (see Chapter 1). That is, they called for a central government with powers over foreign affairs, defense, and currency; a zonal federation for West Pakistan (none was needed for the east); and provincial autonomy of the highest degree. These proposals, though rejected by the rulers in West Pakistan, formed the basis of the Six Points of Mujibur Rahman when they were announced in 1966.

Bengalis found that the new government of Pakistan in Karachi included none of the political figures who had led the Muslim League to its substantial victory in the 1945–1946 election in Bengal. Representatives from Bengal included a Scheduled Caste Hindu and an Urdu-speaking member of the national elite. The pre-independence Muslim League prime minister of Bengal, Husain Shaheed Suhrawardy, was replaced by the Urdu-speaking Khwaja Nazimuddin as chief minister of East Bengal.[2] This dismissal of the talents of Suhrawardy by Jinnah would come back to haunt the West Pakistanis: Suhrawardy founded the party that became the Awami League and led the struggle for autonomy and eventually independence for Bangladesh. The Muslim League ministry that ruled in East Bengal until 1954 became increasingly unrepresentative of the province as it supported the activities of the national Muslim League, seen by many to be inimical to East Pakistani interests.

The formulation of a constitution for Pakistan was a long and difficult task. One of the key points of contention was the level of representation to be given to each wing in the parliament. West Pakistanis tried to find a formula that would result in equality of representation between the two wings. One proposal, eventually abandoned, would have created two houses in parliament, with the lower one representing the people on the basis of population and the upper representing the federating units on the basis of equality. The excess seats in the upper house for the west would have exactly offset the majority for the east in the lower house, so that when the houses met jointly to settle disputes on legislation between them there would be "parity" between the wings.

The word *parity* (or *equality*) became a key slogan in constitution making. To West Pakistanis it meant equality of parliamentary representation only, but to East Pakistanis it carried a broader meaning—not only parliamentary membership (a sacrifice for the Bengalis) but also steps toward parity in representation in the civil and military services and, most important, in investment in the economy. On the understanding that the latter meaning was accepted, the Bengalis agreed to the parity principle in parliament and paved the way for the 1956 constitution as a precursor to a parliamentary system of government. Another argument arose, however, over joint or separate electorates. The Bengalis favored joint electorates (despite their substantial non-Muslim minority) because the then-ruling parties in the east, including the Awami League, believed they would be the beneficiaries of the non-Muslim vote to the evident cost of the Muslim League. The Muslim League constitution barred non-Muslims from membership and clearly did not represent minority interests.

Administrative Problems

The Bengalis were greatly underrepresented in the central civilian services, which included the Civil Service of Pakistan (CSP), and even more so in the military services. The latter problem dates back to the British concept of martial races under which the Bengalis were excluded from military service. Bengali membership in the military services was about 6% in the late 1960s, a figure that led Mujibur Rahman during the 1970 election campaign to suggest that East Pakistan would contribute 6% of its taxes to the maintenance of the Pakistan military. In addition to their concern about membership, the East Pakistanis were worried that their province was defenseless against India. Pakistani military doctrine stated that the defense against India must come from the west wing and that troops should be concentrated there. The conflict of 1965 did not result in an Indian attack on the east, but this fact was of no comfort to the Bengalis.

With respect to civil employment, the pre-independence Indian Civil Service (ICS) did not contain sufficient Muslim Bengalis to staff the positions in Dhaka or to provide for parity in representation in the bureaucracy in Karachi and Islamabad. As a result, high-level posts in Dhaka, including that of governor, were often filled by West Pakistanis or refugees from India who had declared for West Pakistan. A quota system was implemented in the examinations for the various services, but it did not result in numerical parity; nor did it significantly improve the situation in terms of the level of posts held by Bengalis.

Economic Disparity

In the 1950s and early 1960s, East Pakistan maintained with justification that it had earned the majority of the exports of Pakistan, largely through jute exports, but was allocated much less than its share in expending the earnings. This larger amount of exports from the east continued until the mid-1960s; thereafter, exports of cotton, other agricultural commodities and manufactured goods from the west exceeded the total exports of the east. The East Pakistanis also saw substantial amounts of foreign assistance going to the west, especially in the huge Indus basin project, whereas no equivalent project was developed for the east. More important, the industrial development of the east was almost entirely in the hands of West Pakistani entrepreneurs who, it was believed, exported their profits to the west and imported high-level employees to the east. The Bengalis lost out on both reinvestment of profits and jobs at the upper echelons of industry. Banking was also primarily a West Pakistani function.

The west responded to the Bengalis' complaints with two major points. First, the resources of East Pakistan, beyond jute and paper manufacturing and a few other areas, were not attractive to investors. Second, certain expenditures had to be made in the west for governmental infrastructure, including the military. These economic grievances would eventually lead to several of the Six Points of Sheikh Mujibur Rahman.

National and Regional Elites

The reader may recall the reference made in Chapter 16 to "national" and "regional" (or "vernacular") elites in East Pakistan.[3] In the pre-independence period, the national elite was so called because it supported the policies, aspirations, and programs of the Muslim League on an all-India basis. In the post-independence period, the group again supported national issues and the All-Pakistan Muslim League. In each case the national elite was viewed by many (perhaps most) Bengalis as ignoring the special problems of the region and province.

Although we will look at individual leaders in the next chapter, it is here that some generalizations may be drawn concerning the national and regional elites. The national elite was usually associated with the groups that came into eastern Bengal from northern India and even Kashmir as officials of the Mughal and preceding Muslim rulers. Their official positions often gained them grants of land that made the families residents in eastern Bengal, even if they were not originally from the area. In many cases the lands were in eastern Bengal, but the seat of political activities was Calcutta, which also served as a base for education. Often these families used Urdu rather than Bengali as a family language and could not speak the local language well. Representative of these families were those of the nawabs of Dhaka (of whom Nazimuddin was the most prominent member) and Bogra (who also gave Pakistan a prime minister in Muhammad Ali), and the former nawab family of Bengal situated in Murshidabad (whose representative at the highest level was Iskandar Mirza). To the extent that these families were active in post-1947 politics, they generally supported the Muslim League.

The regional elite viewed politics as primarily a Bengali Muslim concern and fought for causes specific to eastern Bengal. For example, opposition to Hindu (and Muslim) landlordism was a frequent cause for which they campaigned. The campaigning was in Bengali and aimed at those less high on the economic scale, even in times of the restrictive franchise before independence in 1947. After independence this group, by far the largest, was in the forefront of autonomist movements and eventually the independence movement. Husain Shaheed Suhrawardy, originally a member of the national elite, converted to the regional elite and joined the "lion of Bengal," Fazlul Haq, in the 1954 United Front to oust the Muslim League from office in East Bengal. As we shall see in the next chapter, Mujibur Rahman was heir both to Suhrawardy, who founded the Awami League, and to Fazlul Haq, who began the popularization of regional Muslim politics in Bengal.

The Rise of the Awami League

Although Suhrawardy is most often credited with the founding of the Awami League in 1949, he, of course, did not act in a vacuum. He soon saw that the national Muslim League was going against his assessment of the best interests of East Bengal and worked with others to begin a movement that would pose a challenge to the Muslim League. At the time, Fazlul Haq was out of the ministry but held office as advocate general of the province. Breakaway parties from the Muslim League were also present in West Pakistan, and there seemed to Suhrawardy the possibility of forming an all-Pakistan opposition. The prime minister, Liaquat Ali Khan, had taken the strong view that oppositionists would be just short of traitors, but Suhrawardy was not dissuaded.

The first party name chosen was the Awami ("people's") Muslim League, a name that implied that the people themselves had little to say about a political system that was still in the hands of those whose electoral mandate pre-dated independence. It also avoided a break with the communal political arrangement that still applied in Pakistan (the leading opposition party was the Pakistan National Congress, a Hindu group from Bengal). Suhrawardy had earlier opposed the communal limitations on membership in the Muslim League, saying that they were contrary to Jinnah's statement that all Pakistanis should consider themselves Pakistanis and leave religion to personal preference.[4] The word *Muslim* was soon dropped from the name of the new party, which became the Awami League.

Suhrawardy's associates included a senior, and somewhat leftist, representative of the Islamic scholars, Maulana Abdul Hamid Khan Bhashani, and a number of his followers. Their views on economic matters differed from those of the conservative Suhrawardy, but their views on regional issues were the same. Suhrawardy also drew to him a number of outstanding lieutenants, including Sheikh Mujibur Rahman, the future leader of Bangladesh, and Ataur Rahman Khan, who became chief minister of East Pakistan (at several times during 1956–1958) and prime minister of Bangladesh (1984–1985). In the west, the party consisted largely of lawyers and other professionals as well as some pre-independence parties that were unsure of their future course after 1947. The total in the west was always small, however.

Suhrawardy and the Awami League joined forces with Fazlul Haq, who revived his former party but called it by a new name, the Krishak Sramik party (KSP) or Peasants and Workers party. They were also joined by a few smaller parties to contest the provincial election in 1954. The resulting United Front won a stunning victory, taking 223 of the 237 Muslim seats (reducing the Muslim League to 10) and had allies among the 72 non-Muslims elected (the poll was held under separate electorates). The twenty-one-point program of the United Front was autonomist in form. Suhrawardy, however, agreed to the 1956 constitution on the basis that it would go well beyond parity in parliament to include steps toward equality in the administration and the economy.

The central government initially denied the United Front the right to govern but eventually agreed to parliamentary government in East Pakistan. When the United Front split, the KSP and the Awami League became rivals, and the tussles of East Pakistan were among the proximate causes of the takeover of the Pakistan government by Muhammad Ayub Khan in 1958.[5] Open politics were suppressed during the Ayub regime (1958–1969), and the national elite staged a comeback by using the indirect electoral system of the period, but this absence of parliamentary politics did not extinguish the feeling of many Bengalis that they were being "colonized" by West Pakistan and that autonomy was the solution to this problem.

This period of Ayub's rule added greatly to the strength of the regionalist political culture in which those active in politics became socialized. As in the earlier period of language-issue agitation, university students and professors and other groups in the elite were alienated from the system of Ayub—a factor critical to our understanding of the political views under which Bangladesh was born.

The failure of Pakistan to reach its goals in the 1965 war with India seemed to many oppositionists to demonstrate Ayub's vulnerability. At a meeting in Lahore in February 1966, Mujibur Rahman (who became operational leader of the Awami League after Suhrawardy's death in 1963) delivered a bombshell in the form of the Six Points. These are summarized as follows: (1) A federal government, parliamentary in form, shall be established, with free and regular elections; (2) the federal government shall control only foreign affairs and defense; (3) a separate currency, or separate fiscal accounts, shall control movement of capital from east to west; (4) all taxation powers shall reside at the provincial level, with the federal government subsisting on grants from the provinces; (5) each province may enter into trade agreements with foreign countries and control the allocation of its earnings of foreign currency; and (6) each unit may raise its own militia.[6] To Mujib these points were a means, perhaps a last means, of keeping a united Pakistan; to others in the opposition, as well as to Ayub, they were a demand for independence.

Ayub fell in 1969 and was replaced by General Agha Muhammad Yahya Khan. Yahya described himself as a caretaker whose primary task, after restoring law and order, was to hold elections to determine the wishes of the people of Pakistan. He also set out his requirements regarding the nature of a new constitution and in doing so paid lip service to the principle of provincial autonomy. Of Mujibur Rahman's Six Points, he opposed the fourth (and for good reason if Pakistan were to survive): denial of the power of taxation to the central government.[7]

Elections were held in December 1970 after nearly a year of open campaigning by all political parties. Yahya had decided that elections should be held on a system of joint electorates and on the basis of population rather than parity. In a 300-member house (313 when 7 indirectly elected women from the east and 6 from the west were added), the east would directly elect 162 members and the west, 138, from single-member constituencies. In the east wing, the Awami League won 160 out of 162, with more than three-quarters of the vote. The west had been divided into four provinces by Yahya—the Punjab, Sindh, The North-West Frontier Province and Baluchistan. The Pakistan People's party led by Zulfiqar Ali Bhutto won a majority in West Pakistan as a whole, with 81 seats of the 138, but a majority in only two provinces, the Punjab and Sindh. Similar results were recorded for the provincial assemblies; in particular, the Awami League won 288 of 300 seats in East Pakistan.[8]

Mujibur Rahman claimed victory as well as the right to frame a new constitution on the basis of the Six Points and the right to form a government for Pakistan. At one point Yahya hailed Mujib as the "future prime minister of Pakistan." But the military was not pleased with this outcome, seeing, if nothing else, a diminution of its power and its budget (under the fourth point). Bhutto, too, was unsatisfied, inasmuch as he saw himself playing second fiddle to a Bengali. Negotiations on a constitution and the transfer of power from the military to the civilians continued through January, February, and early March 1971, with greater opposition from Bhutto and responsive stonewalling by the Awami League amid growing concerns by Yahya and his associates. Bhutto claimed that there were two majorities in Pakistan and that he led one of them and would have to be accommodated in any arrangements made. Mujib came under increasing pressure to separate from Pakistan and allow Bangladesh (the name then being used) to go its own independent way. Meanwhile, Yahya had sworn to uphold the unity of Pakistan. It was clear that Yahya's troops, consisting mostly of Punjabis and Pathans, would prefer to try to repress Mujib and the Bengalis before they attempted to put down Bhutto and the Punjabis if it were necessary to resort to force. In the early part of March, civil disobedience began on a wide scale in East Pakistan, and clashes between the Pakistan army and Awami Leaguers escalated.[9]

Civil War and a New Nation-State

On the night of March 25, 1971, the Pakistan army, strengthened by new manpower from the west, struck at the Awami Leaguers and others in Bangladesh (especially Dhaka) in an effort to end the resistance the military had met. In the past, police and military measures had broken the Bengali opposition, but this time the attack on the Bengalis was so brutal that it stiffened their resolve to become an independent nation. On March 27, an independent state was declared by a Pakistani (now Bangladeshi) officer, Major Ziaur Rahman, at Chittagong. Ziaur Rahman would later become one of the heroes of the civil war and, later still, a president of independent Bangladesh.

The details of the civil war that led to Bangladeshi independence are available elsewhere.[10] Suffice to say here that India assisted the Mukti Bahini (national army) and intervened in the war against Pakistan in November and December 1971. Pakistan army units surrendered to the Indian army on December 16, 1971, and Bangladesh became an independent, sovereign state.

Mujibur Rahman, who had been arrested on the night of the Pakistan army crackdown, taken to West Pakistan, and charged with treason, was released by the new Pakistani government headed by Bhutto, who in turn had succeeded Yahya after the latter resigned in disgrace. Mujib returned to Bangladesh in January and assumed the reins of government as prime minister (see Chapter 18).

The fall of united Pakistan seems to many observers to have been the final act in a play that began in 1947. There was little hope for a final act that would be anything but tragic for Pakistan and triumphant (even in tragic circumstances) for Bangladesh. The differences between the two wings were so great that unity was little more than transient. Who should be placed in the dock? Many would say that Bhutto was responsible in the final act, but others would maintain that Jinnah may have played the key role in the first act. There, nonetheless, remains a community of interests between Bangladesh and Pakistan (see Chapter 31).

*   *   *

In sum, the political culture of Bangladesh cannot be understood apart from the events of the period 1947–1971. Two factors are paramount. First, there was the growing alienation of the Bangladeshis (as they were to be called) from the concept of a united Muslim homeland in the subcontinent. This alienation was the often unintentional consequence of the great disparity in resources between the two wings of united Pakistan. The natural resources of the east were few and the human resources were underdeveloped as a result of centuries of neglect under Muslim and British rulers. Second, there was the concomitant growth of a feeling that might be called "Bengalness." These two factors influenced the process of socialization at almost all levels of the elite, and, during the civil war, flooded throughout the Bangladeshi population. Socialization in the direction of liberal democracy (or even that of statism) did occur but it was secondary to the alienation and regionalism that pervaded the system.

Notes

1. This phrase was attributed, perhaps erroneously, to Henry Kissinger; in any event, it was widely used.

2. The nomenclature of the eastern province of Pakistan can be a bit confusing. In 1947, it was designated East Bengal inasmuch as the portion remaining in India was (and is) West Bengal. With the unification of West Pakistan in 1955, the province became East Pakistan. With independence in 1971, it became Bangladesh, land of the Bengalis, although not all of Bengal was included in Bangladesh. After independence, the people were first called *Bangalees,* but the term *Bangladeshis* is now in general use.

3. See Rounaq Jahan, *Pakistan: Failure in National Integration* (New York: Columbia University Press, 1972), pp. 38ff, for a discussion of the vernacular (regional) and national elites.

4. The statement by Jinnah is contained in a number of publications including Sharif al Mujahid, *Quaid-i-Azam Jinnah: Studies in Interpretation* (Karachi: Quaid-i-Azam Academy, 1981), pp. 247–248.

5. For a short summary of politics during the Pakistan period, see Craig Baxter, *Bangladesh: A New Nation in an Old Setting* (Boulder, Colo.: Westview Press, 1984), Chapter 4.

6. Ibid., p. 45.

7. Legal Framework Order, March 30, 1970.

8. For more detailed results see Craig Baxter, "Pakistan Votes—1970," *Asian Survey,* vol. 11, no. 3 (March 1971), pp. 197–218.

9. For more information see David Dunbar (pseudonym for Craig Baxter), "Pakistan: The Failure of Political Negotiations," *Asian Survey,* vol. 12, no. 5 (May 1972), pp. 444–461; and Craig Baxter, "Pakistan and Bangladesh," in Frederick L.

Shiels, ed., *Ethnic Separatism and World Politics* (Lanham, Md.: University Press of America, 1984), pp. 209–262.

10. For a discussion of the civil war, see Shiels, *Ethnic Separatism;* A.M.A. Muhith, *Bangladesh: Emergence of a Nation* (Dhaka: Bangladesh Books International, 1978); and Mizanur Rahman Shelley, *Emergence of a New Nation in a Multipolar World: Bangladesh* (Dhaka: University Press, 1979).

Suggested Readings

Kamruddin Ahmad. *A Socio-Political History of Bengal* (Dhaka: Zahiruddin Mahmud, 1975).

Maudud Ahmad. *Bangladesh: Constitutional Quest for Autonomy* (Dhaka: University Press, 1979).

Craig Baxter. *Bangladesh: A New Nation in an Old Setting* (Boulder, Colo.: Westview Press, 1984).

_____ . "Bangladesh," in Frederick L. Shiels, ed., *Ethnic Separatism and World Politics* (Lanham, Md.: University Press of America, 1984).

Muhammad Abdul Wadud Bhuiyan. *Emergence of Bangladesh and the Role of the Awami League* (New Delhi: Vikas, 1982).

Rounaq Jahan. *Pakistan: Failure in National Integration* (New York: Columbia University Press, 1972).

Talukder Maniruzzaman. *The Politics of Development: The Case of Pakistan, 1947–1958* (Dhaka: Green Book House, 1971).

A.M.A. Muhith. *Bangladesh: Emergence of a Nation* (Dhaka: Bangladesh Books International, 1978).

Hasan Askari Rizvi. *Internal Strife and External Intervention: India's Role in the Civil War in East Pakistan* (Lahore: Progressive Publishers, 1981).

Richard S. Wheeler. *The Politics of Pakistan: A Constitutional Quest* (Ithaca, N.Y.: Cornell University Press, 1970).

18
LEADERS AND FOLLOWERS

The tendency of the Muslims in Bengal since the beginning of mass politics, about 1920, has been to support a single leader and a single issue—a major factor in Bangladeshi politics, as will be seen in the review of elections below. The issues in question have pertained to the Bengalis in particular and have often gone against the view of the Muslim League at the national level. Even in 1945–1946 Bengalis voted for Bengali issues. The leadership, too, was often drawn from the vernacular elite rather than from the national.

Elections

When the franchise was broadened by the Government of India Act of 1935 (see Chapter 1) and elections were held in the winter of 1936–1937 for the Bengal Legislative Council and Legislative Assembly, much of the eastern Bengal electorate gave its support to Fazlul Haq and his Krishak Praja party (KPP), or Farmers and Peoples party. However, the Muslim League gained an almost equal number of seats as a result of its support from voters in the western part of Bengal, where Hindus predominated. These Muslim voters supported the national Muslim League along with Muslim voters in the Hindu-majority areas of north India. Their leader, Khwaja Sir Nazimuddin of the Nawab of Dhaka family, was a member of the national elite. The Muslim majority of eastern Bengal did not fear numerical Hindu domination; the Muslim minority of western Bengal did, as did the Muslim minority in such provinces as Bihar and the United Provinces (now Uttar Pradesh). The cause on which Fazlul Haq campaigned was that of the smaller farmers against *zamindars* (landlords), who were generally Hindu.

In the election of the winter of 1945–1946, the issue was a national one: the separation of Muslim-majority areas of undivided India from the Hindu-majority territories. The champions of this view were Muhammad Ali Jinnah and the Muslim League, which he led. The Muslim voters in Bengal gave their support to the League, which won overwhelmingly, gaining all 6 seats in the Central Legislative Assembly with 94.01% of the vote and winning 112 of the 119 Muslim seats in the provincial assembly with 82.04% of the vote. The outcome, however, was both regional and national, for at the time the poll was held the concept of a Muslim homeland in India was based on the plural "independent states" of the Lahore resolution of 1940. It was only *after* the election that a single state (with two wings) was sought.

By 1954, the national positions taken by the Muslim League had alienated most Bengalis, and the Muslim League was routed by the United Front, which consisted principally of the Krishak Sramik party of Fazlul Haq and the Awami League of Husain Shaheed Suhrawardy. In this election, two regional elite leaders combined forces and had the cooperation of a third, Maulana Abdul Hamid Khan Bhashani. The single issue in 1954 concerned the ending or, at least, moderation of West Pakistani dominance. These demands were embodied in the twenty-one-point program described in the previous chapter.

Direct elections were suspended during the period of rule by Ayub Khan, but, as already mentioned, direct elections with open and free campaigning were restored by the decrees of Yahya Khan and elections were held in 1970. The leader of the Awami League was now Sheikh Mujibur Rahman, and the issue was provincial autonomy as demanded in the Six Points. Again, the issue and the leader combined to produce a large victory. The issue at the forefront of the post-independence election of 1973, which once more resulted in Mujib's victory, was a request for a confirmation that the policies of Mujibism were those desired by the people. After the elections there was no doubt, despite a measure of tinkering with the results, that the people supported Mujib. The Awami League won 291 seats of the 300 contested and took 73.18% of the popular vote.

Elections were not held again until the time of the regime headed by Major General Ziaur Rahman. Zia, as he was called, won the presidential election of 1978 with 76.63% of the vote, whereas his nearest rival, General M.A.G. Osmani, who had the support of the major faction of the Awami League, won but 21.70% (the remaining votes went to several other candidates). Zia followed this outcome with a major victory in the parliamentary elections held in 1979, when his party, the Bangladesh Nationalist party (BNP), won 207 seats out of 300. The percentage of the popular vote (41.16%), however, was lower than that of the winners in previous elections, perhaps because of the extraordinarily large number of candidates running. The leader was clearly the newly charismatic Zia, and the issue was an endorsement of his nineteen-point program for the development of Bangladesh.[1] In 1981, the BNP successfully elected a successor to Zia, Abdus Sattar, but his term was ended by the military coup led by H. M. Ershad in March 1982. Parliamentary elections held by Ershad's regime in 1986 and 1988 were also one-sided. However, this resulted largely from the boycott of the election by the BNP in 1986 and by both the BNP and the Awami League in 1988.

With this almost sheep-like following of a leader during an election came a quick and dangerous letdown into another aspect of Bangladeshi politics, factionalism. It has often been said that Bengal is the most politicized province in India. But there is also this frequently quoted statement: that one Bengali is one political party; two Bengalis, two political parties; and three Bengalis, two political parties with a dissident faction in one of them. Factionalism caused the victorious Muslim League in 1946 to reject the continuance in office of Nazimuddin and to replace him with the urbane and emerging regional elitist Suhrawardy, although Jinnah's intervention reversed this decision once independence had been won. After the 1954 election the United Front was unable to remain united, and from then until 1958, when Ayub took over, there was a constant tussle between Fazlul Haq's KSP and Suhrawardy's Awami League for control of the provincial government. The defection of Bhashani from the Awami League also hurt that party. Through the imposition of emergency rule Mujib was able to keep most, but not all, of the Awami League together after 1973; but he was merely sweeping factionalism under the rug, given its reemergence after Mujib's death in 1975. Zia's party was also factionalized but this became more evident only after he was assassinated in 1981. Ershad's Janata party, however, has suffered little factionalism in the sense that it has not split into rival factions.

Political Leaders

Several Bengali Muslim political leaders have been mentioned in this introduction; some of these careers began in the British period, some in the Pakistan period, and two, Ziaur Rahman and H. M. Ershad, in the post-independence period. Only Mujibur Rahman spanned all three periods. It will be useful to look briefly at some of these key figures and to analyze their use of political skills.

Maulvi A.K. Fazlul Haq: The Regional Elite

Maulvi Abul Kasim Fazlul Haq (1873–1962) came from the coastal district of Barisal (then called Bakerganj) in eastern Bengal.[2] He was truly a vernacular Bengali in that he had neither the landed aristocracy background of Nazimuddin nor the urbane Muslim intellectual background of Suhrawardy. He completed his education in college and law school in Calcutta, where he qualified to become a *vakil* (local lawyer), and set out to serve people and thereby build up his political reputation. His private legal practice was preceded by government service from 1906 to 1912. His entry into elective politics came a year later, in 1913, when he was elected to the Bengal Legislative Council as it was constituted under the Government of India Act of 1909. He served until 1920 and then was regularly elected to the council as it was set up under dyarchy beginning with the 1921 election, serving until that council ended in 1937. His electoral success continued as he led the Krishak Praja party in 1937 in the election for the new Bengal Legislative Assembly; he had founded the party in 1927, as an expression of the regional interests of Bengali Muslims.

During the period of dyarchy (1921–1937), Fazlul Haq had held a number of ministerial appointments, and after the new government was formed in 1937, he became Bengal's first prime minister (as the office was designated prior to independence; it was redesignated chief minister afterward).[3] He formed a coalition with the Muslim League and some Hindu independents. This coalition fell in 1941, when Fazlul Haq broke with the Muslim League, but he was able to form a new ministry with Hindu associates, including, oddly, the communal Hindu Mahasabha. This lasted until 1943, when the new ministry fell, and the Muslim League under Nazimuddin was able to form a ministry of its own. Fazlul Haq became advocate general of East Bengal after independence but resigned the post to revive his party under the altered name, Krishak Sramik party (KSP); he then led it to victory in the United Front alliance with the Awami League in the 1954 election. After that he served briefly as chief minister of East Bengal in 1954, as a central minister in 1955–1956, and as governor of East Pakistan in 1956–1958.

Given his distinguished and active career, one that ended with the assumption of power by Ayub Khan in 1958, Fazlul Haq clearly earned the title *Sher-i-Bengal* (Lion of Bengal), by which he is still known. During his career he was notable for standing for the interests of his region. He had been a member of the Congress (as was almost everyone in politics in the pre-Gandhi period) and a member of the Muslim League, attending the Lucknow session and serving as president before Jinnah made that position his personal fief.

These ventures into national politics did not make Fazlul Haq any less a regional figure. Nor did his moving of the Lahore resolution at the Muslim League session in 1940. This resolution, as we have already seen, demanded separate states for the Muslims if recognition of their rights was not given by the British and the Hindus. It is noteworthy that Fazlul Haq supported the motion with the use of the plural word *states*; he did not abandon his Muslim Bengali political position. Nor did he abandon it when he opposed Jinnah in 1941, and left the Muslim League permanently. Fazlul Haq had been asked as prime minister of Bengal to join a defense advisory council set up by the viceroy. Jinnah claimed that no Muslim Leaguer could join without Jinnah's permission. Claiming that Jinnah was a dictator, Fazlul Haq resigned both from the advisory council and the Muslim League.

Fazlul Haq gained and maintained his popularity through seemingly endless travels throughout eastern Bengal, the most anyone had taken up to his time; perhaps now he has been exceeded by Mujib, Zia, and Ershad. He knew the problems of his fellow Bengalis and worked diligently to solve them. He supported land reform legislation and greater expenditures on education and health. His legacy of the KSP as a party has all but disappeared, but the policies oriented toward rural development have continued insofar as they have been incorporated into the platforms of the Awami League and Zia's and Ershad's party.

Khwaja Sir Nazimuddin

Of the principal leaders discussed here, the only one to have been knighted by the British was Khwaja Sir Nazimuddin (1894–1964), throughout most of his career the principal rival of Fazlul Haq. Their origins could hardly have been more different. Nazimuddin, a member of the wealthy landed nawab of Dhaka family, was related to an earlier nawab whose palace was the site of the founding of the Muslim League in 1906. The family is Kashmiri in origin, often associated with British rule, Urdu-speaking at home, rarely politically fluent in Bengali, and part of the national elite. Nazimuddin's education was very much different from that of his rival. He attended Aligarh Muslim University and then continued at Cambridge.

In the period of restricted franchise, Nazimuddin, too, was elected to the Bengal Legislative Council and served as a minister (1929–1934) under dyarchy. In the coalition between the KPP and the Muslim League he was home minister (1937–1941), but he became leader of the opposition (1941–1943) before being chosen prime minister (1943–1945). He lost an attempt to return as prime minister in 1946 when his faction was defeated by Suhrawardy's after the election of 1945–1946. Nazimuddin, however, became the winner after independence with the backing of Jinnah and was named chief minister of East Bengal in 1947. He succeeded as governor general of Pakistan on Jinnah's death in 1949 and then stepped down from that position to succeed Liaquat Ali Khan as prime minister when Liaquat was assassinated in 1951. He was dismissed from office in 1953. Under Ayub Khan, Nazimuddin reorganized the Muslim League (council faction) and headed the combined opposition against Ayub at his (Nazimuddin's) death in 1964.[4]

Despite his long service in high positions, Nazimuddin was never looked upon by Bengali Muslims as a representative of them and their interests. He was a member of the national elite and spoke for all-India and later all-Pakistan interests. He was never elected in a direct election, having earlier won in university constituencies where his fellow Urdu-speakers comprised the majority of the electorate.[5]

Although Nazimuddin did not represent the aspirations of the regional elite and the mass of Bengali Muslims, his skills are recognized in Dhaka.

He, Fazlul Haq, and Suhrawardy are buried in adjacent graves in a Dhaka park. A factionalized Muslim League now exists in Bangladesh as a party on the fringe.[6]

Husain Shaheed Suhrawardy

If Nazimuddin was born into a family of great landed prominence, Husain Shaheed Suhrawardy (1893–1963) represented a Muslim Bengali family of exceptional intellectual and artistic talents. The family was also one that spoke Urdu rather than Bengali at home. Suhrawardy was educated in Calcutta and Oxford and entered the bar from Gray's Inn in London. Although he had been born in western Bengal, in Midnapur, Calcutta became the focus of his political career. He achieved prominence as deputy mayor of Calcutta in the 1920s. In 1937, he was elected to the Bengal assembly and served as a minister during the coalition with Fazlul Haq and during the premiership of Nazimuddin, with whom he developed a rivalry. Nazimuddin represented the national elite from eastern Bengal; Suhrawardy the national elite from Calcutta and the west; and Fazlul Haq the regional elite. After the 1945–1946 election, Suhrawardy defeated Nazimuddin for the premiership and gained prominence first for his presumed support of the Muslims in the Great Calcutta Killing in 1946 and then for his close work with Mahatma Gandhi to calm communal disturbances in 1947. He had been the mover of the resolution that amended the Lahore resolution to provide for a single Muslim state, but shortly afterward he turned his attention to the issue of Bengali nationalism when, along with some Congress leaders, he proposed a united Bengal as a third dominion in India. This action alone lowered his standing with Jinnah to the extent that after partition he was excluded from political office and succeeded by Nazimuddin as prime minister.

Suhrawardy remained in Calcutta, where he watched as the Muslim League failed to meet the goals of the East Pakistanis; he then went to Karachi to claim his seat in the Pakistan constituent assembly. He opposed the Muslim League policy of continuing the party's exclusive Muslim membership and proposed the establishment of a new party open to all Pakistanis. He subsequently broke with the Muslim League to form what became the Awami League, a party primarily based in East Pakistan that became the voice of Bengali interests. Suhrawardy never spoke Bengali with the accent of an eastern Bengali, but accompanied by his aides, he canvassed the entire province and led the party, in alliance with the KSP, to victory in 1954.

Suhrawardy's agreement with Fazlul Haq was that the KSP would govern in Dhaka while Suhrawardy went to Karachi to represent Bengali interests there. He nevertheless continued his efforts to make the Awami League an effective party in West Pakistan, where he had a law practice in Lahore at the Supreme Court, but he was largely unsuccessful. He served as prime minister of Pakistan, 1956–1957, in the eyes of many the most skilled prime minister in the pre-Ayub period.

Suhrawardy was a convert to regional elitism. Although his own skills were best used at the national level, he chose a group of locally skilled political figures who built the Awami League into the best organized party in Pakistan (albeit only in the east). His political lieutenant in Dhaka was Ataur Rahman Khan (b. 1907), who was several times chief minister of East Pakistan before Ayub and prime minister of Bangladesh (1984–1985). His organizational lieutenant was Sheikh Mujibur Rahman. At Suhrawardy's death in 1963, the party leadership fell to Mujib, who represented the regional elite to an even greater extent.

Sheikh Mujibur Rahman

Mujib (1920–1975) was born far from the centers of power, in Gopalganj in Faridpur District. He attended but did not graduate from a college in Calcutta, having become involved in politics through the All-India Muslim Students Federation in 1940. He was a member of the Muslim League, but joined Suhrawardy and others in what became the Awami League in 1949. He was general secretary in 1952 after gaining experience at lower levels of the organization and was elected to the East Bengal assembly in 1954. He had very brief stints in the cabinet at Dhaka and at Karachi, but it was evident that his skills were more appropriate in the party organization and campaigning. Having become the de facto successor to Suhrawardy in 1963, Mujib was jailed on several occasions during the Ayub period. His statement of the Six Points in Lahore in 1966 (see Chapter 17) was followed by an accusation of collaboration with India to set East Pakistan free in what was known as the Agartala conspiracy case.[7] During the agitation against Ayub in 1968–1969, demands were made for his release. He was freed in 1969, and the case was never completed. He led the Awami League to victory in 1970 and was arrested in 1971, but he returned to lead Bangladesh in 1972—first as prime minister and then as president. He was assassinated on August 15, 1975, under circumstances that will be described in the next chapter.

Mujib's skills were quite clearly those of an organizer at the party level and of a haranguer of the crowds at public meetings. His roots were in the countryside, and in this respect he was more the successor of Fazlul Haq than the urbane Suhrawardy. The traditions of both the Awami League and the KSP seemed to merge in Mujib, but the KSP strand was probably stronger. His philosophy was expressed in *Mujibbad* (Mujibism), which will be discussed in the next chapter. At the beginning of the independent era in Bangladesh, he was adored by the masses, and was given the title

Bangabandhu (Beloved of Bengal). His skills, however, could not be transferred to the running of an independent government—hence his failure in that realm. His charismatic ability to lead was adaptable only to a movement, but in this he was equalled only, perhaps, by Fazlul Haq and Ziaur Rahman.

Maulana Abdul Hamid Khan Bhashani

Bhashani (1885–1976) is an enigma in Bangladeshi politics. Born in a small village in Tangail District he was a Bengali by birth, but one who gained his first political fame when he wandered as a barely trained Islamic leader (hence his title *maulana*) to Assam and there took up the cause of tenant farmers against landlords. His views were often considered radical within the Assam Muslim League inasmuch as he espoused the needs of the downtrodden, at least as he defined them. After independence he moved back to East Bengal and continued to support these causes. He joined with Suhrawardy in founding the Awami League.

Party discipline and Bhashani were strangers. He stood well to the left of the conservative Suhrawardy, was dubbed the "red Maulana" by some, and worked poorly with the populist Mujib. Bhashani broke with the Awami League to form what became the National Awami party in 1957, and under that umbrella he associated with groups ranging from the remnants of the banned Communist party of Pakistan to moderates who fought for the restoration of democracy to others whose principal demands were the undoing of the single province of West Pakistan. Bhashani supported Ayub to the extent of endorsing Ayub's policy of closer relations with China, but in the end he was one of Ayub's outspoken opponents, as he later would be of Mujib.

Bhashani represented another element in the regional elite, often a group to whom the word *elite* can barely be applied. He and his party never gained significant electoral support, but he was expected to take up the cause of the less fortunate—whether it was against the West Pakistanis or the Awami League in Bangladesh, or even against India on the Farakka water question (see Chapter 31). No one has ever replaced him in his role, as all potential claimants lack his charisma.

Ziaur Rahman

Major General Ziaur Rahman (1936–1981) was the principal leader of Bangladesh from 1975 until his death. He was born in Bogra District and attended the Pakistan Military Academy. His military career was uneventful (although it did include service on the Lahore front in 1965) until he found himself in control of Chittagong on March 27, 1971, and broadcast a Bangladeshi declaration of independence. He was one of the heroes of the liberation war but was not a favorite of Mujib, and he had risen only to the position of deputy chief of the army staff by the time Mujib was assassinated. He was claimed by the *sepoys* (soldiers) as their leader in the series of attempted revolutions in November 1975, and emerged then as the army leader in the martial law government. He subsequently became chief martial law administrator and then assumed the presidency in 1977, a post to which he was elected in 1978.

Despite his war record, Zia seemed an unlikely person to achieve a very high degree of popularity. He was quietly efficient but propelled himself into the public image by a seemingly unending whirl of tours throughout Bangladesh. He exhorted the Bangladeshis to work together—a key demand in a factionalized nation—to develop the resources of the country, limited though they were. Indeed, he preached the politics of hope, winning his position of leadership by this means and through his ability to make quick decisions. There was no reconciliation between Zia and the Awami League, but his nineteen-point program drew on the demands of the regional elite and stated rural development ideas that could be traced to Fazlul Haq. From his start as a shy, almost retiring person, Ziaur Rahman grew to be the most successful of the post-independence Bangladeshi leaders.

Husain Muhammad Ershad

Lieutenant General H. M. Ershad (b. 1930) led a military coup on March 24, 1982, against the regime headed by Abdus Sattar, who had been elected to succeed Ziaur Rahman. Ershad, like Zia, was a career military man. As he was in Pakistan during the civil war, he was unable to participate in the liberation campaign. Upon his repatriation to Bangladesh in 1973, he was appointed adjutant general, and in 1975, after a year at the Indian National Defence College in New Delhi, he was named deputy chief of staff of the army. When Zia relinquished his chief of staff post in 1978, Ershad replaced him and thereby became the principal military person on active duty. After Zia's assassination and Sattar's election, Ershad stated that the military should have a defined role in the governance of Bangladesh, a position that the civilian Sattar opposed. Sattar, however, did accept the appointment of a national security council that would include the three service chiefs as well as the president, prime minister and several ministers. This body was to be advisory in nature, but Ershad saw it as having a much more active role than did Sattar and his civilian colleagues.

As a leader Ershad (first as chief martial law administrator and then combining that position with the presidency) has been unable to develop the charisma that characterized Zia. Ershad did not hold elections until 1986, first for parliament and then for the presidency. His party, the Janata party, won the first and he the second, in both cases without the BNP participating and in the second with no significant organized opposition.

The withdrawal of the Awami League from parliament caused another election for that body in 1988 in which the Janata party won overwhelmingly against little opposition.

Ershad has continued the foreign policy set out by Zia and has made successful visits to several countries including the United States. He has made both rural development and industrialization the cornerstones of his policy and, especially in the former, has seen some progress. He has also carried further the early steps of Zia in decentralization of government by forming districts out of the former subdivisions and by holding nonpartisan elections at the local level (see Chapter 19). These actions, however, have not yet brought him the level of popularity Zia had among the mass of Bangladeshis.

*   *   *

In sum, the leadership line from Fazlul Haq to Ziaur Rahman has demonstrated the success of regional politics in Bangladesh, with the partial exception of the overriding national cause of separation from Hindu India. The roots of leadership are in the rural areas. Fazlul Haq, Suhrawardy, Bhashani, Mujib, Zia, and Ershad campaigned there and built their strength on the villagers and their local leaders. But along with this strengthening has always been the weakening of leadership through factionalism, a political disease that threatens Bangladeshi progress.

Notes

1. For detailed results by subdivisions and data from the earlier elections in 1946, 1954, 1970, and 1973, see Craig Baxter and M. Rashiduzzaman, "Bangladesh Votes: 1978 and 1979," *Asian Survey,* vol. 21, no. 4 (April 1981), pp. 485–500.

2. Biographies of Bengali leaders are scarce. One generally unsuccessful venture is that of A.S.M. Abdur Rab, *A. K. Fazlul Haq: His Life and Achievements* (Lahore: Firozsons, preface dated 1966). Another effort is that by Kazi Ahmed Kamal, *Politics and Inside Stories* (Dhaka: Kazi Giasuddin Ahmed, 1970), which discusses Fazlul Haq, Suhrawardy, and Bhashani.

3. Under the Government of India Act of 1935, and until independence in 1947, the heads of government in the provinces were designated prime ministers (premiers). After independence, in both India and Pakistan the title was changed to chief minister; the title of prime minister was reserved for the head of the central government.

4. Nazimuddin's brother, Khwaja Shahabuddin, was a minister in Ayub's cabinet, however.

5. Nazimuddin was succeeded in Dhaka by Nurul Amin (1897–1974), a fellow member of the national elite, who, although he staunchly opposed Ayub and was one of two nonmembers of the Awami League elected in 1970, remained dedicated to a united Pakistan and ended his career as vice president of Pakistan under Bhutto.

6. Another member of the nawab of Dhaka family, Khwaja Khairuddin, has moved to Karachi and is active in Muslim League politics there. Nazimuddin's brother, Khwaja Shahabuddin (see Note 4), remained in Pakistan after 1971 and died in Karachi in 1977.

7. So called from Agartala, the capital of the Indian state of Tripura where the plot was allegedly hatched.

Suggested Readings

Moudud Ahmed. *Bangladesh: Era of Sheikh Mujibur Rahman* (Dhaka: University Press, Ltd., 1983).

Golam Hossain. *General Ziaur Rahman and the BNP* (Dhaka: University Press, Ltd., 1988).

19
INSTITUTIONS AND
GOVERNMENTAL PROCESSES

Bangladesh has undergone a variety of regimes since it became independent in 1971. The goal of the newly independent nation was to establish a socialist democratic state, but this goal proved short-lived as Mujibur Rahman became increasingly authoritarian and the experiment ended in a one-party, single-leader government under him. Mujib's assassination brought a weak government for a brief period, followed by a military government that gradually liberalized the political system under Ziaur Rahman. In turn, Zia's assassination was followed by a weak system and a further dose of military government that so far has been unable to transform itself fully into something resembling an open democratic regime.

The Progress of Government

The Democratic Regime of Mujibur Rahman

The surrender of the Pakistan Army to the Indian Army on December 16, 1971, was largely an Indian matter in that it took place without the presence of representatives of the Bangladesh government-in-exile. Absent also was Mujibur Rahman, who was a prisoner of the Pakistanis. The surrender was accompanied by the fall of the regime of Yahya Khan in Pakistan. His successor, Zulfiqar Ali Bhutto, released Mujib and permitted him to return to Bangladesh via London and, at Mujib's choice, New Delhi. There the leader met with Indira Gandhi, whose ideas on the political, social, and economic goals of government did not differ substantially from his. Mujib arrived in Dhaka on January 10, 1972, and immediately stepped down from the post of president, which had been assigned to him by the government-in-exile, to become prime minister of the new state.

Mujib piloted the constitution of 1972 through the parliament, a body comprising members of the provincial assembly elected in 1970 along with those National Assembly members elected at the same time from what was then East Pakistan. The new constitution was a model of parliamentary democracy and closely followed that of India—with the exception of the federal provisions, as Bangladesh was to be a unitary state. The document included provisions for the basic rights of the people and contained "directive principles" that do not have the force of law but would, if they worked out, set the tone of the new regime.

These basic principles were often described as "Mujibism" or, in Bengali, "Mujibbad." There were four components to this political philosophy: nationalism, democracy, socialism, and secularism. The participation in one way or another of the overwhelming majority of the people and the almost total absence of non-Bengali minorities made the first "pillar" of Mujibism something that was almost accomplished before it was stated. Democracy—the basic freedoms including regular and fair elections—seems surely to have been an objective of Mujib and many of his associates, even though it would be subverted later. Socialism of the democratic and not Marxist variety, too, was a widely accepted dogma. This was true almost by accident as many industrial properties were owned by West Pakistanis who had fled and the assets came by default into the hands of the new government as "evacuee property." Secularism brought into practical operation the basic tenet of the Awami League that all were equal under the law and that religion and politics should be separate. Pakistan might go along the path toward an Islamic state, but Mujib's Bangladesh would follow the route taken by Nehru's secular India and would not Islamicize its polity.

Problems of Reconstruction, Leadership, and Development

The new government was soon overwhelmed by the enormity of the problem of reconstruction and rehabilitation following the immensely destructive conflict for independence. The social and economic fabric of the nation was badly damaged. Mujib's varying claims of the numbers who were killed, the minorities and Muslims who became refugees in India, and the women who were raped by Pakistanis were no doubt exaggerated, but that fact did not lessen the effect on the country or temper the intensity of the suffering. At independence Bangladesh was described grimly as an "international basket case" by some outside observers, using a term of the Vietnam period for those so severely wounded that they became almost totally dependent on others for assistance. Aid did come in vast amounts, not only in terms of food and medicine to provide succor to individuals but also in forms used to reconstruct the severely damaged infrastructure. In the international arena, the Soviets made themselves too conspicuous and the Indians stayed on too long in the eyes of many Bangladeshis (reviving the 1946 fear of Indian—that is, Hindu—domination). The Americans who were accused of being pro-Pakistani during the liberation war provided much of the assistance along with other Western nations, even though the Americans (and the Chinese) delayed full recognition of the new government longer than seemed necessary.

Very few members of the new government had earlier experience in governing. Mujib had but briefly been a minister, and a rather unsuccessful one at that. His leadership is almost universally judged to have been ineffective. Like many other leaders of independence movements, he was able to direct attention to the evils of what he would call the "colonialism" of Pakistan, but once in the seat of government he was unable to adapt to the new situation that found him—and not the Pakistanis—to be the decision maker. He also saw, as have other new leaders in other new countries, that the resource base of Bangladesh was just the same as that of East Pakistan.

What applied to Mujib personally was a problem for the Awami League as well. Among many local-level Awami Leaguers the expression of Louis XIV of France seemed apt: "The state is ours: let us enjoy it." Corruption was widespread, and Mujib failed to use the talents of many senior members of the civil service who were deemed by him to have remained at their posts in opposition to the freedom movement. As a result of this wastage of personnel, many persons qualified only by political persuasion were appointed to key positions, thereby adding both to inefficiency and to corruption.

Rehabilitation had to take precedence over development. Bangladesh faced critical food shortages and suffered famines during Mujib's period, despite assistance from many in the developed world. Much of the industrial sector was nationalized. Firms that were presumably profitable for West Pakistanis—Mujib had complained of the draining of funds from East Pakistan—now became money-losers and drains on the limited resources of Bangladesh.

The Authoritarian Regime of Mujibur Rahman

Still basking in the glow of being the key to liberation, Mujib and the Awami League went to the polls in 1973 to elect a new parliament. The party won almost all of the seats (307 out of 315), and it appeared that, despite some grumbling, the government of Mujib would be firmly in office for the ensuing five-year term of parliament. Parties said to have opposed the creation of Bangladesh were barred from contesting, but this fact probably made little difference in the continuing euphoric period. The challenge came mainly from the left, and it was weak.

The challenges became greater, however, as the law and order situation deteriorated, the economy failed to return to pre-independence levels, and corruption grew. Liberation of the nation also meant liberation of public opinion. The press began to attack the policies and methods of the government. Members of the opposition and even some members of the Awami League in parliament began to join the press in criticism.

Mujib's response to this situation was to declare a state of emergency in December 1974 and to suspend fundamental rights. He followed that action a month later by amending the constitution to provide for a presidential system with himself as president. In June 1975 he took further actions that made Bangladesh a single-party state and, for all practical purposes, gave absolute power to Mujib.

These steps did not alter the situation. The demands on the political system continued to be far greater than Mujib, his system, or the resources of the country could meet. On August 15, 1975, Mujib was assassinated in a plot led by a group of officers in the Bangladesh army. His system collapsed with his death.

The First Interregnum

With the death of Mujib and the arrest of several of his associates, the presidency was assumed by the next senior person in the cabinet, Khondakar Mushtaq Ahmad, a politician viewed as being one of the most conservative of the Awami Leaguers. Mushtaq promised elections and a return to parliamentary government. He disbanded the single party and promised to allow other parties to resume activities as elections approached. However, he did not take steps to prosecute the assassins of Mujib. In November 1975, a series of coups and attempted coups dislodged Mushtaq but did not permit pro-Mujib forces to gain power. Mushtaq yielded the office of president to the chief justice, A.S.M. Sayem, who also became chief martial law administrator. The key person, however, was one of the deputy chief martial law administrators, Major General Ziaur Rahman.

The Regime of Ziaur Rahman: Gradual Liberalization

Ziaur Rahman ("Zia"), the chief of the army staff, quickly emerged as the leading member of the ruling group. On November 30, 1976, he replaced Sayem as chief martial law administrator, and on April 21, 1977, he assumed the presidency when Sayem resigned on grounds of "ill health." He was confirmed in the presidency in May 1977, when a referendum approved his holding the office. The referendum, however, did not confer legitimacy on him or his system if for no other reason than that no alternatives were presented. In June 1978, he was elected president for a five-year term in a contested election.

Beyond these steps toward power, Zia developed a program that might be called the "politics of hope." The nineteen points of this program called for a revitalization of Bangladesh both economically and socially. Zia emphasized such steps as family planning and especially the expansion of agricultural production, with the goal of reaching self-sufficiency in food grains as soon as possible. Considerable progress was made during his period in office. Zia also had a vision of a subcontinent that would work as a unit to find solutions to the economic, social, and technological problems affecting the entire region. Zia was looked upon as a quiet soldier, albeit a war hero, when he assumed office, but he became a charismatic figure equalling and perhaps exceeding both Fazlul Haq and Mujibur Rahman.

In preparation for his campaign for the elected presidency, Zia had sanctioned the formation of a political party dedicated to his program and to his candidacy. After the election the party was reformed into the Bangladesh Nationalist party (BNP), which became Zia's vehicle for obtaining a majority in the parliamentary elections held in February 1979. The BNP won 207 of 300 directly elected seats; the Awami League was a distant second with but 39 seats. Shah Azizur Rahman was appointed the first elected prime minister under the new parliament.

Zia was not without opponents. The Awami League was opposed to his military rule, to his failure to punish the assassins of Mujib, and to his less than socialistic economic policies. It believed that the principles of Mujibism were being sacrificed, even though Zia's program represented for others a pragmatic stance toward the many problems of Bangladesh. Zia restored to office the civil servants unutilized by Mujib. He also rehabilitated the military officers who had been forced to remain in Pakistan during 1971. A split in the army took place between the groups roughly termed "freedom fighters" and "returnees."

Considerable economic progress was made during the Zia regime, partly, of course, as a result of relatively good weather conditions and partly as the outcome of extensive foreign assistance. Zia's career, however, was terminated suddenly on May 30, 1981, when he was assassinated in Chittagong in a conspiracy in which a freedom fighter general played a part. The details of the conspiracy have not yet been revealed.

The Second Interregnum

Vice President Abdus Sattar became the acting president upon Zia's death. The constitution stated that a new election for president must be held within 180 days. The election was in fact held in November 1981, and Sattar became president. He was an elderly man who, in accordance with the constitution, had been appointed vice president by Zia. In the view of some, especially the military, Sattar was ineffective and had in his cabinet some ministers who were corrupt or incompetent or both. The chief of the army staff, Lieutenant General Husain Muhammad Ershad, demanded a constitutional role for the military in the governance of the country; Sattar refused to comply fully with this demand. On March 24, 1982, Ershad led a coup and dismissed Sattar and his government.

Authoritarianism Returns: H. M. Ershad

With the assumption of power by Ershad, the state returned to the political point it had left with the gradual liberalization by Zia. Parties were banned, the press was controlled, channels of access were closed or narrowed, and martial law was reimposed.

In his statement accompanying the takeover, Ershad, following the record of many military leaders, said that conditions required the only organized force in the nation to assume power, temporarily, to set the government in order. He further declared that elections would be held to restore representative government. Several dates were set for elections to be held, but these came and went without polling. In early 1986 another date was set. In March 1985, Ershad had asked for approval of his policies through a referendum in which the question at root was "Ershad yes or Ershad no." The government reported that he won overwhelming support, although there were allegations that the ballot boxes had been stuffed with yes votes. The "approval" obtained did not necessarily add legitimacy to the Ershad regime. An election was finally held for parliament in May 1986, but the results were inconclusive and there were reports of much irregularity in the polling. The Jatiya party, which supports Ershad, won a slim majority of the 300 seats contested, whereas the opposition Awami League and its allies won just short of 100 seats. Another opposition group, the BNP, now led by Zia's widow, Khaleda, refused to participate in the poll. The remaining seats went to a number of smaller parties and independent candidates. Ershad did not win the large majority he had hoped for.

In the fall of 1987, widespread demonstrations against the Ershad regime led by the BNP and the Awami League cooperating with each other caused Ershad to dissolve parliament and call for a new election. This was held in March 1988, and, as both the Awami League and the BNP boycotted the poll, Ershad's Jatiya party won almost all the seats against scattered and weak opposition. Ershad rules with a tame parliament in what is essentially a presidential system.

The Institutions of Government

The constitution of 1972, as amended under Mujib, has twice been suspended under martial law: once in the Zia period and again by Ershad. Originally it set Bangladesh as a unitary state with a parliamentary system modeled on that of Great Britain. As noted above, Mujib changed this setup first to a presidential system and then to a single-party system. The provisions pertaining to the single-party system have been revoked and Bangladesh now has a multi-party system. The provisions for a strong presidency remain.

Figure 19.1   Bangladesh central government

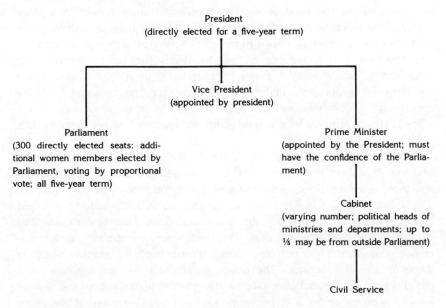

The Central Government

The constitution as amended under Ershad calls for a president and a vice president elected by a plurality popular vote and a single chamber parliament (Jatiyo Sangsad) elected, also by plurality vote, from 300 single-member constituencies (see Figure 19.1). In addition, the parliament itself will elect by proportional vote a number of women members, the number (which at present is 15) to be set by law. The president appoints the prime minister from among the members of the parliament. As the prime minister is subject to a vote of confidence, the president must choose a person who has the support of the majority of parliament. The president also appoints the other members of the cabinet, but he may select not more than one-fifth of the cabinet members from outside the parliament. This provision, it is said, will allow experts to be included in the highest policy-making level of government.

To be enacted, laws must be passed by the parliament and approved by the president, who has the right of veto; he also has the right to dismiss the cabinet. Power is thereby centered in the office of the president. During Zia's parliamentary period, Zia was supported by a large majority of parliamentarians belonging to his own party. It is not at all clear what would happen if the parliament were opposed to the president, especially if the majority were sufficient to override his veto.

The government at the center is organized into a number of departments or ministries. At the head of each is a political minister (who may have authority over one or more departments). The active head of a department or ministry is a secretary drawn from the civil service, although an increase has occurred in the number of persons from the police service and, occasionally, the military serving in secretarial positions. Although the secretary is responsible, under the minister, for the operations of the department as a whole, he or she is assisted by a range of subordinate officers who have lower-level responsibility for segments of the department's work.

The members of the higher civil service (i.e., those who enter at a level that will allow them to become secretaries) are selected through examination, and there is a prescribed system of training at entrance and during service. The unified Bangladesh Civil Service established in 1980 features fourteen "cadres" designed to bring together a number of separate services inherited from Pakistan (and British India). The foreign service operates as a semi-autonomous cadre, although the examination procedures are the same as those for the civil service. The police constitute a service separate from the civil service. Senior police officers also enter by examination; the highest level for a police officer is inspector general, although, as noted above, some become secretaries. There are also a number of boards, commissions, and corporations on an all-Bangladesh level that draw a substantial proportion of their senior officers from the civil service.

The Supreme Court of Bangladesh has two divisions. The Appellate Division, as its name indicates, has only appellate jurisdiction. The High Court Division has both appellate jurisdiction and some original jurisdiction. The Supreme Court has benches in several cities besides Dhaka. However, the point of original jurisdiction in most cases is the district court, with some lesser cases being heard by district magistrates or in the *upazilla* courts.

Local Government

Until the Ershad regime, Bangladesh was organized into twenty districts, which were grouped into four divisions (Chittagong, Dhaka, Khulna, and Rajshahi). Below the district level were smaller units previously called subdivisions. Ershad has decreed that each of the subdivisions be designated as a district. There are sixty-four of these new districts. The former districts are now designated "regions" (see Table 19.1).

Ershad's goal in expanding the number of districts was to move the decision-making power closer to the people. The former districts averaged about 5 million residents each; the new districts will contain many fewer residents (about 1.5 million on the average) and the district headquarters

TABLE 19.1 Bangladesh Local Government

Level	Number	Chief Administrator	Local Government	Elected Representatives
Central	1	President	Parliament	300 directly; 15 women indirectly
Division	4	Commissioner	None	None
Region	20	Not determined	None	None
District	64	Deputy Commissioner	Zilla Parishad	Not determined
Upazilla	460	Upazilla officer	Upazilla Parishad	Chairman elected; chairmen of union parishads automatically members
Union	4,354	Local officer	Union Parishad	Ten (average) elected members

town will be much closer to the typical resident of the district. The districts will also be more uniform in topography, agriculture, and industry, thereby allowing, it is hoped, more efficient use of human and physical resources in the development of the country.

Each district is headed by a deputy commissioner drawn from the civil service. He also has the titles of district collector (of revenue) and district magistrate (responsible for law and order and some judicial functions). In his "minicabinet" he has representatives of most of the central departments (e.g., a superintendent of police, a district judge, a district health officer). He is charged with the overall administration and development of the district. The task is not an easy one, as the other government representatives have a dual loyalty: to him as head of the district administration but, more important, to the head of the central government department in Dhaka, where assignments and promotions are controlled. Coordination can be difficult.

Below the district level is the *upazilla* (literally, subdistrict), of which there are 460 in the country. Ershad has held elections to the councils of these bodies, which correspond approximately to the *thana* (literally, police station area) council that existed before as the lowest level development coordination bodies. Under the Ershad plan of decentralization, the *upazilla* will be the focal point of administration and development. Below that level are unions with territories comprising one or more villages. These also have elected councils.

Urban coordinating bodies cover entire cities. In the largest urban areas (Dhaka, Chittagong, and Khulna) there are municipal corporations with mayors and elected councils. Each also has a government-appointed administrator, who is roughly equivalent to a city manager. Smaller urban areas have elected city or town councils and also may have government-appointed administrators.

Police administration is headed by the inspector general of police, who serves nominally under the authority of the Home Ministry. At the district level there is a superintendent of police, and at the *upazilla,* an inspector of police. Commissioners of police direct the work in the major urban areas and report directly to the inspector general.

*   *   *

In sum, Bangladesh is still developing a structure of government for the long term, as the events described in the first part of this chapter confirm. The central government seems unlikely to change from one centered on a strong president, but a freely elected parliament could conceivably assert its role. Ershad's changes in the local government system may further Zia's urging for national cooperation by starting at the lowest level and working upward.

Suggested Readings

Craig Baxter. *Bangladesh: A New Nation in an Old Setting* (Boulder, Colo.: Westview Press, 1984).

Marcus Franda. *Bangladesh, the First Decade* (New Delhi: South Asian Publishers, 1982).

Rounaq Jahan. *Bangladesh Politics: Problems and Issues* (Dhaka: University Press, 1980).

Zillur Rahman Khan. *Leadership in the Least Developed Nation: Bangladesh* (Syracuse, N.Y.: Maxwell School, 1983).

Talukder Maniruzzaman. *The Bangladesh Revolution and its Aftermath* (Dhaka: Bangladesh Books International, 1980).

————. *Group Interests and Political Change; Studies in Bangladesh and Pakistan* (New Delhi: South Asian Publisher, 1982).

20
PARTIES AND GROUPS

Bangladesh is a nation without highly organized political parties or effective interest groups. The latter are developing, but the party system is one that has seen a number of new parties created to support particular leaders but has not yet been tested in more than a single election or perhaps two (see Table 20.1, which excludes the 1986 and 1988 elections as they were not fully competitive). Moreover, factionalism is endemic in Bangladeshi organizations.

Political Parties

Muslim League

The oldest party still existing, barely, in Bangladesh is the Muslim League. The League was founded in Dhaka in 1906 and won an almost complete victory in the 1945–1946 election on the question of Pakistan or a united India. It was soon deserted by many East Pakistanis, however, as it pursued an all-Pakistan program and seemed to many in East Pakistan to place national (or, to use East Pakistani terms, West Pakistani) interests ahead of those of the province. The Muslim League was trounced in the 1954 election and lost its place as the governing group. A major portion of the Muslim League supported Ayub Khan in the 1960s, and again the party was alienated from much of the Bangladeshi population. Factionalized into three groups, it was also a loser in the 1970 elections. It was barred from contesting the 1973 election. In 1979 it won 19 seats in the parliament, largely owing to the respect given to one veteran leader (Abdus Sobur Khan of Khulna) and to the family of another leader (Fazal Kader Choudhury of Chittagong). The Muslim League is now almost nothing in the political spectrum.

The old rival of the Muslim League, the Congress, existed briefly after 1947 as the Pakistan National Congress. It held seats from East Pakistan in the central assembly and also had seats in the provincial assembly. All of those elected were Hindus. As the party disappeared during the Ayub

TABLE 20.1   Elections in Eastern Bengal, East Bengal, East Pakistan, and Bangladesh

	Seats Won	Percentage of Votes
1946 Bengal Legislative Assembly (Muslim seats)		
Muslim League	114	82.04
Krishak Praja Party	3 ⎱	17.96
Others	2 ⎰	
1954 East Bengal Legislative Assembly (Muslim seats)		
United Front	223	65.72
Muslim League	10 ⎱	34.28
Others	4 ⎰	
1970 National Assembly Seats from East Pakistan		
Awami League	160	75.22
Others	2	24.78
1973 Bangladesh Parliament		
Awami League	292	73.18
Others	8	26.82
1979 Bangladesh Parliament		
Bangladesh Nationalist Party	207	41.16
Awami League (Malik group)	39	24.52
Muslim League	20	10.03
Jatiyo Samajtantrik Dal	8	4.87
Others	26	19.42

Source: Adapted from Craig Baxter and M. Rashiduzzaman, "Bangladesh Votes: 1978 and 1979," Asian Survey, vol. 21, no. 4 (April 1981).

period, most leading Hindus are currently associated either with the Awami League, the Bangladesh Nationalist party, or the Jatiya party.

The Awami League

Having observed the sharp division between the all-Pakistan goals of the Muslim League (and, incidentally, its internal factionalism, especially in West Pakistan) and the aspirations of the East Pakistanis, two prominent pre-independence political figures returned to politics in the early 1950s (see Chapter 18). One of these was Fazlul Haq, who revived his pre-independence Krishak Praja (Farmers and Peoples) party (KPP) under the new name Krishak Sramik (Peasants and Workers) party (KSP). This party, which eventually played an important role in the 1954 election, was very much the personal vehicle of the man who had been dubbed the "Lion of Bengal." But with Ayub's martial law in 1958 and Fazlul Haq's death before the restoration of democracy, the party has all but disappeared. Its former supporters can be found in a number of parties and were mainly in the Awami League at the time of Bangladeshi independence.

The other political figure to return to active politics was Husain Shaheed Suhrawardy, who, though a member of the Pakistan Constituent Assembly, remained in Calcutta after independence. He strongly held the view that the Muslim League had accomplished its goal with the partition of India and that it should now be dissolved in favor of a new national party which would include non-Muslims in its membership. But this option was rejected by the refugees (that is, the Muslims who had migrated from India to Pakistan) and West Pakistani leaders of the Muslim League. In 1951, Suhrawardy and some others from East Pakistan formed the Awami (People's) Muslim League as an opposition group. This was quickly renamed simply the Awami League, and membership was opened to all Pakistani citizens. The new Awami League was unable to make serious inroads into the west wing of Pakistan, although it did form alliances with short-lived opposition groups in the west.

The intellectual leadership of Suhrawardy, a former prime minister of united Bengal and a member of the national elite (now converted to vernacular elitism in East Pakistan), was a major asset of the new party. He was joined by a large number of vernacular elite Muslim League members, but only a few members of the highest echelons of the East Pakistan Muslim League. Among the former were Ataur Rahman Khan (b. 1907), who served as chief minister of East Pakistan several times between 1956 and 1958 and who later became prime minister of Bangladesh in 1984 under Ershad. Another who joined Suhrawardy was Sheikh Mujibur Rahman, who eventually succeeded Suhrawardy in the leadership of the party.[1] Still another was the religious and political leader Maulana Abdul Hamid Khan Bhashani (see Chapter 18).

The 1954 Election

Elections were due in East Pakistan in 1951, but the slippage of Muslim League strength led the central government to delay the poll until 1954. Among the key issues unresolved was the status of Bengali as a co-national language of Pakistan. Jinnah and the Muslim League (including many Muslim League leaders from East Pakistan) favored the single national language formula, which eventually gave that status to Urdu (see Chapter 16). Protests in East Pakistan culminated on February 22, 1952, when police killed a number of student demonstrators—a day that is still observed in Bangladesh as "Martyrs' Day." There were numerous other grievances as well.

Suhrawardy's Awami League and Fazlul Haq's KSP joined hands in a United Front that also included several smaller parties. The result of the election was a crushing defeat for the Muslim League. The United Front won 223 of the 237 Muslim seats (elections were still on a separate electorate basis) and had allies among some of the 72 non-Muslims elected. The

Muslim League won but 10 seats. The problems of retaining the unity of the United Front are not pertinent here; suffice to say that the grand beginning was belied by the intra-front political warfare, which lasted until Ayub's takeover in 1958.

The Awami League Active Again

Politics during the beginning of the Ayub Khan period were sharply curtailed. The Awami League remained the focus of opposition to Ayub and contested the indirect elections of the president's basic democrat system. Several of the leaders, especially Mujibur Rahman, were jailed for significant periods. The quiet work of strengthening the organization continued. When Ayub was dismissed and replaced by Yahya Khan, who promised free politicking and direct elections, the Awami League was ready to resume full and open activity. In the December 1970 election for the National Assembly, the Awami League swept the poll in East Pakistan by winning 160 of the 162 seats at stake and polling about three-quarters of the popular vote. In the election for the provincial assembly it all but duplicated this feat, winning 288 of the 300 directly elected seats.

The Awami League leaders who were able to escape arrest by Pakistan authorities in March 1971 set up a government-in-exile in Calcutta. Syed Nazrul Islam was designated acting president in the absence of Mujibur Rahman, who was in jail in West Pakistan. The Awami League coordinated the resistance to the Pakistan army, in which it was joined by several small leftist parties, although it remained a party of the center. It was prepared to take over the reins of government following the Pakistani surrender in December 1971.

The one-party decree of Mujib in 1975 led to the formation of the Bangladesh Krishak Sramik Awami League (BAKSAL), an amalgamation of the names of the two principal parties in the United Front of 1954. With the assassination of Mujib, BAKSAL was ordered dissolved (although a tiny party now has resurrected the name).

The Awami League was revived when parties were permitted to function again in 1976. It contested the presidential election of 1978 as the leading member of a coalition supporting General M.A.G. Osmany, the loser in a landslide against the incumbent president, Major General Ziaur Rahman. A split in the Awami League did not hurt the party in the parliamentary election of 1979, when it finished a distant second to the Bangladesh Nationalist party. In the presidential election of 1981, the Awami League ran Kamal Hussain, a former foreign minister, against the then incumbent acting president, Abdus Sattar, and again was soundly defeated.

The party is now under the leadership of Sheikh Husina Wajid, a daughter of Sheikh Mujibur Rahman, who was abroad when her father was assassinated and thus was spared. She was in exile in India when asked to return to assume the leadership in 1979. The party opposed elections under Ershad's martial law regime, but reversed that position and participated in the May 1986 election, winning about 70 seats. Sheikh Husina Wajid became leader of the opposition in parliament. However, in the fall of 1987, the party left the parliament, causing its dissolution, and did not participate in the 1988 election. It has returned to the "no vote under Ershad" stance.

The Awami League strongly supports the four pillars of Mujibism: democracy, nationalism, socialism, and secularism. Despite the deviation to authoritarianism in the latter Mujib period, the party claims to support a parliamentary system with regular free and open elections. If it assumes office in the future, it might work for a reversal of some of the denationalization that has taken place under Zia and Ershad. It would also oppose the steps taken by Zia and Ershad (to be noted below) away from what the party might describe as "pure secularism." It is generally felt that the party would take a favorable attitude toward India and the Soviet Union, but this stance, especially with regard to India, might not be given support by the elites or the people in general.

Bangladesh Nationalist Party

The Bangladesh Nationalist party (BNP) was formed in 1978 as a group in support of President Ziaur Rahman. It was built partly on the basis of its predecessor, which used the acronym JAGODAL (National Democratic party). To the JAGODAL were added splinter groups from a wide group of parties, ranging from a portion of the conservative Muslim League to several leftist fragments; these now form the BNP. Abdus Sattar was appointed head of the BNP, although Zia was the real leader. The party supported the nineteen-point program for the reconstruction and development of Bangladesh (see Chapter 19). As the JAGODAL the party was behind Zia's successful election for the presidency; as the BNP it won about two-thirds of the seats in the parliamentary election of 1979. After Zia's assassination, the BNP successfully supported Abdus Sattar in his election to the presidency in 1981.

After Zia's death and even before the Sattar campaign, there were signs of factionalism in the party. Some younger members thought that a younger candidate for the presidency than Sattar should be chosen, but the party was unable to agree on a candidate other than the acting president. Since Ershad took over, the party has further factionalized. It co-opted as party leader Zia's widow, Khalida Zia—a woman who was very much in the background during her husband's term of office. Among the defectors, however, were Zia's and Sattar's prime minister, Shah Azizur Rahman and the current vice president, Moudud Ahmed. Like the Awami League, the

BNP opposes the holding of elections under Ershad—but this is ironic given that Zia had held his elections under the very same conditions. Unlike the Awami League, the BNP did boycott the election of May 1986 and also that of March 1988, a course that has placed its future in question. Also like the Awami League, the BNP heads a coalition of smaller parties.

The policies of the BNP are a moderate reversal of those of the Awami League. It supports a freer economy, maintains the present formulation of "absolute faith and trust in Almighty Allah," and provides for a presidential form of government. In foreign policy, the Zia government built close relations with the United States, China, and the Arab states—relations it wishes to maintain. It also prefers to carry out subcontinental politics in the context of the South Asian Association for Regional Cooperation organization (see Chapter 31).

Jatiya Party

The party formed in 1983 to give support to the program and person of Ershad, which at that time used the acronym JANODAL (People's party), is now known as the Jatiya party (also meaning People's party). It is composed largely of defectors from the BNP, a few former Awami Leaguers and certain others from smaller parties or who were inactive in politics. Ershad had been unable to generate the enthusiasm for himself or for his program that Zia was able to mobilize. He had hoped that the party would popularize the program and its leader and that a sizable majority could be obtained in the promised election. The party would have preferred that a presidential poll be held prior to a parliamentary election in the hope that Ershad could win the first and then use his coattails to pull a majority behind him into parliament. But Ershad, having won confirmation in office in the March 1985 referendum, asserted that a presidential election was no longer necessary and proceeded to a parliamentary poll in May 1986. The Jatiya party did not achieve a large majority; rather, it squeaked by with a bare majority of 152 out of 300 seats.

The policies of the Jatiya party do not differ greatly from those of the BNP. It is clearly a political vehicle for Ershad, although it would perhaps go further in freeing the economy now that Ershad has moved rather extensively in the direction of divesting the government of properties owned by it, even in banking.

The Left

Nowhere is the Bengali penchant for factionalism more evident than in the fragmentation of the already small leftist wing of politics. There is a veritable multitude of such parties, often local groups gathered around a single leader. Although these parties can occasionally win a single seat in parliament, they cannot seriously affect the outcome of elections.

Other than the East Pakistan offshoot of the pre-independence Communist party of India, the organized left can best be traced to the split in the Awami League in 1955. Maulana Abdul Hamid Khan Bhashani objected to the relatively conservative policies of Suhrawardy—especially his foreign policy, which seemed to Bhashani and his associates to be overly pro-Western. Bhashani and certain others withdrew, combined with groups in West Pakistan, and formed the National Awami party (NAP). The power of the new party in East Pakistan was attributed to the fact that it held the balance between the contending KSP and Awami League in the provincial assembly.[2]

Like the other parties, the NAP was unable to work in a free environment during the Ayub period, although Bhashani (who was referred to as the "Red Maulana") strongly supported Pakistan's opening to China. The party began to fragment; indeed, the major division occurred in the mid-1960s, when a Bhashani faction competed in East Pakistan with one led by Muzaffar Ahmad. The former was often described as "pro-Peking" and the latter, as "pro-Moscow," the designation of the Bhashani group having been highly exaggerated.

The tiny Muzaffar group continues to exist, as it has for some time, as a leftist hanger-on of the Awami League. The Bhashani group has experienced continued and repeated fragmentation—to the extent that Bhashani's son was briefly in Ershad's cabinet.

Other Parties

The factionalism of Bangladesh politics has led to a multiplicity of parties in the field—many more, in fact, than those mentioned here. A president, a general secretary, a tiny office, and a telephone seem to be all the requirements for forming a party. More than fifty parties were registered when Zia opened up political activity in 1976. The majority of them still exist and have been joined by many others.

The Press

The Bangladeshi press can be described as weak, although there are notable exceptions to this rule. The two major English language dailies, the *Bangladesh Observer* (formerly the *Pakistan Observer*) and the *Bangladesh Times* were government controlled until recently, and, in the latter case, government owned. However, the *Bangladesh Observer*, the larger and generally more authoritative of the two, has now been restored to its pre-1971 owner and takes an independent stance. These two have now been joined by the *New Nation*, published by the *Ittefaq* organization. The English weekly *Holiday* has a long record of opposition beginning with the Ayub period, for which it has often been penalized.

The newspaper with the highest circulation and the greatest influence is *Ittefaq,* currently published by Anwar Hussain "Manju," the son of the founder, Tofazzal Hussain. Tofazzal Hussain was jailed by Ayub, and the paper was suppressed during periods of the Mujib regime. Other Bengali language newspapers are smaller and generally, but not always, supportive of particular political points of view. Among the rest, *Sangbad* is perhaps the most influential after *Ittefaq.*

Radio and television are state owned and operated, but there appears to be a fairly large audience for non-Bangladeshi radio sources, including All-India Radio, BBC, and VOA.

Bureaucrats Armed and Unarmed

The highly selective nature of recruitment for the upper entry levels of the Bangladesh Civil Service makes that group an elite one with interests it is sure to pursue. Although not as highly selective in its entrance requirements, the military is also a special interest group.[3] The members of these groups are often related by blood or marriage, as is frequently the case with the business elite. It is to the latter group that both civil and military officers often apply for post-retirement positions. An officer seeks this kind of employment after service for much the same reason his counterpart in the United States would do so: He already "knows his way around" the governmental apparatus. Yet another source of employment is to remain on duty after formal retirement "on contract"—that is, to gain an extension in the same or a different post. For example, a number of Bangladeshi ambassadors abroad are retired military officers and some are retired civil service officers.

Both groups are interested in maintaining the select nature of their services and in continuing or expanding the perquisites of office. Free or highly subsidized housing, access to specially priced food rations, posts for spouses, above-standard medical treatment, and university entry for children are among the stated or informal perquisites.

Although recruitment of Bengali Muslims to both the civil and military services was minimal during the British period and not greatly increased during the Pakistan period, there is clearly an old-boy network that acts to preserve privileges and to protect fellow members of the group. The recent recruitment of many officers means that their ties with village Bangladeshis are not likely to become remote in time, but the positions from which they have originated are often among the village elite and those they have entered are in the national elite. The response of these officers to rural problems is thus often less than fully sympathetic. Ershad's program of decentralization, with assignments for new entrants to places that until recently were only subdivisional towns, has not been welcomed. A clearer case of opposition surfaced when he decreed that the High Court, which had had but one bench in Dhaka, would now have additional benches in a number of places outside the capital. This opposition was, expectedly, also joined by the lawyers. The civil service and the military do not always stand together; many civil service officers were angered at the movement of military officers into civilian "preserves" under Ershad.

Students and the Universities

The university community—there are seven universities in the country at Dhaka, Chittagong, Rajshahi, Jahangirnagar (a Dhaka suburb), and Mymemsingh (agricultural), including the medical and engineering universities in Dhaka—has long been a political force. Many Muslim League and Awami League leaders gained their first political experience at Calcutta or Dhaka before 1947. After 1947, students and some professors were in the forefront of the movements for recognition of Bengali, parity for East Pakistan, and, eventually, autonomy and freedom for the east wing of Pakistan. The most vicious attack of the Pakistan Army in March 1971 was made against Dhaka University, and just before the army surrendered there was another round of killings of intellectuals in December 1971.

Student groups today are generally aligned with one or another of the political parties.[4] Leftist strength is often seen by the government and outsiders as greater than that of the Islamic right, but both sides contend for support among the students. It is probably accurate to say that on most issues the bulk of the student body (and the faculty as well) is either neutral or apathetic. Nonetheless the fact that most student groups are located in key urban areas, especially Dhaka, causes concern to whatever government is in power. The students are capable of demonstrations, some violent, that can tie up the city and support general strikes (*hartals*). Arrests of students and at times faculty members during such upheavals are frequent; the police occasionally use tear gas or rifle fire to stop the activities.

The Urban Elite: Business and Law

Before Bangladesh's separation from Pakistan the majority of the manufacturing, banking, and commercial business activities in East Pakistan was in the hands of West Pakistanis. When a study was made of the thirty largest business houses in Pakistan, only one, that of A. K. Khan, a jute and textile entrepreneur from Chittagong, was from East Pakistan.[5] The Mujib period of nationalization of business contributed to the stifling of Bangladeshi entrepreneurship. With the liberalization under Zia and Ershad, however, a number of Bangladeshi business houses have grown up. Some of these now play a prominent role in politics. A few industrialists have entered the political arena as participants; others help finance parties, perhaps more often the BNP or the Jatiya party than the Awami League, although the latter is not devoid of industrial contributors. Business people are often interconnected with civil servants and military officers; moreover, as noted earlier, many of those retired from both groups enter business and others "sponsor" their children in business activity. The interests of the business people are typical of such groups elsewhere: They look for government assistance in the form of loans to establish and maintain enterprises and for policies that will keep costs low and profits reasonably high.

The legal profession, on the other hand, is closely interlinked with politics. Many of the leading political figures are trained in the law. Lawyers also have been among the leaders of the opposition as they set demands for human rights, free elections, and, generally, an open society.

Trade Unions

In nations with surplus labor, trade unions are unlikely to have a major impact on politics. Bangladesh has large numbers of potential laborers, but many of these are unskilled; thus there have been examples in this country of skilled and specialized groups of workers being able to exercise an impact on political and economic policies. Further, the migration of some specialized groups to employment in the Middle East has created additional shortages in some areas. (Bangladesh earned $617 million from migrant workers' remittances in 1987.)[6] Unions are most often closely tied to political parties, although some factory unions do exist.

Strikes are generally discouraged by the government. Workers will, however, join other groups in demonstrations, especially when economic matters, such as changes in the subsidized price of food grains, are at issue. If and when significant industrial growth takes place, more trade union activity can be expected.

Rural Elites: Secular and Religious

In a land-poor country such as Bangladesh, the holder of as little as five acres of land can be an influential person in his village area. Those with the land ceiling of thirty acres are very influential persons indeed. Landlordism in the traditional sense of large estates disappeared in several stages, beginning with the Fazlul Haq ministry in united Bengal and culminating in land reforms during the early years after Pakistan's independence. Nonetheless, there are the traditional elite families to whom respect is given and whose members can draw on vote banks, though to a much more limited degree than earlier. Such elites are likely to oppose further land reform, to support government programs that provide agricultural assistance, and to look for higher government purchase prices for commodities produced. Until the landless and very small landholders and tenant farmers are better organized, these elites are likely to exercise a high degree of domination in the rural areas.

Bangladesh has not yet followed the path of many Islamic majority countries in demanding the establishment of an Islamic state. The constitution was amended by Zia to give recognition to the Muslim majority by amending the "secularist" fundamental principle of state policy to read that the Bangladeshis had "absolute trust and faith in Almighty Allah," and that the Muslims could order their lives according to the *Sunnah*. However, he also made it clear that the rights of the minorities to practice and preach their faiths would not be inhibited. The reason behind the Zia move seems to have been an attempt to assuage the Middle Eastern states that had complained that Bangladesh was not sufficiently Islamic to warrant large doses of assistance from the oil-rich nations.

The religious leaders, the *pirs*, have not played an important role in either East Pakistani or Bangladeshi politics. Although many are respected by their followers, a demarcation seems to have occurred between religion (viewed generally as a private matter) and politics—a demarcation that has become increasingly atypical of Muslim-majority nations. Early in his rule, Ershad did cause the constitution to be amended to declare Islam the state religion but no further steps have been taken.

*   *   *

In sum, political parties and organized interest groups are weak in Bangladesh. The parties have rarely been tested in successive elections. Groups tend to be divided and often transient in organization.

Notes

1. The actual head of the All-Pakistan Awami League was a West Pakistani, but Mujib controlled the bulk of the party through his leadership of the East Pakistan party.

2. The West Pakistan NAP held a similar balancing position in that wing between the Muslim League and the Republican party.

3. Military officer recruitment generally occurs at a somewhat lower social level and does not require the university preparation that is called for at the higher civil service entry levels.

4. See Talukder Maniruzzaman, *The Bangladesh Revolution and Its Aftermath* (Dhaka: Bangladesh Books International, 1980), especially ch. 4.

5. See Hannah Papanek, "Pakistan's Big Businessmen," *Economic Development and Cultural Change,* vol. 21 (October 1972).

6. World Bank, *World Development Report, 1989* (New York: Oxford University Press, 1989), table 18, p. 198.

Suggested Readings

Specific studies on Bangladeshi political parties are yet to appear. The following, however, contain discussions of parties in a broader framework.

Muhammad Abdul Wadud Bhuiyan. *Emergence of Bangladesh and the Role of the Awami League* (New Delhi: Vikas, 1982).

S. R. Chakravarty. *Bangladesh: The Nineteen Seventy-Nine Elections* (New Delhi: South Asian Publishers, 1988).

Talukder Maniruzzaman. *Radical Politics and the Emergence of Bangladesh* (Dhaka: Bangladesh Books International, 1975).

————. *The Bangladesh Revolution and Its Aftermath* (Dhaka: Bangladesh Books International, 1980).

Charles P. O'Donnell. *Bangladesh: Biography of a Muslim Nation* (Boulder, Colo.: Westview Press, 1984).

M. Rashiduzzaman. "The National Awami Party of Pakistan: Leftist Politics in Crisis," *Pacific Affairs,* vol. 43, no. 3 (Fall 1970).

Kirsten Westergaard. *State and Rural Society in Bangladesh* (London: Curzon Press, 1985).

21
THE MILITARY

As noted in the previous chapter, the military plays a role in the politics of Bangladesh. By contrast, in two of the larger nations of South Asia—India and Sri Lanka—the military has not been actively involved in politics; indeed, it has generally accepted a role subordinate to the civilian leadership of the two countries (as would behoove the military in a democratic political system). Although the governmental and military heritage of the British period is common to all four nations, the military in Pakistan and Bangladesh has assumed the governance of those two countries for prolonged periods, initially under martial law but occasionally continuing after martial law was lifted (as when military leaders, such as Ayub Khan, Ziaur Rahman, and H. M. Ershad, have remained in office in what might be described as military-dominant civilian regimes). Ayub Khan in Pakistan never let it be forgotten that he was a field marshal; and Ziaur Rahman in Bangladesh, even though he tried to drop the title of major general and despite his popularity, was also a "soldier-statesman." Ershad, too, has shed his formal military role.

Bengal and the Military Under Britain and Pakistan

In many ways the governing role of the military in Bangladesh might come as a surprise to someone who served in India a century ago—as would, of course, the very concept of a separate Bangladesh itself. The British Indian army prior to the mutiny of 1857 and the consequent transfer of power from the East India Company to the Crown, was organized into three territorial units: Bengal, Bombay, and Madras. It was the Bengal army that mutinied in 1857 (see Chapter 1). This army was largely drawn from Bengal, although new units were being raised in the recently conquered Punjab as well. The citizens of Bengal were rather broadly defined at the time, including personnel from all of the areas under the direct control of the Bengal presidency—that is, including Bihar as well as Bengal proper. Many of the *sepoys* (enlisted soldiers) were drawn from the higher castes of Hindus, and some were Muslims. Both religious groups were offended by the new weapons introduced by the British, which included cartridges greased with either beef or pig fat. The cartridges had to be bitten open to allow placement of gunpowder in the barrels—but this action placed both the Hindus and the Muslims in danger of being polluted by the fat. This fear spread rapidly among the *sepoys* and became one of the important elements leading to the mutiny. (The mutiny is also described by Indians as the first War of Independence even though it failed in that objective.)

The mutiny was quelled principally by British and Punjabi troops (the Punjabis remained loyal to Great Britain). The Bombay and Madras troops did not mutiny and also remained loyal. The upshot was that the British determined that the Bengalis would no longer be recruited to the Indian army. The doctrine of the "martial races" specified that only such races could be enlisted. Within this category were Punjabi Muslims and Sikhs, who eventually dominated the Indian military during both world wars and on into independence in 1947.

The dominance of the Punjabis continued in the post-independence army of Pakistan (although India took steps to broaden the base of recruitment extensively after independence; indeed, the largest single group in its army remains the Sikhs, who constitute about one-eighth of the total).[1] Although some steps were taken to work toward parity between East and West Pakistan in civilian government positions, nothing was done on the same scale to increase the proportion of Bengalis in the military. A report issued in 1956, during the period of limited parliamentary rule in Pakistan, stated that in the army only 1 of 60 officers of the rank of brigadier or higher, and only 12 of 850 in the field grade ranks of colonel, lieutenant colonel, and major, came from East Pakistan. The same report indicated that about 10% of the air force officers and 1% of those in the navy were Bengalis.[2] In 1971, when Bangladesh became independent, only two Bengalis, both in the army, had reached star rank. It has been reported, perhaps apocryphally, that Sheikh Mujibur Rahman, in discussing his new Six Point program in 1970, said that East Pakistan would contribute to the defense budget in direct proportion to its membership in the armed forces—6%!

It must be emphasized, however, that more than reluctance by Punjabi and Pathan military leaders was involved in the slow recruitment of Bengalis (and Baluch and Sindhis as well). In Bengal, after nearly a century in which Bengalis were all but denied admittance to the military (some technical personnel were enlisted during World War II), the tradition among most Bengali families was to avoid looking to the military as a source of employment. Thus the limited recruitment efforts met with equally limited response. A Bengal regiment was raised, but initially its senior officers were from the west. A number of Bengali officers were trained, including both presidents Ziaur Rahman and Husain Muhammad Ershad, who had risen to the rank of major by the time the civil war broke out. The Bangladeshi forces during the war were led by a retired colonel, Muhammad Abdul Ghani Osmany, who was later minister of defense in the cabinet of Mujibur Rahman and the losing candidate against Zia in the 1978 presidential election. Several of the Mukti Bahini (national army) leaders were majors, but, as will be discussed below, some (including Ershad) did not participate because they were stationed in West Pakistan in 1971.

Freedom Fighters and Returnees

As noted, a small number of Bengali officers were assigned by the Pakistani military to positions in both East and West Pakistan. Those assigned in the east almost without exception joined the Mukti Bahini in its conflict against Pakistan. Those in the west were unable do so but, in most cases, were soon isolated and either relieved of duty or assigned routine tasks and then later relieved. There thus developed a split in the Bangladesh military between those who were described as "freedom fighters" and those who, after their eventual repatriation, were called "returnees."

The initial Bangladesh military establishment drew its strength from the Mukti Bahini, which comprised those Bengali officers and enlisted men who were able to escape the initial crackdown by the Pakistan army; similar personnel from the East Pakistan Rifles (EPR), a paramilitary force devoted to border protection; numerous police personnel; and a substantial number of civilians who joined in the resistance against Pakistan. After the conflict ended and Bangladesh became independent, the police and EPR personnel returned to their former units, with the EPR now designated the Bangladesh Rifles (BDR). Most of the civilians also returned to their former occupations, but some, often imbued with deep devotion to Mujibur Rahman personally, expressed their wish to remain in the military. Because they had received no formal military training, however, their retention was frowned upon by those who had served in the Pakistan army.

The freedom fighter group was itself divided, and some members, notably Ziaur Rahman, were not in the good graces of Mujib. It is said that Mujib resented the unilateral declaration of independence by Zia on March 27, 1971, in which Zia, in temporary control of Chittagong radio, proclaimed himself president of Bangladesh. Zia quickly corrected himself, stating that Mujib was president and that he was acting in Mujib's name. Zia, a genuine war hero and an obvious candidate for rapid advancement, was passed over by Mujib for the post of chief of the army staff.

When Zia took effective control of the government after the November 1975 coups, he worked quickly to integrate the returnees into higher-level posts in the military. Several of the freedom fighters were retired and then often compensated with appointments to diplomatic posts abroad. The older Ershad, for example, was advanced to the post of deputy chief of the army staff and eventually, when Zia relinquished the post, to chief of the army staff. The first navy chief, who had made a dramatic escape from Pakistan in 1971, was also displaced by a returnee. There was resentment among the freedom fighters; in fact, it was a freedom fighter who was responsible for the assassination of Zia in 1981.

A Politicized Military: The Rakhi Bahini

Mujib's distrust of the military run by former officers of Pakistan was based partly on their former association but also on his concern that the military heroes of the freedom struggle might command greater respect than he. As his domestic troubles mounted, criticism of him also mounted. At the same time, the military was relatively immune from criticism. Mujib lost the services of the respected General Osmany when he began his moves toward authoritarianism in late 1974, and Osmany resigned in protest. Given the financial constraints of Bangladesh, Mujib also found it difficult to meet the demands of the poorly equipped military.

What Mujib wanted at this time was a praetorian guard that would be loyal to him first and the country second. The officers in this guard would necessarily be persons with military training, but its ranks could be filled by some of those freedom fighters who had been drawn from civilians. The establishment of the Jatiyo Rakhi Bahini (National Security Force) met this need; but it was looked upon as a rival by the regular military. The Rakhi Bahini seemed to receive much greater allotments of funds and to have better facilities and equipment. When the assassination of Mujib was engineered by a group of disaffected army officers, another target was the Rakhi Bahini. It was disbanded and many of its members were jailed. Its elaborate headquarters now serves as the National Defense College. No successor government has attempted to raise a similar praetorian guard.

Weaknesses in Training and Equipment

Discipline and morale have been hindered in the Bangladeshi military through severe weaknesses in training opportunities and lack of supplies and equipment. The financial resources of the country permit neither a large and modern table of organization and equipment nor time and supplies needed for training.

The mission of the armed forces is both external and internal. On the external side its role is to repel or, at least, hinder an attack on the nation (one that for practical purposes could only come from India) until international pressures can be mobilized to bring about a cease-fire and a return to the status quo. Internally, as in each of the states studied in this book, the military may be called upon to give "assistance to the civil"—that is, to aid in the suppression of law and order problems or to help in the handling of natural disasters.

As noted, however, the military is ill-equipped both in manpower and materiel. The army consists of about 75,000 officers and men, most of them assigned to divisions with headquarters located in Dhaka, Chittagong, Comilla, Jessore, and Bogra or to subordinate units located in smaller stations. Recruitment has been greatly expanded since independence, at which time the Pakistani bias against Bengalis in the military had clearly ended. There is a munitions factory north of Dhaka, built during the Pakistan period with Chinese assistance, but most equipment must be imported at great cost (given that the expense cuts into the severely limited foreign exchange resources). No significant amount of military assistance has been made available to Bangladesh other than a small grant from the Chinese.

The navy has added a single British-built frigate to its small fleet of patrol boats, which perform what is essentially coast guard duty. There are about 5,000 men in the navy. The air force numbers about 2,500. The principal aircraft in the inventory are 30 Chinese F-6s (a Chinese version of the Soviet MiG-19) and 8 MiG-21s supplied by the Soviets during the Mujib period; but the latter are believed to be inoperable, partly as a result of the Soviet cutoff of spare parts. The inventory also includes several Soviet transport aircraft, useful in natural disasters, and some Soviet, Indian, and U.S. helicopters, likewise valuable during disasters as well as for transport in a country with few airfields.

Bangladesh has two paramilitary forces. One of these is the Bangladesh Rifles (mentioned above), a unit with border patrol duties and about 25,000 to 30,000 lightly armed personnel. The second force, called the Ansars, is roughly equivalent to a national guard, is based at the village level, and numbers about 15,000 personnel.

Discipline and Intramilitary Disputes

Discipline in the military has been a problem for Bangladesh in another more serious sense. A group of majors was responsible for the assassination of Mujibur Rahman in 1975, and it was a disaffected major general who, it is alleged, was the ringleader in the plot resulting in Ziaur Rahman's assassination in 1981. In addition, the chief of staff, General Ershad, overthrew a fairly elected civilian government headed by Abdus Sattar in 1982.

Aside from these actions, there were several that did not succeed. Perhaps the most notable was the rebellion in October 1977 said to have been led by the Jatiyo Samajtantrik Dal (JSD), which briefly endangered the Zia government. This event took place during a time when the government was stretched by the crisis created by the landing of a hijacked Japanese airliner at Dhaka airport. On September 30, a mutiny broke out in Bogra, that, while apparently quelled quickly, resulted in the loss of several officers. On October 2 a new (but probably related) mutiny began in Dhaka. Zia's residence was successfully defended by his personal guards, but a number of air force officers at the Dhaka airport in connection with the hijacking were killed and the radio station was held briefly. The mutiny ended after a few hours, at least partly owing to the swift action of the ranking officer in the Dhaka cantonment, Major General Muhammad Manzur—the same person alleged to have been the leader of the assassination plot against Zia in May 1981. The failure of the regime to take careful action after the prelude at Bogra can be seen as an almost standard reaction to yet another plot, of which there had been many since the 1975 murder of Mujib and the November coups and countercoups. The record appears to be much better during the Ershad regime.

The disputes that characterized the Mujib and Zia periods between freedom fighters and returnees now have all but ended because of the reduced number of officers who were on active duty in 1971 and remain on duty today. A major portion of the officers (especially those of lower rank) have been recruited and trained at the Bangladesh military academy since 1971. These younger officers do not carry the baggage of the animosity between "freedom fighters" and "returnees"; they are Bangladeshi officers without previous service under Pakistan.

A danger that has been recognized by the governments of both Zia and Ershad is the infiltration of the military by groups, especially the JSD, advocating more radical solutions to the problems of Bangladesh. Early in the Zia period, in 1976, Zia caused the arrest and trial of a leading JSD military officer, Colonel Abu Taher, who was convicted and executed for attempting to overthrow the government. Taher and others who agreed with him wanted to form a "people's army" patterned after the rankless People's Liberation Army of China.[3] Such groups are alleged to have been behind the serious mutinies at Bogra and Dhaka in 1977. Careful selection and retention programs seem to have reduced the danger of such activity, but it cannot be ruled out.

A Praetorian Army?

If we include all of the period from the assassination of Mujib until the assassination of Zia (August 1975–May 1981) and the period of Ershad's rule (since March 1982), we find that Bangladesh was under military rule or domination by the military for three-quarters of the time since its independence. Zia, of course, liberalized his regime markedly and ended martial law, but the people never forgot that he came to power through the military and that the military would *in extremis* be his ultimate support.

Ershad, too, has taken steps toward liberalization and ended martial law, but his military connection is not overlooked by the people.

It is clear that the military has been a major force in Bangladeshi politics. It is also clear that if Ershad's desire is met, the military will be given the constitutional status to remain so. Before he assumed power, Ershad demanded a role for the military through a national security council, invoking what is often called the "Turkish model." His plan for a future Bangladeshi system may still include the same idea.

Even if the government adopted a civilian rule in which the military became constitutionally subordinate to the government and a national security council were not created, the potential for military intervention would remain. Indeed, as history has shown, military establishments that have taken power demonstrate a high propensity for repeating the exercise.

Notes

1. See Robert L. Hardgrave, Jr., "India in 1984: Confrontation, Assassination and Succession," *Asian Survey,* vol. 25, no. 2 (February 1985), p. 132.

2. Talukder Maniruzzaman, *The Politics of Development: The Case of Pakistan, 1947–1958* (Dhaka: Green Book House, 1971), p. 43, citing the Constituent Assembly of Pakistan Debates, vol. 1 (January 17, 1956), p. 1845.

3. For the text of a statement purportedly made by Taher, see Lawrence Lifschultz, *Bangladesh: The Unfinished Revolution* (London: Zed, 1979).

Suggested Readings

Emajuddin Ahamed. *Military Rule and the Myth of Democracy* (Dhaka: University Press, Ltd., 1988).

Craig Baxter. *Bangladesh: A New Nation in an Old Setting* (Boulder, Colo.: Westview Press, 1984).

Stephen P. Cohen. *The Indian Army* (Berkeley: University of California Press, 1971).

_____ . *The Pakistan Army* (Berkeley: University of California Press, 1984).

Golam Hossain. *General Ziaur Rahman and the BNP* (Dhaka: University Press, Ltd., 1988).

Zillur Rahman Khan. *Leadership in the Least Developed Nation: Bangladesh* (Syracuse, N.Y.: Maxwell School, 1983).

Talukder Maniruzzaman. *The Bangladesh Revolution and Its Aftermath* (Dhaka: Bangladesh Books International, 1980).

Philip Mason. *A Matter of Honour: An Account of the Indian Army, Its Officers and Men* (London: Jonathan Cape, 1974).

Edward A. Olsen and Stephen Jurika, Jr. *The Armed Forces in Contemporary Asian Societies* (Boulder, Colo.: Westview Press, 1985) (includes articles by G. L. Wood on India, S. P. Cohen on Pakistan, and J. Lundstead on Bangladesh).

22
MODERNIZATION AND DEVELOPMENT: PROSPECTS AND PROBLEMS

Bangladesh is often described as the "largest-poorest" nation in the world. According to World Bank data Bangladesh comes in fifth from the bottom in the usual measure of wealth or poverty: The gross national product (GNP) per capita was only $160 in 1987.[1] The country is not, of course, the largest either in terms of area or population. Nonetheless, in the sense that it is a densely packed nation with perhaps two-thirds of its population living below the poverty line, Bangladesh qualifies for the term applied to it. The title of a book on political development in Bangladesh uses another term: "least developed nation."[2]

In this chapter, we shall look at the economic and social aspects of political development—an especially problematical concern with respect to Bangladesh if the soaring and geometrically compounding pressure of population on resources is not abated, and abated very soon.

The World's Largest-Poorest Nation

The two principal goals of Bangladesh, as propounded by Zia and Ershad, have been the achievement of self-sufficiency in food grains and a sharp decrease in the rate of population growth. The two are intimately related. The amount of land available for cultivation is basically constant, changing favorably only to the extent that it can be double- or triple-cropped through better water management, including irrigation. Hence, as the population increases, the amount of land per capita decreases. The challenge is to increase production per unit of land at a faster rate than the population growth rate.

In 1984 Ershad introduced a new land reform program under which no family may own more than 20 acres of land. This new ceiling is a reduction from the earlier 33 acres. It will mean little, however, to the majority of

Bangladeshis.[3] According to the 1977 agricultural census, only 0.4% of the farmers owned more than 25 acres and collectively held but 3.45% of the cultivated land. The average farm holding among those who held land was 3.5 acres, but when the landless are factored into this calculation the average holding is only 2.3 acres. The landless, if they have no other regular occupation, are dependent for income, in cash and kind, upon farm labor opportunities. Of those who hold land by ownership or rental, 58.3% own all the land they till; about 0.5% rent all the land they farm. The remainder farm a combination of owned and rented land. As the inheritance laws of both Hindus and Muslims tend to lead to rapid fragmentation of land holdings, the average 3.5-acre holding does not usually exist in a single consolidated piece. The census showed that most holdings contain 6 to 9 fragments, and about 10% contain 20 or more.[4]

A growing proportion of the arable land is now tilled two or three times a year, thus accounting for the expansion of effective cultivated acreage. However, 55% of the land is still single-cropped, while 38% is double-cropped and 7% is triple-cropped. Irrigation is the key to multiple-cropping. The national average for cropping is 1.5 (that is, the average piece of farm land is cropped 1.5 times), but the regions vary widely. In 1977, about 30% of the holdings reported using irrigation water, covering about 31% of the cropped area. This total has increased since 1977, but there is much more to be done. A major program initiated during the Zia period and continued since then has been the reopening of silted irrigation channels, most of the work done by hand under the "food for work" program for which the food payment is funded by international bodies.

New strains of rice and wheat have increased production to a degree, but not as extensively in the case of rice as the wheat "Green Revolution" accomplished in Indian and Pakistani Punjab. Much basic research was done at the International Rice Research Institute in the Philippines, and additional development has taken place in Bangladesh. The use of new seeds, for instance, requires a carefully coordinated supply of ingredients beyond seeds. Fertilizer is needed at specific times. Bangladesh has been able to use its abundant natural gas supply to manufacture nitrogenous fertilizers to supplement the animal fertilizers used for centuries, but phosphate and potash fertilizers must be imported. The 1977 agricultural census reported that 51% of landholders used chemical fertilizers, but also that this figure accounted for only 29% of the land. In addition, farmers need credit facilities (over and beyond the traditional village moneylenders) to finance the inputs until their harvests can be sold. Price incentives can be used to spur farmers on to higher production, but they may also cause political liabilities when the increased costs are passed on to urban consumers. At one time, many urban dwellers were placed on a subsidized price system for rice, although international assistance providers opposed the arrangement. The Ershad regime, to its credit, has sharply reduced the subsidy and raised the standard procurement price for rice paid to farmers.

Weather is a key factor in the increased output of rice. Too much rainfall results in flooding that washes crops away; too little stunts the development of rice and causes a decrease in production. On the whole, however, the strong development programs of the Zia period, which have carried over into the Ershad regime, have produced a steady increase in rice harvests. In the ten-year period from 1973–1974 to 1983–1984, rice production rose from 10 million tons to more than 14 million tons. Nevertheless, much wheat and some rice is imported each year to meet shortfalls and to build buffer stocks. Per capita availability of food grains is about one pound per day. Indeed, there are serious shortages in the average diet, not only also in quantity but in quality of nutrients. Much of the protein consumed is derived from lentils, but production of these crops has declined since independence. Production of fish, another important part of the traditional Bengali diet, has declined as well, relative to the years before 1971. Meat and poultry production has increased in total, but on a per capita basis it has declined.

A World Bank study in 1979 began with a statement that is as valid today as it was several years ago: "Rapid industrial growth is a necessary condition for the eventual solution of Bangladesh's problems of slow GDP [gross domestic product] growth, mass poverty and heavy dependence on foreign investment resources."[5] Mujib's experiments with socialism were a disaster for the economy. Then, under Zia there was some liberalization. But the Ershad regime has moved rapidly toward denationalization of many areas of the economy, including portions of the banking field, the nationalization of which was especially dear to Mujib and much of the Awami League. Zia and Ershad also made foreign investment easier to accomplish, but owing to the lack of resources in Bangladesh, it has primarily been a paper exercise rather than a practical step. Between 1973–1974 and 1980–1981, industrial production rose 45%, but this is a questionable figure as the starting base was so low. Growth in the private sector was 64%, but in the public (government-owned) sector only 39%. Although it cannot yet be measured, some significant further growth in the private sector seems to have occurred since Ershad assumed office.

The political implications of this dismal picture are very serious for the government. Ershad has taken steps, as did Zia before him, to involve the rural population in the development program and, not coincidentally, to build a personal support base (see Chapter 19). Much of his effort has revolved around the more affluent groups in the rural areas. So far these groups have been able to maintain traditional leadership in the countryside. How long this dominant position in the rural areas will continue is a major question for the government. In the urban areas, however, unrest has occurred under every government. The ending of the ration system, for instance, took political courage, but it was done under martial law and without discussion in a parliamentary body. So far, the governments in Bangladesh have shown greater concern about the present endemic urban unrest than about the potential rural unrest.

Limitations on Resources, Human and Natural

Bangladesh is a nation with few natural resources beyond its highly fertile soil. Much of the soil is replenished each year with silt deposited by rivers during annual floods. The delta on which most of the country is situated serves as an interconnected outlet for much of the flow of the Ganges River system as well as the only outlet for the Brahmaputra and the Meghna. Other rivers include the Teesta, which falls into the Ganges in northwest Bangladesh, and the Karnaphuli in the southeast. The latter has been harnessed as Bangladesh's only hydroelectric station (see Chapter 16).

As noted, a major source of power for Bangladesh is the abundant natural gas found in the eastern part of the country and off shore. However, as neither gas nor electric power distribution systems yet cross the Ganges River, although such are projected by the planned Jamuna River bridge, the southwestern part of the country is dependent on foreign oil for power generation. Although there has been much searching, the hopes for the discovery of oil have thus far been unmet. Some limited supplies of coal are known to exist but have not been economical to mine. There are no other feasible mineral deposits.

The rivers of Bangladesh are not an unmixed blessing. They are essential for the supply of water and for use as an intricate transportation system. But they also divide the country and are often so wide as to create hazards for travellers in storms; moreover, the flooding from them can be devastating as was seen in 1988. Finally, India and Bangladesh are at odds on the division of the waters of the Ganges, a topic that will be discussed in Chapter 31.

Bangladesh is also beset by problems in the area of human resources—particularly in terms of the skills available to utilize modern technology. It is estimated that about 80% of Bangladeshi adults are illiterate, even relative to the somewhat low standards by which literacy is measured. The government maintains that 60% of the eligible students are attending primary school, but this figure is probably inflated inasmuch as it represents the number attending at some time during the reporting year. Female literacy and school attendance rates are much lower than those for males, thus reflecting (and creating) additional problems with respect to the dissemination of information about family planning.

More than 400,000 students attended institutions of higher learning in 1983–1984. About 18% of the university and college students are women thus reflecting a higher rate for them at the upper levels of education than at the lower. Many Bangladeshi students take courses of study that, however culturally enriching they may be, are not likely to contribute directly to development; technical education lags behind the liberal arts. In 1983–1984, the total budget for education (current and development) was only 1.37% of the overall budget.

The population growth rate was 2.8% from 1965 to 1980—the rate is said to have dropped to 2.3%, but this figure may be too low. Considerable effort is being given to population planning programs, with sizable contributions from foreign governments and public and private organizations. In 1988, Ershad was given an award for family planning by the United Nations. The population growth, which places heavy pressure on development programs as well as on education, employment, food, and health, cannot help but lead to serious long-term political difficulties.

Like the other countries of South Asia, Bangladesh is host to a wide range of endemic and potentially epidemic tropical diseases. Malaria, cholera, and other intestinal diseases are chief among these. Coupled with malnutrition, these diseases lead to serious debilitation of much of the population, which in turn lowers the level of human resources. Fortunately, international groups have provided aid in the form of health delivery systems and drinking water. Dhaka itself is the site of the largest laboratory in the world studying cholera and other intestinal diseases.

Rapid urbanization has also caused both economic and political problems. With good reason, governments in Bangladesh, as elsewhere, are concerned about the potential for urban unrest. Accordingly, urban areas receive greater attention than others from political leaders and economic planners.

Weaknesses of the Administrative System

Bangladesh inherited from the Pakistan period a number of highly skilled officers of the Civil Service of Pakistan (CSP). Some of these men (at the time, there were no women) were denied employment by the Mujib regime as they had not quit their posts and joined the freedom movement. This situation was reversed by Ziaur Rahman, who employed almost all the CSP officers. In the mid-1970s new entrants to the highest level of the civil service began to assume key positions. These echelons—comprising the former CSP personnel and the upper ranks of the Bangladesh Civil Service—continue to be highly skilled and well trained in the generalist tradition of the Indian Civil Service. Newly established in-service training programs maintain and develop these skills.

The civil service group is small, however, and its directions must be carried out by subordinates who often have neither the skills nor the drive to be effective. With the devolution of much government power to the *upazilla* (subdistrict) administration, it is essential that government employees be carefully selected, trained, and retrained to carry out the directions coming from Dhaka. But much must yet be done to accomplish this end. Corruption, for instance, remains a serious problem; at least part of it is "traditional" but another part is certainly the result of poor selection and pay.

Bangladesh now has a unified civil service, somewhat similar to the United States "General Schedule," in which almost all government employees are graded in a single salary schedule; also as in the United States, different categories of newly recruited employees enter at different points on the schedule. The system in Bangladesh is perhaps even more analogous to the British arrangement of clerical, executive, and, at the highest level, administrative employees. The phasing in of the new system will take some time. It met with some opposition from the former CSP group, which saw its high status being eroded.

Political Uncertainty

The frequent changes of government in Bangladesh and the swings in economic policy have acted as disincentives to investors, both domestic and foreign. The Zia and Ershad regimes have moved far from the doctrinaire socialism espoused (even if not fully implemented) by the Mujib government. The divestitures of many government-held enterprises during the Ershad period has given some confidence to local entrepreneurs.

Entrepreneurship, however, is not a widely held skill in Bangladesh. Before 1971, most of the larger industrial concerns were owned by West Pakistani business houses. As previously noted, a study of the thirty largest houses in the 1960s showed that only one was of East Pakistan origin— that of A. K. Khan of Chittagong. This house remains important but has been surpassed, especially by the Islam group based in Dhaka. The lack of willing and capable Bangladeshi investors has contributed to the nationalization of "evacuee properties," as the firms formerly owned by West Pakistanis were termed. It is interesting to note that some Pakistani investors have returned to Bangladesh.

Before independence, many of the small shops were owned and much of the skilled labor provided by the small Bihari group, which comprised about 0.6% of the population. This group of Urdu-speakers migrated in 1947 mainly from the Indian province of Bihar to East Pakistan, rather than following the more general pattern of migration of Urdu-speakers to West Pakistan. The group generally supported Pakistan in 1971 and has paid an internationally publicized penalty since. Some Biharis have been transported to Pakistan and some remain in camps, but many, though they may live separately, have integrated themselves into the Bangladeshi economy.

The Bangladeshi interest in business seems to be increasing. Children of government employees and military men often join retirees from both groups in entrepreneurship. The political uncertainty facing the country, however, inhibits many of these people from making large investments that may have slower returns—a problem particularly true of foreign investors. Added to this has been the feeling that Bangladesh has little to offer in labor, markets, and resources, especially when compared with the huge potential of neighboring India.

The Future

Bangladesh has received large amounts of foreign assistance in efforts to ease its immediate problems and to build for the future. Almost all of the aid in the period just after independence came in the form of relief and rehabilitation for an economy and society shattered by the experience of civil war. In more recent years, too, a substantial portion of foreign aid has been received in the form of food supplies rather than assistance for long-term development. For example, U.S. assistance in 1980–1981 was $131 million but of this 55% ($72 million) was in Public Law 480 food aid, while 27.5% ($36 million) was nonproject help and only 17.5% ($23 million) was project aid.

Almost every nation and public and private international organization in existence has assisted Bangladesh. The United States, the European Community, and a few other countries have supplied food for survival, whereas the Islamic oil states have lent funds to help with energy; some, especially Saudi Arabia, have provided money for Islamic religious projects as well. Meanwhile, many of the private groups, such as the U.S. CARE and the British OXFAM, have worked more directly on developmental programs in agriculture, family planning, and health. As noted, however, the economic situation in Bangladesh is such that the immediate problems must be given priority. That is, development receives attention—often well-planned attention—but it must come second.

The economic future for Bangladesh is bleak indeed. The population, unless a miraculous turnabout occurs, will rise from 110 million (1990) to 217 million by 2025. And it is doubtful that agricultural production could continue to advance at a rate to maintain current food supplies, which are already below those considered necessary. It is equally doubtful that non-agricultural employment opportunities will expand at anywhere near the rate needed to provide for a population even now severely un- or underemployed.

Indeed, only Malthusian limitations of war, plague, and famine seem to be able to forestall this truly dismal forecast.

The political consequences of Bangladesh's future are uncertain at best. Bangladesh rebelled against Pakistan, but it was not so much a rebellion of the rural masses, as one spearheaded by the urban middle class. Whether a rural rebellion will occur in the future is impossible to predict. Whether the governments of the future will be able to meet at least the minimal urban demands is equally hard to predict. What can be foretold with reasonable certainty, however, is that a government following any revolution will face the same problems with the same inadequate resources.

Notes

1. The World Bank, *World Development Report, 1989* (New York: Oxford University Press, 1989), Table 1, p. 164. There are probably some poorer countries than Bangladesh for which figures are not given in the table.

2. Zillur Rahman Khan, *Leadership in the Least Developed Nation: Bangladesh* (Syracuse, N.Y.: Maxwell School, 1983).

3. See Peter J. Bertocci, "Bangladesh in 1984: A Year of Protracted Turmoil," *Asian Survey*, vol. 25, no. 2 (February 1985), pp. 155–168, especially p. 165 for the land reform question.

4. Unless otherwise stated in the text, the data in this chapter are taken or developed from the *Statistical Yearbook of Bangladesh, 1984–85*, published by the Ministry of Planning in Dhaka.

5. *Bangladesh: Current Trends and Development Issues* (Washington, D.C.: International Bank for Reconstruction and Development, March 1979), p. 41.

Suggested Readings

Craig Baxter. *Bangladesh: A New Nation in an Old Setting* (Boulder, Colo.: Westview Press, 1984).

Just Faaland and J. R. Parkinson. *Bangladesh: The Test Case of Development* (London: C. Hurst and Co., 1976).

Marcus Franda. *Bangladesh: The First Decade* (New Delhi: South Asian Publishers, 1982). See especially Part 3, "Population and Resources."

F. Thomasson Jannuzi and James T. Peach. *The Agrarian Structure of Bangladesh: An Impediment to Development* (Boulder, Colo.: Westview Press, 1980).

Zillur Rahman Khan. *Leadership in the Least Developed Nation: Bangladesh* (Syracuse, N.Y.: Maxwell School, 1983).

PART 4

SRI LANKA

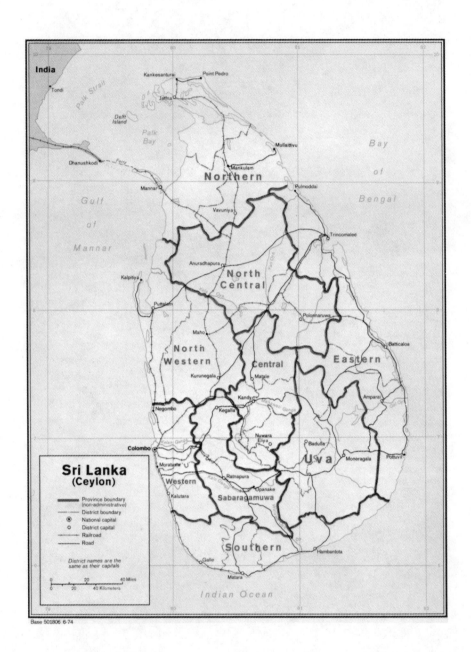

Sri Lanka
(Ceylon)

Province boundary
(non-administrative)
District boundary
⊛ National capital
○ District capital
Railroad
Road

*District names are the
same as their capitals*

0   20   40 Miles
0   20   40 Kilometers

India

Tondi

Palk Strait

Kankesanturai
Point Pedro
Jaffna
Delft Island
Palk Bay
Mullaittivu
Bay
Mankulam
Northern
Pulmoddai
of
Dhanushkodi
Mannar
Vavuniya
Bengal

Gulf
Anuradhapura
Trincomalee

of
**North
Central**
Kalpitiya

Mannar
Puttalam
Polonnaruwa

Maho
Batticaloa
**North
Western**
Central
Eastern
Kurunegala
Matale

Amparai
Kandy
Negombo
Kegalla

Nuwara
Eliya
Badulla
Colombo
Uva
Moneragala
Pottuvil
Moratuwa
Ratnapura
Western
Opanake
Kalutara
Sabaragamuwa

Southern
Hambantota
Galle
Matara

Indian Ocean

Base 501806 6-74

23
SOCIETY'S HERITAGE
AND ITS MEANING
FOR THE PRESENT

The political systems of the Third World are marked by violent upheaval, revolution, and military intervention in politics. There are only a few nations among the developing countries that have been able to maintain a system of stable and representative government. From 1948 until the 1980s, Sri Lanka was one of these countries. How was Sri Lanka able to maintain this record of political stability and representative democracy? Indeed, it is one of the poorest nations in the world, with a per capita gross national product of $400 per year.[1] In addition, a wide gap exists between the rich and the poor. And yet representative government and stability have persisted. An examination of Sri Lanka reveals many factors that have led to the political stability the country has experienced as well as other factors that one would expect to lead to instability and violence. Despite the violence Sri Lanka is currently experiencing, it has been able to maintain its democratic institutions. The following chapters explore why Sri Lanka has been successful thus far in establishing a stable political system; they also describe the threats to that stability. Specifically, they examine the cultural and historical heritage of Sri Lanka, the nature of its political institutions, the style of leadership exhibited by its leaders, and the ethnic problems and divisions in the society that threaten to destabilize it.

The present chapter describes some of the basic features of the country and its historical heritage. The island now known as Sri Lanka has long been known for its natural beauty and lush vegetation. Located at the foot of the South Asian subcontinent, it is a teardrop-shaped island about the same size as the state of Massachusetts (25,300 square miles). In 1988, its population was estimated to be 16.6 million people; the concentration of these people on a small land area thus makes it one of the most densely populated countries in the world, over 655 people per square mile.[2] The population density is intensified by the concentration of population in the southwest corner of the island.

Despite its small size Sri Lanka exhibits a great deal of geographic and climatic diversity. The southwest corner of the island, known as the wet zone, normally receives 100 to 200 inches of rain annually. The rest of the island—the north and east—has an arid climate with 50 to 70 inches of rainfall concentrated into a brief three-month period (October through December), during which the northeast monsoons blow rain clouds ashore. The southwest is affected by the monsoon during June and July and receives significant amounts of rainfall throughout the rest of the year.

The island also exhibits sharp topographical differences. The south-central portion of the island is marked by a series of mountains and high plateaus, with cities and villages located above the 5,000-foot level. This region is known for its tea plantations; in fact, most of the mountains have been stripped of their natural vegetation and replanted with tea. The rest of the island is a relatively level coastal plain with rolling hills and a land mass that rises as one travels toward the center of the island.

Within this environment of geographic diversity and tropical climate, a strong cultural heritage developed on the island of Sri Lanka. Ancient traders coming to Sri Lanka marveled at the natural beauty and friendly natives of the island they called Taprobane or Serendib, which stood at the crossroads of the Indian Ocean. A highly developed civilization emerged in the north-central part of the island, an area from which spices and other products were made available to the traders coming from the Orient and the Middle East. The arrival of the first Europeans in 1505 signaled a change in the nature of life on the island. The Sri Lankans lost their independence first to the Portuguese in 1505, then to the Dutch in 1656, and finally to the British in 1802 (see Chapter 1), but they did not lose their strong sense of national identity and pride. This national pride, coupled with the political institutions left by the British, helped create the stable and competitive political system mentioned earlier.

The strong sense of national identity and pride among Sri Lankans today is the result of the deep cultural and historical heritage of the island. The island's inhabitants claim that their heritage can be traced back more than 2000 years.[3] Most modern-day Sri Lankans are descended from one of two cultural-linguistic groups—the Aryans of northern India, or the Dravidians of southern India. The Aryans are descended from migrants from north India, who are believed to have arrived around 500 B.C., whereas the first Dravidians are believed to have come across from south India about the same time. The early Sri Lankans settled in the north-central regions of the country in an area that is now called the dry zone. The original inhabitants of the area, called Veddahs, were an aboriginal people who intermarried with the migrants and largely disappeared from the island as a distinct cultural group. Today, small groups of Veddahs can still be found in the eastern jungles of Sri Lanka. It was an arid region that spawned the growth of a major irrigation system to support the agriculture of the area. A great civilization flourished from the third century B.C. until the twelfth century A.D. Two of the major civilizations were centered in the present-day cities of Anuradhapura and Polonnaruwa. In the thirteenth and fourteenth centuries, the civilizations began to decline. The reason for this decline is unknown, but several theories suggest such causes as the increase in the prevalence of malaria in the region due to the many irrigation tanks that fostered the breeding of mosquitos, the inability of the society to maintain the thousands of miles of irrigation canals and reservoirs, and the decline of the groundwater levels as a result of the overpopulation of the region.[4]

Buddhism and Hinduism were introduced to the island from India at the time of the development of the great civilizations of the north-central parts of Sri Lanka. Buddhism is believed to have been introduced during the reign of King Devanampiya Tissa (307–267 B.C.);[5] Hinduism appears to have been established even earlier.[6] Hinduism and Buddhism were readily accepted by many of the people, and many Sri Lankan Buddhists today consider themselves to be the protectors of the faith.

These early civilizations thrived in the harsh climate with the development of the widespread system of irrigation tanks and canals to support the growing population of the region. With the success of the civilizations came a series of invasions from the Indian empires to the north, but by the thirteenth century, the Sri Lankan civilization of the dry zone was crumbling. These invasions led to the establishment of a Tamil kingdom on the Jaffna peninsula in the north. At the same time the Sinhalese were abandoning the dry areas of the north-central island and moving into the forested southwest section of the island and the hill region of the south-central portion of the island.

When the Portuguese arrived in 1505, they found the island divided between three kingdoms. Two were Sinhalese, with their capitals at Kotte (near present-day Colombo) and at Kandy in the central hill country. The third was a Tamil kingdom located on the northern Jaffna peninsula. The Portuguese arrival marked the beginning of a 300-year period of colonialism on the island. The Portuguese brought with them a desire to establish trade and to spread the Roman Catholic religion. They became embroiled in Sri Lankan politics and were ultimately deeded the Kotte kingdom upon the death of the king in 1597. In 1697, the Portuguese conquered the Jaffna kingdom and ruled all of the island except the Kandyan kingdom in the central hills, which repelled all of their efforts to conquer it.[7]

The desire to control the cinnamon trade of South Asia led the Dutch to challenge the Portuguese for control of the island. First the Dutch set up a trading post in Batticaloa on the east coast of the island (1602). A series of battles followed, in which the Dutch allied themselves with the king of Kandy to attack the Portuguese forts on the island. The last fort was overrun in 1658, and the Portuguese were forced off the island. The Dutch turned the administration of the island over to the Dutch East India Company, which continued to transform the island into a Christian nation by spreading the faith of the Dutch Reformed Church and to transform the economy into an export-oriented economy by establishing cinnamon plantations and cultivating coffee, cotton, tobacco, and sugar.[8]

The arrival of the British in Sri Lanka was a consequence of England's fear of French influence in South Asia. In particular, the British were concerned that the port of Trincomalee on the east coast would fall into French control. As a result, the British began negotiating with the Dutch in the late eighteenth century over the status of the port. Finally the Dutch were forced from the island in 1795. The British turned the administration of Ceylon over to the British East India Company, which ran the country until Ceylon became a crown colony in 1802. The British administration soon sought to unify the island by bringing the Kandyan kingdom under British control. The kingdom had persisted throughout the Dutch and Portuguese eras protected from the colonial armies by the rugged hill country of central Sri Lanka. The armies of the Dutch and the Portuguese tried to conquer the Kandyan kingdom but the Kandyan armies, commanding the higher points, were able to turn back armed attacks. As a result of the isolation of the landlocked Kandyan kingdom, the people of the region developed a distinct culture and set of traditions that have persisted until the present time.[9] The British brought the Kandyan kingdom under their control in 1815 and consolidated their rule over the whole island. From this time until their voluntary departure in 1948, the British ruled the island with only two serious challenges to their rule—the armed revolts of 1818 and 1848.

The British era was marked by further attempts to transform the Sri Lankan economy into an export-oriented economy and by efforts to establish British customs and beliefs in the country. English became the language of both government and the Sri Lankan elite, while Christianity, this time in the form of the Anglican Church, was fostered. It became customary for upper-class Sri Lankans to adopt the Christian religion and to speak the English language in their homes.

The British made several major changes in the economic life of the country. They used the hill country to establish first a coffee industry and then, after a disease destroyed the coffee plants, a tea industry. At the same time they established rubber and coconut plantations in the lower elevations of the hill country and in the coastal areas. The development of the plantations led to the growth of a landed aristocracy based on the ownership of the plantations. This aristocracy included British settlers and

Sri Lankans who were given the land because of their loyalty and/or service to the British. The development of the plantation economy transformed peasant agriculture by removing land that had once been used for vegetable cultivation from the use of the peasants.[10]

During the period of British rule, Sri Lankan cultural traditions and beliefs were neglected. The Buddhist and Hindu religions were ignored by the British and damaged when traditional temple lands were taken over by the British as "crown" or government lands. The English language was used as the language of government and commerce, whereas the languages spoken by most of the population—Tamil and Sinhala—were associated with a backward and primitive peasantry. In addition, the government operated with British traditions in mind. Sunday replaced the Buddhist day of prayer (the *poya* day) as the weekly day of rest, and Christian religious holidays were celebrated as national holidays.

After independence, attempts were made to reassert Sri Lankan control over the society. These attempts reflected the influence of the dominant ethnic group in the society—the Sinhalese. In the mid-1950s, there was a movement among the rural peasantry to restore the traditional values of the society and to remove the influence of the alien British culture. In 1956, the Official Language Act made Sinhala the national language, thus replacing English as the official language of government. Buddhism was later given special status by a series of laws passed in the 1960s and by the constitution of 1972. These attempts to restore Sinhala and Buddhism to a position of dominance in the society were accompanied by actions intended to return the traditional culture to a position of respect in the society. The wearing of traditional forms of dress as well as the use of Sinhala in commerce and government soon became popular among politicians.

However, these actions to restore the cultural heritage of Sri Lanka have proven to be disruptive to the political system. As noted in the next chapter, not all Sri Lankans agree about what constitutes the traditional Sri Lankan cultural, linguistic, and religious heritage.

Notes

1. World Bank, *World Development Report—1989* (New York: Oxford University Press, 1989), p. 164.
2. Ibid.
3. K. M. De Silva, *A History of Sri Lanka* (Berkeley: University of California, 1981), chapter 1.
4. Ibid., chapter 7.
5. K. M. De Silva, "Historical Survey," in K. M. De Silva, ed., *Sri Lanka: A Survey* (Honolulu: University Press of Hawaii, 1977), p. 33.
6. C. S. Navaratnam, *A Short History of Hinduism in Ceylon* (Jaffna: Sri Sanmuganatha Press, 1964). The question of which religion was the first on the

island is highly controversial and an important part of the debate concerning the Tamil-Sinhala conflict.

7. See George Davison Winius, *The Fatal History of Portuguese Ceylon: Transition to Dutch Rule* (Cambridge: Harvard University Press, 1971).

8. See K. M. De Silva, *A History of Sri Lanka*, chapters 10–14.

9. For a description of the Kandyan kingdom, see Robert Knox, *An Historical Relation of Ceylon,* published as the *Ceylon Historical Journal*, vol. 6 (July 1956–April 1957).

10. See Asoka Bandarage, *Colonialism in Sri Lanka* (New York: Mouton, 1983).

24
THE SOCIAL AND ECONOMIC FABRIC OF THE SOCIETY

The social and economic environment in which a political system operates can have a great impact on how well the government performs and on how politically stable the government is. In Sri Lanka several features of the socioeconomic environment have influenced the conduct of government and politics.

Socioeconomic Development

The quality of life in Sri Lanka is quite high despite the fact that the country is one of the poorest in the world on the basis of per capita gross national product.[1] It also has one of the best educational systems in Asia. The literacy rate in 1988 was estimated to be about 87%, and a very high percentage of school-age children attend school.[2] Education through the university level is free, and the average Sri Lankan is well aware of the value of education. The university system in the country is well developed, and competition to get into the institutions of higher learning is very stiff; only about 6% of those taking the entrance examinations actually gain admission.[3]

Health standards in Sri Lanka are quite high. Life expectancy at birth is 70 years—only five years lower than that for life expectancy in the United States and nine years higher than the average of other low-income countries.[4] This high life expectancy reflects the quality of medical services in the country. All medical care is free, and most Sri Lankans have easy access to doctors and hospitals. In addition, the government provides a system of nutritional care. Prior to 1979, every Sri Lankan was given a free measure of rice each week as well as reduced prices on other commodities. The size of the free measure of rice varied over time but was generally 2 kilograms. Since 1979, however, the free measure of rice has been replaced

TABLE 24.1   Voter Turnout Rates in National Elections

Year	Percent of electorate voting
1947	55.8
1952	70.7
1956	69.0
1960 (March)	77.6
1960 (July)	75.9
1965	82.1
1970	85.2
1977	86.7
1982 (presidential)	80.1
1982 (referendum)	70.8
1988 (presidential)	55.4
1989	63.6

All elections are parliamentary unless otherwise noted.

Sources: H.B.W. Abeynaike, Parliament of Sri Lanka (Colombo: Lake House); and Island, December 19, 1988, and February 18, 1989.

with a system of food stamps for the needy. Although the value of food stamp benefits increased very slowly after 1979, the nutritional requirements of the population are still generally met.

Accompanying these high levels of education and health has been a more equitable distribution of income and wealth than is found in other Third World countries. Although there is a wide gap between the rich and the poor in Sri Lanka, the gap is not as large as that in other developing nations.[5] Moreover, the gap decreased throughout much of the 1960s and 1970s. A strong sense of egalitarianism runs through the political culture of Sri Lanka and is reflected in the political behavior of the population.

In addition to this apparent strong sense of egalitarianism, the Sri Lankan people exhibit strong support for participatory democracy. As noted in Chapter 28, Sri Lankans frequently contact their elected representatives for the resolution of political problems. They also appear to exhibit widespread interest and involvement in the open and free elections held since independence. Voter turnout in Sri Lanka has been the highest in South Asia, rising from a low of 55.8% in the first parliamentary elections shortly before independence in 1947 to a high of 86.7% in the 1977 parliamentary elections (see Table 24.1). The turnout rates in the four national elections since 1977 have been lower. Yet the presidential elections of 1982 resulted in an 81.1% turnout rate and the national referendum held later in that year resulted in a 70.8% turnout rate. Even more surprising is the turnout in the presidential election in December 1988 and the parliamentary elections in February 1989. Despite death threats against anyone voting in these elections by two

TABLE 24.2   Ethnic Population of Sri Lanka

Ethnic Group	Percent of population
Sinhalese	74.0
Sri Lanka Tamils	12.6
Sri Lanka Moors	7.1
Indian Tamils	5.6
Burghers	.3
Malays	.3

Source: Statistical Abstract of the Democratic Socialist Republic of Sri Lanka—1982 (Colombo: Department of Census and Statistics, 1982), p. 32.

rebel groups, turnout was 55.3% in the presidential election and 63.6% of the voters in the parliamentary elections.

The Sri Lankan people exhibit strong support for open and free elections. In 1981, the country triumphantly celebrated the fiftieth anniversary of universal adult suffrage. Even more surprising is the fact that when the first elections in Sri Lanka permitting universal adult suffrage were held in 1931, it was only two years after Great Britain held its first election with universal adult suffrage.

Ethnicity

Despite its small size, the island of Sri Lanka is marked by a relatively wide diversity of ethnic groups. Two thousand years of invasion and foreign interference have resulted in a highly diverse ethnic structure in which individual Sri Lankans display a strong allegiance to their ethnic groups. The result of this has been a great deal of competition and conflict among the groups. This has affected the conduct of politics in Sri Lanka. The society is divided by language, culture, religion, and caste. The first three cleavages in particular tend to reinforce each other. In other words, the members of each major linguistic group tend to share the same culture and religion.

The largest ethnic group on the island is the Sinhalese, who comprise almost three-fourths of the population (see Table 24.2). They trace their origins to north India, claiming to be the earliest "civilized" inhabitants on the island and to have been responsible for the dry-zone civilizations of Anuradhapura and Polonnaruwa. The Sinhalese speak an Indo-European language similar to Hindi and are the only people in the world to speak this language. Most Sinhalese practice Buddhism and consider themselves to be the protectors of the faith. Over two-thirds of the population of the island practice Buddhism (see Table 24.3), which was brought to Sri Lanka in the third century B.C. and subsequently spread quickly through the dry-

TABLE 24.3   Religious Composition of the Sri Lankan Population

Religion	Percent of population
Buddhism	69.3
Hinduism	15.5
Islam	7.6
Christianity	7.5
Others	.1

Source: Statistical Abstract of the Democratic Socialist Republic of Sri Lanka—1985 (Colombo: Department of Census and Statistics, 1987), p. 34.

zone civilization. It persisted in Sri Lanka even after Buddhism had lost much of its influence in India. On their arrival the Europeans challenged Buddhism, and a significant minority of the Sinhalese adopted Christianity as its faith. Some of their descendants continue to practice Christianity today, and there are significant numbers of both Roman Catholics and Protestants.

The next largest ethnic community is the Sri Lanka Tamils, who trace their ancestry to the same period as that of the Sinhalese arrival and challenge the Sinhalese versions of the historical origins of Sri Lanka. They are religiously and culturally related to the Tamil community of south India and speak the same Dravidian language, Tamil (see Table 3.2). Most of the Tamils practice Hinduism, although significant numbers converted to Christianity after the arrival of the Europeans. Thus, the Tamils are distinct from the Sinhalese on the basis of culture, religion, and language. Although there is a significant population of Sri Lanka Tamils in the capital city of Colombo, most are found in the northern and eastern regions of the island. The northern Jaffna peninsula and the land areas immediately to its south are populated almost exclusively by Sri Lanka Tamils.

The Indian Tamils consider themselves to be culturally distinct from the Sri Lanka Tamils even though they speak the same language, practice the same religion, and trace their cultural origins to south India. The Indian Tamils arrived in Sri Lanka at a much later date than did the Sri Lanka Tamils. The Indian Tamils trace their origins to the coffee and tea estate workers brought from India by the British in the nineteenth and early twentieth centuries. They are found in the estate areas of the Kandyan hill country in central Sri Lanka, where they make up an overwhelming majority of the tea estate workers on the island.

Shortly after independence, the government passed legislation that made it very difficult for Indian Tamils to be Sri Lankan citizens. The rationale behind this action was based on the argument that even though many of the Indian Tamils were born in Sri Lanka, they were only temporary residents of the island and did not have any long-term ties to the country. The government then sought to deport most of the Indian Tamils and other noncitizens to India and Pakistan. The governments of both of these countries initially resisted this move, and the Indian Tamils remained in Sri Lanka as a stateless body of people. Then an agreement between Sri Lankan Prime Minister Sirimavo Bandaranaike and Indian Prime Minister Lal Bahadur Shastri in 1964 arranged for the granting of citizenship to approximately 300,000 of the 975,000 Indian Tamils in the country and the deportation to India of 525,000 of them. The status of the remaining 150,000 was to be the subject of further negotiations. This agreement has been implemented very slowly, and a significant number of Indian Tamils remain stateless.

An additional ethnic community of importance is the Moors, who are descended from early Arab traders to the island. The Moors practice Islam and, for the most part, speak Tamil. They are found in the important trading centers and along the east coast of Sri Lanka. The Moors of the east coast constitute a backward community with low levels of income and literacy while the Moors found in the trading centers tend to be wealthy and often literate in several languages.

Several smaller ethnic communities also inhabit Sri Lanka. These include the Burghers and the Malays. The Burghers are of mixed European and Sri Lankan descent. Their native tongue is usually English, and most are Christians. The majority are found in the capital city of Colombo and make up part of the economic elite of the island. The Malays are descended from the Malay traders and guards brought to the island during the colonial era. They are largely found in Colombo and practice Islam.

Both the geographic diversity of the island and its colonial history have contributed to the development of subcultures within the two major ethnic groups—the Sinhalese and the Tamils. The Sinhalese are divided between the low-country Sinhalese and the Kandyan Sinhalese. During the 200 years of colonial rule, during which the Kandyan kingdom resisted the European powers, the people in the hill country developed a culture that differs widely from that of the people living in the lowland areas. In recent years, however, the distinction between the two groups of Sinhalese has decreased as contact between the two groups has increased.

The Sri Lanka Tamil community is divided between those Sri Lanka Tamils living on the Jaffna peninsula and those living along the east coast of the island. The east coast Tamils tend to be poorer and less educated than the Jaffna Tamils and are often thought to be more traditional in their outlook.

The Caste System

The Sri Lankan caste system is similar to that in India (see Chapter 3); in its general structure, however, it is different in two very important respects. In Sri Lanka, by contrast to India, the various caste groups generally are concentrated geographically such that an overwhelming majority of the population in any area are members of the same caste. In addition, the highest-status caste is also the largest in size among both the Tamils and the Sinhalese. Each of these groups has a different caste structure.

Since no census of Sri Lankan castes has been taken in this century, the size of the caste groups can only be estimated. However, it is generally agreed that the Sinhalese caste structure is dominated hierarchically and numerically by the Goyigama (cultivator) caste, which is estimated to comprise about one-half of the Sinhalese population. Beneath the Goyigamas are three castes of lesser status. These are the Karawa (fishermen) caste, the Salagama (cinnamon peeler) caste, and the Durawa (toddy tapper) caste. These three castes are found along the southwest coast of the island and generally constitute a majority in the regions where they are found. Untouchability is rare among the Sinhalese, although several important castes of very low status do exist. Among these are the Wahumpara (jaggery/palm sugar maker) and the Batgam castes (of uncertain occupational origin). These castes, too, are geographically concentrated. Both are found in inland regions in the transition zones between the lowlands and the Kandyan hill country.[6]

The Sri Lanka Tamil caste structure is also dominated by the cultivator caste, known as the Vellala. The Vellala are believed to comprise about one-half of the Sri Lanka Tamil population in the northern Jaffna peninsula.[7] Beneath the Vellala are several other important castes including the Koviyar (domestic servants) and two castes associated with fishing—the Karayar, whose members generally live along the northern coast, and the Mukkuvar, whose members generally live along the east coast. Untouchability is much more common among the Tamils than it is among the Sinhalese, and it is estimated that one-fourth of the population of the Jaffna peninsula is composed of members of the untouchable castes. These include the Palla (agricultural laborers), Ambattar (barbers), Valava (toddy tappers), and the Paraya (scavengers) castes. With the exception of the Indian Tamils, the Moors and the other small ethnic groups—like the Muslims in Pakistan, India, and Bangladesh—do not recognize caste distinctions.

*   *   *

The consequence of the ethnic divisions in Sri Lanka has been communal strife. Since independence, the conflict between the Sinhalese and Tamils has escalated, and smaller conflicts have been waged between the Roman Catholics and Buddhists as well as among the various caste groups. The most serious conflict has been the Sinhalese-Tamil dispute. Both ethnic groups fear the intentions of the other group. The Tamils, as a minority in Sri Lanka, feel that they have not received fair treatment from the Sinhalese and believe that the Sinhalese are trying to turn the country into a Sinhala-speaking Buddhist state. The Sinhalese, on the other hand, despite their majority status within the population, also feel threatened. The Sinhalese culture and language is found only on the island of Sri Lanka and is much smaller than the Tamil-speaking culture and society to the north of Sri Lanka in the Indian state of Tamilnadu. The fear of the Sinhalese has led them to be suspicious of the actions of the Tamil community in Sri Lanka. Some Sinhalese fear that their culture and nation might be absorbed by the Tamils.

This conflict became more violent after 1977 and upset the political stability of the country when it erupted into open civil war in 1984. Since then, the Sri Lanka Tamil regions of the country, especially the Jaffna peninsula, have been in a state of open revolt against the government. Violence and bloodshed increased rapidly in the 1980s (see Chapter 29).

Many of the efforts of the Sri Lankan leaders to establish a stable society are directed at a resolution of the ethnic conflict facing the country. But government attempts to resolve the conflict have been draining resources that could be utilized elsewhere to help further develop the economic and social achievements described earlier in this chapter.

Notes

1. World Bank, *World Development Report—1989* (New York: Oxford University Press, 1989), p. 164.

2. Ibid., p. 22.

3. Swarna Jayaweera, "Education," in Robert N. Kearney and Tissa Fernando, eds., *Modern Sri Lanka: A Society in Transition* (Syracuse, N.Y.: FACS Publications, 1979), pp. 147–148; and Sunil Bastian, "University Admission and the National Question," in Social Scientists Association, eds., *Ethnicity and Social Change in Sri Lanka* (Colombo: Social Scientists Association, 1984), p. 174.

4. World Bank, *World Development Report–1989*, p. 164.

5. Ibid., p. 222.

6. Bryce Ryan, *Caste in Modern Ceylon* (New Brunswick, N.J.: Rutgers University Press, 1953).

7. Bryan Pffafenberger, *Caste in Tamil Culture: The Religious Foundations of Sudra Domination in Tamil Sri Lanka* (Syracuse, N.Y.: FACS Publications, 1983).

25
LEADERSHIP AND FAMILY

Two additional factors affecting the political system of Sri Lanka are the role of kinship in the society and the cultural attitudes of the people toward their leaders. The features that stand out when one examines these factors are (1) the role and influence of family and other kinship ties in political affairs of the country, and (2) the dominating personality of and the influence exercised by the politicians who have occupied the highest political office in the country.

The Political Role of Family and Kinship

As in the other South Asian countries, Sri Lankan politics have been marked by what can be called the politics of personality: Much of the political conflict in the country has been accentuated by kinship and the role of individual personalities. Kinship may take the form of allegiance to family and to the broader form of affiliation known as caste.

Family ties have played a very important role in Sri Lankan politics. The status of a family has always been an important factor in Sri Lankan social and political life. During colonial times certain families gained an important economic position, which carried a great deal of status with it. The descendants of these families are still treated with respect and are given a high level of status in the society. Politics in the first forty years (1947–1987) of the post-colonial era were dominated by a few families, and the political and economic elite of the country has been populated by a relatively small number of family groups.[1] This differs from India where the Nehru family has been the one dominant family, or Pakistan where a large number of families have formed semipermanent alliances. It is not surprising that the largest political party in Sri Lanka, the United National party (UNP), was once known as the "Uncle-Nephew party" because of the kinship ties among the party's leaders. The political history of Sri Lanka since independence has been a history of a few dominant personalities, all representing a few important families.

The first prime minister of Sri Lanka was an independence movement leader, Don Stephen Senanayake. He was elected as prime minister in 1947 as the leader of the United National party. The 1947 elections were a contest between the UNP, a loose grouping of pre-independence personalities, and several Marxist parties led by the Lanka Sama Samaja party (LSSP). The UNP received the most votes in the election but failed to poll over 40% of the vote, winning only 42 seats out of the 95 seats in parliament. Senanayake made agreements with several independent members of parliament and was able to form a government. In 1952, upon his unexpected death while horseback riding, D. S. Senanayake was replaced by his son, Dudley, who almost immediately called new elections. These elections were won by the UNP, which captured 54 of the 95 seats elected. Dudley experienced several political setbacks during his first few months in office and resigned as prime minister in 1953.

The strength of the Senanayake family ties in the UNP continued as the party selected Dudley's uncle, Sir John Kotelawala, as prime minister. Kotelawala remained in power until the 1956 elections, which represented a major turning point in Sri Lankan post-colonial history. From 1948 until 1956, the UNP ruled the country, with no major opposition party threatening its parliamentary majority.[2]

In 1956, a new party and personality emerged in Sri Lankan politics, and the UNP lost the election. The Sri Lanka Freedom party (SLFP) won 51 seats in parliament, while the UNP was reduced to 8. A new family was interjected into the leadership of Sri Lankan politics. The new prime minister was Solomon West Ridgeway Dias Bandaranaike. Bandaranaike was not related to the Senanayake family, although until 1951, he had been a member of the UNP and a close associate of the former prime ministers. A very charismatic and dynamic leader, he was able to put together a populist coalition, which drew its support from the rural Sinhalese peasantry.[3] Bandaranaike's leadership was very short lived. He was assassinated by a disgruntled Buddhist monk in 1959. The conspiracy behind his death was a consequence of the disappointment of some of his radical supporters, who expected him to do more for the restoration of Sinhalese Buddhism. He led Sri Lanka for little more than three years; yet his impact continues to affect Sri Lankan politics and society. His name is invoked by members of both of the country's major political parties as a source of inspiration and guidance.

Bandaranaike was replaced for a brief time by Wijayananda Dahanayake, the minister of education in Bandaranaike's cabinet. For approximately the next six months Sri Lanka was led by a man who was not related to either the Senanayakes or the Bandaranaikes. Dahanayake was unable to hold Bandaranaike's coalition government together, and elections were held in March 1960. The UNP recovered from the defeat it had suffered in 1956 by winning a plurality of seats in parliament. However, as it did not win a majority, Dudley Senanayake could not form a government. In new elections in July 1960, Bandaranaike's widow, Sirimavo, became prime minister—the first woman ever to be elected head of government in a democratic system. She did not have the same charisma as her husband but was able to invoke his name and promised to continue his policies.

Sirimavo ruled until 1965, when the SLFP lost the parliamentary elections of that year to the UNP, once again led by Dudley Senanayake. As had been the case in the previous five elections, the governing party lost the next parliamentary elections, this time in 1970. Sirimavo Bandaranaike again became prime minister. And this time she won an overwhelming victory. The SLFP and its coalition partners won 116 of the 151 seats contested in the election and dominated politics for the next seven years. In 1973, the leader of the UNP, former Prime Minister Dudley Senanayake died. A leadership battle immediately erupted in the UNP for control of the party between Rukman Senanayake, Dudley's nephew, and Junius Richard Jayawardene, a distant relative of Dudley. Jayawardene had been an associate of D. S. Senanayake and had first been elected to the state council, parliament's colonial predecessor, in 1943. He had been a leader of the UNP since independence and had been biding his time while the Senanayake family passed the party leadership among themselves. Upon becoming the president of the UNP, Jayawardene began to restructure the party in his image. He made efforts to bring younger people into the party and to build a strong party organization. His efforts were successful, and he became prime minister after the UNP won the 1977 elections in a landslide unprecedented in Sri Lankan electoral history. The UNP won 140 of 168 seats. The SLFP was reduced to 8 seats. After coming to power, Jayawardene directed the rewriting of the constitution and the creation of a presidential system (discussed in Chapter 26). He became the first president under the new constitution and assumed commanding control of the government machinery and his party.

The SLFP itself was also in a state of change. The Jayawardene-led UNP government accused the former prime minister Sirimavo Bandaranaike of abusing her power while in office from 1970 to 1977. In October 1980, her right to participate in politics was removed for a period of seven years, and the SLFP needed a new leader. They chose her son Anura after a long and divisive battle within the party. Anura Bandaranaike was soon thrust into the role of the keeper of his father's legacy. Unfortunately, he inherited a political party torn apart by factionalism and reduced to a minimal role in the parliament.

In 1988, Jayawardene decided to retire, and his party, the UNP, nominated his prime minister, Ranasinghe Premadasa, a member of a low caste, to contest the next presidential election. Premadasa defeated Sirimavo Bandaranaike in the election in December 1988 and began a new era in Sri

TABLE 25.1   Heads of Government of Sri Lanka

	Party	Date of Birth	Date of Death	Term of Office	Caste
Don Stephen Senanayake	UNP	10/20/84	3/22/52	Sep. 1947–Mar. 1952	Goyigama
Dudley Senanayake	UNP	6/19/11	4/13/73	Mar. 1952–Sep. 1953 Mar. 1960–July 1960 Mar. 1965–May 1970	Goyigama
John Kotelawala	UNP	4/04/97	10/02/80	Sep. 1953–Apr. 1956	Goyigama
S.W.R.D. Bandaranaike	SLFP	1/08/99	9/26/59	Apr. 1956–Sep. 1959	Goyigama
Wijayananda Dahanayake	SLFP	10/22/02	–	Sep. 1959–Mar. 1960	Goyigama
Sirimavo Bandaranaike	SLFP	4/17/16	–	July 1960–Mar. 1965 May 1970–July 1977	Goyigama
J. R. Jayawardene	UNP	9/17/06	–	July 1977–Dec. 1988	Goyigama
Ranasinghe Premadasa	UNP	6/23/24	–	Dec. 1988–	Hinna

Lankan politics in which the family dominance of the Senanayakes and Bandaranaikes was gone. More importantly, Premadasa was of humble origins and was not part of the English-speaking elite as were the Senanayakes, Jayawardenes, and Bandaranaikes.

Thus, until 1989, the highest leadership position in the government of Sri Lanka had been dominated almost exclusively by three families: the Senanayakes, the Bandaranaikes, and the Jayawardenes. More important, the governments formed since independence have revolved around the personalities of these party leaders.

Caste and Politics

An additional feature of kinship and its role in Sri Lankan politics is the influence of the caste system. (The Sri Lankan caste system is discussed in Chapter 24). This system has played a very important role in the political development of the country. Traditionally, Sinhalese society has been dominated by the Goyigama caste, which in addition to being the highest-status caste in the Sinhalese caste hierarchy is the largest caste on the island. The members of the Goyigama caste have dominated the politics of independent Sri Lanka.[4] Until 1988, all of the executive leaders of the country (prime ministers and now the president under the current presidential system) were members of the Goyigama caste (see Table 25.1). The constitution of 1978 placed executive power in the hands of the president and reduced the power of the prime minister, who had had considerably more power under the provisions of the two earlier constitutions of the country. (These constitutions are discussed in Chapter 26.) The current president (elected in 1988), Ranasinghe Premadasa (born June 23, 1924), is a member of a small lower-status caste rather than a Goyigama. His prime minister, D. B. Wijetunga, is a member of the Goyigama caste. By the same token, the Tamils have been politically dominated by the cultivator caste in their caste hierarchy, the Vellala.[5] In fact, most of the Tamil members of parliament and their leaders have been members of this caste grouping.

Caste has also played a very important role in Sri Lankan elections. Voters in parliamentary elections do not often support candidates who are from different castes than their own. Until 1989, the impact of this caste allegiance was tempered by the fact that most Sinhalese electoral constituencies were overwhelmingly populated by the members of one caste. Thus, caste was not an overt factor in the recruitment of candidates running for office. When 90% of the electorate was of the same caste, one could expect that all of the candidates would be from the majority caste. However, the 1989 parliamentary elections were conducted using proportional representation, and multi-member electorates corresponding to the administrative district became the electoral constituency. The impact of this system on caste voting is still unknown.

Prior to 1989, the major parties very rarely nominated a candidate from a minority caste group and almost never nominated a candidate from a numerically small caste group. In the few electorates in which the castes were relatively evenly split, a candidate's caste affiliation was an extremely important factor in the election campaign.[6] In this situation, the UNP and the SLFP would frequently run candidates from different castes.

Once elected, members of parliament and cabinet members are often more responsive to the members of their caste group. Patronage benefits such as jobs and job transfers, as well as the placement of development projects such as roads and bridges, are often affected by the caste affiliation of the recipients. Thus, caste plays a very large role in the politics of Sri Lanka.

Patron-Clientism

A significant element in the relationship between the leaders of Sri Lanka and its population is the existence of what has been called patron-client relationships.[7] These relationships are found in many Third World nations and some industrialized democracies. They consist of a dominant patron who provides clients with political favors or material benefits in return for their political support or assistance in times of need. Patron-clientism is frequently found in areas such as Pakistan, Bangladesh, and India, where a traditional landed aristocracy exerts its power and influence in a politically modernizing environment.[8] In short, the patrons utilize their sources of power to provide benefits to those who support them. In many cases, the members of the Sri Lankan parliament have assumed the role of the traditional patron by dispensing government patronage in return for the support of their constituents. The constituents (clients) try to ally themselves with a particular member of parliament (patron) and disassociate themselves if it appears that the MP is going to lose the next election.[9] The MPs try to provide as many benefits as they can to their clients in order to develop a network of faithful supporters. The system is fueled by the use of the MP as an employment agent in charge of dispensing government jobs.

The consequence of the role of family, caste, and patron-client relationships in Sri Lanka is a highly personalized sense of politics. An MP's constituents often feel that they can freely approach their representative as if he or she were a friend or close associate.[10] As a result, the MPs are inundated by constituents who come to their offices or homes to make requests of them. This personalization of politics is carried to the point where national leaders are frequently referred to by their first names by the populace and in the press. As noted in Chapter 28, this practice often leads to highly personalized demands made on the governmental representatives. It is certainly a significant element of the success of democratic rule in the country.

Summary

The dominating presence of the prime ministers and executive president of Sri Lanka resembles the traditional attitudes toward the pre-colonial leadership of the country.[11] In the era of the Kandyan kings, the populace showed great deference to the leader, who came from a family lineage of rulers. The leader acted as protector of his people, a relationship not unlike that of the patron and client or the MP and his or her constituents. While the king led the country, the people were to give him the authority and obedience deserving of someone in that position. The prime ministers and executive president have a similar degree of authority and in many ways demand that authority from the people. The result is a powerful and generally dynamic leader drawn from the economic and social elite of the society. The structure of government in which these leaders operate is discussed in the next chapter.

Notes

1. Janice Jiggins, *Caste and Family in the Politics of the Sinhalese, 1947–1976* (London: Cambridge University Press, 1979), p. 96.

2. See A. Jeyaratnam Wilson, "Politics and Political Development Since 1948," in K. M. De Silva, ed., *Sri Lanka: A Survey* (Honolulu: University of Hawaii Press, 1977), pp. 292–300.

3. W. Howard Wriggins, *Ceylon: Dilemmas of a New Nation* (Princeton, N.J.: Princeton University Press, 1960), pp. 119–124.

4. Jiggins, *Caste and Family*, p. 25.

5. Bryan Pfaffenberger, *Caste in Tamil Culture: The Religious Foundations of Sudra Domination in Tamil Sri Lanka* (Syracuse, N.Y.: FACS Publications, 1982), pp. 92–93.

6. Robert Oberst, *Legislators and Representation in Sri Lanka: The Decentralization of Development Planning* (Boulder, Colo.: Westview Press, 1985), p. 114.

7. See James C. Scott, "Patron-Client Politics and Political Change in Southeast Asia," *American Political Science Review*, vol. 66, pp. 91–113.

8. Robert E. Gamer, *The Developing Nations: A Comparative Perspective,* 2nd ed. (Boston: Allyn and Bacon, 1982). (See chapter 4 for a thorough discussion of patron-client relationships.)

9. See Oberst, *Legislators and Representation,* pp. 55–65.

10. Ibid.

11. Ibid., chapter 4.

26
THE POLITICAL
PROCESS AND
GOVERNMENT INSTITUTIONS

The influence of powerful individuals and personalities in the politics of Sri Lanka is best reflected in the country's current constitution. The constitution was the work of the man who became the first executive president under the provisions of the constitution, Junius Richard Jayawardene, who was initially elected to parliament during the colonial era and gradually established himself in a dominant role in Sri Lankan politics. Many of his personal views and ideas are enshrined in the constitution. For instance, a few years before the constitution was promulgated, he argued for a strong national government with more power concentrated in the executive, in order to pursue economic development adequately.[1] The overall impact of the new constitution has been to concentrate power in the hands of the executive and to make the president a dominating figure in the government.[2]

The powerful executive in Sri Lanka emerged very slowly. During the colonial era Sri Lankans were not given very much influence in the government. Although there have been many arguments concerning the contribution of the colonial experience in Sri Lanka, most writers agree that two elements of the British rule left a major impression on today's Sri Lanka—namely the structure of government established by the British, and the educational system created during the colonial period.[3] During the colonial era the British created political institutions modeled on their own. They set up a parliamentary system and gave the Sri Lankans a limited degree of self-rule before granting independence. Sri Lanka, along with India, became one of the first British colonies to be allowed elected representatives from the local population in a colonial legislature. In 1912, they were permitted to elect 3 members out of a 21-member Legislative Council. The number of elected members was increased to 4 in 1917, and to 23 out of 37 members in 1920. (These proportions roughly parallel the development of indigenous representation in India.) This experience with self-rule during the colonial era provided the Sri Lankans a limited experience with self-government.

Just prior to independence a three-man commission of Englishmen headed by Lord Soulbury wrote a constitution modeled on the British Westminster system of government, which is very similar to India's constitution without the federal provisions (see Chapter 5). The Sri Lankans adopted the Soulbury constitution and governed with it until its replacement in 1972. This constitution provided for a parliamentary system with a bicameral legislature.[4] The lower house, or House of Representatives, became the dominant chamber of government. It was elected directly by the people in a combination of single and multi-member electoral districts. The number of multi-member districts was limited, never exceeding 5 districts with either 2 or 3 members elected. The House of Representatives was given the responsibility to select the prime minister and to approve the cabinet. The upper house, or Senate, consisted of 30 members, 15 nominated by the governor general on the recommendation of the cabinet and 15 elected by the lower house by proportional representation. Its power was quite limited, and its main function was to provide the means for political parties to reward their supporters. In addition, the Senate's members could be named to the cabinet of ministers.

The government created by the Soulbury constitution was criticized by many because of its similarity to the governmental structure of Sri Lanka's former colonial ruler, Great Britain. The SLFP-led United Front government elected in 1970 was dedicated to changing the structure of government to fit the Sri Lankan society more effectively than the "alien" Soulbury government had done. In 1972, a new constitution was promulgated. It had been written by a constitutional convention consisting of the members of parliament elected in 1970. The fact that the majority of seats were won by the United Front gave the coalition a free hand in determining the changes in the new constitution. The major changes introduced by the constitution included the abolition of the Senate and provisions that not only accorded Buddhism a special place in the society but also affirmed the role of Sinhala in governmental actions.[5]

The 1972 constitution was very unpopular with the two major opposition parties, the UNP and the leading party of the Tamil ethnic group, the Federal party (FP). The Federal party opposed the constitution because it designated Sinhala as the official language and bestowed special status on Buddhism. In addition, it did not provide the Tamil language with any special status. The UNP opposed the 1972 constitution because of fears it would lead to an authoritarian government.

The UNP's 1977 election manifesto promised a new constitution and the creation of a presidential form of government. The new constitution unveiled in 1978 drastically altered the nature of Sri Lankan government.[6]

The Westminster-style parliamentary system was replaced by a government modeled after that of France. Its main features are as follows:

1. A provision for an executive presidency that, unlike India's presidency, carries a great deal of power. The position commands many more powers than did the prime ministers under the two previous constitutions of Sri Lanka. The president is now elected by a direct vote of the people for a fixed term of six years. (The third amendment to the constitution, passed in 1982, allows the president to call a new presidential election at any time after serving four years of his or her term.) The parliament also has a term of six years, but the president is permitted to dissolve it and call new elections at any time.

2. The president appoints the prime minister and the cabinet subject to parliamentary approval. In addition, the president rather than the prime minister presides over the cabinet when it meets.

3. The single-member system of electoral constituencies was replaced with a system of proportional representation in the 1989 parliamentary elections.

4. All vacancies in parliament are filled by the party of the member who vacated the seat and not through by-elections, as was done in the past. In addition, the party has the right to expel any of its members from parliament and to replace them with another member of the party. (The second amendment to the constitution, passed in 1979, allows the whole parliament to decide if an MP can either be expelled by his or her party or switch party allegiance. Thus far, the provisions of the amendment have allowed several opposition members to cross over to the government, although no government members have been permitted to join the forces of the opposition.)

5. Finally, the constitution provides for national referenda on issues of importance.

The structure of the government created by the constitution is presented schematically in Figure 26.1.

The unique feature of the 1978 constitution is the power placed in the office of the president.[7] On paper, it divides governmental authority among the executive, legislature, and judiciary. The executive president created by the constitution exercises a great deal of power. He or she may declare war and peace, grant pardons, and carry out any actions approved by the legislature or ordered by the Supreme Court. However, the main powers of the president are, in fact, the informal powers that a president may wield to control the legislative branch. As the highest elected official of his or her party, the president may exert influence over the members of parliament

Figure 26.1   Structure of the Sri Lankan government

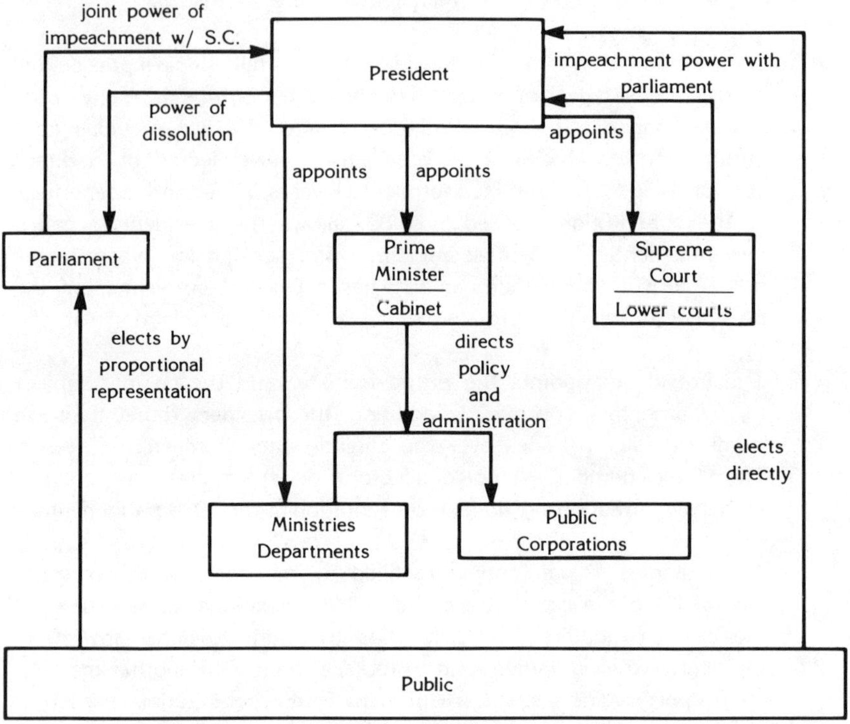

through the party's power to replace them. In fact, both presidents (Jay-awardene and Premadasa) elected since the system began have wielded a great deal of influence and power over the parliament through their control of the members of parliament.

   The constitution states that the president is responsible to parliament and that parliament may impeach the president. However, the Supreme Court must approve the impeachment. The president also wields a great deal of control over the Supreme Court, given the presidential power to nominate and remove members. In addition, as a party leader, the president is in a position to remove from parliament any party members whom the president does not like or disagrees with. As a result, the parliament may be reduced to little more than a rubber stamp, if the president is in a position to control both the cabinet and the party.

   Several other provisions of the constitution help maintain stability and the maintenance of one party in power. Prior to 1978, the governing party had lost each of the previous seven elections. The new constitution created a system of proportional representation that contains an unusual provision. The leading party in each of the electoral districts receives a bonus seat before the seats are distributed on the basis of proportional representation. Jayawardene's party, the UNP, had been the leading vote getter in almost every election since independence. The successful elections of the SLFP have always involved electoral agreements with smaller parties in which the parties have decided not to contest each other in the same constituencies. Following the elections of 1956 and 1970, the parties joined together in a coalition government. Under proportional representation, it would be unlikely for the parties to join together to contest the election under the same party banner. Thus, the constitution helps ensure the possibility of a UNP victory in future parliamentary elections.[8]

The system of proportional representation also includes provisions for the electoral list of candidates to be determined by the voters. At the ballot box, voters select a party and a candidate from that party. The votes for the party determine how the seats are divided among the parties while candidate preferences determine who within that party wins the seat. Thus if the SLFP wins eight seats in an electoral district, the top eight vote getters of the SLFP will be elected to parliament.

When government power became concentrated in the president, the parliament, which had been the center of power under both the Soulbury constitution and the constitution of 1972, lost much of its power and influence.[9] It currently has 196 members and since 1977 has been dominated by the UNP.

The Sri Lankan parliament, like that of Great Britain, maintains a rigorous separation between government supporters and the opposition. As in most parliamentary systems, the benches of each side face each other on opposite sides of the floor of parliament. Constitutional provisions barring crossovers from one party to another have limited what was once very common behavior under the provisions of the earlier constitutions. Each side of the parliament chooses a leader: The majority selects the prime minister, and the opposition selects the leader of the opposition. A strict code of party loyalty ensures that the members will vote as the party leaders want them to, unless they are released by the party leadership to vote their consciences— an alternative that does not happen very often. Thus, most votes of parliament are highly predictable. Members who do not do as the party leaders wish are often expelled from the party and can be expelled from parliament as well under the provisions of the current constitution. The party leaders hold group meetings of their party's parliamentary members, thus providing the backbenchers—who are otherwise not allowed to express negative opinions about government policy—an opportunity to complain; at the same time, the party leaders are given the chance to determine the sentiment of their members on legislative proposals.[10]

The members of parliament represent the privileged elite of the country. Most speak fluent English and cabinet meetings are often held in English.

Most come from the upper economic classes—hence the overrepresentation by MPs from the professional occupations and the landowning elite. The ethnic minorities are fairly well represented as well, although the Indian Tamils have elected only one representative to parliament (in 1977) since the denial of their citizenship after electing 6 members to the first parliament in 1947.

Although the constitution went into effect in 1978, its electoral provisions were not applied at the national level until 1982. In the first presidential elections, held in October 1982, the incumbent president, Jayawardene, won reelection to office.[11] After his election triumph, Jayawardene decided to use the constitutional provision for referenda to ensure for his party the kind of dominance it had exercised from 1977 to 1982. It was generally believed that a parliamentary election might result in a UNP defeat but definitely would not result in the five-sixths majority that the 1977 elections had given the UNP. An election victory with a reduced UNP majority would have taken away the UNP's power to amend the constitution at will as it had been able to do since the 1977 elections. Thus, the first and (thus far) only national referendum in Sri Lankan history was held in December 1982, shortly after the presidential elections. The issue voted on was the question of whether the parliament elected in 1977 should be allowed to sit until 1989 without general elections, which were required by law to be held no later than 1983.

More than 54% of the electorate supported the proposition, and the parliament was allowed to sit until 1989. But the referendum was the first national election in Sri Lankan history to be marked by allegations of widespread vote fraud.[12] Many voters opposed to the proposal had been intimidated into not coming to the polls. In addition, many poll watchers had been forcibly removed from the polling stations and irregularities had occurred after they were forced out of the stations.[13]

On December 19, 1988, a new presidential election was held. President Jayawardene had announced in September that he would not run for reelection. His prime minister, Ranasinghe Premadasa, was nominated by the UNP and faced former SLFP prime minister Sirimavo Bandaranaike and the United Socialist Alliance candidate Ossie Abeygunasekera. Premadasa won a narrow victory polling 50.4% of the vote to Bandaranaike's 45.0% of the vote (see Table 26.1). The leftist Abeygunasekera was not a factor in the election. The election was marked by widespread bloodshed as two rebel groups, the Janatha Vimukti Peramuna (JVP) and the Liberation Tigers of Tamil Eelam (LTTE), tried to intimidate voters and candidates by carrying out assassination campaigns.

After his election, President Premadasa immediately arranged for parliamentary elections to be held in February 1989. This election was also marred by widespread violence and became the bloodiest election in Sri

TABLE 26.1   1988 Presidential Election Results

Candidate	Party	Total Votes	Percent Polled
Ranasinghe Premadasa	UNP	2,569,190	50.4
Sirimavo Bandaranaike	SLFP	2,289,860	45.0
Oswin Abeygunasekera	USA	235,719	4.6

Source: Based on data in Island, December 19, 1988.

Lankan history. However, it was held and 63.6% of the electorate turned out to vote. The UNP won 125 of the 225 seats contested (see Table 27.1).

An important element of both elections was that they were relatively honest compared to the 1982 referendum and local elections held from 1982 to 1988. There was widespread violence and intimidation by the rebel groups but government supporters were not as active in ensuring a UNP victory.

The Public Service and Administration

The national government oversees a large bureaucracy, which is in charge of carrying out the decisions of parliament and the executive. By contrast to the U.S. system, employment as a bureaucrat in most of South Asia carries with it a great deal of status, and government jobs are thus highly sought after. The Sri Lankan administrative system is modeled on the British system of administration.[14] But it has been severely criticized by some politicians who attribute their problems with it to the introduction of an alien (British) system of administration into the country. In particular, the bureaucracy is frequently accused of being partisan, lethargic, and insensitive to public needs.

The administrative system is overseen by cabinet ministries in which political appointees at the very top of the hierarchy make policy decisions. Beneath each of the approximately twenty-five ministries are a series of government departments that carry out functional activities such as irrigation projects, road construction and repair, and statistics gathering. These departments, which are highly centralized, have main offices in Colombo, where most decisions regarding the tasks of field officers are made.

The public service is hierarchical in nature, with an elite corps at the top of the administrative structure. This upper elite is a highly professional and well-trained cadre that carries with it a great deal of social status. Beneath it are subordinate and minor employees who carry out most of the decisions made from above.

At the top of the administrative structure is the Sri Lanka Administrative Service (SLAS), which is similar to the Indian Administrative Service (described in Chapter 8). The SLAS is staffed according to the results of competitive merit examinations and has three levels of hierarchy. Promotion in the SLAS is handled by the secretaries of the ministry in charge of the SLAS position. The secretaries are the highest-ranking public officials in the ministry. Under the constitutions of 1972 and 1978 they have been political appointees rather than being drawn from the civil service, as was done from 1947 until 1972.[15]

In addition, a significant number of public corporations oversee government businesses and industries. The government of Sri Lanka operates corporations in such industries as tea, rubber, and coconut estates (e.g., the Janatha Estates Development Board and the Sri Lanka State Plantations Corporation), leather (Ceylon Leather Products Corporation), and chemicals (Paranthan Chemicals Corporation). Many of these corporations are profitable, and the Jayawardene government sold to the private sector a number of corporations that consistently failed to generate profits.

Despite criticisms about the performance of the public service, however, few efforts were made to change the system of administration after Sri Lanka received independence. The only major change has occurred in the administrative apparatus, which has been politicized. That is, all of the governing parties have been guilty of trying to bring the civil service under their political control; as a result, promotions and hirings are often handled on the basis of political criteria.

Local Government

As Sri Lanka is a unitary state, its local government has been very weak. Government decisions are made in Colombo and are sent to the rural areas of the country. In addition, the national government has control over most of the revenues generated by the government.

The country is divided into nine provinces, which were significant units of local governmental administration during the colonial era. Today, the system of local government is in a state of change. The district, which had been the main unit of local administration, has been partially replaced by provincial governments created in 1988. There are eight provincial governments (at the moment the Eastern and Northern Province are combined). Each province has a popularly elected council with a chief minister and ministers approved by the council.

The first elections to provincial councils were held in 1988. However, the SLFP opposed the creation of the councils on the grounds that they were unnecessary and refused to participate in the elections. The strong SLFP opposition to the councils has raised serious issues about their future if the SLFP should come to power.

In addition, the councils did not receive adequate funding authority when they were first created under the government of President Jayawardene. By the time that President Premadasa was able to appoint his Minister of Local Government, U. B. Wijekoon, the task of transferring authority and power from the central government departments to the provincial governments had become very difficult.

The creation of the provincial councils is expected to lead to the removal of the former system of local administration, the *kachcheri* system. Each province is divided into two or three administrative districts, which add up to twenty-four throughout the island. Each of the districts has a set of government offices called a kachcheri, which occupies the center of government administration in each district. Most government departments have district offices in the kachcheri, and the highest official in each kachcheri is the government agent (GA).[16] The GA is supposed to be the chief coordinator of government activities in the district in addition to being in charge of development projects.

Government agents were very important figures in the colonial administration of Great Britain. They were the most powerful officials in the provinces of their administration (during the colonial administration, the government agents oversaw the provinces rather than the districts). Although they were primarily revenue agents, they were soon given extensive powers to control almost all government activities in their regions. After independence, however, the influence of the government agents declined as they had to compete with the members of parliament and the main offices of the departments in Colombo for influence over the running of government activities in the district.[17] Because of the high degree of centralization in most government departments, the officials in the departments were more likely to listen and respond to those who made the decisions about their promotions and transfers—namely, the department heads in the main offices in Colombo rather than the government agents.

The members of parliament also eroded some of the power of the GAs. The development of a patronage system in which the members of parliament are the main distributors of benefits has focused citizen interest on the MPs and away from the government agents. The government agents no longer have the power and influence to resolve complaints. Rather, the MPs have sought this power in order to enhance their position with their electorates. In addition, the MPs have much more influence with the bureaucracy and are better able than the GAs to resolve citizen problems with government departments and agencies.[18] The future of the kachcheri system and the government agent is in doubt as the government tries to create the provincial councils. However, the failure to create the council system has resulted in doubts about whether the kachcheri system will prevail.

In addition to the kachcheri and the provincial councils, there are several elected local government councils in each district. Prior to 1981, local government revolved around a system of councils at the village, town, urban, and municipal levels. These governments carried out a relatively small number of functions. With limited tax revenues to work with, they were reduced to overseeing public works in the city or village under their jurisdiction.

In 1981 the government abolished the village and town councils and replaced them with district development councils (DDCs),[19] with the intention of replacing the village and town council system with one council for every administrative district. These councils were not very successful and were eventually replaced by the provincial councils.

The creation of the DDCs in 1981 did not affect the urban and municipal councils that had existed prior to that time. The twelve municipal councils function in most of the largest cities on the island, and the thirty-eight urban councils preside over the medium-sized cities. Both types of councils are elected by proportional representation and both select the mayor and deputy mayor of the city from among the council members.

The creation of the DDCs in 1981 and the provincial councils in 1988 were part of a broader attempt to decentralize the administrative process in Sri Lanka. Since Sri Lanka is a unitary state, most of its important decisions are made in the capital city of Colombo. In recent years, the idea of decentralization has become quite popular among Sri Lankan and international experts of development and governmental administration.[20] What decentralization involves is a transfer of decision-making authority from the central government machinery to local units of government or to citizen groups. It is generally believed that the people who will be affected by administrative and development decisions should have more power to affect what happens to them. In other words, decentralization is conceptualized as a means of providing these people with the power to affect the decisions that deal directly with their lives.

Serious attempts to decentralize development administration were begun in the 1970s, when a scheme later called the decentralized budget (DCB) was created.[21] This was a plan to provide each of the members of parliament with block grants for development projects in their electoral districts. A council called a district ministry (it was called the political authority under the SLFP government from 1970 to 1977) was created in each district and headed by the district minister (political authority). The district ministry reviewed the projects of the MPs and gave them final approval. The MPs were in charge of project selection, administering the project once it was accepted by the technical staff undertaking the work and ensuring that the project was completed properly. In many cases, the projects involved small-scale development works that were not feasible for the centralized government departments. Many projects were turned over to villages to complete and on occasion were done with volunteer labor. Since the creation of the DCB, other attempts were made to decentralize development work. These included the DDCs, as well as a scheme to carry out development work at the district level by means of an integrated district-level plan. These projects offer Sri Lankan villagers hope for more realistic development projects and greater influence over the government actions that directly affect their lives.

*   *   *

In summary, the Sri Lankan government has been structured in such a way as to provide the people with opportunities to become involved in government decisions. The highly partisan nature of politics (discussed in Chapter 27) has led to a very strong patronage system in which the members of parliament try to please the people by meeting their demands. Both the high level of citizen input into the government and the open structure of the government have contributed to the political stability experienced by Sri Lanka.

Notes

1. J. R. Jayawardene, "Parliamentary Democracy—the Role of the Opposition in a Developing Nation," *Parliamentarian,* vol. 52, no. 3 (July 1971), pp. 191–194.

2. A. Jeyaratnam Wilson, *The Gaullist System in Asia: The Constitution of Sri Lanka (1978)* (London: Macmillan, 1980), p. 62.

3. James Jupp, *Sri Lanka: Third World Democracy* (London: Frank Cass, 1978), pp. 28, 218.

4. See ibid., pp. 258–271, for a discussion of the constitution.

5. See K. M. De Silva, "The Constitution and Constitutional Reform Since 1948," in K. M. De Silva, ed., *Sri Lanka: A Survey* (Honolulu: University of Hawaii Press, 1977), pp. 312–329.

6. See Wilson, *The Gaullist System,* for a thorough discussion of the constitution.

7. Ibid., p. 62.

8. Robert C. Oberst, "Proportional Representation and Electoral System Change in Sri Lanka," in James Manor, ed., *Sri Lanka in Change and Crisis* (London: Croom Helm, 1984), pp. 118–134.

9. Wilson, *The Gaullist System,* p. 96.

10. See Robert C. Oberst, *Legislators and Representation in Sri Lanka: The Decentralization of Development Planning* (Boulder, Colo.: Westview Press, 1985), pp. 77–81.

11. For a discussion of the 1982 elections see W. A. Wiswa Warnapala and L. Dias Hewagama, *Recent Politics in Sri Lanka: The Presidential Election and the Referendum of 1982* (New Delhi: Navrang, 1983); and Manor, *Sri Lanka,* chapters 2–5.

12. Warnapala and Hewagama, *Recent Politics,* chapter 8; and Priya Samarakone, "The Conduct of the Referendum," in Manor, *Sri Lanka,* pp. 84–117.

13. Government of Sri Lanka, *Sessional Paper no. II, Report on the First Referendum in Sri Lanka* (Colombo: Department of Government Printing, 1987).

14. For the best description of the development of the administrative system, see W. A. Wiswa Warnapala, *Civil Service Administration in Ceylon: A Study in Bureaucratic Adaptation* (Colombo: Department of Cultural Affairs, 1974).

15. Wilson, *The Gaullist System,* pp. 138–139.

16. For a description of government agents, see G. R. Tressie Leitan, *Local Government and Decentralized Administration in Sri Lanka* (Colombo: Lake House, 1979), chapter 6.

17. Neil Fernando, *Regional Administration in Sri Lanka* (Colombo: Academy of Administrative Studies, 1973), pp. 12–14; and Robert C. Oberst, "Administrative Conflict and Decentralization: The Case of Sri Lanka," *Public Administration and Development,* vol. 5, no. 4.

18. Oberst, *Legislators and Representation,* chapter 4.

19. Bruce Matthews, "District Development Councils in Sri Lanka," *Asian Survey,* vol. 22 (November 1982), pp. 1117–1134.

20. See Dennis Rondinelli, John R. Nellis, and G. Shabbir Cheema, *Decentralization in Developing Countries: A Review of Recent Experience* (Washington, D.C.: World Bank, 1983).

21. See Oberst, *Legislators and Representation,* chapter 7.

27
THE POLITICAL
PARTY SYSTEM

The Sri Lankan political party system is quite distinctive. It has been very volatile, given the emergence and demise of many new small parties with each election.[1] Yet the system has been dominated by several important and long-lasting parties. The election of 1977 appears to have marked a major change in the party alignment. The dominant parties—the United National party (UNP) and the Sri Lanka Freedom party (SLFP)—survived the election, but two important Marxist parties appear to have suffered major setbacks that threaten their future influence in the political system.

It can be argued that the Sri Lankan party system has actually involved two party systems rather than one—one system for the Sri Lanka Tamils and another for the other communities on the island. Despite many appeals by the major parties to gain Tamil support, the Sri Lankan Tamils have chosen to support their own political parties, which do not receive a significant amount of electoral support from the other ethnic communities. The rest of Sri Lankan politics has been dominated by the two major parties, which have frequently required the support of smaller parties in order to govern effectively.

The Sinhalese Party System

The United National Party

The United National party is the party of the right in Sri Lankan politics. It has generated such personalities as Don Stephen Senanayake, Dudley Senanayake, and J. R. Jayawardene. Its emergence as an umbrella party from the colonial era was similar to the formation of the Congress party of India (see Chapter 6) insofar as it represented a union of many different ideologies and personalities that rose out of the independence movement. The domination of the party by the independence movement politicians ended with the retirement of J. R. Jayawardene in 1988. A new generation

TABLE 27.1   Results of Sri Lanka Parliamentary Elections

	Elections							
	1947		1952		1956		March 1960	
	Seats Won	Percent Polled	Seats Won	Percent Polled	Seats Won	Percent Polled	Seats Won	Percent Polled
UNP	42	39.8	54	44.1	8	27.9	50	29.4
SLFP	–	–	9	15.5	51	40.0[a]	46	20.9
LSSP	15	16.8[b]	9	13.1	14	10.5	10	10.5
CP	3	3.7[c]	4	5.8	3	4.6	3	4.8
MEP	–	–	–	–	–	–	10	10.6
TC	7	4.4	4	2.8	1	.3	1	1.2
FP	–	–	2	1.9	10	5.4	15	5.7
CIC	6	3.8	–	–	–	–	–	–
Others	22	31.4	13	16.9	8	11.4	16	16.7

[a]Results for the Mahajana Eksath Peramuna coalition of S.W.R.D. Bandaranaike and his SLFP.
[b]Includes two LSSP factions contesting the election separately.
[c]Includes the united front of the CP and the VLSSP.

	July 1960		1965		1970		1977		1989	
	Seats Won	Percent Polled	Seats Won	Percent Polled	Seats Won	Percent Polled	Seats Won	Percent Polled	Seats Won	Percent Polled
UNP	30	37.6	66	38.9	17	37.9	140	50.9	125	50.7
SLFP	75	33.6	41	30.2	90	36.6	8	29.0	67	31.8
LSSP/USA[d]	12	7.4	10	7.4	19	8.8	0	3.6	3	2.9
CP[d]	4	3.0	4	2.7	6	3.4	0	1.9	–	–
MEP	3	3.4	1	2.7	0	.9	0	.4	–	–
FP(TULF)	16	7.2	14	5.4	13	5.0	18	6.8	10	3.4
TC	1	1.5	3	2.4	3	2.3	–	–	–	–
EROS	–	–	–	–	–	–	–	–	13	2.7
SLMC	–	–	–	–	–	–	–	–	4	3.6
Others	10	6.4	7	7.0	2	5.1	2	6.6	0	1.8

[d]The LSSP, CP, and SLMP united to form the USA in 1989.

of politicians led by President Premadasa has sought to lead the party into the 1990s.

The UNP has been the strongest vote-getter in Sri Lankan elections (see Table 27.1). It dominated the first two elections after independence in 1947 and 1952, before losing the 1956 elections to the SLFP, and returned to power for a brief period in 1960 after the March elections of that year. Since the March 1960 election results did not give the UNP a working parliamentary majority, it was unable to obtain a vote of confidence from parliament for its government. In the elections of July 1960, the UNP once more lost to the SLFP. It returned to power in 1965 and governed until 1970, when it lost the election. In 1977, the UNP was returned to power with a commanding five-sixths majority in parliament. The scheduled 1983 elections were canceled following a referendum held in 1982 over the question of whether the present parliament elected in 1977 should be continued until 1989. The 1989 parliamentary elections gave the UNP control over parliament but with a smaller majority (125 out of 225 seats).

As noted in Chapter 25, the UNP has been dominated by four major personalities. The current party is headed by Ranasinghe Premadasa who is trying to restructure the party after the dominating influence of J. R. Jayawardene. He has brought a new and different generation of leadership into the party by promoting younger party members to positions in the party leadership. Premadasa has developed a populist image because of his housing and poverty alleviation programs. This contrasts sharply with the party under Jayawardene who moved it to the right. In many ways Premadasa's policies are similar to those of the Senanayake family which led the party to a moderate center-of-the-road economic policy that advocated the creation of a minimal welfare state and strict government involvement in the economy. Premadasa has not, however, reversed most of the policies of Jayawardene who opened the economy to free enterprise by limiting government controls, privatizing government corporations, and cutting social welfare subsidies along with other social welfare benefits.[2]

The Sri Lanka Freedom Party

The Sri Lanka Freedom party is the chief opposition to the United National party. After its formation by S.W.R.D. Bandaranaike in 1951, it received relatively limited support in 1952, when it elected only 9 members to parliament. In 1956, however, Bandaranaike put together a strong coalition of leftist and anti-UNP parties and personalities. Many of these united because of their personal opposition to the UNP. The party was swept overwhelmingly into power in the 1956 elections. It tapped a strong sense of discontent among the rural Sinhalese, who felt that they had been discriminated against by the British and the first two governments of independent Sri Lanka. It therefore committed itself to restoring the Sinhalese culture, language, and religion (Buddhism) to a position of dominance in the society. As a result, the government's first act was to make Sinhala the language of government, thus replacing English.

The coalition was held together until Bandaranaike was assassinated in 1959. After his death the coalition fell apart, and the SLFP was unable to provide a cohesive force in the March 1960 elections. Many small parties emerged out of Bandaranaike's 1956 coalition and split the party's support. By the July 1960 elections, the SLFP was able to pull its supporters together under the leadership of Bandaranaike's widow, Sirimavo, who, as noted, became the first woman ever elected as head of a democratic government. She ruled until 1965 and again from 1970 until 1977.

Under the guidance of Sirimavo Bandaranaike, the SLFP has remained the party of the moderate left, although its membership includes both leftists and rightists. Many of the members of its right wing would probably feel comfortable in the UNP, whereas many of its left-wing members are closely allied to the parties of the far left in Sri Lankan politics. During the period of coalition between the Communist party and the Trotskyite Lanka Sama Samaja party in the 1970s, Sirimavo Bandaranaike performed a balancing act between the SLFP's right- and left-wing members and the coalition's leftist parties. The SLFP has advocated greater government involvement in the economy, increased social welfare, and a foreign policy of nonalignment.

The SLFP's success in elections has always been accompanied by electoral agreements with the major parties of the left. This was the case in 1956, 1960, and 1970. The main elements of the 1970 United Front coalition were the Lanka Sama Samaja party (LSSP) and the Communist party (CP). Since its stunning loss in 1977 the SLFP has undergone a split, with a number of factions emerging at different times. At present, one such faction is the Sri Lanka Mahajana party, established by several members of the left wing of the SLFP. Its future is questionable.

The Lanka Sama Samaja Party

At one time, the Lanka Sama Samaja party was billed as the world's only successful Trotskyite party. Its ideology is based on that of Leon Trotsky, the loser to Josef Stalin in the power struggle that followed Lenin's death in 1924 in the Soviet Union. Its support comes from many Marxists who object to the Communist party's close association with the Soviet Union and thus prefer the independent Marxism of the LSSP. Moreover, it represents an independent doctrine of Marxism adapted to the specific culture and needs of Sri Lanka rather than the Soviet-oriented Marxism of the Sri Lanka Communist party.[3]

After the 1947 elections, the LSSP was the main opposition to the governing UNP. But the emergence of the SLFP provided many voters on the left wing of Sri Lankan politics with a moderate alternative to the Marxist LSSP and Communist party. The result was a sharp decline in LSSP support; the LSSP has elected a member to parliament in every parliamentary general election except that in 1977.[4]

The LSSP was an important element of the 1970 United Front coalition established by Sirimavo Bandaranaike. Three cabinet positions were given to LSSP MPs in the government formed after the 1970 elections. These included the important ministry of finance. All three cabinet posts were held until the LSSP left the coalition in 1975 over a series of policy disputes with the other members of the coalition. Today its support is weak and it has had to unite with three other leftist parties into the United Socialist

Alliance (USA) in order to remain competitive in elections. The USA consists of the Communist party, the Sri Lanka Mahajana party founded by a faction of the SLFP, and the Nava Sama Samaja party founded by a faction of the LSSP led by charismatic Vasudeva Nanayakara.

The Communist Party

The Communist party of Sri Lanka has maintained close ideological ties with the Soviet Union. The impact of the changes in the Soviet Union on the party are still not known. It has received strong support in the southern regions of the country, where it has been associated with the Durawa caste. Like the LSSP, the Communist party won several seats in parliament in every election until that of 1977, when it failed to win any seats. In 1981, however, it won a by-election and gained one seat in parliament. Like the LSSP, it was given an important cabinet post in the 1970 coalition government, which it held until it left the coalition shortly before the 1977 elections. The platform of the party has closely followed Soviet policies and has been highly critical of the current UNP government's domestic and foreign policies.

Other Leftist Parties

The left wing of Sri Lankan politics has usually been splintered with ideological rifts and factions. As a consequence, many small left-wing parties have emerged at different times during the post-colonial period. Of current significance are the following.

1. The Janata Vimukthi Peramuna (JVP) and its founder and leader until his death in November 1989, Rohana Wijeweera, were responsible for a youth-led insurrection against the government of Sirimavo Bandaranaike in 1971. Formed in the late 1960s, the JVP (known in English as the People's Liberation Front) came perilously close to overthrowing the government with a series of well-planned attacks against police stations and government positions.[5] Official estimates placed the death toll at around 1,200 people, while unofficial reports placed it much higher. In addition, more than 16,000 suspected insurgents were taken into custody after the aborted revolt.[6] As a result, many of the leaders and followers of the JVP were sentenced to jail. Wijeweera was sentenced to twenty years in prison; however, the UNP released him shortly after the 1977 elections.

The UNP legalized the JVP and the party emerged as a moderate leftist party, but without the Maoist beliefs it had proclaimed at the time of the insurrection. After its legalization, it contested local council elections and Wijeweera ran for president. In the 1982 presidential elections Wijeweera was able to poll 4.2% of the total vote, or about 270,000 votes. Following severe anti-Tamil riots in 1983, the party was accused of fomenting the violence; then it was banned. Until 1987, the JVP was active creating an underground organization. After the July 1987 Indo-Lanka Accords that made concessions to the Tamil insurgents in the north of the island, the JVP began a campaign of assassinations of government supporters. At the height of the violence (June to August 1989), over 800 people per month were being killed. Not all of the deaths were at the hands of the JVP however. Death squads of government supporters and security forces are believed responsible for many of the deaths.

In November 1989, the government captured Wijeweera and claimed that he was shot dead by his own supporters as he led government security forces to JVP hideouts. In any case, all of the JVP politburo and most of its district leaders were either captured or killed during November 1989. This did not destroy the movement however. Violence continued in 1990 although it was not as widespread as before.

2. The Mahajana Eksath Peramuna (MEP) was founded by one of Sri Lanka's early and most important leftists, Philip Gunawardena. Like so many of the important Sri Lankan political actors, he was a highly charismatic individual. He originally formed a splinter party, called the Viplavakari Lanka Sama Samaja party (VLSSP), from elements of the LSSP in 1950. The VLSSP contested the 1952 elections and entered into an electoral agreement with the Communist party. In 1956, it joined S.W.R.D. Bandaranaike's coalition, which was called the Mahajana Eksath Peramuna. After Bandaranaike's death, Gunawardena adopted the name of the 1956 coalition as the name of his party. The MEP has been known by this name ever since. After 1960, the party moved to the right and joined a coalition government with the UNP; later, after Gunawardena's death, it moved back to the left. The party was without parliamentary representation from 1970 until a by-election in 1983, when its leader Dinesh Gunawardena, Philip's son, was elected to parliament. Dinesh and two other party members were returned to parliament in the 1989 parliamentary elections.

The Tamil and Muslim Party System

In Sri Lanka (as in India), some regional minority groups have formed their own political parties. The Sri Lanka Tamils, for example, have consistently supported their own parties and tried to win the support of the Sri Lanka Muslims. As a result, there is a separate party system operating in areas where the Sri Lanka Tamils are in the majority. The Tamil party system at the moment is in a state of transition because of its transformation by the ethnic conflict that developed into a civil war in the 1980s.

Immediately following independence, there was only one important Tamil party in Sri Lanka—the Tamil Congress (TC) led by G. G. Ponnambalam. The TC cooperated with the UNP in the first government after independence.

It was during this government that the Indian Tamils were denied citizenship and the right to vote. Several members of the Tamil Congress deserted their party in opposition to its support of this action and formed a new party called the Federal party. Under the leadership of S.J.V. Chelvanayagam, this party demanded the establishment of a federal system in Sri Lanka, with home rule for the Tamils in the eastern and northern parts of the island.

The Federal party soon replaced the Tamil Congress as the dominant party among the Sri Lanka Tamils. Its members included Marxists and capitalists united under the banner of federalism for the Tamil areas. Shortly after the 1970 elections, the Tamil parties, comprising both the Indian and the Sri Lanka Tamils, came together in a coalition to form the Tamil United Liberation Front. A significant element of the TC opposed the union and reappeared as the Tamil Congress after the 1977 elections.

The TULF increased its demands for regional self-rule in 1976 and began demanding an independent state (*Eelam*) for the Tamil people. In the 1977 general elections, and in the local council and presidential elections in the early 1980s, the TULF received the overwhelming backing of the Sri Lankan Tamils in the north and along the east coast.

The call for *Eelam,* accompanied by the increasing violence by Tamil youths in the north and east of the island, led the government to pass the sixth amendment to the constitution in 1983. This amendment specifically banned the advocacy of separatism. All of the sixteen TULF MPs were expelled from parliament for failing to recite a loyalty oath required by the amendment. The government then refused to hold by-elections in the areas represented by these opposition members because of the youth-led violence, and the Sri Lanka Tamils remained without representation in parliament until 1989.

The TULF originally included the largest Indian Tamil political organization, the Ceylon Worker's Congress (CWC). After the 1977 elections, however, the leader of the CWC was offered a cabinet post in the UNP government. As a result, the CWC has disassociated itself from the TULF. In any case, the calls for *Eelam* are largely ignored by the Indian Tamils, who reside outside the territory that has been claimed for the state of *Eelam.*

As the tensions between the the Sinhalese and the Sri Lanka Tamils increased, Sri Lanka Tamil youths resorted to violence and joined several political groups commonly called "tigers." These organizations challenged the leadership position of the TULF in the Sri Lanka Tamil community, and became the dominant force in Sri Lankan Tamil politics in the late 1980s.

Although there were a large number of "tiger" groups, only a few were an important political force. Most of these groups had sophisticated training camps in southern India and were financed by the proceeds from bank robberies in Sri Lanka and drug sales in Europe, as well as by donations from wealthy Tamils living in the United States and Great Britain.

The political strength of the tigers became apparent after the July 1987 Indo-Lanka Accords that called for a ceasefire between the tigers and the government with the Indian army acting as a peacekeeping force. It also established a system of provincial councils. All but one of the major tiger groups went along with the treaty and turned over their arms and became legal political organizations. The one exception was the most powerful group, militarily, the Liberation Tigers of Tamil Eelam (LTTE). They continued to fight against the Indian forces.

In provincial council elections in November 1988 and the parliamentary elections of February 1989, the now-legal tiger groups contested and became the dominant political force in the Tamil areas. In the Northern and Eastern province council elections in November 1988, most of the tiger parties boycotted the election and the Eelam People's Revolutionary Liberation Front (EPRLF) won a majority of seats in the council. Varatharajaperumal became the chief minister of the Eastern and Northern Province council and began to promote Tamil interests from his party's position of power in the provincial government.

In the 1989 parliamentary elections, the Eelam Revolutionary Organizaton of Students (EROS) ran as an independent slate of candidates while the Tamil Eelam Liberation Organization (TELO) and the EPRLF ran with the TULF as the Tamil United Liberation Front. Under the Sri Lankan electoral system, voters cast votes for both the party and then for candidates nominated by that party. EROS easily captured a majority of the votes in the Jaffna peninsula. However the TULF slate dominated the Tamil areas in Trincomalee, Batticaloa, Ampara, Vavuniya, Mullaitivu, and Mannar districts. In the preference voting for TULF candidates, the EPRLF won seven seats and TELO won two. The TULF candidates were completely rejected by the voters, although the TULF leader A. Amirthalingam was nominated to occupy the TULF bonus seat the party won.

The LTTE boycotted the elections and continued its guerrilla campaign against the government and Indian forces. However, the EROS slate of candidates ran with LTTE support and their strong showing reflects the popularity of the LTTE among the Tamils. The party is led by Velupillai Prabhakaran, a member of a middle-level caste, the Kariayar or fisherman caste, and thus differs sharply from the Vellala (farmer caste)-dominated TULF. Ideologically, the LTTE does not espouse a concise and coherent economic ideology. Its main goal is the protection of the interests of the Tamil people from the Sinhalese-dominated government of Sri Lanka.

In 1988 another force emerged in Sri Lankan politics, the Sri Lanka Muslim Congress (SLMC). For many years, Sri Lanka Muslims tended to support the UNP in elections although the Tamil parties and the SLFP had tried to win their support. The SLMC was the first successful attempt to form a Muslim political party in Sri Lanka. The Muslim community has remained one of the poorest in Sri Lanka with very low levels of education. It is not surprising that the SLMC was formed to represent the community. It was created by Muslims who felt a need to protect Muslim interests. They have feared that the Sinhalese-dominated government and the Tamils would not act in the best interests of the Muslims. In the 1989 parliamentary elections, the SLMC won two seats.

A Party System in Change

The many changes in the party system in Sri Lanka since 1977 have created a highly volatile situation that could pose a serious threat to the political system. Among the Tamil parties, a new generation of leadership appears to have emerged. The TULF, representing the older generation of leadership, appears to have been dealt a fatal blow with the LTTE assassination of its leader A. Amirthalingam in July 1989. The younger generation of leaders represented by the tigers appears to have taken a leading role in Tamil politics. Many of the older generation of Tamils appear to have acknowledged that the "boys," as the guerrilla fighters have been called, have earned the right to lead the Tamils because of their sacrifices for the Tamil people.

The Sinhalese party system has also been in a state of change. Perhaps the most important change has been the apparent demise of the Sri Lankan "old left." The "old left" consists of the USA and its allies. Since the 1977 parliamentary elections, the parties of the "old left" have not been able to compete competitively with the UNP and the SLFP. The growth of the JVP and the widespread support for the party among the young appear to reflect the inability of the LSSP and CP to win the support of youths as they did in the 1950s and 1960s.

Although the future of the parties of the "old left" in Sri Lanka is still in doubt, the relatively significant percentage of the population that has followed left-wing politics in Sri Lanka may not be willing to sit by peacefully and watch as their parties lose the influence they once wielded in Sri Lankan politics.

Change has not been confined to the parties of the left. The SLFP and the UNP have both experienced pressure for change. When SLFP leader Sirimavo Bandaranaike was stripped of her right to participate in politics and to lead the SLFP, a power vacuum in the party led to a conflict between the party's left and right wings. Although the dissension in the party has not been as open as it was in the early and mid-1980s, the party is still split ideologically and personally between the left and right factions and between the supporters of Sirimavo's children and their opponents.

The UNP has been taken over by the populist politics of Ranasinghe Premadasa who has moved the party to the center of the political spectrum and away from the right it occupied during the Jayawardene years. His more moderate policies, especially his support for the welfare state, have alienated many of the Jayawardene supporters in the party and created a climate in which factions of the party may break away and form their own parties or join with the opposition.

The next few years will be very important to the future of democracy in Sri Lanka as the party system struggles with the forces that have been changing it. The nature of the changes are still not known although their consequences will have a major impact on the structure that Sri Lankan politics takes in the future.

Notes

1. For a description of the party system see Calvin A. Woodward, *The Growth of a Party System in Ceylon* (Providence, R.I.: Brown University Press, 1969); and Robert N. Kearney, "The Political Party System in Sri Lanka," *Political Science Quarterly,* vol. 98 (Spring 1983), pp. 17–33.

2. Robert C. Oberst, "The Politics of Change: Ideology and Structure in Sri Lanka," *Asian Thought and Society,* vol. 9 (March 1984), pp. 57–64.

3. For a thorough description of the early history of the party, see George Jan Lerski, *The Origins of Trotskyism in Ceylon* (Stanford, Calif.: Hoover Institution, 1968).

4. The LSSP leader, Colvin R. De Silva, was awarded the bonus seat won by the USA.

5. See Robert N. Kearney and Janice Jiggins, "The Ceylon Insurrection of 1971," *The Journal of Commonwealth and Comparative Politics,* vol. 13 (March 1975), pp. 40–65; and A. C. Alles, *Insurgency—1971* (Colombo: Colombo Apothecaries, 1976).

6. Gananath Obeyesekere, "Some Comments on the Social Backgrounds of the April 1971 Insurgency in Sri Lanka (Ceylon)," *Journal of Asian Studies,* vol. 33, pp. 367–384.

28
GROUPS AND INTEREST ARTICULATION

Constituent demands in a political system are a way of linking the governed with the governors. In every successful democracy, there is a considerable amount of communication between the constituents who bring their needs to their representatives and the representatives who, because of their accountability in elections, must respond to the demands.

Demands may be presented to the government by two broad categories of constituents—individuals and interest groups. As noted later in this chapter, Sri Lankan members of parliament receive a large number of individual requests from their constituents. In addition, government officials are approached by various groups in the society.

Interest Groups

National Groups

It has been argued that the emergence of broad-based national interest groups is a part of the development process that Third World democracies are undergoing.[1] Interest groups provide governmental representation for the various interests in the society. In Sri Lanka, interest groups are both unorganized and weak. They do not exert a great deal of pressure on lawmakers and bureaucrats. Their weakness can be attributed to several factors.

First, many interest groups find that it is not worthwhile to approach the elected members of parliament with their demands. Thus, they try to influence the administrative rather than the policy-making process. Public policy in Sri Lanka is the result of a party's election platform and the party's ideology. Many groups know in advance that the government's ideology is not favorable to their demands and direct their demands to the administrators who may be more responsive and can circumvent the rules to assist their demands. But this practice is limited by a general sense of

339

hostility among the governing Sri Lankan political parties toward what they call "sabotage by public officials" hostile to the governing party's policies.[2] Attempts are frequently made to transfer or suspend bureaucrats who may be sympathetic to the opposition party. There is a strong belief held by many politicians that bureaucrats work for either one of the major parties. As a result, the elected politicians try to limit the amount of policy interpretation exercised by the bureaucrats. This limits the amount of influence the interest groups can exert over government decisions by approaching the bureaucracy.

A second factor is that the major parties establish interest groups that they are then able to control. In fact, most interest groups are closely connected with either the government or an opposition party and, thus, do not need access to the politicians. Interest groups in Sri Lanka are frequently extensions of political parties. This is especially the case among trade unions, in which the electoral triumph of the union's party is believed to lead to the union's political objectives[3]—thus, the all-or-nothing view of the political process by the unions. If the wrong party is in power, the unions do not expect to receive government cooperation and benefits. There is little bargaining and compromise between the government and the interest groups. The interest group either receives what it wants from its party when the party is in power or it is denied its objective.

A third factor is that policy-making power is concentrated in a few important ministries and thus the number of people who may influence that policy is limited.[4] The domination of Sri Lanka by a few charismatic personalities has resulted in a small "inner circle" consisting of people who are given significant amounts of policy-making power.

A fourth factor is the nature of power and influence in Sri Lanka. Much pressure is exerted through family networks and friends.[5] As noted earlier, Sri Lankans tend to view power in personal terms; thus, when an individual, no matter how unimportant, goes to a person with power, he or she expects to be granted a personal meeting with that official. No mere representative of that official would be acceptable. Access to power is indeed a personal affair.[6] Thus, a lobbyist in Sri Lanka is effective only if he or she can establish a set of personal contacts. At the same time, the highly partisan nature of politics in Sri Lanka makes it very difficult for an individual to maintain close personal contacts with powerful members of both parties.

A fifth factor is that interest groups tend to be ad hoc.[7] Groups may initially become active over an emotional issue, but once their initial objectives are achieved or the issues lose their emotional appeal, the groups become inactive and disappear. This is especially the case with village-level interest groups. For instance, an important person in the village with a demand may gather some of his clients and go to the government official as a delegation representing the village. Many of the clients go with him because of the opportunity to present their own demands if the opportunity avails itself. Thus, the important person's demand appears to reflect a broader segment of the village population than it actually does.

Nevertheless, the people in positions of power do not generally feel pressured by these groups since they are usually dealing with *friends* who are leading the groups.[8] This practice has been reinforced by the creation of ministries that cater to a specific clientele such as the Ministry of Cultural Affairs, which was set up to deal with the demands of the All-Ceylon Buddhist Congress, or the Ministry of Regional Development, which was established to deal with the Tamil ethnic group in the eastern and northern parts of the island.

In short, the relationship between national interest groups and people in positions of power is not one of compromise and bargaining but rather one of cooperation and accommodation. The effectiveness of these groups in affecting policy, although limited by poor organization, is enhanced by close ties to the political parties as well as by the personal relationships created by the leaders of the groups with people in positions of power.

Local Groups

Local interest groups function in a slightly different way and are much more influential than the national organizations. South Asian life revolves around the village. More than 78% of the Sri Lankan population live in rural areas. The average villager is very active in village-level organizations, and a large number of village-level organizations have developed. These include development-oriented organizations, such as rural development societies, religious societies, parent-teacher associations, cooperatives, and occupational groups, which are quite active and vigorously lobby for policies and government actions that will benefit their group.

These organizations are dominated by a small elite of the village-level society and often revolve around one or two important people in the village. Villagers in Sri Lanka often look to people with high economic standing, a good background, the right caste, educational attainment, and a certain amount of religious piety to lead them. Many of the organizations in the village often have the same people leading them,[9] thus limiting the influence and input of the villagers themselves.

In addition, these groups tend to be highly politicized, with their leadership allied to one of the major political parties. After elections, the leaders are often replaced by people acceptable to the newly elected national leaders or MPs. There have been cases in some rural development societies in which the old leaders have refused to yield power in the organization after a national election and the government has recognized a new organization led by the supporters of the government. On the whole, however, the village-level groups tend to deal with village-level concerns and not national concerns. They seek new roads, village electrification, bridges, development projects, and so on. The amount of influence they exert depends, once again, on how closely they are aligned with those who wield power.

Individual Demands

Most demands made on the Sri Lankan political system are made by individuals. Many Sri Lankans expect their government representatives to respond to their needs. Most of these needs are of a personal nature, and the benefits they receive are called particularized benefits. Sri Lankan members of parliament set aside time to meet personally with their constituents. As a result, they are inundated by constituents with highly personalized requests for such things as jobs for their children or themselves. The average member of parliament may meet with more than 700 people a week, and the ministers, who have a large number of patronage jobs available to them, may see several thousand constituents each week.[10] The constituents will begin lining up outside the meeting place before sunrise and wait for hours for their opportunity to speak to the member of parliament. The MP will usually deal with each request quickly and move on to the next petitioner. Ministers are assisted by several staff people, who type letters of recommendation, call government servants who have refused to act on a government form, and take down information to follow up on requests.

The most frequent request received by MPs is for help with employment.[11] The petitioner, his or her son or daughter, or another relative may request help in finding a job, obtaining an employment transfer to a better location, or getting an improved appointment. Beyond this, the member of parliament may be faced with requests to resolve family feuds or even to speak to a husband who has been sleeping with other women. Very rarely do the demands deal with national issues or questions of community development. (Even when they do deal with community development they often involve projects that will personally benefit the petitioner, such as a paved road past his house or a new irrigation canal to his fields.) Another important aspect of these demands is that both men and women come to make them, with women composing more than 40% of the petitioners.[12]

The members of parliament have a limited number of jobs and other benefits to provide to their constituents. They base their decisions on patronage. Almost all government jobs are given on the basis of who one knows rather than on merit. The patronage system has undergone considerable expansion since the 1960s. This expansion has resulted in increased con-stituent demands and expectations as well as dissatisfaction from the supporters of the opposition parties.

The net consequence of this pressure for personalized treatment is overburdened legislators who spend most of their time dealing with petitioners' requests. In fact, the legislators are often left with the feeling that their time should be spent with more important activities such as development work and national issues. Efforts to reduce the constituent pressure on legislators have not been successful. During the Jayawardene years the creation of a computerized "job bank" to dispense government jobs turned into a fiasco that rewarded those with access to the computer "bank." The creation of proportional representation was intended to be a means of controlling job seekers. However, the use of the preferential ballot requires that members of parliament be popular in their electoral districts. The main effect of the change was to enlarge the size of the electoral district to include a whole administrative district.

* * *

In summary, interest articulation and demands, like other aspects of Sri Lankan society, are a highly personalized process. The government representatives frequently respond to the personal needs of the people and for most of the people, this is what they expect of their representatives. Yet the most important part of this system of demands and government responses is its high level of institutionalization and effectiveness, especially where individual demands are concerned. Sri Lankans have access to their leaders, and they take advantage of this access.

Notes

1. Gabriel A. Almond and G. Bingham Powell, *Comparative Politics: System, Process and Policy* (Boston: Little, Brown, 1978), pp. 196–197.
2. Robert N. Kearney, *Trade Unions and Politics in Ceylon* (Berkeley, Calif.: University of California Press, 1971), pp. 83–84.
3. Ibid., p. 2.
4. Robert C. Oberst, "Democracy and the Persistence of Westernized Elite Dominance in Sri Lanka," *Asian Survey*, vol. 25 (July 1985).
5. Janice Jiggins, *Caste and Family in the Politics of the Sinhalese, 1947–1976* (New York: Cambridge University Press, 1979); and James Jupp, *Sri Lanka: Third World Democracy* (London: Frank Cass, 1978), p. 194.
6. Robert C. Oberst, *Legislators and Representation in Sri Lanka: The Decentralization of Development Planning* (Boulder, Colo.: Westview Press, 1985), pp. 34–35.
7. Urmila Phadnis, *Religion and Politics in Sri Lanka* (New Delhi: Manohar, 1976), p. 273.

8. Oberst, *Legislators and Representation,* pp. 40–41.
9. Ibid., pp. 41–44.
10. Ibid., p. 59.
11. Ibid., p. 37.
12. See ibid., chapter 3.

29
MODERNIZATION AND DEVELOPMENT: PROSPECTS AND PROBLEMS

This final chapter on Sri Lanka examines the effectiveness of the Sri Lankan government in resolving the problems facing it. Two serious problems stand out. The first is the crisis of economic development and the difficulty involved in meeting the material needs of the people. The second is a resolution of the two civil wars that have engulfed the country since 1983. Both of these problems pose a serious threat to the maintenance of stable and representative government in Sri Lanka.

Economic Development

Most of the political systems of the Third World are faced with an economic development crisis. They are trying to meet the needs of their societies with a limited amount of resources. But their failure to develop economically can lead to dissatisfaction among the population and the potential for political violence and unrest. The developing nations of the world are faced with a series of cruel choices, none of which offer clear-cut solutions.

Sri Lanka faces a similar dilemma: Should the country try to take care of the immediate needs of its people by investing its scarce resources in nutrition, health, and educational programs (basic needs)? Or should it strive to develop productive industries that will lead to greater economic growth and well-being in later years? The government of J. R. Jayawardene made a very controversial and determined response to this quandary that appears to be in the process of being reversed by President Premadasa.

Sri Lanka has had a long experience investing in the basic needs of its population. These efforts have led to very high levels of social well-being although growth rates of gross national product have been very low. The literacy rate in Sri Lanka is 87%, the life expectancy of its citizens at birth is 70 years, and yet the per capita income is only about U.S.$400 per year.[1]

As noted, the government of S.W.R.D. Bandaranaike (1956–1959) expanded the social welfare programs that contributed to these high measures of social well-being,[2] which have included pension programs, free medical care, nutrition programs, and a series of subsidies of important food and fuel items. But these programs became extremely expensive—and they threatened to drain the nation's treasury. A country as poor as Sri Lanka has limited resources, and if it is to fund social welfare programs it must divert its resources away from other investments into these programs. This diversion of resources is complicated by the large role that the government plays in the economy. Such efforts as the nationalization of important industries, the restriction of foreign investors, and a land reform program in the 1970s that redistributed land to landless peasants and took away plantations from private owners (often foreigners) and placed them in the hands of government corporations have cost a great deal of money and made further demands on the already limited resources in the national treasury.

The UNP has generally believed that the social welfare programs of the SLFP should be restricted and that savings should be invested in more productive enterprises. After winning the 1977 elections, the government of J. R. Jayawardene called for a major change in the economic policies of Sri Lanka. The new policies were a sharp departure from the policies of previous governments, even those of his own party.

In short, the government cut social welfare programs. It ended the ration of free rice distributed to every citizen and replaced it with a food stamp program whose benefits did not increase in value from its creation in 1979 until 1987. In addition, the program did not permit the addition of a single new recipient during this period. This all occurred despite inflation rates of 10–20% a year.[3] The result has been a general decline in the benefits provided and a great savings for the government. In addition, government subsidies on other commodities were cut back or ended. The government's policy was accompanied by a shift toward a free enterprise system, including the sale of unprofitable government corporations and the establishment of tax holidays to lure foreign corporations to place manufacturing enterprises on the island. The government also embarked on a major investment program to accelerate the building of a hydroelectric and irrigation project in the hill country. All of these policies have generated a great deal of controversy.

Among Jayawardene's most important initiatives was the Mahaveli project, a massive irrigation scheme that was discussed for many years prior to its start during the United Front government in the 1970s. The SLFP government planned for the project to take thirty years. The project was expected to create a series of dams in the hill country—specifically to divert water to the dry zone in the north and east. It was hoped that the lands once irrigated during the Anuradhapura and Polonnaruwa periods would once again be opened up to cultivation. In a sense, the plan called for a restoration of an irrigation system that had once been the lifeblood of the golden age of Sri Lankan civilization.

The UNP planned an accelerated Mahaveli project that called for completion of the system in five years instead of thirty. It scaled the project down to four major dams and several irrigation zones. Although the project ran slightly behind schedule, four dams were completed and several areas opened up for cultivation. As the reservoir projects are completed, the water is diverted to the dry zone to the north and east. The government then oversees the distribution of newly irrigated lands to settlers from the more heavily populated regions of the southwest and the hill country. Unfortunately, the project has required the diversion of large amounts of resources to its construction in addition to the large national debt created as a result of the international loans used to fund it.

After his election, President Premadasa embarked on a major poverty alleviation program that sought to provide a basic standard of living for all Sri Lankans. At the time of his election, Sri Lanka was engulfed in two civil wars, the ethnic conflict between the Tamils and his government, and the JVP terror campaign against the government. The JVP campaign had its roots in the poverty and desperation that Sri Lankan young people have been experiencing. The Jayawardene years (1977–1989) did not do a lot to alleviate these conditions. Although there was strong economic growth in Colombo, many rural areas did not experience that growth. The civil war drained economic resources that could have gone into development while the cutbacks of social welfare expenditures increased malnutrition among children and removed the safety net of the free ration system. As a result, Premadasa directed his efforts toward the poor in the first year of his administration.

A cornerstone of the free market economy of the Jayawardene administration was its "investment promotion zone," or free trade zone. A 180-square-mile area was set up north of the capital city of Colombo near the city's international airport. In an effort to lure multinational corporations, it offered potential investors several benefits:

1. The right to import all equipment and inputs duty free.
2. No taxes on all royalty payments.
3. Exemption from taxes on the income of all foreign personnel attached to the project.
4. Exemption from taxes on all dividends paid to all foreign and Sri Lankan investors in the project.

5. A tax holiday for up to ten years depending on the nature of the project.
6. An additional period of reduced taxes following the ten-year tax holiday.[4]

The program got off to a slow start given the limited number of foreign corporations that took advantage of the tax holidays. However, over 80,000 jobs were created. Most of these have involved the sewing of clothing for markets in Western Europe and North America.

Civil War

As serious as they are, Sri Lanka's economic problems have been overshadowed by the ethnic conflict between the Tamils and Sinhalese and the second JVP insurrection. In the summer of 1984, the country entered a period of open warfare between the Tamil guerrilla fighters and the government. The Jaffna, Vavuniya, Mannar, Batticaloa, Ampara, and Trincomalee districts became a battleground, with almost daily clashes between the Tamil guerrillas and the Sinhalese soldiers.

The sources of this conflict can be traced back to prehistoric times, when the first civilized groups began appearing on the island.[5] However, only the situation since independence in 1948 will be discussed here. As noted in Chapter 23, the Sri Lanka Tamils have never provided very much support to the SLFP and the UNP. The emergence of the Federal party as the dominant party in the Sri Lankan Tamil areas was the result of their strong advocacy for federalism and regional autonomy for the Tamils. The Federal party was created to advocate federalism and its success in replacing the Tamil Congress as the dominant Sri Lanka Tamil party can be attributed to this advocacy. Until the 1970s, the Federal party demanded a federal system of government in Sri Lanka so that the Tamils could control their own affairs. In the mid-1970s, with the creation of the TULF, they escalated their demands to include the creation of an independent state for the Tamils. Their demands for greater autonomy were fueled by several concerns.

The first concern was the language issue. As long as the British ruled Sri Lanka, an alien language—English—was imposed upon the people. As soon as the British left the island, the issue emerged as an important point of confrontation. When the Official Language Act of 1956 specified Sinhala as the sole official language of Sri Lanka, the Tamils feared that they would be denied employment in government jobs that would now require proficiency in Sinhala for employment, that they would be unable to understand government legal proceedings that would now be held in Sinhala, and that they would be left out of the commercial life of the society that would now be conducted in Sinhala. The government responded by passing a resolution allowing for the use of Tamil in government transactions involving people who spoke Tamil. The resolution also provided government employees whose mother tongue was Tamil the time to learn Sinhala. However, the implementation of these requirements, which were passed in 1959, has not yet been enforced. Many government communications to Tamil-speaking people still appear in Sinhala. Moreover, although the Constitution of 1978 gave the Tamil language special status in some government dealings, it maintained the superiority of Sinhala in the society; in addition, its designation of Tamil as a "National Language" while Sinhala remained the only "Official Language" failed to placate the Tamil leadership, and the problem remains a point of confrontation.

A second concern has been the education issue. As noted in Chapter 25, Sri Lankans value the importance of education. Admissions to university education are very limited and much in demand. After independence, admissions were determined on the basis of examinations in the three languages used in the country—Sinhala, Tamil, and English. Only those receiving the highest scores were admitted. For many years the number of students admitted on the basis of the Tamil language exams exceeded the number that would have been expected from this group on the basis of their percentage of the population. Many Sinhalese felt that the Tamil examiners were inflating the scores so that more Tamil students would be admitted to the universities. In the 1970s, the United Front government of Sirimavo Bandaranaike became concerned with the superior performance of the Tamil students. Quotas based on the size of each ethnic community were set, and university exams became an issue of dispute. The UNP sought to defuse the issue by altering the system to one based both on quotas and merit, but this effort was very slow in easing resentment.

A third concern pertains to employment. The government sector is the main source of high-status jobs. As Sinhala has become more important as the language of government, the Tamil speakers have become more concerned with the access of their community to government employment. But there has been a severe shortage of jobs for educated young people from all ethnic communities since the early 1960s. The lack of jobs has been cited as a cause of the youth insurrection led by the JVP in the early 1970s. This uprising involved many more Sinhalese youths than Tamil youths. The government's language and education policies helped to create a sense of deprivation among the Tamil youths, who now also had the Sinhalese and the government to blame for their plight. They also fueled the guerrilla warfare that has engulfed the northern and eastern regions of the country.

A fourth concern has been the Sinhalese colonization of traditional Tamil areas. In Trincomalee, Vavuniya, and Batticaloa districts, recently irrigated lands have been opened for settlement. In many areas, especially Trincomalee, the lands have been given to Sinhalese. This has had the effect of reducing the Tamil percentage of the population in these areas. The problem has been amplified by the Mahaveli development project, which has opened up newly irrigated lands at a rapid pace. Most of the irrigated farmland created by the Mahaveli project has been distributed to Sinhalese settlers.

The fifth concern has been regional autonomy or control over significant policy decisions directly affecting the Tamils. One of these decisions relates to the number and type of development projects in Tamil areas. The Tamils feel that they have not received their fair share of the projects available. This was especially the case with the Jayawardene government's two major development initiatives—the Mahaveli Project, which, for the most part, affects Sinhalese areas, and the Free Trade Zone, which is located near Colombo in the Sinhalese heartland. In short, the Tamils believe that they are not benefiting from the income and jobs generated by these projects.

A second issue raised by the question of regional autonomy concerns the maintenance of law and order. The majority of police and armed forces in the Tamil areas are members of the Sinhalese ethnic group. Many of the attacks carried out by the "tiger" groups were directed against the Sinhalese police and soldiers. On several occasions since 1977, the police and soldiers have gone on rampages in which they attacked innocent bystanders. There have been charges that hundreds of innocent bystanders have been killed, numerous women have been raped, and homes and businesses have been looted and burned during these attacks. The government claims to have punished those responsible for the attacks, but it has failed to produce enough evidence of this claim to satisfy the Tamil leaders.

In addition, since the UNP came to power, the country has suffered major outbursts of anti-Tamil rioting (specifically in 1977, 1981 and 1983). Once again large numbers of Tamils have lost their lives and personal belongings. Moreover, some Tamil leaders have claimed that the police cooperated and assisted the rioters in their attacks against the Tamils.

The five preceding concerns led Tamil leaders to intensify their demands for an independent state, and the Tamil youths to encourage further violence. Communication between the Sinhalese and Tamils broke down, and the militant tiger leaders gained more influence in the Tamil community.

From 1984 until 1987, the two sides negotiated with the Indian government acting as an intermediary. These negotiations met with very little success. In July 1987, the Sri Lankan and Indian governments signed the Indo-Lanka Accords that brought Indian troops to Sri Lanka to enforce a cease-fire. The tigers were never involved in the negotiations and the LTTE never agreed to the accords. Open warfare between the Indian Peace Keeping Forces and the LTTE erupted in October 1987 and continued until the Indian departure in March 1990.

In 1989, President Premadasa began the first direct negotiations between the Sri Lankan government and the LTTE, and reached an agreement with them in June 1990 to lay down their arms, renounce separatism and negotiate further on regional autonomy. He then asked the Indian troops to leave the country by the second anniversary of their arrival. They refused and continued their war against the LTTE.

The Indians feared that their departure from Sri Lanka would result in LTTE attacks against the tiger groups (primarily the EPRLF and TELO) that had agreed to the Indo-Lanka Accords and laid down their arms to become legal political parties. As a result of these concerns, they initially refused to leave although in September 1989 they agreed to a slow withdrawal that was completed in March 1990. To protect the EPRLF, the Indians helped the Eastern and Northern Provincial Council to create the Tamil National Army. This military organization came into conflict with the Sri Lankan government and increased tension between the two sides. The demands of the Tamils were still not satisfied at the time of the Indian departure; however, Sri Lanka was as close as it had been at any time in the previous decade to integrating the Tamils into the national political framework.

The 1987 Indo-Lanka Accords and the 1989 Indian refusal to leave the country stirred Sinhalese nationalist emotions. The JVP, which had been organizing for armed struggle since 1983, emerged with a campaign of assassinations against supporters of the government and the Accords. This campaign was intensified in June, July, and August 1990 after the Indian refusal to leave the country. By 1989, the JVP insurrection had become bloodier than the Tamil conflict. In addition, pro-government death squads emerged and by July and August of 1989 were responsible for most of the deaths in the country. Thousands of low-caste youths and university students were murdered during the summer and fall of 1989 by the death squads, which consisted of off-duty security personnel and UNP supporters. In November, the leader of the JVP, Rohana Wijeweera, and most of the JVP leadership were captured and most were killed shortly after their capture or during it. Although the JVP lost almost all of its leadership, the organization was able to continue its military operations, although at a much reduced level.

The Future of Democracy in Sri Lanka

At no time since independence from Great Britain has the future of Sri Lanka been so clouded with the threat of violence and anarchy. A total breakdown in communication has occurred between the two major ethnic groups, the Sinhalese and the Sri Lanka Tamils, and between the youth of Sri Lanka and the older generation. The agreement between the LTTE and the government of Sri Lanka and the killing of the JVP leadership offer some hope for an end to the two conflicts. However, the refusal of the

Indian government to remove its troops from Sri Lanka seriously destabilized the political system. It increased the support for the ultra-nationalist JVP which argued that the Indians would never leave and prevented the government of Sri Lanka from coming to an agreement with the LTTE.

Despite the Indian government's withdrawal in March 1990, there are serious questions about whether the conflicts can be resolved in the long run. In the case of the Tamils, the central issue of Tamil autonomy has not been resolved. The Sri Lankan government has not been willing to grant enough autonomy to regional governments in the past to satisfy Tamil demands and may not be able to offer enough now. In addition, the issue of Sinhalese colonization of areas traditionally inhabited by the Tamils has been exacerbated by a surge of settlers into Trincomalee and Vavuniya districts in the 1980s.

The forces that led to the creation of the JVP still remain despite the demise of the JVP's leadership. There is a strong sense of alienation among members of the younger generation in Sri Lanka. The extensive death squad killings and torture of Sri Lankan young people, especially university students, have inflamed the younger generation. Even government supporters among the youths have found it difficult to support the brutality of the death squads' indiscriminate attacks. The damage done by the extra-legal methods employed by the government to eradicate the JVP will take a long time to heal.

The future of Sri Lanka depends on the resolution of the violence in the country. However, after peace is brought to the country, the nation will face the prospect of building its economy. In the long run, the economic issues will be the key to Sri Lanka's future. The youth-led civil wars have, in part, been fueled by the inability of the economy to provide jobs and a secure future to Sri Lanka's educated youths. The failure to accelerate economic development may lead to another JVP insurrection in the future and an unending ethnic crisis.

Notes

1. World Bank, *World Development Report—1989* (New York: Oxford University Press, 1989).

2. W. Howard Wriggins, *Ceylon: Dilemmas of a New Nation* (Princeton, N.J.: Princeton University Press, 1960), chapter 8.

3. Government of Sri Lanka, *Sri Lanka Socio-Economic Data, 1984.*

4. Government of Sri Lanka, *A Guide to the Foreign Investor* (Colombo: Ministry of Finance and Planning, n.d.), p. 2.

5. For contrasting views of the ethnic crisis, see Satchi Ponnambalam, *Sri Lanka: The National Question and the Tamil Liberation Struggle* (London: Zed, 1983), for the Tamil perspective, and T.D.S.A. Dissanayaka, *The Agony of Sri Lanka* (Colombo: Swastika, 1984), for the Sinhalese perspective.

Suggested Readings

Bandarage, Asoka. *Colonialism in Sri Lanka* (New York: Mouton Press, 1983).

De Silva, Colvin R. *Sri Lanka: A History* (New Delhi: Vikas Publishing, 1987).

_____. *Ceylon Under the British Occupation 1795–1833: Its Political, Administrative and Economic Development,* 2 vols. (Colombo: Colombo Apothecaries, 1962).

De Silva, K. M. *Managing Ethnic Tensions in Multi-Ethnic Societies: Sri Lanka 1880–1985* (Lanham, Md.: University Press of America, 1986).

_____. *A History of Sri Lanka* (Berkeley: University of California Press, 1981).

DeSilva, K. M., ed. *Sri Lanka: A Survey* (Honolulu: University of Hawaii Press, 1977).

Dubey, Swaroop Rani. *One-day Revolution in Sri Lanka: Anatomy of 1971 Insurrection* (Jaipur: Aalekh Publishers, 1988).

Fernando, Tissa, and Robert N. Kearney, eds. *Modern Sri Lanka: A Society in Transition* (Syracuse, N.Y.: FACS Publications, 1979).

Jiggins, Janice. *Caste and Family in the Politics of the Sinhalese. 1947–1976* (New York: Cambridge University Press, 1979).

Jupp, James. *Sri Lanka: Third World Democracy* (London: Frank Cass, 1978).

Kearney, Robert N. "Territorial Elements of Tamil Separatism in Sri Lanka." *Pacific Affairs,* vol. 60 (Winter 1987), pp. 561–577.

_____. *Trade Unions and Politics in Ceylon* (Berkeley: University of California Press, 1971).

_____. *Communalism and Language in the Politics of Ceylon* (Durham, N.C.: Duke University Press, 1967).

Kearney, Robert N., and Janice Jiggins. "The Ceylon Insurrection of 1971," *Journal of Commonwealth and Comparative Politics,* vol. 13 (March 1975), pp. 40–65.

Kearney, Robert N., and Barbara Diane Miller. "The Spiral of Suicide and Social Change in Sri Lanka." *Journal of Asian Studies,* vol. 45 (November 1985), pp. 81–101.

_____. *Internal Migration in Sri Lanka and Its Social Consequences* (Boulder, Colo.: Westview Press, 1987).

_____. "Women's Suicide in Sri Lanka." In Patricia Whelehan, ed. *Women and Health: Cross-Cultural Perspectives* (Granby, Mass.: Bergin and Garvey Publishers, 1988).

Knox, Robert. *An Historical Relation of Ceylon,* published as the *Ceylon Historical Journal,* vol. 6 (July 1956–April 1957).

Leitan, G. R. Tressie. *Local Government and Decentralized Administration in Sri Lanka* (Colombo: Lake House, 1979).

Manogaran, Chelvadurai. *Ethnic Conflict and Reconciliation in Sri Lanka* (Honolulu: University of Hawaii, 1987).

Manor, James, ed. *Sri Lanka in Change and Crisis* (London: Croom Helm, 1984).

Matthews, Bruce. "District Development Councils in Sri Lanka," *Asian Survey,* vol. 22 (November 1982), pp. 1117–1134.

Oberst, Robert C. "Sri Lanka's Tamil Tigers." *Conflict,* vol. 8 (Winter 1988), pp. 185–202.

_____. "Federalism and Ethnic Conflict in Sri Lanka." *Publius,* vol. 18 (Summer 1988), pp. 175–193.

————. *Legislators and Representation in Sri Lanka: The Decentralization of Development Planning* (Boulder, Colo.: Westview Press, 1985).

————. "Democracy and the Persistence of Westernized Elite Dominance in Sri Lanka," *Asian Survey,* vol. 25 (July 1985), pp. 760–772.

Pfaffenberger, Bryan. *Caste in Tamil Culture: The Religious Foundations of Sudra Domination in Tamil Sri Lanka* (Syracuse, N.Y.: FACS Publications, 1983).

Phadnis, Urmila. *Religion and Politics in Sri Lanka* (New Delhi: Manohar, 1976).

Rogers, John. "Social Mobility, Popular Ideology, and Collective Violence in Modern Sri Lanka." *Journal of Asian Studies,* vol. 46 (August 1987), pp. 583–602.

Ryan, Bryce. *Caste in Modern Ceylon* (New Brunswick, N.J.: Rutgers University Press, 1953).

Tambiah, S. J. *Ethnic Fratricide and the Dismantling of Democracy* (Chicago: University of Chicago Press, 1986).

Wilson, A. Jeyaratnam. *The Gaullist System in Asia: The Constitution of Sri Lanka (1978)* (London: Macmillan, 1980).

Wiswa Warnapala, W. A., and L. Dias Hewagama. *Recent Politics in Sri Lanka: The Presidential Election and the Referendum of 1982* (New Delhi: Navrang, 1983).

PART 5

SOUTH ASIA

30
NEPAL, BHUTAN, AND THE MALDIVES

Nepal

The Himalayan kingdom of Nepal is a small country the size of the state of Illinois, with a population of 16 million. Sandwiched between its two giant neighbors, the People's Republic of China and India, it is landlocked and thus has access to the sea only through Indian territory (see Map 30.1). Linked with both China and India by all-weather motorable roads, Nepal today occupies a strategic position in the South Asian subcontinent.

Nepal achieved its territorial consolidation in the eighteenth century under a dynamic Gurkha king, Prithvi Raj Narayan Shah, who organized the Nepali army along Western lines. He also promulgated a new, uniform legal and administrative system for the efficient rule of his kingdom. In the 1814 war with the British rulers of India, Nepal not only suffered a defeat but also lost considerable territory to British India, although it gained British recognition of its sovereignty in return. Even though Nepal was never occupied by the British rulers of India, it was rarely in a position to assert its complete independence. When India became independent in 1947, however, Nepal, too, declared its independent status and sought relations with the outside world as a sovereign state. After 1947 Nepal emerged from its seclusion and became active in regional politics.

Ethnic and Religious Plurality

The ethnic composition of Nepal's population and its cultural heritage have been deeply influenced by India and Tibet, two of its immediate neighbors. Its population is divided into two predominant racial groups, Caucasoid and Mongoloid.[1] The Caucasoids possess predominantly Indo-Aryan traits as their ancestors migrated to Nepal mainly from north India. More specifically, in the twelfth and thirteenth centuries frequent Muslim invasions of India spurred high-caste Hindus to migrate to Nepal. The Malla dynasty, which ruled the Kathmandu Valley from the thirteenth century until

Map 30.1

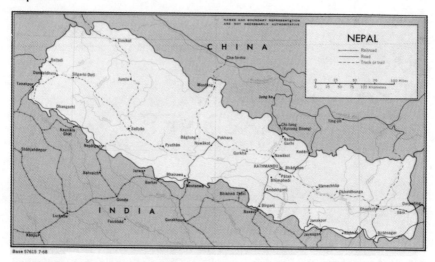

Base 57615 7-68

1768–1769, and the Shah dynasty, which is the current ruling family of Nepal, originated from the same clans as those Rajput chiefs who left Rajasthan while seeking shelter in Nepal to save their religion from the Muslim onslaughts.[2] Their number increased when population pressure forced many north Indians to seek land and livelihood in the Terai area of Nepal. The people of Mongoloid origin, on the other hand, originated mainly in Tibet and the southern provinces of China.

The Nepalese population of both racial stocks is subdivided into many ethnic groups. Predominant among the Indo-Nepalese are the following groups: (1) The upper-caste Hindus are made up of Brahmins and Kshatriyas. Among this group the Thakuri, or Rajput, subcaste of Kshatriyas constitutes the ruling elite of the country, whereas the Brahmins provide the country's intelligentsia. Both subgroups have built distinctive Nepali traditions and aspects of culture based upon the Nepali version of Hinduism and the Nepali language. Nepali, spoken by the country's majority, belongs to the Indo-European group of languages. (2) The recent Nepalese migrants are people of Indian origin who work mainly as farmers and laborers in the Terai area and bear a close resemblance to their brothers in north India. Their values, language, and culture are hard to distinguish from those of the people of north India. (3) The Newaris constitute another important subgroup among the Indo-Nepalese, who, though predominantly Hindu, include some Buddhists among their ranks. The Newaris are highly literate and urbane and dominate Nepal's trade and commerce.

Among the Mongoloids the following groups are prominent: (1) The Magars and the Gurungs are mainly Hindus who have produced Nepal's famed Gurkha soldiers. (2) The Kiratis possess a distinct ethnic identity based upon their language and regional affiliation. They seek regional autonomy within Nepal. (3) The Thakalis constitute another group of Tibetan origin that has recently adopted many practices of Hinduism. (4) The Sherpas are Buddhists well known for their mountaineering skills; in fact, they often serve as guides. (5) The Tamangs constitute a tribal group whose members work mainly as porters and farm laborers. They are of Tibetan origin and follow Buddhism.

Over the last fifty years or so, many of these groups have given up their tribal customs and gradually embraced the dominant Nepali culture based upon Hinduism. During this period the process of social change has "fostered the integration of Nepali society by standardizing religious and social practices and by providing a common perception of social values and attitudes as well as limited social and economic mobility."[3]

Nepal is a Hindu kingdom, and the king is looked upon as the protector and promoter of the Hindu religion. In fact, the provisions of the 1959 and 1962 constitutions declare that Nepal is a Hindu monarchy and stipulate that "the ruler must be an adherent of Aryan culture and a follower of Hindu religion."[4] This central place of Hinduism in Nepal's political setup has been accepted by all segments of the society, even by those who belong to the extremist revolutionary groups.[5]

Political Institutions

The history of Nepal's institutional development can be divided into three phases:

The Rana Regime. This first phase was characterized by a feudalistic society in which the landed aristocracy occupied the key positions in the court, the army, and the administration. The overall system resembled closely those existing in other Asian kingdoms of the nineteenth century. Owing to the feudal nature of the Nepali society and the intrigues and conspiracies existing in the palace and among the members of the nobility, the king was reduced to titular head of the state. The effective power passed into the hands of the Rana family, who provided the various hereditary prime ministers of the country. The Ranas, an upper-caste family of Nepali nobles, starting with Jang Bahadur in 1856, settled an order of succession that left little choice to the king in the selection of the prime minister. Even though the succession order set by Jang Bahadur was often disregarded, the relatives of the various branches of the Rana family continued to occupy the key positions in the court, the administration, and the army. The efforts of the king to break out of this order and to establish himself as an effective ruler of the country always ended in failure. The Ranas exercised despotic power and left no room for democratic reforms.

Nepal did not remain in complete isolation, however. The social and cultural revival in India and the rise of the nationalist movement under the Indian National Congress deeply influenced the middle-class Nepalese. The Rana regime's suppression of the modernist aspirations of the educated classes gave birth to an anti-Rana movement. Many of the educated young Nepalese living in India in the early 1940s were influenced by such Indian socialist leaders as Jaya Prakash Narayan and Ram Manohar Lohia. Close contact with the freedom movement in India encouraged the young Nepali leaders, such as B. P. Koirala and D. R. Regmi, to organize the Nepali *rashtriya* (national) Congress in Calcutta in 1947. It was this organization that spearheaded the anti-Rana movement and demanded the democratization of Nepal. The Ranas, unaware of the extent of middle-class alienation, responded with increased suppression. The break for the Nepali nationalists came in 1950 when King Tribhuvan and his family sought asylum in India. Various anti-Rana organizations then joined together under the banner of the Nepali Congress, launched an armed struggle against the Rana regime, and set up a parallel government. The king fled, thereby depriving the Ranas of their legitimacy. Faced with this popular upsurge and the tough attitude of the government of India, which was sympathetic to the aspirations of both the Nepali Congress and King Tribhuvan, the Ranas yielded. The 1950 upsurge brought an end to the Rana regime.

The Monarch and Experimentation with Democracy. The return of King Tribhuvan to the position of an effective ruler of the country raised the hope for democratic reforms. The second phase in the institutional development of Nepal started with the Interim Constitution of 1951. The new constitution, although it promised free elections, set up a coalition government consisting of the representatives of the Nepali Congress and members of the Rana family. The king was to serve as the head of the state as well as of the government. But King Tribhuvan was not an activist monarch; indeed, he aroused the hope that effective powers would soon be transferred to the people's representatives. That hope evaporated, however, with the disintegration of the coalition between the Nepali Congress and the Ranas.

The Nepali Congress, the main reformist and modernist party in the country, became divided into various factions and was thus unable to provide a united leadership. Amidst the quarreling politicians and factional squabbles, the people looked upon the monarch not only as the symbol of national unity but also as the saviour of the country.[6]

King Mahendra, who succeeded his father in March 1955, promulgated a modified form of parliamentary government through the 1959 constitution. This new constitution provided for a bicameral legislative body consisting of the *Pritinidhi Sabha* (representative assembly), with 109 members to be elected directly on the basis of universal suffrage, and the *Maha Sabha* (the great assembly), the upper house, consisting of 36 members. The Maha

Sabha was to be a permanent body with partly elected and partly appointed members serving terms of six years, one-third of whom would retire every two years. The new constitution also provided for a cabinet responsible to both the parliament and the king. The ministers and the parliament were, of course, subordinate to the king, who was the ultimate source of authority.

In the first free elections to parliament held in February 1959, the Nepali Congress won an absolute majority with 74 out of 109 seats. Its leader, B. P. Koirala, became the prime minister and formed a cabinet consisting of Nepali Congress members. Nepal's experiment with parliamentary government did not last long, however. On December 15, 1960, King Mahendra dismissed the Koirala government and arrested the prime minister as well as his cabinet colleagues. The king felt that Nepal was not yet ready for some of the changes, especially land reforms, that had been introduced by the Koirala government. Instead, Nepal remained basically a feudal society. Traditional ruling elites still occupied powerful positions within the army and the administration. The Nepali Congress leaders lacked not only solidarity but also an extensive organizational network to mobilize the masses against the sporadic revolutions and defiance of the national authority by members of the landed aristocracy. The king was concerned about the stability in the country and could not afford to alienate the landowning segment of the society, which had held power for such a long time. King Mahendra and his prime minister also had serious personal and political differences. The king feared that a popular prime minister backed by a popularly elected parliament might impose severe restraints on his personal power and reduce him to a figurehead. The idea of a constitutional monarchy did not have any appeal for the king.

The Panchayati Raj: The Experiment with Guided Democracy. Like many rulers in Third World countries, King Mahendra believed that a democratic system and parliamentary government are products of the Western cultural milieu and are thus not suitable for societies such as Nepal. At the same time, he found it hard to rule without some sort of popular association with the administration. The *panchayat* (council) system, which is believed to have existed in the past Nepali society, is considered more suited to its people than the representative institutions of the Western societies. In 1962, therefore, the king issued a constitutional ordinance introducing a new set of popular institutions based upon an indirect system of election. The *panchayats* were to be elected at the village, town, and district levels; but only the lowest level, the village *panchayat,* was to be directly elected by the people. At the national level stood the *Rashtriya Panchayat* (national council or parliament), which was to be elected indirectly by the members of the local *panchayats* as well as by the members of professional and class organizations. A council of ministers, to be selected from the members of the national parliament, was to serve as an advisory body to the king. The real power remained with the king, who had the authority not only to amend the constitution but also to suspend it by royal proclamation during emergencies. Another important feature of the new constitution was the abolition of all political parties; parties were not allowed to operate or to put up candidates for public offices.

King Mahendra's efforts, however, failed to satisfy either the politicians, the intellectuals, or the students—the most articulate segments of Nepali society. The resultant demonstrations, which often led to considerable unrest, finally forced King Birendra, the successor to King Mahendra, to call in May 1979 for a nationwide referendum to determine the future form of Nepal's government. The referendum gave two choices to the people: (1) a partyless *panchayat* system with the prospect for future reform, or (2) a "multiparty system." Although no clear definition of "multiparty system" was provided, the implication was that it stood for a parliamentary system of government run on a party basis.

The supporters of the *panchayati raj* (rule) and of the "multiparty system" were provided ample opportunities to campaign for their preferred form of government. The referendum was held on May 2, 1980, and 67% of the eligible voters participated.[7] The *panchayat* system won by a narrow majority of 54.7% of the votes,[8] making it evident that there was still considerable support for the free operation of political parties and a parliamentary system of government.

Even though the new institutional system created after the 1980 referendum failed to lift the ban on political parties, it nevertheless represented a significant departure from the constitutional arrangements existing since 1962. Under the new system, the 112 members of the national *panchayat* (parliament) are elected directly by the people on the basis of universal adult suffrage. Furthermore, the prime minister is elected by the *Rashtriya Panchayat* (national parliament), from which he selects the council of ministers. Both hold office as long as they enjoy the parliament's confidence. The constitutional reforms, however, have not altered the status of the king, who still holds the sovereign power in the kingdom of Nepal.[9]

The elections to the national *panchayat* were held in May 1981. Even though the political parties could not contest the elections, their leaders were not restricted against seeking seats in the national legislature. Some former party leaders were elected to the *Rashtriya Panchayat*.

In the absence of officially sanctioned parties, groups and factions organized around powerful members of the national parliament have become common. Since the referendum of 1980, even though the monarch has not been reduced to a mere constitutional head of the state, the people's participation in the political process has evidently increased. The faction leaders now vie with each other to control power; they are even able to change governments if the prime minister and his cabinet fail to meet their demands. Moreover, the voters are apparently able to bring about changes in the composition of the national *panchayat* if they so decide. Despite this liberalization, however, Nepal continues to be a guided democracy in which the king wields the ultimate power. In February 1990, the Nepali Congress, joined by the Leftist United Front and human rights activists, launched a movement for the legalization of political parties and restoration of a parliamentary system of government. This was the latest expression of Nepali opposition to the king's partyless democracy that led to another round of repression and political violence. However, in April, the king reversed his position and agreed to permit party-based elections. Indeed, the country still has a long way to go before it becomes a full-fledged democracy.

Parties, Factions, and Groups

The sociopolitical structure in Nepal has not been conducive to the development of a sound party system. The domination of the political and administrative life of the country by a few high-caste families and the hostile attitude of the monarchy toward parties and political leaders have hampered the growth of a competitive party system in the country. The public behavior of the party leaders, continual interparty conflicts, and the politicians' inability to build a viable party organization have led to a poor image of party leaders in Nepali society. Yet, despite these limitations and the royal ban on the parties, it is possible to identify certain parties with which the politicians and the people associate themselves.

The Nepali Congress is one of the oldest and best-known political parties of Nepal. As an umbrella organization founded in 1950 by the anti-Rana intellectuals residing in India, it sought to overthrow the Rana regime and democratize the society. After the 1950 revolution, the Nepali Congress became the ruling party, though only for a short period. Under the leadership of the powerful B. P. Koirala, however, it survived as a major political force in the country, even after its government had been dismissed and its leaders were jailed.

The party is a moderately socialist, basically reform-oriented organization that seeks to liberalize Nepali society along democratic lines. In the 1980 referendum it supported the "multiparty" option in opposition to the *panchayat* system. Although Koirala himself was ambivalent toward the new institutional setup of the post-referendum period, his party decided to boycott the 1981 *Rashtriya Panchayat* elections.[10] Thus the Nepali Congress adopted a rejectionist posture toward the new regime.

On July 22, 1982, Koirala died. His death created a major void both in the Nepali Congress and in the politics of his country, as Koirala had played a central role in national politics since 1950. He had been instrumental in securing many constitutional reforms, including the 1981 democratization of the Nepali political institutions. He had also been a moderating force within his party and consistently advocated a policy of national reconciliation in Nepal. Although his death has left the Nepali Congress without a widely accepted leader, the party is expected to maintain its support among the different sections of the population of the country.

The Nepal Communist party is another organization that maintains a stable base in the country. The Communist movement in Nepal has been deeply influenced by the Communist party of India. Many young Nepali intellectuals who were in residence in Bengal came under the influence of the Indian Marxists, whose guidance in 1949 helped them found the Nepal Communist party in Calcutta. Like their counterparts in India, the Nepali Communists looked upon the Nepali Congress leaders as collaborators who were willing tools of international imperialism. They called for a broad-based alliance of the "progressive forces" to fight the Nepali Congress and an expansionist India. The establishment of people's democracies based upon the Chinese model, relentless opposition to the king and his feudalistic regime, and radical social and economic reforms are the hallmarks of the party's program.

Not unlike the Communist movement in India, the Nepal Communist party suffers from interfactional conflicts and strong ideological schisms that have produced deep divisions within its leadership. In addition to its various minor splinter groups, the Nepal Communist party is divided into pro-Moscow and pro-Beijing factions, the two largest ideological groups.

The Communists in Nepal are able to maintain their support because of their strong hold on the peasants and the workers. They maintain this support through the All-Nepal Kisan Sabha (All-Nepal peasants union) and the Nepal Trade Union Congress.

King Mahendra's partyless *panchayat* system was accompanied by the Back to Village National Campaign (BVNC), an organization created to mobilize the Nepalese masses to carry out the ideological goals set by their monarch. Even though BVNC was not called a political party, it was assigned a ten-point program to achieve changes in the social, political, and economic life of the country. The ministers, the *panchas* (members of the *panchayats*), and the administrative officials were asked to work toward national con-solidation, to achieve agrarian reforms, and to perform voluntary labor in the villages. The BVNC gave the appearance of an officially sanctioned party headed by the king, who was determined to provide direct leadership to the masses.[11]

In addition to the BVNC, the administration launched the Rashtriya Swatantra Vidyarthi Parishad (RSVM), or independent nationalist students association, to control the students and their political activities. The students constitute one of the most vocal and volatile groups in Nepal. In 1979, students at the various campuses of Tribhuvan University began an agitation in which they demanded the abolition of the RSVM; they also called for many other educational and political reforms. The agitation took a violent turn, forcing the king not only to abolish the RSVM but also to provide constitutional reforms by holding a national referendum.

Modernization and Development: Problems and Prospects

Since the revolution of 1950 the monarchy has become the key to the political development and modernization process in Nepal. The crown not only provides a link with the country's traditional past; it also serves as a major force in ushering Nepal into the twentieth century.

The key to the ultimate survival of these institutions, however, lies in the economic development of the country. Nepal is still one of the poorest countries in the world, with one of the lowest per capita incomes—$120 per year—among the countries of South Asia. The infant mortality rate is high, and much of the Nepali population suffers from serious malnutrition. Consequently, life expectancy is low, just around 43 years.[12]

The rulers of Nepal, however, have been conscious of the need for economic development and modernization of the country. In 1950 Nepal did not possess any significant infrastructure for modernization. Since 1956, however, the country has launched various economic development plans that have resulted in the expansion of roads, the building of several airports, enhanced power generation capacity, and increased irrigation facilities. Nepal has also built several educational institutions to increase its technically skilled manpower and made noticeable improvements in its health care facilities. It has been the recipient of economic and development aid from its two giant neighbors, India and the People's Republic of China, which continue to vie with each other to woo the Himalayan kingdom. In addition, Nepal has benefited from the development assistance provided by the United States and the Soviet Union. Despite these efforts, Nepal's economic growth rate continues to be dismal. According to the World Bank's 1987 *World Development Report,* "Nepal's economic growth on a per capita basis was only .1% per year during 1965–85, with a per capita income of $160 in 1985, the fifth lowest in the world."[13] Long-term economic development prospects, however, are dependent on continuous political stability, population control, and the cooperation of its neighbors.

Bhutan

Bhutan is another Himalayan kingdom that escaped direct British rule before India became independent. Unlike Nepal, which is predominantly Hindu and constitutes an extension of Indo-Aryan culture, Bhutan is pre-

Map 30.2

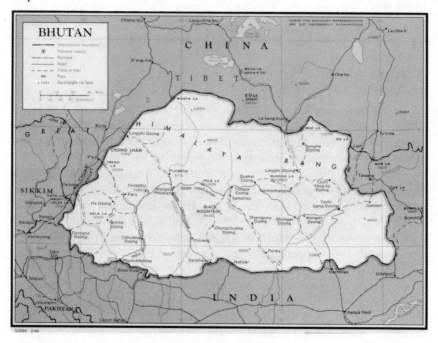

dominantly a Buddhist country with strong cultural and religious ties to Tibet, its northern neighbor (see Map 30.2). Having proved itself capable of maintaining a distinct national identity, it has been spared the impact of Indo-Aryan culture, dominant in South Asia. Mahayana Buddhism, which constitutes the state religion of Bhutan, was brought into the country from Tibet in the eighth century. Subsequently, many Buddhist Lamas from Tibet came to Bhutan as missionaries to propagate their religion, to build monasteries, and to settle in the country. Ultimately, they helped build the distinct cultural and national identity of Bhutan.

Ethnic Composition of the Population

There is considerable diversity in the ethnic composition of the population of Bhutan. The Bhutanese of Tibetan origin constitute the most important group (though not the majority) of the population inasmuch as they provide the country's dominant political and religious elites. The Indo-Mongoloids, who migrated from the Himalayan parts of the present-day Indian state of Assam, constitute the second most important ethnic group. The aboriginal tribal population, consisting of the Lepcha, Drokpa, and Doyas tribes, makes up only a small part of the overall population of the country, whereas the

Bhutanese of Nepali origin, who have been residents of the country for generations, constitute a very significant portion.

Bhutan, though a small country with an area of only 18,000 square miles (the size of Vermont and New Hampshire combined) and a population of about 1 million, contains many linguistic groups within its boundaries. Aside from Dzongkha and Nepali, the two most prominent languages of the country belonging, respectively, to the Tibetan and Indo-European families of languages, there are a host of dialects used by different groups within the country that do not belong to either one of the major groups. Dzongkha is the language of the dominant elite and has become the language of the administration. As it is also the most widely understood language in the country, it is used as the primary medium of education and communication in Bhutan. Nepali is used mostly in those areas where Bhutanese of Nepali origin have settled in large numbers. Recent years have also witnessed an increase in the popularity of English, which has become an important medium of instruction, especially for the upper strata of Bhutanese society.

Political Development and Modernization

Before 1907 Bhutan was ruled by chiefs, headmen, and the lamas who also owned the country's land and constituted its aristocracy. For all practical purposes Bhutan could be classified as a theocracy in which the chief lama held the country's highest spiritual and political authority. In 1907 this order came to an end when Ugyen Wangchuck, the founder of the current ruling dynasty and the most influential and powerful chief of the country, consolidated his powers and with the consent of the country's lesser chiefs, noblemen, and religious leaders became His Highness the Maharaja (the king)—the first Druke Gyalpo of Bhutan. The British, who were concerned about Chinese designs on Bhutan, encouraged the establishment of a centralized administration under a hereditary monarch. It has been the rulers of this dynasty who have provided Bhutan with political stability and have also moved Bhutan out of its medieval isolation into the twentieth century.

In 1910 Ugyen Wangchuck signed a treaty with the British rulers of India in which he "agreed to be guided by the advice of the British Government in regard to its external affairs."[14] In return, the British government pledged not to interfere in the internal affairs of Bhutan. Ugyen Wangchuck was assisted by Kazi Ugyen Dorji, the head of another important noble family and a close friend of the ruler, in the transition of Bhutan from its fragmented feudal state into a centralized kingdom. But it was during the regime of the third ruler of the dynasty, the Third Druke Gyalpo Jigme Dorji Wangchuck, that the country made rapid strides toward modernization. In the words of Leo Rose, between the Third Druke's succession to the throne in 1952 and his death two decades later, the entire political and administrative system was restructured. A popular assembly and the nucleus of a cabinet system of government was introduced; the administrative machinery was modernized; and an economic development program was inaugurated with specialized economic departments established for the purpose. In twenty years Bhutan was transformed from a society marked by almost total political, economic, and intellectual isolation from the rest of the world to one in which an intensive effort is being made to relate the country to modernization processes introduced in most other developing societies.[15]

Despite these efforts, however, Bhutan is still dominated by a traditional value system. Its political institutions are fragile, and it faces a serious threat to its internal cohesion from the Nepali Bhutanese, whose values, culture, and traditions have not yet been fully integrated into the mainstream of Bhutan's political culture. Bhutan has also been rocked by political assassinations and unsuccessful attempts at coup d'état resulting from interelite political rivalries.

Bhutan, India, and the World

In 1947, when the British withdrew from India, Bhutan viewed the new rulers of India with a mixture of caution and suspicion. Bhutan would have liked to assert its complete independence and reorient its relations with India. As Bhutan represented a major security concern for India, however, India declined to change the treaty provisions of 1910. In 1948, when Bhutanese officials approached the successors of British rule in India seeking to review Bhutan's relations with the new government, the government in New Delhi agreed to respect Bhutan's autonomy provided that Bhutan adhered to treaty obligations from the British period. In 1949 the ten-article treaty replacing the 1910 treaty, signed by Bhutan and India, confirmed the treaty obligations of the two nations; that is, Bhutan accepted Indian advice on foreign affairs and India pledged not to interfere in Bhutan's internal affairs. In short, India and Bhutan, each faced with a threat from the People's Republic of China, needed each other. Furthermore, the Bhutanese rulers seem to have recognized that Bhutan had a far better chance of survival as an independent country if it aligned with India than if it sought distance from it. They also seem to have concluded that, by not undermining India's security and by not seeking to assert their independence, they would gradually be able to expand their relations with the outside world. They were correct in their assumptions. By 1971 Bhutan, with Indian support, had become a member of several international organizations, including the United Nations.

Maldives

An island country with only 115 square miles of territory and a population of 150,000, Maldives is one of the most densely populated nations in the world. It is located in the Indian Ocean, and Sri Lanka and India are its closest neighbors. A majority of its people are of Sinhalese or Tamil origin, with some mixture of Arab blood.

Until the middle of the twelfth century the Maldivian population followed Buddhism, which was brought to the country from Sri Lanka. In 1153, however, the king of the island country was converted to Islam which had been introduced into Maldives from Morocco. Subsequently, the king forced his subjects to renounce Buddhism and to become followers of Islam. Today 100% of the population is Sunni Muslim, although the predominant cultural traits are still of Sri Lankan rather than Arab origin. The people of Maldives speak Devehi, an Indo-European language that is related to Sinhala (the main language of Sri Lanka). The Maldivian national identity has been strengthened by the insular nature of the society, the distinct language, and the Islamic traditions and values.

The economy of the island is still primitive; the country's main sources of income are fishing and tourism. A majority of the tourists come from the Western European countries rather than from the United States. In addition, the country grows coconuts, fruits, and millet.

The island country was a British protectorate from 1867 to 1966, when it became independent. During this period, the sultan, the country's monarch, had complete freedom in the management of its internal affairs. The first constitutional reforms were introduced in 1932, when a legislative assembly called the Majlis was created and a cabinet was installed. This constitutional experiment did not last very long, however. Between 1934 and 1943 two sultans were deposed. In 1945 Abdul Majeed, a highly respected nobleman, was elected the new sultan of the country. He brought about considerable liberalization in the society and is frequently referred to as the father of the modern Maldives. After he died in 1952, the country under his successor Muhammed Amin Didi made major rapid strides in modernization. The new ruler not only expanded educational facilities, especially for women, but he also introduced telephones and electric power in Male, the national capital. Then, following Muhammed Amin's death in 1954, Prince M. Fareed Didi became sultan of the country and abolished the first republic, which his predecessor had established.

After 1957 the country experienced the reconstitution of the Majlis, the abolition of the sultanate, and the reconstitution of the republican form of government (1968). Today the country is headed by a president who exercises virtually absolute power and acts the part of sultan, even though he was elected by the Majlis. In turn, the Majlis, the legislative body of the country, is elected for five years. The constitution, however, does not allow the operation of political parties, and the members of the legislature enjoy little independence. The Majlis passes without much discussion every piece of legislation that is sent to it by the president.[16] The current president, Maumoon Abdul Gayoon, is a nobleman who assumed his office in 1978. In 1989, there was an attempted coup against the president by mercenaries hired by a discredited business man. However, the coup attempt failed because of the intervention of Indian armed forces. The Gayoon government still faces some serious problems, including the control of runaway population growth in a traditional and orthodox Muslim society, increasing income disparities between the elites and the masses, the need for educational reforms, and the role of Islam in the politics and culture of the society.

Notes

1. Leo E. Rose and Margaret W. Fisher, *The Politics of Nepal: Persistence and Change in an Asian Monarchy* (Ithaca, N.Y.: Cornell University Press, 1970), p. 9.

2. Rishikesh Shaha, *Nepali Politics: Retrospect and Prospect* (Delhi: Oxford University Press, 1975), p. 19.

3. Ibid., p. 18.

4. Rose and Fisher, *The Politics of Nepal*, p. 35.

5. Ibid.

6. Anirudha Gupta, *Politics in Nepal: A Study of Post-Rana Political Development and Party Politics* (Bombay: Allied Publishers, 1964), p. 95.

7. Douglas Heck, "Nepal in 1980: The Year of the Referendum," *Asian Survey*, vol. 21, no. 2 (February 1981), p. 183.

8. Herka Gurung, "The Sociology of Elections in Nepal, 1959 to 1981," *Asian Survey*, vol. 22, no. 3 (March 1982), p. 304.

9. Tulsi P. Uprety, "Nepal in 1982: Panchayati Leadership in Crisis," *Asian Survey*, vol. 23, no. 2 (February 1983), p. 143.

10. Devendra Raj Panday, "Nepal in 1981: Stagnation Amidst Change," *Asian Survey*, vol. 22, no. 2 (February 1982), p. 156.

11. Lok Raj Baral, "Party-Like Institutions in Partyless Politics: The GVNE in Nepal," *Asian Survey*, vol. 16, no. 7 (July 1976), pp. 672–681.

12. Sukhdev Shah, "Developing an Economy: Nepal's Experience," *Asian Survey*, vol. 21, no. 10 (October 1981), p. 1060.

13. Quoted in Sukhdev Shah, "Nepal's Economic Development: Problems and Prospects," *Asian Survey*, vol. 28, no. 9 (September 1988), p. 945.

14. Ram Rahul, *Modern Bhutan* (Delhi: Vikas Publications, 1971), p. 51.

15. Leo Rose, *The Politics of Bhutan* (Ithaca, N.Y.: Cornell University Press, 1977), p. 38.

16. Clarence Maloney, "The Maldives: New Stresses in an Old Nation," *Asian Survey*, vol. 16, no. 7 (July 1976), pp. 654–671.

Suggested Readings

Baral, Lok Raj. *Oppositional Politics in Nepal* (Columbia, Mo.: South Asia Books, 1970).

Gupta, Anirudha. *Politics in Nepal: A Study of Post-Rana Political Developments and Party Politics* (Bombay: Allied Publishers, 1964).

Joshi, Bhuwanlal, and Leo E. Rose. *Democratic Innovations in Nepal: A Case Study of Political Acculturation* (Berkeley: University of California Press, 1966).

Misra, H. N. *Bhutan: Problems and Policies* (New Delhi: Heritage, 1988).

Rose, Leo E. *The Politics of Bhutan* (Ithaca, N.Y.: Cornell University Press, 1977).

Rose, Leo E., and Margaret W. Fisher. *The Politics of Nepal: Persistence and Change in an Asian Monarchy* (Ithaca, N.Y.: Cornell University Press, 1970).

Seddon, David. *Nepal: A State of Poverty* (New Delhi: Vikas, 1987).

Shah, Rishikish. *Nepali Politics: Retrospect and Prospect* (Delhi: Oxford University Press, 1975).

Singh, Nagendra. *Bhutan: A Kingdom in the Himalayas* (New Delhi: Thompson Press India, Ltd., 1972).

31
SOUTH ASIA AS
A REGION AND IN
THE WORLD SYSTEM

The strategic location of South Asia makes it an area of importance in the world system. Pakistan is almost as much a part of Southwest Asia as it is of South Asia, given its proximity to the Gulf and its border with Iran. It has Islamic ties with the important Muslim nations of the Gulf area. It is also a neighbor of Afghanistan and in some respects has inherited the guardianship of the historic invasion routes from Central Asia to the Indo-Gangetic plain. India, as the second most populous nation in the world, is important not only in terms of its geographic location but also as a potentially huge market, as a rapidly growing technological power, and as a long-time leader among Third World nations. Sri Lanka, which extends south into the Indian Ocean, sits athwart some of the world's important shipping lanes. Finally, Bangladesh lies adjacent to the volatile eastern areas of India.

The Inheritors of British Rule

Many of the features just described were present when the British ruled South Asia. In fact, they were seen by the British as important attributes of their governance of the region. The establishment of Afghanistan and Tibet as buffer areas between the British dominions and the empires of Russia and China were included among these attributes. Today, neither Afghanistan nor Tibet is a buffer zone, and the successor Chinese power borders directly on South Asia through the Chinese incorporation of Tibet. The Soviet Union attempted from 1979 to 1989 to occupy Afghanistan, which would have placed Soviet power on the borders of South Asia. India, as the largest and strongest power in the region, has inherited much of the British role—although it plays that role in a very different way.

The Predominance of India

However much the smaller powers in the region may resent the importance of India, they have no choice but to live with their huge neighbor as best they can. In this section we will look briefly at some of the outstanding problems between India and the other nations that border it. India dwarfs the other nations by almost any measure of power (see the Statistical Appendix); indeed, it has the largest and best-equipped military force by far (although Pakistan also possesses some modern weapons), and in 1974 demonstrated its nuclear capability.

As we have seen, the division of the British Indian Empire in 1947 was accomplished in violence, leaving India and Pakistan as rivals in bitterness rather than as parts of a united country or even as cooperating successors to Britain. The further division of Pakistan in 1971 and the creation of Bangladesh was accompanied by war between India and Pakistan. India gained much more than its rival as a consequence of its three wars with Pakistan. India has at times seen itself as Britain's successor in its relations with Nepal and Bhutan. It has also had problems with Sri Lanka, the most important of which pertain to the future of the Tamil-speaking community on that island.

Conflict Between India and Pakistan

The issue of contention between India and Pakistan that has caused the greatest difficulty and drawn the most international attention is that involving Jammu and Kashmir. In brief, at the time of independence in 1947, the ruling princes of the Indian states (see Chapter 1) were given the choice as to which of the two successors, India or Pakistan, they wished their states to join. Joining at this early stage meant the cession of powers over defense, foreign affairs, and communications to one or the other dominion: as it turned out, it would also mean full integration into the new nation chosen. All but 3 of the more than 500 princes decided quickly to accede to one nation or the other, taking into consideration primarily the geographic location of the state and the religious majority of the people of the state. Two that delayed, Hyderabad (the most populous of the princely states, whose ruler desired independence) and Junagarh (a small state with a Muslim prince who acceded to Pakistan despite its majority Hindu population), were eventually merged with India.

The third, Kashmir (as it is usually called, although officially it is the State of Jammu and Kashmir), remains a problem that has not been formally and finally settled. Had the states been subject to partition as the provinces were, Kashmir might have been divided inasmuch as its minority Hindu population lived in a rather clearly defined area bordering India. Moreover, the majority Muslim community and its also fairly well-defined area could have joined Pakistan; although that action would have left a sparsely populated Buddhist area, Ladakh, on the Chinese border to be argued about. However, the maharaja wished to continue to control the state and continued to desire independence, while the British made it clear that they were not willing to consider this a possibility. The maharaja then concluded "standstill" agreements with both India and Pakistan. These agreements stipulated that the services, such as posts and transport, passing through the new nations' territories into the state would continue unhindered. The maharaja also faced internal demands for constitutional rule from the multicommunal party known as the National Conference, led by Sheikh Muhammad Abdullah, a close friend of Nehru.

In October 1947, Muslim tribesmen from Pakistan began a series of raids into Kashmir and detached some of the northern and western areas of the state as "governments" independent of the ruler in the capital of Srinagar. The northern areas have since been incorporated into Pakistan; the western areas, including Muzaffarabad, have been designated independent "Azad" (free) Kashmir, an entity not recognized by any nation except Pakistan. The threat to Srinagar caused the maharaja to appeal to India for assistance, which was given only after the maharaja acceded to India in October 1947. The accession was accepted only with the proviso that the will of the people would be ascertained after the state returned to normal. The maharaja subsequently installed a new government under Sheikh Abdullah. Because Indian troops were involved, Pakistani troops also entered the war.

India brought the matter of what it called "Pakistani aggression" to the United Nations in January 1948. Resolutions of the Security Council in August 1948 and January 1949 made provisions for a Pakistani withdrawal and the withdrawal of the bulk of the Indian troops preparatory to the holding of a plebiscite under United Nations auspices. A cease-fire became effective on January 1, 1949. A United Nations peacekeeping force was set up in the area (and remains to this day). Several attempts were made by Security Council representatives to implement the plebiscite agreement, but all failed. In 1954, Prime Ministers Jawaharlal Nehru of India and Muhammad Ali Bogra of Pakistan met in an attempt to resolve the difficulties, but they, too, were unsuccessful. Earlier, in 1953, Abdullah had been removed as prime minister of Jammu and Kashmir and arrested on the charge that he was in opposition to the integration of the state into the Indian Union. (Abdullah was released in 1964 and returned to the state as chief minister in 1975, a post he held until his death in 1982.) In 1958, another face-to-face meeting was held between Nehru and Prime Minister Firoz Khan Noon, but this also failed to achieve a mutually satisfactory settlement of the issue.

The question of Kashmir continues to plague Indo-Pakistan relations. Pakistan still demands that the plebiscite be held, as required by the Security Council resolutions. Pakistan's confidence in gaining the state in this manner is probably misplaced, however, given that Abdullah and his immediate successors (his son first, then his son-in-law, and then the son again) appear to have accepted a close relationship with India as best for the state. In turn, India maintains that the regular elections in the state have returned parties favoring integration with India and that these elections have served as a surrogate for the plebiscite; in the view of many observers, however, the elections were far from "free and fair." India has thus responded that the only issue still to be resolved is the "vacation" of the Pakistani "aggression" in the northern area and in Azad Kashmir.

In the summer of 1965, disturbances in Kashmir signified (falsely, as it turned out) to the Pakistanis that Muslim Kashmiris in the Srinagar area, the Vale of Kashmir, were prepared to rebel against Indian rule and, that, with some help from Pakistan, they would be successful. Apparently at the urging of the foreign minister, Zulfiqar Ali Bhutto, President Ayub Khan authorized Pakistani troops to cross the 1949 cease-fire line and to invade Indian-held Kashmir. The result was a disaster for Pakistan. The Pakistanis had initially caused the Indian military situation in the Vale to become difficult by threatening the key land communications line, but India responded by attacking Pakistani Punjab at Lahore and Sialkot in early September. Within two and a half weeks, a cease-fire was arranged. Ayub and Indian Prime Minister Lal Bahadur Shastri met under the auspices of Soviet Prime Minister Kosygin at Tashkent in January 1966 and arranged for a mutual withdrawal both in Kashmir and along the international boundary.

Kashmir also played a limited role in late 1971 when India entered the Bangladesh civil war. The cease-fire in December covered both the eastern (Bangladesh) and western (Kashmir and the Punjab) fronts. The 1949 cease-fire line was modified to a limited extent by the 1972 line of control that separates the territories administered by India and Pakistan (or Azad Kashmir). The issue continued to fester: No Pakistani politician can publicly accept the status quo in Kashmir and expect to survive politically; whereas India could perhaps accept the present line of control as an international boundary. In 1989 and 1990, dissident younger Muslims in the Indian part of Kashmir have raised demands, often violently, that the government of Farooq Abdullah, the Sheikh's son, be dismissed. The new prime minister, V. P. Singh, dismissed Farooq but this did not quiet the situation. It has appeared that many young demonstrators are demanding independence, while others look for union with Pakistan. One thing is clear: They oppose continuation of the union with India, maintaining that India has failed to develop the state and that Farooq and Rajiv Gandhi denied democracy. There is clear "moral" support to the dissidents from Pakistan, but Pakistani help in arms is unproven. The Kashmir issue is, therefore, not settled.

A number of other unresolved disputes have been waged between India and Pakistan over such issues as compensation for refugee properties and the status of minority groups in each country. On the latter issue, Pakistan often complains about the rioting between Hindus and Muslims, with Pakistan taking the view that the former are the perpetrators. The dispute over the boundary in the Rann of Kutch area between the Indian state of Gujarat and the Pakistani province of Sindh was successfully referred to British arbitration.

One major dispute was resolved successfully, however, through international intervention—namely, the division of the waters of the Indus River system. Immediately after partition the rivers from which irrigation canals branched were those running through India (i.e., the Ravi, the Sutlej, and the Beas rivers); but the areas using the water were principally in Pakistan. India naturally wished to utilize these waters to develop and expand its irrigation systems, but in doing so (beginning in the late 1940s) it would leave the Pakistan areas without water. In response, Pakistan threatened to go to war. The flow was restored, but the Indian desire to use the waters was clearly communicated. During the 1950s, the World Bank became involved and offered the two countries several plans for solving the problem. A treaty was signed by Nehru and Ayub Khan in 1960 under which the waters would be divided and international donors, including the Bank, India, and most Western nations would finance the building of replacement works in Pakistan. These works included two large storage dams at Mangla on the Jhelum and Tarbela on the Indus, several barrages designed to divert the waters of those two rivers and the Chenab, and a series of link canals to carry the water from the western rivers into the irrigation system formerly supplied by the eastern Ravi, Beas, and Sutlej. In turn, India was permitted to utilize the waters of the three eastern rivers. The plan, which was completed by the end of the 1960s (except for the dam at Tarbela) has worked exceptionally well. It has also demonstrated that the application of engineering solutions to a problem not charged with communal issues (as was Kashmir) could lead to a settlement that would meet most of the interests of each party.

India in 1971: The Question of Bangladesh

The outbreak of civil war in East Pakistan (see Chapter 17) confronted India with some difficult choices. Many Indians thought that the loss of East Pakistan would greatly weaken Pakistan's threat to India, although the actual outcome does not fully support those expectations. Some groups in India quickly gave support to the Bangladeshis, including those with strong

Hindu orientations and those in West Bengal. Muslim groups were less enthusiastic and often opposed Indian interference in the civil war.

Refugees, many (but certainly not all) Hindu, arrived in India in great numbers—as many as 10 million, according to some estimates. India supported these refugees at great cost, although international assistance eased the burden somewhat. In addition, it was host in Calcutta to the provisional government of Bangladesh.

India provided sanctuary and eventually training and equipment to the Mukti Bahini (national army). And it was gradually brought into the civil war. In early December Indian military formations entered East Pakistan. Dhaka fell to the Indians on December 16, 1971. The third Indo-Pakistan War also entailed several naval engagements in the Bay of Bengal and the bombardment of Karachi. Pakistan initiated the conflict in the west (in the Punjab and in Kashmir) by attacking several Indian airfields, but by the time of the cease-fire India had the initiative there as well. India took custody of an estimated 90,000 Pakistani troops in East Pakistan (now Bangladesh). By all accounts, Pakistan suffered a crushing defeat—a defeat that quickly led to the displacement of the martial law regime of General Agha Muhammad Yahya Khan by the civilian government of Zulfiqar Ali Bhutto.

India had signed a treaty with the Soviet Union in the summer of 1971, and the Soviets supported Indian assistance to the Mukti Bahini; they apparently also cautioned against any Indian attempt at a "final solution" in West Pakistan. The U.S. government, despite strong public opinion to the contrary, appeared to support Pakistan, at least to the extent that it believed that nations should not be divided through the military action of another nation. The same view was taken by the U.N. General Assembly, which debated the issue in December under the Uniting for Peace resolution after the Security Council was unable to act owing to Soviet vetoes. In fact, India's invasion of Pakistan was condemned by the General Assembly; only India and the Soviet group voted against the condemnation. That vote, however, meant little in practical terms as the creation of Bangladesh was by then a *fait accompli.*

India and Pakistan: Simla and After

In some ways India and truncated Pakistan were now back where they had been in 1965: needing an agreement to restore relations and to facilitate a withdrawal. Neither side, but especially India, wanted an international mediator as Kosygin had been in 1966. Prime Minister Indira Gandhi and President Bhutto (as he was then) met in Simla in July 1972 and with difficulty worked out an agreement. Bangladesh, though involved, was not present. The agreement led to the release of both the Pakistani prisoners of war and the much smaller number of Indians held by Pakistan; it also provided for the withdrawal of troops on both sides to the international boundary in the Punjab and Sindh and for a new line of control in Kashmir. Bangladesh eventually acquiesced in the agreement and withdrew its demand that some Pakistani troops be tried as war criminals.

The fall of Bhutto in July 1977, and the replacement of his government by the martial law regime of General Muhammad Zia ul-Haq followed the defeat of Indira Gandhi in the March 1977 election in India. Pakistan, among other South Asian countries, had become concerned over what it perceived to be Indira Gandhi's imperial attitude, and grew even more worried when the new government led by Morarji Desai installed Atal Behari Vajpayee as foreign minister. Vajpayee was leader of the Bharatiya Jana Sangh, a Hindu-oriented party, that in the past had included among its campaign slogans a demand for the reunification of India. Vajpayee and the Desai government, however, took deliberate steps to improve relations with all of India's neighbors, including China. Vajpayee made a successful visit to Pakistan and called for the complete implementation of the Simla agreement. Steps were also taken to establish joint Indo-Pakistan committees on a number of subjects such as tourism and trade. These committees were continued by Indira Gandhi upon her return to office in 1980, as well as by Rajiv Gandhi, who succeeded his mother after her assassination in 1984, and now by V. P. Singh.

This is not to say that India and Pakistan have completely avoided conflict; in verbal form, at least, the conflict persists. To the annoyance of India, Pakistani officials still bring up the Kashmir issue. The two countries also disagree on the Afghan issue. India complains about Pakistani arms purchases and insists that Pakistan is preparing to test a nuclear weapon. Pakistan sees to its own satisfaction Indian interference in the internal problem it has in Sindh, and India reciprocates by seeing a Pakistani hand in the Sikh disturbances in the Punjab and more recently the Muslim opposition in Kashmir. In 1984, before Rajiv Gandhi took office, he predicted that India and Pakistan would be at war before the end of a year. The fact that this did not happen can be considered a measure of the success of the small moves between the two countries. India also welcomed the appointment of Benazir Bhutto as prime minister, with some in each country predicting a new and friendly phase in Indo-Pakistan relations as both she and Rajiv Gandhi were not "burdened" with the memory of partition. These hopes were dashed. Rajiv Gandhi in his last visit to Pakistan in 1989 publicly argued with Benazir Bhutto on such matters as army control of the Pakistani government, nuclear preparations, and assistance to the Sikhs. The Kashmir demonstrations have precluded similar predictions about a V. P. Singh–Bhutto relationship.

India and Bangladesh: Water Problems
and Other Issues

In its initial period of independence, Bangladesh expressed a strong feeling of gratitude for India's aid in the civil war. But this feeling dissipated quickly, despite the twenty-five-year treaty signed in March 1972. The Bangladeshis were hurt by the failure of India to include a Bangladeshi representative at the surrender ceremony in Dhaka on December 16, 1971. They also felt that the Indians were staying on too long after the war, especially in the Chittagong Hill Tracts, to the extent that they had almost become an occupying army. India, the Bangladeshis claimed, had taken charge of the prisoners and had removed almost all of the captured Pakistani military equipment. And the Indian building of the Farakka Barrage, which was completed in 1975, aroused strong anger toward India as well as toward Mujibur Rahman, who seemed unable to do anything to protect Bangladeshi interests.

The reader should understand that during most of any given year, the flow in the Ganges is sufficient that the withdrawal of 90,000 cubic feet per second (cusecs) would make no significant impact on the flow received downstream in Bangladesh. But during the low flow period in April and May, such a withdrawal would all but dry up the Ganges below Farakka. Clearly the needs of both India and Bangladesh could not be met during this low-flow period.

It might be thought that the upper-riparian/lower-riparian conflict could be settled along the lines of the Indus settlement. The political differences involved make that unlikely, however. According to the terms of the Indus settlement, India and Pakistan have almost total control over the rivers that are assigned to them. But this solution could not be applied to the Ganges waters, even if the Brahmaputra waters were taken into account, because both rivers then would be subject to Indian control. The Indians have proposed the building of a link canal that would run from the Brahmaputra at a point just inside Indian territory, across about sixty miles of Bangladeshi territory, and then empty into the Ganges just above Farakka in Indian territory. But the Bangladeshis have objected on the grounds that this plan would give India control of the intake on the Brahmaputra as well as the outflow on the Ganges, and would also displace a large number of Bangladeshis. In turn, Bangladesh has proposed that the flow of the Ganges be controlled by means of storage dams in Nepal on tributaries of the river. But India has objected on the grounds that as the matter is bilateral, a third party should not be introduced into the discussions. The issue has become the subject of regular meetings of a joint rivers commission, but it seems no closer to resolution than it was in the 1970s. In the interim, an agreement has been reached to divide the low-flow run of the river about equally, but, of course, it satisfies neither side.

India and Bangladesh are in dispute over a number of other issues as well. For instance, the land boundary (a question going back to 1947) has not been settled, and the sea boundary is also unresolved. Moreover, in 1984, India proposed to build a fence along its border to prevent Bangladeshis from crossing into Assam and the other eastern hill states—an action Bangladesh considers an affront.

India and Sri Lanka

Some of the problems India has with Pakistan and Bangladesh are avoided in the case of Sri Lanka because the two countries were not governed together as parts of the British Indian Empire and because there is a fairly well-defined sea boundary between the two. Even so, India and Sri Lanka have argued over the ownership of small islets in the Palk Strait. Moreover, the two countries compete over the production of tea, Sri Lanka's most important export crop, but one that is also important to India.

The principal point of contention has been the status of the Tamil-speaking, predominently Hindu population of Sri Lanka (see Chapters 23 and 24). There are two distinct groups of Tamils in Sri Lanka. The "Indian Tamils" (who make up about 6% of the total population[1]) are descendants of Tamil laborers imported into Sri Lanka in the nineteenth century to work on the tea plantations in central Sri Lanka. At a meeting between Prime Ministers Lal Bahadur Shastri of India and Sirimavo Bandaranaike of Sri Lanka in 1965, it was agreed that India would repatriate a substantial proportion of these Indian Tamils while others would be given Sri Lankan citizenship. The agreement has operated sporadically, and many Indian Tamils subject to repatriation remain in Sri Lanka.

On the other hand, the "Sri Lanka Tamils" (about 13% of the population) are descended from Tamils who migrated to Sri Lanka centuries ago, and settled primarily in the northern and eastern parts of the island (although many live in cities such as Colombo). As noted in Part 4, many Tamils feel that they have not been given a proper share in the politics and economy of the island state, and some have resorted to violence, including terrorism, in their demand for a separate state. Much sympathy is given to the Tamil separatists (and autonomists) by residents of the south Indian state of Tamil Nadu.

The Indian government has denied any direct involvement in the agitation and has taken steps to limit or to eliminate support that may be given by the Tamils in India. The non-Congress government of the Tamil Nadu state has also denied any involvement, although for local political reasons it cannot say unequivocally that it opposes Tamil separatism in Sri Lanka—only that it opposes the means being used by the extremists to attain independence. In 1985, India did become directly involved in a diplomatic sense inasmuch as it consulted frequently with Sri Lankan officials. Meetings also took place between Prime Minister Rajiv Gandhi and President Jayawardene, who agreed that the Sri Lankan government should hold a round table conference regarding the terms for a settlement with the Tamil autonomists. Their objective was to reach a settlement with the Tamils acceptable both to them and to the majority Sinhala population on the island. The conferences failed to accomplish their goal and fighting continued. Under an agreement between Sri Lanka and India an Indian "peacekeeping force" was introduced into Sri Lanka in 1987. This, too, failed to pacify the Tamils, although elections did take place in the Tamil areas under Indian protection. Opposition grew throughout Sri Lanka to the Indian presence and the Sri Lankan government demanded withdrawal. Indian troops completed their withdrawal in March 1990.

India and Nepal

Nepal's relations with India are very much rooted in questions of trade and transit and of defense. Regarding the latter issue, India has had troops stationed in Nepal to monitor Chinese movements across the Himalayas in the Tibet region of China. This arrangement has ended, however, as Nepal (which tries to maintain equal relations with its two neighbors) objected.

The trade and transit issue represents a much more pressing problem. The border between China and Nepal is such that commerce is severely restricted by topographical factors. Nepal traditionally trades with India, and its imports and exports (except for the limited amount transported by air) must necessarily go through India. The usual port is Calcutta. India wants Nepal to buy from India all goods that can be obtained there, rather than going elsewhere for less expensive goods. The regular discussions for renewal and revision of trade and transit agreements between the two countries involve a great deal of hard bargaining, and India holds most of the levers of power. India has also permitted a transit agreement with Bangladesh that permits limited use of Chittagong and Chalna as ports and duty-free transport from Bangladesh to Nepal. In 1989, the most recent trade and transit agreement expired. India refused to agree to Nepalese suggestions for changes and imposed a limited blockade on Nepal. The V. P. Singh government has set improved relations with Nepal as one of its goals. It remains to be seen whether the bureaucracy will accept this and also accept a less domineering role for India with regard to Nepal.

Nepal does have leverage in one respect that is of importance to India and potentially to Bangladesh: the rising of many key tributaries of the Ganges in Nepal. Storage and hydroelectric dam sites in Nepal can regulate the flow of the Ganges and can provide power for export from Nepal to India. They could also be part of a solution to the Farakka barrage problem between Bangladesh and India.

Pakistan and Bangladesh

Perhaps to the surprise of many, relations between Pakistan and Bangladesh have improved considerably over the years. Pakistan initially refused to recognize Bangladesh and for a limited time broke diplomatic relations with nations that did accord recognition, a process that was stopped when most of the major countries began relations with Dhaka. The Islamic summit conference in Lahore in February 1974 saw the mediation of several Muslim leaders and the eventual invitation to Mujibur Rahman to join the conference. Bhutto paid a state visit to Bangladesh in June of the same year, following a conference among India, Pakistan, and Bangladesh in April. During that latter conference, Mujib dropped his demand for the trials of 195 Pakistani prisoners of war, and Bhutto expressed "regret" for "any crimes" that may have been committed. The exchange of military and civil detainees followed. Formal relations were established in 1976. Presidents Ziaur Rahman and Ershad have visited Pakistan and President Zia-ul-Haq and Prime Minister Benazir Bhutto have visited Bangladesh. The two countries often agree on "Islamic" positions, some of which oppose the views of India. For example, both Pakistan and Bangladesh supported the complete withdrawal of Soviet troops from Afghanistan under a negotiated settlement, while India voted with the Soviets in the United Nations.

Trade between Pakistan and Bangladesh has increased. Travel is relatively free; each nation's airline regularly flies to the other. Pakistani banks have reopened in Bangladesh, and there is some prospect of Pakistani investment as well. But problems do remain, including the division of the assets of united Pakistan between the two successors and the transfer of "Biharis" to Pakistan. Nonetheless, the very strong feelings that understandably characterized Bangladeshi opinion in the immediate aftermath of the civil war have all but dissipated, as has the hope in Pakistan of a reunited Muslim state in South Asia.

South Asian Association for Regional Cooperation (SAARC)

In August 1983 the seven South Asian nations signed an agreement in New Delhi formally establishing the South Asian Regional Cooperation (SARC). The group was renamed when the 1983 agreement was ratified at a summit meeting in Dhaka in December 1985. It is now the South Asian Association for Regional Cooperation (SAARC).

SAARC was founded on the efforts of President Ziaur Rahman, who was the first head of government to visit each of the other four major states of South Asia (India, Pakistan, Sri Lanka, and Nepal). Ziaur Rahman preached the importance, as he saw it, of the states coming together to work on economic, social, and technological matters as a prelude to political cooperation. India resisted at first as it saw SAARC as a limitation on its strength; meanwhile, Pakistan feared that India would dominate the group. However, both were eventually persuaded that a limited regional group would be advantageous to all.

SAARC generally avoids political matters and strictly bilateral issues, but it has agreed to explore a wide range of social, economic, environmental, and technological matters. Though it is a far cry from a common market, it does represent a promising start toward restoring a level of cooperation that has been absent since the departure of the British. The reader should note, however, that trade among the countries of South Asia (with the exception of Nepal and India) is quite limited; each of the nations trades more with developed countries than with its neighbors. If trade within South Asia were to expand, however, India would surely benefit the most. Further, the annual summit meetings provide a means for private discussions between heads of government; these discussions do breach the formal ban on political consultations.

South Asia and the World

The perception of most nations outside South Asia is that India was the successor state to the British when imperial power in the region was ended in 1947. Pakistan has been viewed by many as a state created simply to satisfy the desire to combine religion and state—a stance appalling to many Western democracies which had long since divided church and state. Yet, Pakistan was admitted to the United Nations with only a single negative vote, from Afghanistan—as a result of that country's dispute with Pakistan over the future of the Pushtun-speaking area in the North-West Frontier Province.

India thus started with a great advantage over both Pakistan and Ceylon (as Sri Lanka was then called). Its major leaders, Mahatma Gandhi and Jawaharlal Nehru, were hailed as outstanding among many intellectual and political observers, whereas Muhammad Ali Jinnah was (erroneously) viewed as a religious fanatic. India was an original member of the League of Nations (one of its delegates, the Aga Khan, had been president), and its military personnel (many of them Punjabi Muslims who became Pakistanis) had performed with great distinction in World War II. Hardly a minor advantage was India's inheritance of the name *India,* although some Indians were willing to lose the advantage and call the nation *Bharat.*

India's Relations Outside the Region

It is interesting to note that India rejected dominion status within the British Commonwealth of Nations in its Lahore resolution of 1930 but accepted that status at independence in 1947. When India determined to become a republic under the constitution of 1950, the pattern of the Commonwealth was altered. Previously, all members of the Commonwealth had accepted the British monarch as monarch of the Commonwealth member as well (as in the case of Canada or Australia). It was agreed that India could remain a member of the Commonwealth as a republic but accept the British monarch as occupying a symbolic position as "Head of the Commonwealth." The pattern applied to India has been followed by a large number of the members of the Commonwealth that have become independent since World War II.

India had already set another precedent for the colonies of Great Britain by organizing a political party that looked beyond the achievement of freedom to the creation of a polity, economy and society to follow the initial step of independence. Many of the parties in other colonies used the word "Congress" to denote a party seeking freedom. Relations between the Indian National Congress and other freedom movements were often close—a fact that India could build on after independence to assert its leadership in what is now called the Third World. Nehru, who participated in the Bandung (Indonesia) Conference in 1955, is credited with being one of the three principal leaders involved in forming the Non-Aligned Movement (the other two are Nasser of Egypt and Tito of Yugoslavia).

Nonalignment was a part of Nehru's creed. To him it meant avoidance of alignment with either of the two blocs led by the superpowers, the United States and the Soviet Union. What it did not mean was neutrality. Nehru maintained that India reserved the right to take whatever position on an issue that best served the country's interests. However, such interests often, indeed usually, seemed to U.S. governments to favor the Soviet view over the American.

Nehru's stance on nonalignment was seriously eroded when his daughter, Indira Gandhi, signed a treaty of friendship with the Soviet Union in 1971. The agreement stated that the two countries would consult with each other when either was threatened by a third party. India under Nehru had protested strongly when Pakistan joined the CENTO and SEATO alliances with the West in the 1950s on the basis that the alliance arrangements would bring one of the superpowers into the subcontinent. This prospect apparently did not concern Indira Gandhi in 1971.

India's close relations with the Soviet Union were reinforced by the visit of Rajiv Gandhi to Moscow in 1985, very soon after his assumption of power. The Soviet Union is by far the major supplier of military equipment to the Indian military as well as an important trading partner. It also provided both diplomatic and military support during India's conflict with China in 1962 and its conflict with Pakistan over Bangladesh in 1971. India, however, maintained a somewhat more neutral stance during its leadership of the Non-Aligned Movement beginning in 1983, although it is possible that this neutrality is evident only in comparison to India's predecessor, Cuba. India favored the Soviet withdrawal from Afghanistan but continues to support strongly the Soviet puppet regime in that country. The difficulties the Soviets face within the Warsaw Pact area and within the Soviet Union itself have not affected Indo-Soviet relations. Nonetheless, India does find itself looking to the industrialized countries for much needed technology in contrast to earlier contacts with the Soviets, especially in the military field.

India's relations with China appeared to be close after the communist forces gained power in 1949. The slogan *Hindi-Chini bhai bhai* ("Indians and Chinese are brothers") was frequently heard. However, relations cooled when India discovered that China had built a road between Sinkiang and Tibet across the Aksai Chin in Jammu and Kashmir, which India believed to be its territory. China also disputed the line in the northeast, the McMahon Line, which Britain, Tibet, and China agreed upon in an meeting at Simla in 1914. India accused China of committing "cartographic aggression" because the latter claimed much of northeast India, all of Bhutan and parts of Nepal, Kashmir, and Uttar Pradesh. In October 1962 war broke out between China and India, and the Indian forces suffered a humiliating defeat—especially in the Northeast Frontier Agency (now Arunachal Pradesh). China withdrew unilaterally but made it clear to all that India had been given a "black eye." Relations have since improved somewhat (e.g., ambassadors have once again been exchanged) but India remains adamant in its demand that the territory occupied by China in the Aksai Chin must be returned to India. China has proposed the application of the "watershed principle" in both the northeast (i.e., essentially the McMahon Line) and in the Aksai Chin, because this would give China the area of the road.

India and the United States have what might be called a "love-hate" relationship. U.S. investment in India has been slight compared with that of the British, for historical reasons as well as those related to conditions of investment, regulation, controls of returns, and, often, the corruption of the Indian bureaucracy. India, as mentioned above, strongly opposes the United States' relationship with Pakistan, especially its provision of sophisticated military equipment to Pakistan. At the official level India has also opposed the United States on such issues as Korea and Vietnam. At the same time, India is eager to obtain technological information from the United States (a major point in the 1985 visit of Rajiv Gandhi to Washington). Investment by U.S. firms has increased and in many cases is in highly technological fields such as computer software. Some relaxation of Indian regulations has contributed to this. However, the ideological positions of some members of the Singh cabinet who oppose or fear foreign investment could stem or reverse this flow of technology. The United States remains for most Indians the preferred place of study and eventual migration.

Many Americans will recall the idealistic lectures delivered by Nehru and his UN representative, Krishna Menon. Although Mahatma Gandhi is remembered as a successful practitioner of nonviolent protest (a stance adopted by Martin Luther King, for example), the sanctimonious statements of Nehru, Menon, Indira Gandhi, and even Rajiv Gandhi are viewed by many Americans as tiresome at best. They are not likely to forget that India has, indeed, resorted to violence to meet its national interests, as in 1961 in case of Goa, Daman, and Diu, areas legally held by Portugal.

Pakistan Draws on Its Islamic Card

Faced with the disadvantage of being the new country in the division of India and of being in conflict with its larger co-inheritor of the British raj, Pakistan believed that it had to look outside the subcontinent for possible allies in defending itself against what it thought would eventually be an Indian bid to reunify South Asia. That this was not India's goal failed to mitigate Pakistan's fears.

Pakistan accepted Western offers to join the ring of security pacts built in the 1950s to close the gap between U.S. commitments in Europe (through NATO) and those in East Asia (following the Korean war experience). Pakistan in 1955 joined the South East Asia Treaty Organization (SEATO) along with Thailand and the Philippines, and the Central Treaty Organization (CENTO, originally the Baghdad Pact) along with Iraq (briefly, until 1958), Iran, and Turkey. Its negotiations with the United States also brought U.S. military assistance, through agreements initiated in 1954. This assistance met with strong objections from India, which perceived that the purposes of the United States and Pakistan were very different. Pakistan accepted the weapons as a protection against India, whereas the United States provided them in an effort to build strength against possible Soviet or Chinese action.

The course of United States–Pakistan relations has been rocky. The United States cut off military supplies to both India and Pakistan in 1965, and has never significantly supplied India since that time. (The U.S. military supply relationship with India was brief, following the Sino-Indian conflict of 1962.) Supplies to Pakistan resumed on a very limited basis in the late 1960s but were curtailed again during the Bangladesh civil war in 1971. It was not until the Soviet invasion of Afghanistan in December 1979 that a new offer was made to Pakistan—the Carter administration had declared that Pakistan was a "frontline" state. Pakistan rejected the Carter offer but accepted the larger bid by the Reagan administration in 1981 to provide

Pakistan $1.6 billion in military supplies and a similar amount in economic aid over a five-year period. On the expiration of the agreement, a new program began that includes more economic than military assistance.

Worrisome to both the United States and India has been Pakistan's nuclear program, as it is thought to be aimed at the development of nuclear weapons, despite Pakistani denials. India successfully tested a nuclear device in 1974, prompting a drive by Pakistan for equivalence. A number of U.S. laws pertaining to nonproliferation appear to have been violated. In early 1979, the United States terminated economic assistance to Pakistan (there was no military assistance at that time). The program of both economic and military assistance begun in 1981 has required a number of presidential waivers of the provisions of these laws. In the post-Soviet withdrawal period, it seems likely that these provisions may be more strictly applied to Pakistan. It must be stated, however, that Pakistan has made a number of proposals that aim to end both Indian and Pakistani arms programs; these have been rejected by India.

Pakistan's relations with the Soviet Union, never very close to begin with, were severely damaged by the invasion of Afghanistan. By contrast, Pakistan has had close and valuable relations with China proceeding in particular from an agreement regarding the international border concluded in 1962. The conflict between China and India also brought Pakistan and China closer. The Chinese supported Pakistan diplomatically in 1965 and 1971, and China has provided an important amount of military assistance. It is also reported, but not confirmed, that China may have assisted Pakistan in its development of nuclear technology. Moreover, Pakistan played a key role in facilitating the visit of Henry Kissinger to China in 1971.

Particularly since 1971, Pakistan has expanded its ties with the Islamic countries of the Middle East. The religious ties are close, but the economic ties have been of even greater importance. Trade has expanded greatly, and Pakistani migrant workers have found employment in the Gulf states, Libya, and Iran. Remittances from workers abroad account for the largest single item in Pakistan's foreign exchange earnings. Pakistan also has military relationships with several countries including Saudi Arabia, Jordan, Oman, and the United Arab Emirates. In addition, a Pakistani, Syed Sharifuddin Pirzada, is the secretary general of the Islamic Conference organization.

Bangladesh Emerges

At independence Bangladesh found itself in close association with India and the Soviet Union and was subject to delayed recognition by the United States and China. The cooling of relations with India has been mentioned above; there was a similar cooling of relations with the Soviet Union, especially over the number of Soviets engaged in such projects as the clearing of Chittagong harbor. Relations are now correct but not cordial.

The United States recognized Bangladesh in early 1972, and the anger that resulted from the presumed U.S. "tilt" toward Pakistan in the freedom war has largely dissipated. Some of Mujibur Rahman's cabinet colleagues were opposed to close ties with the United States, but U.S. assistance was deeply needed and, in fact, available. Visits to the United States by Mujib, Ziaur Rahman, and Ershad have helped bring about developmental assistance, but the occasionally requested military assistance has not been forthcoming.

China's recognition of Bangladesh followed that of Pakistan. The Chinese have provided some economic assistance as well as a small amount of military aid, primarily for the air force.

The location of Bangladesh has prompted it to reach out to Southeast Asia while its majority religion has drawn it close to the countries of the Middle East. Southeast Asia provides a limited market and is a source of open market purchases of rice, whereas the Middle East has been a source of economic assistance and is an outlet for migrant workers from Bangladesh. Of course, Bangladesh receives economic assistance from many other donors, as well. A highly skilled diplomatic endeavor keeps this assistance flowing.

Sri Lanka: From Ties East to Ties West

Following independence, Sri Lanka, under the leadership of the United National party of D. S. Senanayake and Sir John Kotelawala, generally maintained close ties with the West—especially with Great Britain, which provided the largest market for Sri Lankan goods and also maintained a naval base at Trincomalee. The somewhat leftist regimes of the two Bandaranaikes ended the naval arrangement and Sri Lanka began to associate more closely with the East, including several close trade ties with China. This, at least, was the view of many in the West, although many Sri Lankans would aver that Sri Lanka was actually moving toward a stance of more balanced nonalignment. Sri Lanka annoyed India in 1962 by joining in a Third World proposal to end the Sino-Indian War—one that called for mediation rather than an acceptance of the Indian view. Sri Lanka also became the leader of the Non-Aligned Movement in 1976 and gained greater recognition of its position in the world.

The latest return to power of the United National party has resulted in a tilt toward the West in international positions (the reverse was true perhaps during the period of Sirimavo Bandaranaike). The tendency of Presidents Junius Jayawardene and Ranansinghe Premadasa to look more toward a market economy has been interpreted, not necessarily correctly, as reflecting a Western bias in international relations. At the same time, Sri Lanka remains at the forefront of a movement to declare the Indian Ocean a nuclear-free zone and to remove superpower activity from the region.

Afghanistan and the Direct Presence of a Superpower

The Soviet invasion of Afghanistan in December 1979 resulted, for the first time since the departure of the British, in the direct involvement of a superpower on the border of South Asia. Americans have described Pakistan as a "frontline" state and have provided economic and military assistance to Pakistan and military supplies to the Afghan *mujahidin* (freedom fighters). Nearly 3 million Afghans have fled to Pakistan and perhaps another million to Iran. Pakistan, despite international assistance, has found the cost of supporting these refugees to be a great burden on its economy and on its political and social systems. It has worked through the United Nations in an effort to find a means by which Soviet troops can be removed from Afghanistan and a nonaligned government free of outside interference can be established in Kabul. The first of these goals has been met as the Soviets completed their withdrawal in 1989. But the prospect of an end to the civil war and a peaceful, nonaligned Afghanistan seems remote.

India has not specifically condemned the Soviet action in Afghanistan, having seemingly accepted the Soviet argument that the Soviets were invited into the country by the government of Babrak Karmal. India has maintained instead that Afghanistan should be free of all foreign interference, implying that Pakistani, Iranian, and U.S. assistance to those Afghans who opposed the communist regimes prior to Karmal (those of Taraki and Amin) began before the Soviets were asked in by Karmal.

Interests of the Superpowers

U.S. interests in South Asia fall into four categories. First, the United States would like to see the nations of South Asia settle disputes through negotiations rather than open conflict. Second, the United States supports democratic regimes responsive to the wishes of the people in each nation. Third, U.S. support will be provided to the extent possible for the economic development of each nation with the goal of reasonable standards of living for all. Finally, the United States neither seeks a position of primacy in the area nor wishes to see any other outside power gain such a position. There is, of course, little direct action the United States could take to achieve these goals other than providing economic and technical assistance. Indeed, U.S. security requirements tend to take precedence over the goals for the region, as many observers have assumed to be the case to the military assistance provided to Pakistan—a country that, at the time, had a poor record on democratic institutions and human rights.

The interests of China are generally compatible with those of the United States. China fears an expanded Soviet presence in South Asia and accuses both the Soviet Union and India of seeking "hegemony" in the region. China therefore works closely with Pakistan and Bangladesh on many issues. China maintains that it is prepared to negotiate its outstanding border problems with India, but not in accordance with India's demands for recognition of Indian sovereignty on the basis of Indian maps.

The Soviet Union has anchored its policy toward South Asia on its close relationship (and, now, a treaty) with India. In return, it receives diplomatic support from India on a wide variety of issues ranging from Afghanistan to Kampuchea. India finds the alliance useful as the Soviets not only constitute a good market, but more important they supply military equipment. At the same time, some Indians believe that the Soviet Union is far behind the West in industrial, if not also military, technology.

A Regional Block: Pitfalls and Promises

The formal establishment of SAARC in 1983 raised the hope that disputes within the region would be moderated and solutions found—in short, that there would be no repetition of the three wars fought between India and Pakistan in 1948, 1965, and 1971. However, the economic links between the member countries are minimal inasmuch as intraregional trade is infrequent (Indo-Nepal and Indo-Bhutanese trade are exceptions). Cultural links are also minimal, as the three largest states have been separated from each other for more than forty years. Calcutta, for instance, is no longer the prime magnet for Bangladeshi Bengalis, nor is Lahore for Indian Punjabis; and although there are many Islamic pilgrimage sites in India and some Sikh shrines in Pakistan, they are important to only a small number of people. Still, SAARC plays a great potential role in such areas as technology, tourism, meteorology, and trade. The realization of its potential would, in fact, do much to lessen conflict and improve relations in the region.

The problem for the six smaller states is the dominance of India. Leo Rose has described India's views as constituting the "Indira doctrine" for the subcontinent. This doctrine holds that the other states should recognize India's preeminent place in international affairs and should not take positions at variance with those taken by India.[2] It also insists on bilateral political relations with its neighbors and opposes "internationalization" of disputes. The smaller states are truly under India's shadow.

Notes

1. These percentages were provided in Robert N. Kearney, "Sri Lanka in 1984: The Politics of Communal Violence," *Asian Survey,* vol. 25, no. 2 (February 1985), p. 257, citing Department of Census and Statistics, *Census of Population and Housing, Sri Lanka, 1981* (Colombo: Department of Census and Statistics, 1981).

2. Leo Rose used the term *Indira doctrine* during a session on Bangladesh at the Foreign Service Institute, Arlington, Virginia, November 27, 1984.

Suggested Readings

The reader should consult *Asian Survey,* vol. 25, no. 4 (April 1985), which is devoted to articles on the South Asian Association for Regional Cooperation, and the February issues of *Asian Survey* each year, which contain country articles on the South Asian nations (except Bhutan and the Maldives). Each of these latter articles includes a section on the foreign policy of the preceding year.

B. M. Abbas A. T. *The Ganges Water Dispute* (Dhaka: University Press, Ltd., 1982).

William J. Barnds. *India, Pakistan and the Great Powers* (New York: Praeger Publishers, 1972).

Craig Baxter. *Bangladesh: A New Nation in an Old Setting* (Boulder, Colo.: Westview Press, 1984).

Zulfikar Ali Bhutto. *The Myth of Independence* (Lahore: Oxford University Press, 1969).

Jayasree Biswas. *US-Bangladesh Relations* (Calcutta: Minerva, 1984).

S. M. Burke. *Mainsprings of Indian and Pakistani Foreign Policies* (Minneapolis: University of Minnesota Press, 1974).

————. *Pakistan's Foreign Policy: An Historical Analysis* (London: Oxford University Press, 1973).

Carnegie Endowment for International Peace. *Nuclear Weapons and South Asian Security* (Washington, D.C.: Carnegie Endowment for International Peace, 1988).

Sudarshan Chawla. *The Foreign Relations of India* (Encino, Calif.: Dickenson, 1976).

A. J. Cottrell and R. W. Burrell. *The Indian Ocean: Its Politics, Economics and Military Importance* (New York: Praeger Publishers, 1972).

Robert H. Donaldson. *Soviet Policy Toward India: Ideology and Strategy* (Cambridge, Mass.: Harvard University Press, 1974).

V. P. Dutt. *India's Foreign Policy* (New Delhi: Vikas, 1985).

Sumit Ganguly. *The Origins of War in South Asia* (Boulder, Colo.: Westview Press, 1986).

Sisir Gupta. *Kashmir: A Study in India-Pakistan Relations* (Bombay: Asia Publishing House, 1966).

Robert L. Hardgrave, Jr. *India Under Pressure: Prospects for Political Stability* (Boulder, Colo.: Westview Press, 1984), especially chapter 3 on foreign policy.

Selig Harrison. *In Afghanistan's Shadow: Baluch Nationalism and Soviet Temptation* (New York: Carnegie Endowment, 1981).

Robert Jackson. *South Asian Crisis: India-Pakistan-Bangladesh* (New Delhi: Vikas, 1978).

Rodney W. Jones. "The Military and Security in Pakistan," in Craig Baxter, ed., *Zia's Pakistan: Politics and Stability in a Frontline State* (Boulder, Colo.: Westview Press, 1985).

Alastair Lamb. *Crisis in Kashmir, 1947–1966* (London: Routledge and Kegan Paul, 1966).

Chih H. Lu. *The Sino-Indian Border Dispute* (Westport, Conn.: Greenwood Press, 1986).

Surjit Mansingh. *India's Search for Power: Indira Gandhi's Foreign Policy, 1966–1982* (Beverly Hills, Calif.: Sage, 1984).

Neville Maxwell. *India's China War* (London: Jonathan Cape, 1970).

Aloys A. Michel. *The Indus Rivers: A Study of the Effects of Partition* (New Haven, Conn.: Yale University Press, 1967).

Norman D. Palmer. *The United States and India: The Dimensions of Influence* (New York: Praeger, 1984).

Hasan Askari Rizvi. *Internal Strife and External Intervention: India's Role in the Civil War in East Pakistan [Bangladesh]* (Lahore: Progressive Publishers, 1981).

Leo E. Rose and John T. Scholz. *Nepal: Profile of a Himalayan Kingdom* (Boulder, Colo.: Westview Press, 1980).

Lloyd I. Rudolph and Suzanne Hoeber Rudolph. *The Regional Imperative: U.S. Foreign Policy Towards South Asian States* (New Delhi: Concept, 1980).

S. Nihal Singh. *The Yogi and the Bear: A Study of Indo-Soviet Relations* (Riverdale, Md.: Riverdale Co., 1986).

Anwar H. Syed. *China and Pakistan: Diplomacy of an Entente Cordiale* (Amherst, Mass.: University of Massachusetts Press, 1974).

Shirin Taher-Kheli. *The United States and Pakistan: The Evolution of an Influence Relationship* (New York: Praeger Publishers, 1982).

Shashi Tharoor. *Reasons of State: Political Developments and India's Foreign Policy Under Indira Gandhi, 1966–1977* (New Delhi: Vikas, 1982).

Raju G.C. Thomas. *Indian Security Policy* (Princeton, N.J.: Princeton University Press, 1986).

Yaacov Y.I. Vertzberger. *Misconceptions in Foreign Policy Making: The Sino-Indian Conflict, 1959–1962* (Boulder, Colo.: Westview Press, 1984).

————. *The Enduring Entente: Sino-Pakistan Relations, 1960–1980* (New York: Praeger Publishers, 1983).

Lawrence Ziring, ed. *The Sub-continent in World Affairs: India, Its Neighbors and the Great Powers* (New York: Praeger Publishers, 1982).

CONCLUSION: DEMOCRACY AND AUTHORITARIANISM IN SOUTH ASIA

It is often said that India is the world's largest democracy; that Pakistan is a model of a praetorian state; that Bangladesh, reputedly an "international basket case" economically, is also one politically; and that Sri Lanka is a model democracy inasmuch as it has a two-party system and changes rulers often. It is also frequently noted that each of these nations has inherited various liberal British traditions, despite the fact that they have also been bequeathed the heritage of viceregal rule and the "steel frame" that accompanied it. Each of these descriptions contains a kernel of truth, perhaps— but they all omit a reference to the social backgrounds of the four nation-states.

Before looking more closely at the four countries together, we must review two definitions that are pertinent to this chapter. The term *democracy,* for instance, is used in a broad sense, with no differentiation made between such adjectival prefixes as *representative, constitutional,* and *liberal.* What is meant, therefore, is a system of government (a regime, if one prefers) in which the authorities are responsible to elected representatives of the people and operate under a freely enacted constitution, in a climate which is characterized by open channels of access such that interest groups, political parties, and the press are free to speak and act. The term *South Asia* refers, of course, to the seven nations joined together in the South Asian Association for Regional Cooperation (SAARC).

Preceding chapters have dealt with the regime developments in each of the four major countries (including brief descriptions of those in the other three). They have also revealed the social background and political cultures of each state. Now we turn to a summary of comparisons and contrasts among those states as well as a proposal of some tentative ideas regarding the future course of each of the countries.

South Asia in 1990:
The Crisis of Nation Building

As this chapter is being written, the record may seem especially dismal. India is facing major problems with nation building in such areas as the Punjab, Kashmir, and Assam. Pakistan is attempting to transform its regime from one of martial law to one in which a president and a prime minister share power but with the military in the background. How successful this will be is not yet known. Bangladesh remains under a military ruler despite the trappings of a democratic system. Sri Lanka and Pakistan also face serious nation-building problems: The conflict between the Sinhalese and the Tamils continues in Sri Lanka, and Pakistan has to contend with Sindhi, Baluch, and Pathan subnationalisms. Thus the tenuous process of nation building in South Asia is far from complete.

Structural Differentiation

The record reflecting the establishment of specialized structures in governmental and nongovernmental areas is a mixed one. India became an independent state in 1947 with a number of advantages over other nations that would achieve independence in the following decades. It had in place most of the attributes of an efficient state: a functioning civil service, a capable and proven military, rather well-defined borders, and a system of representative government that, while it was not created on the basis of direct adult suffrage, nonetheless reflected the political views of the nation. More than this, it had sufficiently developed nongovernmental structures, such as an established political party that performed many of the roles required for interest aggregation. Few countries, certainly neither Pakistan nor Bangladesh, could boast either a party or a leader whose continuity and dedication to democratic norms over a long period could match this combination. The Congress brought under its umbrella a wide variety of Indians (admittedly only a small fraction of the Muslims) who were united not only in their demand for Indian independence but also on what shape India should take after independence. By contrast, the Muslim League and the Awami League were in essence single-issue and single-leader parties that lacked differentiated substructures. Elites in both nations had thought little about the form Pakistan and Bangladesh should take politically, economically, and socially after independence. Sri Lanka's United National party lay somewhere between these two poles, perhaps closer to the Congress.

Constitution Making: Institution Building

The enactment of a constitution was for India a relatively rapid and unanimous process, even given the disagreements that arose on certain issues and the significant modifications that were soon needed in answer to political requirements, such as the reorganization of India into linguistically based states. Nehru was able to enshrine his four principal objectives: democracy, socialism, secularism (in its broadest meaning), and nonalignment. Sri Lanka was also able to frame its constitution along well-trodden democratic lines. But Pakistan was unable to do so and has thus experienced a series of constitutions; the place of Islam and the question of parity between the two widely separated wings were basic issues of dispute. Finally, Bangladesh wrote a document quickly but, like Pakistan, has subverted it regularly.

Free, fair, and timely elections and the willingness of the party in power to accept the results of the elections are essential for legitimacy and stability in a political system. They are also among the measures of an open society. In the 1950s, the Congress acknowledged defeats in some states, although the instability of the non-Congress governments usually required early elections in which the Congress was the winner. But this system did not continue. The future was perhaps foreshadowed when the first toppling of a state government through central (Congress) manipulation, Kerala in 1959, took place. What thereafter became an almost regular practice was the tendency of a central government, whether Congress or Janata, to seize on any sign of weakness to displace elected state governments headed by rival parties or coalitions. Pakistan, the only other federal government in South Asia, has regularly followed the pattern of dismissing provincial governments and forcing changes in provincial leadership. Both actions were taken in the pre-Ayub period as well as under Bhutto. In the former case, even the central government was changed at the whim of the head of state. Such frustration of the aspirations of the regional elites by central governments has frequently led to the installation of state and provincial governments in India and Pakistan that have been contrary to the expressed will of the people.

Periods of Authoritarianism

The dismissal of a state government in Gujarat and the strong popular opposition to a poorly run ministry in Bihar were contributing factors to the nineteen-month emergency imposed by Indira Gandhi in June 1975. The emergency was retained until after her defeat in the delayed parliamentary election of March 1977. A number of constitutional amendments were enacted, a retroactive one that prohibited calling into question the election of high officers of state, especially the prime minister, and another that greatly extended the powers of the government with respect to detention of opponents. The parliament also approved an extension of the term of the lower house from five years to six, thus avoiding an election scheduled for 1976. Hence, a crisis of legitimacy was created in India. It is to Indira Gandhi's credit, however, that when she permitted the election to be held in 1977 (perhaps through miscalculation), the voting was fair and she accepted the result—her crushing personal and party defeat—without challenge. Indeed, her action restored the legitimacy of the system.

Pakistan has avoided or voided elections on occasion. Its government delayed a poll for three years (from 1951 to 1954) in East Bengal when it became clear that the Muslim League had lost influence there. The military struck in 1958 before the scheduled 1959 elections could be held. And in 1977, Bhutto used fraud to gain the desired result and then was ousted. Meanwhile, Bangladesh now cannot agree on a framework for a new election following the questionable elections of the Ershad period. In both countries there are forces that pose challenges to the stability and legitimacy of their systems. In Sri Lanka, a constitutional referendum extended the life of parliament well beyond its original five years, as was done earlier when Sirimavo Bandaranaike lengthened the term of the seventh parliament by two years. Such actions, however, do not bode well for the stability and legitimacy of the Sri Lankan government.

Each of the South Asian countries inherited laws from the British that both permitted preventive detention and could be used to restrict severely the right of assembly. These laws have been used frequently because they were not repealed after independence.

Toleration of opposing views is a standard by which the degree of political participation and level of openness of a political system can be tested. Nehru, for instance, vigorously opposed political parties and politicians who themselves opposed the Congress. But he did so within the limits of a free society, both in public and on the floor of parliament. Toleration fell to a new low when his daughter imposed the emergency in India, and there remained, even under Rajiv Gandhi, the concern that an emergency once tried could be repeated again. Sri Lanka, with its reputation for political openness, suffered a setback when it banned political activity by former Prime Minister Sirimavo Bandaranaike, expelled from parliament members of the Tamil United Liberation Front, and then failed to hold by-elections for the seats. The authoritarian regime of the later Mujib period and the subsequent periods of martial law in Bangladesh have restricted expression of dissent in that country. However, among the four nations the record of Pakistan on political participation and individual rights must be judged the poorest. The term *enemy of Pakistan* was used in Jinnah's time to describe those who oppose Urdu as a national language and has been used freely since to describe those who oppose almost any policy of the leadership. During Bhutto's regime it seemed that opposition had literally become treason.[1] Now, following the steps taken by Zia-ul-Haq toward Islamization of law, opposition could become heresy as well.

The British Heritage

British supremacy in the subcontinent is often dated from 1757, when the battle of Plassey was fought in Bengal. But that event did not bring all of British India under the East India Company; indeed, most of what is Pakistan today was not taken by the British until the mid-nineteenth century. Thus the areas that make up Pakistan and much of northern and western India have had a much briefer spell of British rule than Bengal and the areas immediately adjacent to Madras and Bombay. There are important differences. For example, British control over the Punjab was exercised very largely through key "Punjab chiefs," who, though not quite Indian princes, were hereditary landlords of great power in their local areas. Most were Muslim or Sikh; only a small number were Hindus. In the Punjab, Sindh, the NWFP, and British Balochistan, this system did not encourage the development of democratic rule; rather, it reinforced traditional authoritarianism, which persists. The liberal ideas that the Nehrus and other early Congress leaders drew upon, supported by the Morleys in London, did not apply to Pakistan. They also did not apply fully to what is now Bangladesh, where the Muslims were most often subservient to absentee Hindu landlords. The point of all this is that the people of these areas have as a common heritage an authoritarian system instituted or prolonged by the British—a system that, when combined with the "steel frame" aspects of British rule, severely diminishes the prospects for liberal democracy.

The British government system in India was also anything but democratic. As it evolved, certain rather liberalizing concessions were made, such as those permitting Indians to become elected members of councils and to enter the civil services. Similar acts applied to Sri Lanka. But the final act for India, that of 1935, still left the ultimate authority at the center squarely in the hands of the viceroy/governor general. India and Sri Lanka very quickly curtailed the power of the governor general, but Pakistan did not.

As noted, the British ruled India and Sri Lanka through a "steel frame," at the top of which were the elitist civil services and other central services. At the base of a pyramid that culminated in governorships and memberships in the governor general's council was the district administration, where young Britishers and later Indians and Sri Lankans became masters of an area which even then averaged more than a half-million people (in India). The tasks of this "steel frame" were revenue collection, maintenance of law and order, and coordination of other governmental operations. The new states of Sri Lanka, Pakistan, and India (and later Bangladesh) inherited these tasks as well as the partially rooted liberal principles held by the Congress and the United National party. The military, too, was disciplined and authoritarian. In two of the countries—namely, Pakistan and Bangladesh—

it has violated the boundary between civilian and military authority and has assumed governing powers.

A balance sheet drawn up shortly after independence for Pakistan, India, and Sri Lanka shows that in state-building functions and institutions the British tradition was strong but not necessarily liberal-democratic. Thus, the frequently mentioned liberal background supposedly available to Pakistan, India, and Sri Lanka in 1947 and 1948 may be very much overstated.

Prospects for the Development of a Secular Political Culture

The place of religions in South Asia is a point that needs to be reiterated. The doctrine of Islam, as a revealed religion, is believed to be immutable but is nonetheless subject to many interpretations. Revealed, pervasive religions are not, it can be argued, conducive to democracy and a secular political culture as we in the West know it. Unreformed Islam, like unreformed Christianity, allows little or no room for dissent or alternative proposals. Jinnah's cry of "enemies of Pakistan" can be taken to mean "enemies of Islam" for those who have ventured to disagree with Zia-ul-Haq's policy of Islamization.

Bangladesh has not yet moved toward Islamization of its society and politics and, indeed, it may never do so. Those who have lived in each of the two Muslim successors to the British Indian Empire are often struck by the personal nature of Bangladeshi Islam, by the sense that one's relationship with one's god is one's own affair and not that of the state. The situation is, of course, quite different in Pakistan where many wish the state would assume the role of enforcer of Islamic purity. Bangladesh thus may have better prospects than Pakistan for the development of a political culture based on secular principles.

Hinduism appears to be much less inhibiting of democratic ideas and more inclined toward separation of politics from religion. Caste associations[2] can be and are used as interest groups and as mobilizers of votes, but, as India modernizes, many competing interests will place claims on the political behavior of Indians and cut across the ascriptive boundaries that separate them. Religion divides India sharply just as language and the cleavage between "caste Hindus" and "untouchables" (Gandhi's Harijans, the Children of God) have done. But despite the recent violence in the Punjab, Kashmir, and Assam, the repeated oppression of the Harijans, and the ethnic demands made in Bombay, Assam, and elsewhere,[3] interest articulation may yet begin to cross ascriptive lines in a process that should result from expanding economic and educational opportunities. Such competition should be healthy for democracy, whereas a continuation of conflict along such basic divisions as caste, community, and religion would threaten both Nehru's concept of "unity in diversity" and his model of a secular polity.

A strong modern middle class is likely to express its views along secular lines economically and socially,[4] but none of the countries of South Asia had developed such a class prior to independence. Farthest along the road were India and Sri Lanka, with their substantial Hindu or Sinhala shares of the government services and their larger groups of professionals, teachers, and modern sector business people. As we have seen, Muslim shares in the Indian government and in other areas of endeavor were much smaller. This was particularly the case in what was to become Bangladesh, where business, the professions, and landownership were very much in the hands of the Hindus, many of whom eventually migrated to India. A similar but less numerically strong case could be made for the areas now comprising Pakistan.

All of the nations of South Asia are undergoing a process of economic development. India, Sri Lanka, and Bangladesh have been reasonably successful in introducing modest land reforms, although Pakistan's reforms have been less successful. Similarly, India and Sri Lanka have been able to expand their middle classes in the past two decades, and living conditions have improved in each of the countries. Nevertheless, the processes of industrialization and agricultural revolution have increased income disparities throughout the region. Hundreds of millions of people live in abject poverty while members of a small upper class enjoy unprecedented prosperity. Such income inequities could trigger a crisis of distribution and thus cause political instability, even in those political systems with reasonably well-differentiated structures.

The Future

India has a fair chance of continuing along democratic lines, although dangers do exist and there will no doubt be stumbles. Sri Lanka may find even greater pitfalls as it tries to reintegrate the Tamils, who were so thoughtlessly driven out of the system. Bangladesh is hindered by its weak economic and social base, but it might prove capable of creating a strong presidential system, that, while likely to draw criticism from the outside, could lead to greater liberalization. And, finally, Pakistan seems unlikely to liberalize its society so long as an Islamic state is the stated goal.

Notes

1. David Dunbar [Pseudonym for Craig Baxter], "Bhutto—Two Years On," *The World Today,* vol. 30, no. 1 (January 1974).

2. See Lloyd I. Rudolph and Susanne Hoeber Rudolph, *The Modernity of Tradition,* Part 1 (Chicago: University of Chicago Press, 1967), and, for a discussion of the pre-independence period, Ainslie T. Embree, *India: Search for National Identity* (New York: Knopf, 1972).

3. See Myron Weiner and Mary Fainsod Katzenstein, *India's Preferential Policies: Migrants, the Middle Classes and Ethnic Equality* (Chicago: University of Chicago Press, 1981).

4. Included in the meaning of *middle class* is the concept of the bureaucratic and bourgeois middle class as described by James A. Bill and Carl Leiden, *Politics in the Middle East,* 2nd ed. (Boston: Little, Brown, 1984), pp. 116ff. The categories used by these authors seem to fit South Asia as well.

STATISTICAL APPENDIX

	India	Pakistan	Bangladesh	Sri Lanka
Population (1987), millions	797.5	102.5	106.1	16.4
Area, thousand square miles	1,229	343	55	25
GNP per capita, 1987, dollars	300	350	160	400
Average annual growth in GNP per capita, dollars, 1965–1987	1.8	2.5	0.3	3.0
Growth rate, GDP, 1980–1987				
Overall	4.6	6.6	3.8	4.6
Agriculture	0.8	3.4	2.4	3.1
Industry	7.2	9.1	4.7	4.2
Service	6.1	7.1	5.2	5.7
Total GDP, 1987, dollars, million	220,830	31,650	17,600	6,040
Distribution of GDP, 1987				
Agriculture	30	23	47	27
Industry	30	28	13	27
Service	40	49	39	46
Gross domestic savings, 1987, percentage of GDP	22	11	2	13
Cereal imports, 1987, thousand metric tonnes	46	378	1,781	533
Food and cereal assistance, 1986/7, thousand tonnes	208	456	1,589	284
Energy per capita, 1987, kg. of oil equivalent	208	207	47	160
Merchandise trade, 1987, million dollars				
Exports	12,548	4,172	1,074	1,393
Imports	18,985	5,822	2,620	2,085
Balance	−6,437	−1,650	−1,546	−692
Balance of payments, 1987, million dollars	−3,750	−336	−309	−378
Remittances, 1987, million dollars	2,000	2,172	348	617

	India	Pakistan	Bangladesh	Sri Lanka
Capital transfers, 1987, million dollars				
Gross inflow	6,191	982	923	387
Repayment of principal	2,680	807	191	228
Net inflow	3,511	174	733	159
Debt service ratio, 1987				
Percent of GNP	1.7	3.5	1.8	5.4
Percent of exports	24.0	26.3	24.2	20.2
Population growth, average				
percent, 1980–1987	2.1	3.1	2.8	1.5
Projected, 1987–2000	1.8	3.3	2.4	1.1
Estimated population, 2000, millions	1,010	156	144	19
Urbanization, percent, 1987	27	31	13	21
Life expectancy, 1987				
Male	58	55	51	68
Female	58	54	50	73
Infant mortality rate, 1987	99	109	119	33
Health, 1984				
Population per physician	2,520	2,900	6,730	5,520
Population per nurse	1,700	4,900	8,980	1,290
Caloric intake, per day, 1986	2,238	2,315	1,927	2,401
Education, 1986, percent of age group in attendance				
Primary, total	92	44	60	103
Primary, male	107	55	69	104
Primary, female	76	32	50	102
Secondary	35	18	18	66
Higher	N/A	5	5	4
Central government expenditure, percent of total, 1987				
Defense	21.5	29.5	10.0	9.6
Education	2.7	2.6	10.6	7.8
Health	1.9	0.9	5.0	5.4
Welfare	5.7	8.7	9.8	11.7
Central government Expenditures as percent of GNP, 1987	18.1	21.4	12.2	32.4
Income distribution				
For year	1975–76	NA	1981–82	1980–81
Lowest 20%	7.0	NA	6.6	5.8
Second quintile	9.2	NA	10.7	10.1
Third quintile	13.9	NA	15.3	14.1
Fourth quintile	20.5	NA	22.1	20.3
Highest 20%	49.4	NA	45.3	49.8

Source: World Bank, *World Development Report* (New York: Oxford University Press, 1989), tables on pp. 164–227.

ABOUT THE BOOK AND AUTHORS

This text establishes a sound interdisciplinary context for understanding the political framework of the seven South Asian nations in terms of the history, social structure, and cultural heritage of the region.

The authors make use of the rich comparative possibilities afforded by the subcontinent, exploring examples of political development ranging from the relatively open, democratic systems of India and Sri Lanka to the frequently authoritarian governments of Pakistan and Bangladesh as well as the changing traditional polities of Nepal, Bhutan, and the Maldives. All seven countries face the challenges of nation building, state building, political participation, and economic development, but they also share a common political heritage of relations with Great Britain, as described in the introductory chapter. India, Sri Lanka, Pakistan, and Bangladesh are discussed in detail in sections written by area specialists; Nepal, Bhutan, and the Maldives are grouped together in a brief overview chapter. Concluding chapters survey the subcontinent as a whole, focusing on regional cooperation and conflict, international relations, and ongoing struggles with authoritarianism and democracy. Each chapter is supplemented with suggested readings.

This second edition especially reflects the changes that have occurred in India and Pakistan in 1988 and 1989 and the continuance of ethno-religious strife in Sri Lanka. The section on regional and international politics has been expanded and considers the growing importance of India and Pakistan in the world and regional arenas.

Designed as a core text for courses on the region, *Government and Politics in South Asia* will also be valuable for courses in political development and comparative politics.

Craig Baxter is professor of politics and history at Juniata College; **Yogendra K. Malik** is professor of political science at the University of Akron; **Charles H. Kennedy** is associate professor of politics at Wake Forest University; and **Robert C. Oberst** is associate professor of political science and chair of the Global Studies Program at Nebraska Wesleyan University.

INDEX

Abdali, Ahmad Shah, 25
Abdullah, Farooq, 74, 98, 116, 375
Abdullah, Mohammad (sheikh), 36, 74, 116, 374, 375
Abeygunasekera, Oswin, 323(table)
Adi Granth, 46
Advani, L. K., 112
Afghanistan, 162, 184, 223, 372, 383
   war in, 2, 185–186, 216, 217, 224, 378, 382, 385, 386, 387, 389, 390
Aga Khan Muslims, 176, 233
Agarawal, R. D., 124
Agartala conspiracy case, 252, 256(n7)
AGP. *See* Assom Gana Parishad
Agriculture. *See* Land reform; *and under specific countries*
Ahmad, Fakhruddin Ali, 83(table), 84
Ahmad, Mirza Ghulam, 177
Ahmad, Muzaffar, 273
Ahmadiyya, 177, 194
Ahmed, Moudud, 271
AIADMK. *See* All-India Anna DMK
AICC. *See* All-India Congress Committee
AIMO. *See* All-India Manufacturers Organization
AITUC. *See* All-India Trade Union Congress
Akali Dal, 36, 99, 106, 116–117, 124, 131
   civil disobedience campaign of, 46, 47, 74, 75, 117
Akbar (emperor of India), 6, 25, 26
AL. *See* Awami League (AL)
Ali, Chaudhury Rehmat, 167
Aligarh Muslim University, 30, 31
All-Ceylon Buddhist Congress, 341
All-India Anna-DMK, 104, 115
All-India Congress Committee (AICC), 59, 107, 109, 148
All-India Kisan Sabha (Farmers Association), 125
All-India Manufacturers Organization (AIMO), 122, 123
All-India Muslim League. *See* Muslim League

All-India Muslim Students Federation, 252
All-India Sikhs Students Federation, 131
All-India Trade Union Congress (AITUC), 123
All-Nepal Kisan Sabha, 364
All-Pakistan Awami League (AL), 277(n1)
All-Pakistan Muslim League, 239
Amdedkar, B. R., 128
Amin, Nurul, 255(n5)
Amirthalingam, A., 336, 337
Amritsar resolution, 113
Annadurai, C. N., 73, 115
ANP. *See* Awami National Party
Antulay, A. R., 127
Aryans, 22–23, 298
Arya Samaj, 29
Assamese language, 48(table), 49(map)
Associated Chamber of Commerce and Industry of India (Assocham), 122, 123
Association of Islam. *See* Jamaat-i-Islami
Assom Gana Parishad (AGP), 104, 111, 116
Aurangzeb (emperor of India), 6
Awami League (AL), 191, 205, 238, 253, 254, 255, 259, 272, 273, 276, 288, 394
   electoral success of, 242, 247, 249, 261, 262
   factionalism in, 248
   and Mujibur Rahman, 247, 252, 258, 260, 269, 270, 277(n1)
   rise of, 240–243
   Suhrawardy's involvement in, 237, 240, 251–252
Awami National Party (ANP), 193(table), 194
Ayub, Gohar, 212
Ayub Khan, Muhammad, 174, 193, 197(table), 199–200, 202, 214, 215, 247, 248, 252
   authoritarianism of, 206, 209, 211–212
   foreign policy of, 212, 224, 375, 376
   political parties under, 241, 250, 267, 268, 270, 273
Azad, Maulana Abdul Kalam, 86

Babur (emperor of India), 6, 25

Back to Village National Campaign (BVNC), 364

Badal, Prakash Singh, 117

Baghdad Pact. *See* Central Treaty Organization

Bahadur, Jang, 359

BAKSAL. *See* Bangladesh Krishak Sramil Awami League (AL)

Baloch, 162, 164, 165(table), 186–187, 194, 394

Balochistan National Alliance (BNA), 193(table), 194

Balochistan War, 214

Bandaranaike, Anura, 312

Bandaranaike, Ossie, 322

Bandaranaike, Sirimavo, 307, 312, 313(table), 323(table), 331–332, 333, 337, 349, 380, 388, 396

Bandaranaike, Solomon West Ridgeway Dias, 311, 313(table), 331, 334, 346

Bandung Conference, 384

Banerjea, Surendranath, 31, 32

Bangladesh, 2, 7, 162, 184, 202, 229–293, 314, 372
  agriculture in, 230, 234, 276–277, 286–288, 292, 399
  British influence on, 2, 262, 291
  civil service of, 135, 143, 259, 261, 264, 274–275, 276, 277(n3), 290–291
  constitution of, 257–258, 260, 261, 262–263, 277, 395
  creation of, 65, 126, 130, 154, 168, 243, 373, 377
  democracy vs. authoritarianism in, 246–248, 257–262, 393, 394, 395, 396, 397–398, 399
  economy of, 1–2, 230, 238–239, 261, 286–289, 292–293
  elites in, 239–240, 275–277
  foreign relations of, 255, 376–377, 379–380, 381, 382, 385, 387–388
  geography of, 229–230
  governmental institutions in, 262–266
  governments of, 257–262
  grievances against Pakistan, 181, 229, 232–233, 236–239, 244
  and India compared, 100, 135, 143, 279
  interest groups in, 273–277
  leaders of, 248–255
  military of, 126, 135, 253–254, 260–262, 274–275, 276, 277(n3), 279–285, 388, 397–398
  modernization and development of, 286–293
  and People's Republic of China, 387, 390
  political parties of, 237, 238, 240–243, 246–248, 260, 261, 262, 267–273, 276
  population of, 230–232
  relations with India, 258, 271, 376–377, 379–380, 387
  religions in, 129, 233–234, 398
  resources of, 289–290
  Six Point program for, 236, 237, 239, 241–242, 247, 252, 280

Bangladesh Krishak Sramik Awami League (AL) (BAKSAL), 270

Bangladesh Nationalist party (BNP), 247, 254, 261, 262, 268, 270, 271–272, 276

Bangladesh War, 65, 126, 130, 154, 243, 281, 373, 376–377

Banias. *See* Caste System

Barnala, Surjit Singh, 47, 117

Basic Democrats (BD), 206, 211, 213, 216, 270

Basu, Jyoti, 95, 99, 114

Bengali language, 48(table), 49(map), 232, 233, 236, 239

Bengalis, 181, 231, 232, 233, 237, 238, 243, 279–280, 390

Besant, Annie, 30

Bhagavadgita, 23

Bhandari, N. B., 116

Bhandarkar, R. C., 30

Bharatiya Jana Sangh, 378

Bharatiya Janata party (BJP), 70, 104, 105(table), 108, 109, 111–113, 123, 129

Bharatiya Lok Dal, 68, 110. *See also* Janata Dal

Bharatiya Mazdoor Sabha (BMS), 123

Bharat Sevak Samaj (Indian Service Association), 125

Bhashani, Maulana Abdul Hamid Khan, 240, 247, 248, 253, 255, 269, 273

Bhindranwale, Sant Jarnail Singh, 46, 74–75

Bhutan, 2, 16, 17, 365–368, 373, 385, 390

Bhutto, Benazir, 176, 195, 196, 197(table), 201–202, 209, 217, 222, 223, 378, 382
  and regional interests, 183, 184, 185, 187, 217

Bhutto, Shahnawaz, 200

Bhutto, Zulfiqar Ali, 197(table), 200–201, 202, 203(n10), 207, 222, 223, 255(n5), 375, 377, 378
  authoritarianism of, 185, 200–201, 395, 396
  and Bangladesh, 242–243, 257, 382
  and Pakistan People's Party, 195, 196, 200
  reforms of, 182–183, 212–214, 215, 221

Birendra (king of Nepal), 362

Birlas, 123, 132(n3)

BJP. *See* Bharatiya Janata party

BLD. *See* Bharatiya Lok Dal

BMS. *See* Bharatiya Mazdoor Sabha

BNA. *See* Balochistan National Alliance
BNP. *See* Bangladesh Nationalist party
Bogra, Muhammad Ali, 239, 374
Brahmins. *See* Caste system
Brahmo Samaj, 29
Brecher, Michael, 86
British East India Company, 6, 7, 8, 16, 17,
    27, 279, 300, 397. *See also* Colonial
    period; Great Britain
Brohi language, 162, 164, 165(table), 186
Buddha, Gautama, 23
Buddhism, 3, 23–24, 45, 358, 359, 366,
    369
  in Bangladesh, 231, 233, 234
  in Sri Lanka, 299, 301, 305–306,
    306(table), 308, 311, 318, 341
Bugti, Nawab Akbar, 187
Burghers, 305(table), 307
Burma, 14, 232
BVNC. *See* Back to Village National
    Campaign

Carter, Jimmy, 386
Caste system, 3, 23, 29, 42–44, 46, 53,
    56(n1), 122, 132(n3)
  in Bangladesh, 233, 234
  and Indian political process, 44, 52, 79,
    94, 128, 140, 146, 151–152, 398–399
  in Sri Lanka, 307–308, 313–314
  See also Hinduism
Central Treaty Organization (CENTO), 2,
    384, 386
Centre of Indian Trade Unions (CITU), 123
Ceylon, Crown Colony of, 2, 5, 15–16, 17.
    See also Sri Lanka
Ceylon Leather Products Corporation, 324
Ceylon National Congress, 16
Ceylon Worker's Congress (CWC), 335
Chamber of Commerce and Industry, 121
Charles II (king of England), 6
Chelmsford, Lord, 11
Chelvanayagam, S.J.V., 335
Chief Khalsa Diwan, 131
China, People's Republic of, 114, 115, 146,
    149, 372
  and Bangladesh, 259, 272, 283, 387, 388,
    390
  and Bhutan, 368, 385
  and Nepal, 357, 358, 365, 381, 385
  and Pakistan, 200, 212, 214, 273, 387,
    390
  relations with India, 65, 126, 378, 385,
    386, 388, 390
  and Sri Lanka, 388
Choudhury, Fazal Kader, 267
Christianity, 29, 45, 121, 131, 166(table),
    231, 233, 234

  in Sri Lanka, 299, 300, 306, 307, 308
CITU. *See* Centre of Indian Trade Unions
Civil liberties, 79–80, 111, 112, 396
Civil Service of Pakistan (CSP), 209, 211,
    212–213, 215, 238
CML. *See* Convention Muslim League
Colebrooke Commission, 16
Colonial period, 5–18, 27–37, 38, 162, 186,
    357, 367, 369
  annexation of India, 7–10, 27
  Bengal army mutiny, 279–280
  British reforms during, 10–14, 33
  civil service during, 136–137, 138, 139,
    142, 143
  cultural revivalism during, 28–31
  democratic vs. authoritarian heritage of,
    397–398
  education during, 27–28, 32
  elections during, 9–13, 14, 32, 33, 35
  European expansion during, 5–7
  nationalist movement during, 31–37
  in Sri Lanka, 298, 299–301, 317–318,
    325
Communal violence
  in Bangladesh, 234
  in India, 37, 46–47, 74–75, 112, 147,
    152–153, 251, 376
  in Pakistan, 176, 177, 183–184, 194
  in Sri Lanka, 308–309, 333–334, 335,
    348–352
Communist party of India (CPI), 64, 70, 88,
    104, 113, 123, 125, 273, 364
Communist party of India (Marxist)(CPM),
    104, 105(table), 114, 123
Communist party of India (Marxist-Leninist)
    (CPI[ML]), 114–115
Communist party of Pakistan, 253
Communist party of Sri Lanka, 330(table),
    332, 333, 334, 337
Congress (I), 65, 67, 72(table), 73, 83(table),
    88, 107–109, 123, 124, 142
  electoral success of, 89, 105(table), 108,
    110, 111, 116
  leadership of, 86, 106, 107–108
  and other parties, 68–69, 110, 111, 112,
    115, 116
  and state governments, 70, 95, 98, 99,
    153
  See also Indian National Congress
Congress (S), 111
Convention Muslim League (CML),
    191(table), 211
Cornwallis, Lord, 8
CPI. *See* Communist party of India
CPI(ML). *See* Communist party of India
    (Marxist-Leninist)

CPM. *See* Communist party of India
  (Marxist)
Cripps, Stafford, 14
CSP. *See* Civil Service of Pakistan
CWC. *See* Ceylon Worker's Congress

Dahanayake, Wijayananda, 311, 313(table)
Dalhousie, Lord, 8
Dange, S. A., 114
Darshanas, 23
Dayanand Anglo-Vedic (DAV) college
  movement, 29
Dayanand (Swami), 29
Defense of Internal Security of India Act
  (1971), 80
Democracy, defined, 393. *See also under
  specific countries*
Desai, Morarji, 63, 65, 67–68, 72(table), 85,
  93, 378
Dev, Nanak (Guru), 46
Development, 38–39, 61, 87, 148–151, 154–
  155, 220–221, 286–293, 345–348, 365.
  See also Industrialization; Modernization
Didi, M. Fareed, 369
Didi, Muhammed Amin, 369
Directive Principles of State Policy, 80
DMK. *See* Dravida Munnetra Kazhagam
Dorji, Kazi Ugyen, 367
Dravida Munnetra Kazhagam (DMK), 73–74,
  104, 111, 115
Dravidian Progressive Federation, 73–74
Dravidians, 21, 22–23, 298
Dulles, John Foster, 53
Durand Line, 185
Dutch East India Company, 15, 300
Dyer, R.E.H., 34
Dzongkha language, 367

East Pakistan Rifles (EPR), 281
Education, 27–28, 32, 50–51, 93, 176, 289–
  290, 303, 317, 337, 349
Eelam People's Revolutionary Liberation
  Front (EPRLF), 336, 351
Eelam Revolutionary Organization of
  Students (EROS), 330(table), 336
Eisenhower, Dwight, 53
Enforcement of Shariah Ordinance, 178(n7)
English language, 163, 367
  in India, 27–28, 48, 49(table), 50–51, 64,
    90, 138
  in Sri Lanka, 300, 301, 321, 348, 349
EPR. *See* East Pakistan Rifles
EPRLF. *See* Eelam People's Revolutionary
  Liberation Front
EROS. *See* Eelam Revolutionary
  Organization of Students

Ershad, Husain Muhammad, 234, 248, 250,
  255, 269, 283, 290, 382, 388
  career of, 254–255, 280, 281–282
  decentralization program of, 274–275
  economic policies of, 271, 275–276, 286–
    289, 291
  elections under, 247, 262, 272, 396
  government under, 261–262, 263, 264
  and military, 279, 284, 285

Family. *See* Kinship
Farakka Barrage, 379, 382
Farmers and Peoples party. *See* Krishak
  Praja party
Farmers' Forum, 125
Federal party (FP), 318, 330(table), 335, 348
Federal Shariat Court (FSC), 175
Federation of Indian Chambers of
  Commerce and Industry (FICCI), 122
Field, John Osgood, 52
FP. *See* Federal party
France, 5, 7, 15, 223, 319
FSC. *See* Federal Shariat Court

Gandhi, Feroze, 76(n7)
Gandhi, Indira, 11, 63, 72(table), 76(n7), 87,
  91, 93, 113, 115, 154
  assassination of, 46–47, 108, 112, 148,
    152
  and Congress party, 106, 107–108, 109,
    148
  electoral popularity of, 63, 65, 86, 89,
    107, 147
  emergency rule under, 65–66, 67, 80, 84,
    86, 89, 107, 114, 395–396
  foreign policy of, 257, 377, 378, 384, 386
  and Janata party, 67, 69, 110
  leadership style of, 64–66, 85
  and presidency, 84–85, 107
  and separatist movements, 46–47, 74,
    116
  and state governments, 95, 98–99
Gandhi, Mohandas Karamchand (Mahatma),
  38–39, 44, 66, 69, 76(n7), 79, 251,
  383, 386
  civil disobedience campaigns of, 11, 34,
    35, 36, 113, 196
  leadership style of, 54, 58–60, 61
  and untouchables, 53, 234, 398
Gandhi, Rajiv, 11, 69–70, 71, 72(table),
  76(n7), 85, 148, 396
  and Congress (I), 69, 70, 86, 108, 109
  foreign policy of, 111, 378, 381, 384,
    385, 386
  and national unity, 47, 75, 89, 147, 375
Gandhi, Sanjay, 66, 69, 108, 152
Gayoon, Maumoon Abdul, 370

Ghaffar Khan, Khan Abdul, 185
Ghose, Aurobindo, 32, 33
Ghosh, Atulya, 63
Giri, V. V., 83(table), 84, 85, 107
Gokhale, Gopal Krishana, 32, 33
Golwalkar, M. S., 129
Government of India Act (1909), 10–11, 32, 248–249
Government of India Act (1919), 12–13, 14, 16, 33, 35, 196
Government of India Act (1935), 13–14, 15, 35, 79, 167, 204, 205, 234, 246, 255(n3)
Great Britain, 155, 164, 166, 186, 357, 365, 367, 369, 374
    expansion into South Asia by, 5–7
    granting of independence by, 14–17
    India as successor to, 372–373, 383
    and Indian civil service, 31, 136–137, 138, 139, 142, 143
    political legacy of, 2, 81, 89–90, 262, 291, 397–398
    and Sri Lanka, 298, 300–301, 317–318, 321, 323, 325, 388
    See also Colonial period
Green Revolution, 53, 110, 151, 153, 287
Gujarati language, 48(table), 49(map)
Gunawardena, Dinesh, 334
Gunawardena, Philip, 334
Gurungs, 358–359

Hadith, 172
Haq, Maulvi Abul Kasim Fazlul, 240, 241, 246, 247, 248–250, 251, 253, 254, 255, 261, 268, 276
Harijans. See Caste system
Hastings, Warren, 8
Hedgewar, Keshav Baliram, 129
Hindi language, 26, 47–48, 49(map), 50, 64, 73, 90, 112, 232
Hindko language, 165(table)
Hinduism, 3, 23–24, 41–42, 45, 54, 398–399
    in Sri Lanka, 299, 301, 306(table), 380
    See also Caste system
Hindus, 25–26, 33, 61, 129–130, 279–280, 373, 378, 397
    in Bangladesh, 223, 234, 267–268, 377, 399
    and communal violence, 37, 152, 234, 376
    nationalism of, 26, 28–30, 32, 37, 70, 111–112, 129
    in Nepal, 357, 358–359
    in Pakistan, 129, 166(table), 185, 399
    and partition, 166, 167
Husain, Altaf, 184

Hussain, Anwar, 274
Hussain, Kamal, 270
Hussain, Tofazzal, 274
Hussain, Zakir, 83(table), 84, 85

IAS. See Indian Administrative Service
ICS. See Indian Civil Service
IJI. See Islami Jamhoori Ittehad
Ilbert Bill (1883), 31
India, 2, 21–157, 232, 314, 370, 372
    agriculture in, 1, 22, 38, 93, 124–125, 149, 150–151, 153, 154, 287, 399
    and Bangladesh compared, 100, 135, 143, 279
    and Bhutan, 17, 368, 390
    bureaucratic structure in, 136–140
    communal violence in, 37, 46–47, 74–75, 112, 147, 152–153, 251, 376
    constitution of, 78–81, 92–93, 99, 147, 153, 394–395
    corruption in, 142–143, 152
    democracy in, 27–28, 52, 53, 393, 394–395, 397, 398–399
    development in, 38–39, 61, 87, 148–151, 154–155
    economic interest groups in, 122–125, 151
    education in, 27–28, 32, 50–51, 93
    emergency powers in, 65–66, 67, 80, 82, 84, 86, 87–88, 89, 91, 107, 114, 395–396
    executive branch in, 81–87
    family and kinship in, 44, 310
    geography of, 21–22
    income distribution in, 150, 151–152, 153
    independence of, 14–15, 37
    institutional stability in, 78, 147–148, 202
    interest groups in, 120–121, 131–132. See also specific interest groups
    Islam in, 24–26, 42, 130, 131
    leaders of independence movement in, 58–62
    linguistic and cultural divisions in, 47–50
    military of, 126, 279, 280, 373, 383, 384–385, 394, 397
    modernization of, 37–39, 61, 146–155
    nationalist movements in, 31–37, 48–50, 53
    and Nepal, 357, 360, 365, 381–382, 383, 390
    and Pakistan compared, 59, 100, 135, 143, 187, 202
    Parliament of, 81, 87–92, 104
    and People's Republic of China, 385, 386, 390
    Planning Commission, 87, 95, 149, 150
    political culture of, 51–55

political parties of, 102–106, 116–117.
  See also specific parties
post-Nehru leaders of, 62–71, 72(table)
press in, 3, 66, 67
regionalism in, 3–4, 48–50, 58, 61–62,
  71, 73–75, 99, 104, 115–116, 153–154
regional predominance of, 372–373, 383,
  390
relations with Bangladesh, 258, 271, 376–
  377, 379–380, 387
relations with Great Britain, 214, 217, 384
relations with Pakistan, 214, 217, 373–
  378, 387. *See also* Indo-Pakistani Wars
relations with Soviet Union, 384–385,
  389, 390
relations with Sri Lanka, 307, 350–352,
  373, 380–381
religious interest groups in, 128–131. *See
  also* Hindus; Muslims; Sikhs
role of bureaucracy in, 135–136, 140–143,
  148
social mobility in, 50–51, 54
and Sri Lanka compared, 100, 117, 310,
  317, 318, 319, 329
state governments in, 93–99
students and intelligentsia in, 125–127
Supreme Court of, 79, 81, 82, 92–93,
  148
Tamils in, 73–74, 336
tribal groups in, 131, 153
and United States, 14, 155, 384–385,
  385–386
  See also Caste system; Colonial period;
  Hinduism; Partition
India Councils Act, 9
Indian Administrative Service (IAS), 8, 87,
  136–137, 138–140, 143, 323
Indian Civil Service (ICS), 8, 9, 13, 31, 136,
  140, 143, 209, 238, 290
Indian Independence Act, 15, 204, 205
Indian Liberation Federation, 34
Indian Mutiny, 8
Indian National Congress, 63, 72(table),
  83(table), 84, 86, 93, 106–109, 130,
  152, 185, 329, 394, 397
  divisions within, 12–13, 32–33, 34, 62,
    102
  dominance of, 63, 102, 104
  founding of, 9, 31
  and institutional stability in India, 78,
    147–148, 202
  and interest groups, 120–121, 123, 124,
    125, 151
  international influence of, 360, 384
  and Muslim League, 10–11, 102, 196
  and nationalist movement, 32–33, 34–35,
    36–37, 113

Nehru's leadership of, 60, 396
  and partition, 15, 37, 164, 167
  and state governments, 95, 98, 395
  See also Congress (I)
Indian National Trade Union Congress
  (INTUC), 123
Indian People's party, 68
Indian Police Service (IPS), 136–137, 138,
  140
"Indira doctrine," 390, 391(n2)
Indo-Lanka Accords, 334, 336, 350, 351
Indo-Pakistani Wars, 5, 53, 223, 390
  over Bangladesh, 65, 126, 154, 169, 243,
    373, 374, 377, 385
  over Kashmir, 64, 126, 169, 200, 212,
    224, 238, 241, 374, 375
Indus River settlement, 212, 239, 376, 379
Industrialization, 53, 61, 93, 149–150, 153,
  155, 211–212, 255, 288
International Rice Research Institute, 287
INTUC. *See* Indian National Trade Union
  Congress
IPS. *See* Indian Police Service
Iqbal, Muhammad, 166
Iran, 176, 372, 386, 387, 389
Iraq, 386
Islam, 3, 24–26, 42, 130, 131, 306(table),
  307, 369
  in Bangladesh, 129, 234, 258, 275, 277,
    398
  in Pakistan, 129, 164, 166–167, 172–178,
    185, 214–215, 221, 222, 396, 398, 399
  See also Muslim League; Muslims
Islamic Conference organization, 387
Islamic Democratic Alliance. *See* Islami
  Jamhoori Ittehad
Islamic Law and Constitution, The
  (Maududi), 199
Islami Jamhoori Ittehad (IJI), 183, 184, 191,
  193(table), 195, 217
Islamization. *See* Nizam-i-Mustafa
Islan, Syed Nazrul, 270
Ismailis, 176
Ithna Ashari Muslims, 176, 233

Jagmohan, 98
JAGODAL. *See* National Democratic party
Jainism, 23, 24, 42, 45
Jallianwala Bagh massacre, 11, 34
Jamaat-i-Islami, 130, 191(table), 192(table),
  193–194, 199
Jamiat-ul-Ulema-i-Islam (JUI), 185,
  191(table), 192(table), 193(table), 194
Jamiat-ul-Ulema-i-Pakistan (JUP), 191(table),
  192(table), 194
Jammu. *See* Kashmir

Jammu and Kashmir National Conference, 116
Jana Sangh, 111–112. *See also* Bharatiya Janata party
Janata Dal, 72(table), 88, 104, 105(table), 109–111, 124
Janata party (Bangladesh), 248, 254, 255
Janata party (India), 67, 68, 72(table), 84, 86, 93, 98, 395
  decline of, 108, 110, 147
Janata Vimukthi Peramuna (JVP), 333–334, 337, 347, 348, 349, 351, 352
Janatha Estates Development Board, 324
Janatha Vimuki Peramuna (JVP), 322
Jan Morcha (People's Front), 71, 109–110
JANODAL. *See* Jatiya party
Jatiya party, 262, 268, 272, 276
Jatiyo Rakhi Bahini, 282
Jatiyo Samajtantrik Dal (JSD), 283–284
Jatiyo Sangsad, 263
Jatoi, Ghulam Mustapha, 195, 197(table)
Jats. *See* Caste system
Jayawardene, Junius Richard, 312, 313(table), 317, 320, 343, 381, 388
  economic policies of, 324, 345, 346, 347–348, 350
  and United National party, 321, 322, 329, 331, 338
Jharkhand Mukti Morcha, 116
JI. *See* Jamaat-i-Islami
Jinnah, Fatima, 211
Jinnah, Muhammad Ali, 11, 13, 35, 59, 182, 196–198, 240, 248, 249, 250, 383
  and Bangladesh, 232–233, 237, 243, 269
  death of, 169, 190, 192, 197
  demand for partition by, 167, 246
  and dissent, 31, 396, 398
Jiye Sindh, 194
JSD. *See* Jatiyo Samajtantrik Dal
JUI. *See* Jamiat-ul-Ulema-i-Islam
Junejo, Muhammad Khan, 193, 208
JUP. *See* Jamiat-ul-Ulema-i-Pakistan
JVP. *See* Janatha Vimukti Peramuna

Kabir, 26, 46
Kannada language, 48(table), 49(map)
Karmal, Babrak, 389
Karunanidhi, M., 74, 95, 99
Kashmir, 35–36, 74, 168, 217, 373–376, 378, 385, 394. *See also* Indo-Pakistani Wars
Kashmiri language, 48(table), 49(map)
Kashmir National Conference, 35–36, 74
Kasuri, Ahmad Raza, 196
Kerala, 395
Khairuddin, Khwaja, 256(n6)
Khalistan, 46

Khan, A. K., 275, 291
Khan, Ghulam Ishaq, 195, 197(table), 209, 210(table)
Khan, Syed Ahmad, 30–31
Khrushchev, Nikita, 113
Kidwai, Rafi Ahmad, 86
King, Martin Luther, Jr., 386
Kinship, 44, 191, 310–313
Kiratis, 359
Kirk, W., 153
Kissinger, Henry, 244(n1), 387
Kochanek, Stanley, 122
Koirala, B. P., 360, 361, 363–364
Konar, Hare Krishna, 114
Kosygin, Alexi, 375
Kotelawala, John, 311, 313(table), 388
Kothari, Rajni, 106
Krishak Praja party (KPP), 246, 249, 250, 268, 268(table)
Krishak Sramik party (KSP), 241, 247, 248, 249, 252, 268, 269, 273
Kshatriyas. *See* Caste system
KSP. *See* Krishak Sramak party
Kurananidhi, M., 115

Labor organizations, 123–124, 151, 276, 340
Lahore resolution, 167, 197, 237, 247, 249, 251, 384
Lal, Chaudhary Devi, 110, 124
Lanka Sama Samaja party (LSSP), 311, 330(table), 332–333, 334, 337
Leftist United Front, 363
Liaquat Ali Khan, 169, 182, 190, 192, 197(table), 198, 199, 240, 250
Liberation Tigers of Tamil Eelam (LTTE), 322, 336, 337, 350, 351, 352
Lohia, Ram Manohar, 360
Lok Dal, 124. *See also* Janata Dal
Lok Sabha, 87–90, 91, 92, 104, 105(table), 107, 108, 112, 117
Longowal, Sant Harcharan Singh, 47, 74, 117
LSSP. *See* Lanka Sama Samaja party
LTTE. *See* Liberation Tigers of Tamil Eelam
Lucknow Pact, 11, 196

MacDonald, Ramsey, 13
McMahon Line, 385
Magars, 358–359
Mahabharata, 23
Mahajana Eksath Peramuna (MEP), 3, 334
Mahanta, Prafulla, 116
Mahasabha, 249
Maha Sabha, 360–361
Mahaveli project, 346–347, 350
Mahavir, Vardhaman, 24

Mahendra (king of Nepal), 360, 361, 362, 364
Mahmud of Ghazni, 25
Maintenance of Internal Security Act (MISA)(1971), 80
Majeed, Abdul, 369
Majlis, 369–370
Majlis-i-Shura, 207, 210(table)
Majlis Tamir-i-Millat, 130
Malayalam language, 48(table)
Malays, 305(table), 307
Maldive Islands, 2, 16, 17, 369–370
Malla dynasty, 357–358
Mann, Simranjit Singh, 117
Manor, James, 148
Manzur, Muhammad, 284
Marathi language, 48(table), 49(map)
Maududi, Maulana, 194, 198–199
Mazumdar, Charu, 114
Mehta, Pherozshah, 32
Mellor, John, 149
Menon, Krishna, 386
MEP. See Mahajana Eksath Peramuna
MGR. See Ramchandran, M. G.
Minto, Lord, 10
Mirza, Iskander, 197(table), 199, 205, 206, 240
MISA. See Maintenance of Internal Security Act
Modernization, 220–222, 365, 367–368
  in Bangladesh, 286–293
  in India, 37–39, 61, 146–155
  in Sri Lanka, 345–352
Mohammadan Anglo-Oriental College, 30, 31
Montagu, Edwin, 11
Montagu-Chelmsford reforms, 12–13, 14, 16, 33, 35, 196
Mookerjee, Shyama Prasad, 111–112
Moors, 305(table), 307, 308
Morley, Viscount, 10, 11, 397
Morley-Minto Act, 10–11, 32, 248–249
Morris-Jones, W. H., 54, 92, 95
Mountbatten, Lord, 15
Movement for the Restoration of Democracy (MRD), 183
MQM. See Muhajir Qaumi Mahaz
MRD. See Movement for the Restoration of Democracy
Mughal empire, 6, 8, 25–26, 27
Muhajir National Movement, 183
Muhajir Qaumi Mahaz (MQM), 183, 184, 191, 193(table), 195, 196, 217
Muhajirs, 162, 164, 182, 183–184, 195
Muhammad, Ghulam, 197(table), 199, 205
Muhammad (prophet), 172, 177
Mujibism, 234, 252, 258, 261, 271

Mujibur Rahman (Mujib), 234, 240, 243, 248, 250, 252–253, 255, 261, 290, 382, 388
  and Awami League, 247, 252, 258, 260, 269, 270, 277(n1)
  economic policies of, 259, 275, 288, 291
  government of, 257–260, 262
  and military, 238, 280, 281, 282, 283
  Six Points of, 236, 237, 239, 241–242, 247, 252, 280
Mukti Bahini, 243, 281
Mushtaq Ahmad, Khondakar, 260
Muslim League, 9, 14, 15, 33, 36–37, 106, 113, 130, 167, 197, 277(n2)
  and Bangladeshi elite, 232, 233, 239, 240
  Bengali rejection of, 233, 241, 246–247, 267–268, 396
  disintegration of, 102, 190, 192–193, 205, 394
  factionalism in, 248, 250, 251, 253, 269
  and Indian National Congress, 10–11, 33, 35, 36–37, 59, 167
  Jinnah's leadership of, 13, 35, 59, 167, 190, 192, 196–198
  Nazimuddin's leadership of, 248, 249, 250
Muslims, 162, 166, 308, 336–337, 374, 375
  in Bangladesh, 232, 233–234, 240, 246–247, 274, 277, 279–280
  during colonial period, 9–11, 13, 30–31, 33, 36–37, 279–280, 397
  in independent India, 45–46, 61, 79, 121, 129, 130–131, 152, 376, 377, 399
  nationalism of, 30–31, 33, 35, 36–37, 164, 166–167, 197
  See also Islam; Muslim League

Nadar, Kumaraswami Kamaraj, 62–63, 107
Nadir (shah of Persia), 25
Namboodiripad, E.M.S., 114
Nanak, 26, 46
Nanayakara, Vasudeva, 333
NAP. See National Awami party
Narayan, Jaya Prakash, 65, 67, 68, 112, 360
Nasser, Gamal Abdel, 384
National Awami party (NAP), 185, 186, 191, 194, 213, 253, 273, 277(n2)
National Conference party, 35–36, 104, 374
National Democratic Party (NDP), 192(table), 194, 271. See also Bangladesh Nationalist party
National Front, 70, 111, 114, 124
Nationalism, 28–37, 53, 120, 258, 271
  four phases of, 31–37
  Hindu, 29–30, 32, 37, 70, 111–112, 129
  Muslim, 30–31, 33, 35, 36–37, 164, 166–167, 197

and regionalism, 48–50, 58
National Volunteer Organization. *See*
    Rashtriya Swayamsevak Sangh
Nauroji, Dadabhai, 32
Nava Sama Samaja party, 333
Nawaz Sharif, Mian, 183, 195
Nazimuddin, Khwaja, 197(table), 198, 237,
    246, 248, 249, 250–251, 255(nn 4, 5)
NDP. *See* National Democratic Party
Nehru, B. K., 98
Nehru, Jawaharlal, 11, 15, 26, 58, 67, 69,
    72(table), 86, 113, 383, 386, 399
    and democratic process, 60–61, 64, 85,
        91, 396
    and economic development, 39, 149
    and Indian National Congress, 60, 106,
        107, 120, 147
    and Indus River settlement, 376
    neutralist policy of, 53, 384, 395
    political objectives of, 395
    and Rajendra Prasad, 82, 84
    and Sheikh Abdullah, 74, 374
    and state governments, 95, 98
Nehru, Motilal, 11, 13
Nepal, 2, 16–17, 357–365, 373, 379, 383,
    385, 390
    ethnic and religious composition of, 357–
        359
    political institutions of, 359–363
Nepal Communist party, 364
Nepali Congress, 360, 361, 363–364
Nepali language, 358, 367
Nepal Trade Union Congress, 364
Netherlands, 5, 15, 17, 298, 299–300
Newaris, 358
Nijalingappa, S., 63
Nizam-i-Mustafa, 174–176, 178, 215, 221
Nonalignment, 53, 111, 224, 384, 385, 388,
    395
Noon, Firoz Khan, 374
Nuclear programs, 53, 154, 223, 373, 378,
    387

Official Language Act (Sri Lanka), 301, 348
Oriya language, 48(table), 49(map)
Osmany, Muhammad Abdul Ghani, 247,
    270, 280–281, 282

Pakistan, 2, 7, 14, 161–226, 314, 383, 397
    and Afghanistan, 2, 216, 217, 223, 224,
        382, 386, 387, 389
    agriculture in, 162, 182, 195, 211, 213,
        216, 287, 399
    Bangladeshi grievances against, 181, 229,
        232–233, 236–239, 244
    bureaucracy of, 135, 143, 209, 211, 212–
        213, 215, 238

civil war in, 65, 126, 130, 154, 169, 243–
    244, 281, 373, 376–377, 385
constitutions of, 173–174, 177–178, 198,
    201, 202, 204–209, 211, 213, 217,
    237–238, 241, 395
courts of, 175, 178(n6), 205, 207,
    210(table), 215
defense expenditures of, 170, 223
democracy vs. authoritarianism in, 393,
    394, 395, 396, 397–398, 399
disabilities of, 168–169
economy of, 1–2, 169, 170, 211–212,
    214, 216, 224
education in, 176
elections in, 184, 191(table), 192(table),
    193, 195–196, 199, 206, 207, 208, 211,
    215–216, 242, 396
ethnic and linguistic diversity in, 162–164,
    165(table), 168, 181
geography of, 161–162, 170
government structure of, 204–209,
    210(table)
Hindus in, 129, 166(table), 185, 399
immigrants to, 130, 162, 166, 168, 182
income distribution in, 182, 212, 221
and India, 390
and India compared, 59, 100, 135, 143,
    187, 202
and Indian Muslims, 61
Indian relations with, 385
institution building in, 221–222
Islam in, 129, 164, 166–167, 172–178,
    185, 214–215, 221, 222, 396, 398, 399
kinship in, 191, 310
leaders of, 196–202, 209, 211–217
military alliances of, 384, 386, 387
military dominance in, 126, 135, 199,
    201, 206–207, 209, 211, 215, 217, 222,
    279, 397–398
military strength of, 168, 206–207, 213,
    223
modernization of, 220–222
National Assembly, 178(n7), 184,
    191(table), 192(table), 193(table), 195,
    196, 205, 206, 207, 210(table), 211,
    216
One Unit Plan, 182, 186, 205
and People's Republic of China, 212, 387,
    390
political parties in, 183–184, 185, 186,
    190–196, 205–206, 211, 213, 214, 215,
    217, 242. *See also specific parties*
regionalism in, 3–4, 181–188, 190–191,
    280
relations with Bangladesh, 382

relations with India, 214, 217, 373–378, 387. *See also* Indo-Pakistani Wars; Kashmir
and Soviet Union, 200, 214, 216, 223, 387
and Sri Lanka, 187, 307, 310
strategic location of, 2, 372
taxes in, 173, 174, 175, 242
and United States, 212, 214, 216, 217, 223–224, 385, 386–387, 388, 389–390
See also Partition
Pakistan International Airlines, 229
Pakistan Muslim League, 191(table), 195
Pakistan National Alliance (PNA), 192(table), 196, 214
Pakistan National Congress, 267–268
Pakistan People's party (PPP), 185, 190–191, 194, 195, 200, 202, 213, 214, 217
electoral strength of, 183, 187, 191(table), 192(table), 193(table), 195–196, 242
Pakistan Student's Federation, 184
Pal, Bipan Chandra, 32, 33
Pant, Govind Ballabh, 86
Paranthan Chemicals Corporation, 324
Partition, 80, 130, 162, 164, 168–169, 182
demand for, 31, 36–37, 166–167, 197
Patel, Sardar Vallabhbhai, 58, 61–62, 67, 78, 86, 102, 120, 137, 147
Pathans, 162, 164, 182, 184–186, 194, 243, 280, 394
Patil, S. K., 63
Peasants and Workers party. *See* Krishak Sramik party
People's Front. *See* Jan Morcha
People's Liberation Front. *See* Janata Vimukthi Peramuna
People's Republic of China. *See* China, People's Republic of
People's Works Program, 213
Pirzada, Syed Sharifuddin, 387
Pitt, William, 8
PNA. *See* Pakistan National Alliance
Ponnambalam, G. G., 334
Population, regional, 1
Portugal, 5, 6–7, 15, 17, 298, 299–300, 386
PPI. *See* Punjabi Pushtun Ittehad
PPP. *See* Pakistan People's Party
Prabhakaran, Velupillai, 336
Prasad, Rajendra, 82–84
PRC. *See* China, People's Republic of
Premadasa, Ranasinghe, 312–313, 314, 320, 322, 323(table), 325, 330, 331, 338, 345, 347, 350–351, 388
Press, 66, 67, 127, 213, 217, 262, 273–274
Preventive Detention Act (1950)(India), 80
Prithvi Raj Narayan Shah, 16, 357
Pritinidhi Sabha, 360

Public Law 480 (U.S.), 292
Punjabi language, 47, 48(table), 49(map), 74, 162, 164, 165(table), 186, 232
Punjabi Pushtun Ittehad (PPI), 195
Punjabis, 162, 164, 181, 182, 183, 184, 187–188(n4), 194, 243, 280, 390
Pushto language, 162, 163, 164, 165(table), 186

Qasim, Mohammad bin, 25
Quit India movement, 14, 36, 113
Quran, 45, 172, 173, 174, 175, 234

Radhakrishnan, Sarvapalli, 83(table), 84, 85
Rahman, Khaleda, 262
Rahman, Shah Azizur, 261, 271
Rahman, Ziaur. *See* Ziaur Rahman (Zia)
Rahman Khan, Ataur, 241, 252, 269
Rai, Lala Lajpat, 32, 33
Rajya Sabha, 87, 90–91, 137
Rakhi Bahini, 282
Ramayana, 23
Ramchandran, M. G., 73–74, 115
Ranade, M. G., 30, 32
Ranadive, B. T., 113
Rana family, 359–360, 363
Rao, N. T. Rama, 111, 115, 116
Rashtriya Panchayat, 361, 362, 363
Rashtriya Swatantra Vidyarthi Parishad (RSVM), 364–365
Rashtriya Swayamsevak Sangh (RSS), 112, 129–130
Reagan, Ronald, 386
Reddy, Neelam Sanjiva, 63, 83(table), 84
Regmi, D. R., 360
Republican party of India, 128
Republican party of Pakistan, 193, 277(n2)
Research and development. *See* Technology
Ripon, Lord, 9
Rose, Leo, 367–368, 390, 391(n2)
Rowlatt acts, 11
Roy, Raja Ram Mohan, 29
RSS. *See* Rashtriya Swayamsevak Sangh
RSVM. *See* Rashtriya Swatantra Vidyarthi Parishad

SAARC. *See* South Asian Association for Regional Cooperation
Samant, Datta, 123
Sanskrit, 29, 48(table), 232
Sanyal, Kanu, 114
SARC. *See* South Asian Regional Cooperation
Sarkaria, Ranjit Singh, 99
Sattar, Abdus, 247, 254, 261, 270, 271, 283
Satyagraha, 11, 34, 55, 196
Saudi Arabia, 292, 387

Sayem, A.S.M., 260
Scott, James, 55
Seal, Anil, 128
SEATO. *See* South East Asia Treaty Organization
Senanayake, Don Stephen, 311, 312, 313(table), 329, 388
Senanayake, Dudley, 311, 312, 313(table), 329
Senanayake, Rukman, 312
SGPC. *See* Shiromani Gurudwara Prabhandak Committee
Shah, G. M., 116
Shahabuddin, Khwaja, 255(n4), 256(n6)
Shah dynasty, 358
Shastri, Lal Bahadur, 63–64, 67, 71, 72(table), 85, 91, 93, 307, 375, 380
Sherpao, H. M., 185
Sherpas, 359
Shia Muslims, 175–176, 176–177, 185, 233. *See also* Islam; Muslims
Shiromani Akali Dal. *See* Akali Dal
Shiromani Gurudwara Prabhandak Committee (SGPC), 117, 131
Shiva Sena, 106
Sikh Forum, 131
Sikhs, 4, 37, 45, 108, 121, 131, 166, 280, 397
   and communal violence, 46–47, 74–75, 112, 147, 152
   and Indo-Pakistani relations, 378, 390
   as separate electorate, 10, 11, 33
   See also Akali Dal
Sikkim Sangram Parishad (SSP), 116
Simla Agreement, 214, 377–378
Simon, John, 13
Sindhi language, 162, 163, 164, 165(table), 182, 186
Sindhis, 4, 162, 164, 182–183, 184, 394
Singh, Ajit, 110
Singh, Charan, 65, 68–69, 72(table), 93, 110
Singh, Giani Zail, 83(table), 84–85
Singh, Gobind (guru), 46
Singh, Tara, 36
Singh, Vishwanath Pratap, 70–71, 72(table), 89, 93, 109, 111, 114, 202, 375, 378, 381
Sinhala language, 301, 305, 318, 331, 348–349, 369
Sinhalese, 299, 301, 305–306, 307, 313, 369
   political parties of, 329–334, 337–338
   and Tamils, 308–309, 348, 349–350, 351, 394
Sino-Indian War, 65, 126, 385, 386, 388
Siraiki language, 165(table), 186

Six Point program, 236, 237, 239, 241–242, 247, 252, 280
SLAS. *See* Sri Lanka Administrative Service
SLFP. *See* Sri Lanka Freedom party
SLMC. *See* Sri Lanka Muslim Congress
Sobur Khan, Abdus, 267
Socialism
   in Bangladesh, 258, 261, 271, 288, 291
   in India, 27, 38, 62, 64, 150, 395
   in Pakistan, 195, 200, 214, 221
Somjee, A. H., 44
Soulbury, Lord, 318
South Asia
   population of, 1
   regional cooperation in, 2–3, 382–383, 390
   strategic location of, 2, 372
   superpower interests in, 389–390
   See also specific countries
South Asian Association for Regional Cooperation (SAARC), 2–3, 272, 382–383, 390, 393
South Asian Regional Cooperation (SARC), 382
South East Asia Treaty Organization (SEATO), 2, 384, 386
Soviet Union
   and Afghanistan, 185, 224, 372, 382, 385, 386, 387, 389
   and Bangladesh, 258, 271, 377, 387–388
   and Indian Communist parties, 113, 114
   and Nepal, 365
   and Non-Aligned Movement, 384
   and Pakistan, 200, 214, 216, 223, 387
   presence in Indian Ocean, 2
   relations with India, 384–385, 389, 390
   and Sri Lanka, 333
Sri Lanka, 297–354
   agriculture in, 301, 346–347, 350, 399
   authoritarianism in, 396
   and Bangladesh compared, 279
   British influence on, 2
   caste system in, 307–308, 313–314
   civil war in, 309, 333–334, 335, 347, 348–352, 380–381
   colonial period in, 298, 299–301, 317–318, 325
   constitution of, 395
   cultural heritage of, 298–299, 301
   cultural revitalization movement in, 31
   democracy in, 393, 394, 395, 397, 398, 399
   economy of, 1–2, 297, 300–301, 303–304, 345–348
   electoral participation in, 304–305
   ethnic groups in, 305–309
   foreign relations of, 388–389

geography of, 297–298
government structure in, 317–323
and India compared, 100, 117, 310, 317, 318, 319, 329
Indian Peace Keeping Force in, 111
interest articulation in, 339–343
kinship in, 310–313
local government in, 324–327
military in, 279
national unification in, 3–4
and Pakistan compared, 187, 202
patron-clientism in, 314–315
political succession in, 58
press in, 3
public service in, 323–324, 339–340, 341
relations with India, 307, 350–352, 373, 380–381
Sinhalese party system in, 329–334, 337–338
strategic location of, 2, 372
Tamil and Muslim party system in, 334–337
See also Ceylon, Crown Colony of
Sri Lanka Administrative Service (SLAS), 323–324
Sri Lanka Freedom party (SLFP), 202, 314, 318, 322, 324, 329, 331–332, 337, 346, 348
electoral strength of, 311, 312, 321, 330, 332
Sri Lanka Mahajana party, 332, 333
Sri Lanka Muslim Congress (SLMC), 336–337
Sri Lanka State Plantations Corporation, 324
Srinivas, M. N., 132
SSP. See Sikkim Sangram Parishad
Stalin, Josef, 332
Sudras. See Caste system
Sufism, 26, 164
Suhrawardy, Husain Shaheed, 237, 240–241, 247, 248, 251–252, 255, 269, 273
Sunnah, 172, 173, 174, 175, 234
Sunni Muslims, 175–176, 176–177, 185, 233, 369
Swaraj party, 13

Tagore, Debendranath, 30
Tagore, Rabindranath, 232
Taher, Abu, 284
Tamangs, 359
Tamerlane, 25
Tamil Congress (TC), 330(table), 334–335
Tamil Eelam Liberation Organization (TELO), 336, 351
Tamil language, 48(table), 49(map), 115, 301, 318, 349
Tamil National Army, 351

Tamils, 4, 21, 73–74, 314, 341, 347, 369, 373, 399
origin of, in Sri Lanka, 305(table), 306–307, 380
political representation of, 318, 322, 334–337
and Sri Lankan civil war, 308–309, 333–334, 335–336, 347, 348–351, 352, 380–381, 394
Tamil United Liberation Front (TULF), 335, 336, 337, 348, 396
Tandon, Purushottam Das, 60
Tashkent Agreement (1966), 64, 212
Tatas, 123
Taxes, 93, 125, 150, 173, 174, 175, 242, 347–348
TC. See Tamil Congress
Technology, 39, 61, 154–155, 289. See also Development
TELO. See Tamil Eelam Liberation Organization
Telugu Desam, 104, 111, 115–116
Telugu language, 48(table), 49(map)
Thakalis, 359
Theosophical Society, 29–30
Tibet, 17, 357, 358, 366, 372, 381, 385
Tilak, Bal Gangadhar, 32–33, 34
Tito, Josip Broz, 384
Trade unions. See Labor organization
Tribal groups, 131, 153, 231–232, 366
Tribhuvan (king of Nepal), 16, 360
Tribhuvan University, 364
Trotsky, Leon, 332
TULF. See Tamil United Liberation Front

Unionist party, 14
Union Public Service Commission, 137–138
Unions. See Labor organizations
United Front (Bangladesh), 233, 240, 241, 247, 248, 249, 268(table), 269–270
United Front (Sri Lanka), 318, 332, 346, 349
United National party (UNP), 16, 202, 318, 332, 337, 388, 394, 397
economic policies of, 338, 346, 347
electoral success of, 321, 322, 323, 329–331
kinship ties in, 310, 311–312, 314
and other parties, 332, 333, 334
and Tamils, 348, 349, 350, 351
United Nations, 17, 290, 368, 374, 377, 382, 383, 389
United Socialist Alliance (USA), 322, 330(table), 332–333, 337
United States, 2, 365
and Bangladesh, 255, 258–259, 272, 291, 292, 377, 387, 388

and India, 14, 155, 384–386
interests in South Asia, 389–390
and Pakistan, 212, 214, 216, 217, 223–
224, 385, 386–387, 388, 389–390
UNP. See United National party
Untouchables. See Caste system
Urdu language, 26, 47, 48(table), 49(map),
130–131, 162, 165(table), 250
as official language of Pakistan, 163–164,
182, 232–233, 236, 269, 396
USA. See United Socialist Alliance
Ushr. See Taxes

Vaishyas. See Caste system
Vajpayee, Atal Behari, 378
Varatharajaperumal, 336
Vasco da Gama, 5
Vedas, 23, 29
Veddahs, 298–299
Venkataraman, R., 83(table), 85
Victoria (queen of England), 9
Viplavakari Lanka Sama Samaja party
(VLSSP), 334
Vivekanand (Swami), 30
VLSSP. See Viplavakari Lanka Sama
Samaja party

Wajid, Husina (sheikh), 270–271
Wali Khan, Khan Abdul, 185
Wangchuck, Jigme Dorji, 367–368
Wangchuck, Ugyen, 367
Warsaw Pact, 385
Wavell, Lord, 15

Weiner, Myron, 137
Wijekoon, U. B., 325
Wijetunga, D. B., 314
Wijeweera, Rohana, 333, 334, 351
World Bank, 1, 286, 288, 365, 376
World Development Report (World Bank),
365

Yahya Khan, Agha Muhammad, 206, 214,
242, 247, 257, 270, 377

Zakat. See Taxes
Zia, Khalida, 271
Zia-ul-Haq, Muhammad (Zia), 197(table),
201, 203(n10), 210(table), 213, 216–217,
223, 378, 382
constitution under, 207–209
economic policies of, 175–176, 216
Islamization program of, 174–176, 177,
178, 214–215, 221, 396, 398
political restrictions under, 191, 195, 196,
202, 215–216
regionalism and, 183, 185, 187
Ziaur Rahman (Zia), 243, 247, 248, 250,
255, 261, 263, 270, 279, 283–284
agricultural policies of, 230, 261, 286,
287, 288
career of, 253–254, 280, 281
civil service under, 261, 290
economic policies of, 261, 271, 275–276,
288, 291
foreign policy of, 382, 383, 388
government program of, 260–261, 262